1,000,000 Books

are available to read at

www.ForgottenBooks.com

Read online
Download PDF
Purchase in print

ISBN 978-1-5279-0562-7
PIBN 10915954

This book is a reproduction of an important historical work. Forgotten Books uses state-of-the-art technology to digitally reconstruct the work, preserving the original format whilst repairing imperfections present in the aged copy. In rare cases, an imperfection in the original, such as a blemish or missing page, may be replicated in our edition. We do, however, repair the vast majority of imperfections successfully; any imperfections that remain are intentionally left to preserve the state of such historical works.

Forgotten Books is a registered trademark of FB &c Ltd.
Copyright © 2018 FB &c Ltd.
FB &c Ltd, Dalton House, 60 Windsor Avenue, London, SW19 2RR.
Company number 08720141. Registered in England and Wales.

For support please visit www.forgottenbooks.com

1 MONTH OF FREE READING

at

www.ForgottenBooks.com

By purchasing this book you are eligible for one month membership to ForgottenBooks.com, giving you unlimited access to our entire collection of over 1,000,000 titles via our web site and mobile apps.

To claim your free month visit:

www.forgottenbooks.com/free915954

* Offer is valid for 45 days from date of purchase. Terms and conditions apply.

English
Français
Deutsche
Italiano
Español
Português

www.forgottenbooks.com

Mythology Photography **Fiction**
Fishing Christianity **Art** Cooking
Essays Buddhism Freemasonry
Medicine **Biology** Music **Ancient Egypt** Evolution Carpentry Physics
Dance Geology **Mathematics** Fitness
Shakespeare **Folklore** Yoga Marketing
Confidence Immortality Biographies
Poetry **Psychology** Witchcraft
Electronics Chemistry History **Law**
Accounting **Philosophy** Anthropology
Alchemy Drama Quantum Mechanics
Atheism Sexual Health **Ancient History**
Entrepreneurship Languages Sport
Paleontology Needlework Islam
Metaphysics Investment Archaeology
Parenting Statistics Criminology
Motivational

THE
PUBLICATIONS
OF THE
𝕾𝖊𝖑𝖉𝖊𝖓 𝖘𝖔𝖈𝖎𝖊𝖙𝖞

περὶ παντὸς τὴν ἐλευθερίαν

VOLUME I.

FOR THE YEAR 1887

Selden Society

FOUNDED 1887

TO ENCOURAGE THE STUDY AND ADVANCE THE KNOWLEDGE
OF THE HISTORY OF ENGLISH LAW.

Patron:
HER MAJESTY THE QUEEN.

President:
THE LORD CHIEF JUSTICE OF ENGLAND.

Vice-President:
THE LORD JUSTICE FRY.

Honorary Secretary for America:
PROFESSOR J. B. THAYER, Cambridge, Mass.

Honorary Secretary and Treasurer:
P. EDWARD DOVE, 23 Old Buildings, Lincoln's Inn.

JUDICIAL COMBAT, *temp*. HENRY III.

See Page xxix.

Select Pleas of the Crown

VOLUME I.

A.D. 1200—1225

Gt. Brit. Curia regis

Selden Society

SELECT PLEAS OF THE CROWN

VOLUME I.

A. D. 1200 — 1225

EDITED

FOR THE SELDEN SOCIETY

BY

F. W. MAITLAND

First published 1888
Reprinted 1955

CONTENTS.

	PAGE
INTRODUCTION	vii
DESCRIPTION OF FRONTISPIECE	xxix

I. PLEAS BEFORE THE JUSTICES IN EYRE IN THE REIGN OF KING JOHN.

PLEAS AT LAUNCESTON IN THE THIRD YEAR OF THE REIGN OF KING JOHN (A.D. 1201)	2
PLEAS AT LINCOLN IN THE FOURTH YEAR OF THE REIGN OF KING JOHN (A.D. 1202)	6
PLEAS AT NORTHAMPTON IN THE FOURTH YEAR OF THE REIGN OF KING JOHN (A.D. 1202)	20
PLEAS AT BEDFORD IN THE FOURTH YEAR OF THE REIGN OF KING JOHN (A.D. 1202)	23
PLEAS AT LICHFIELD IN THE FIFTH YEAR OF THE REIGN OF KING JOHN (A.D. 1208)	28
PLEAS AT SHREWSBURY IN THE FIFTH YEAR OF THE REIGN OF KING JOHN (A.D. 1208)	31
PLEAS AT LINCOLN	36

II. PLEAS BEFORE THE JUSTICES OF THE BENCH AND PLEAS BEFORE THE KING DURING THE REIGN OF KING JOHN.

PLEAS OF MICHAELMAS TERM, A.D. 1200	38
PLEAS OF EASTER TERM, A.D. 1201 (?)	40
PLEAS OF MICHAELMAS TERM, A.D. 1201	43
PLEAS OF MICHAELMAS TERM, A.D. 1202	44
PLEAS OF HILARY TERM, A.D. 1203	45
PLEAS OF EASTER TERM, A.D. 1203	47
PLEAS OF MICHAELMAS TERM, A.D. 1203	48
PLEAS BEFORE THE KING, A.D. 1205	49

	PAGE
PLEAS BEFORE THE KING, EASTER TERM, A.D. 1206	50
PLEAS OF EASTER TERM, A.D. 1206	50
PLEAS OF MICHAELMAS TERM, A.D. 1206	51
PLEAS OF MICHAELMAS TERM, A.D. 1207	54
PLEAS OF TRINITY TERM, A.D. 1208	56
PLEAS OF MICHAELMAS TERM, A.D. 1211	58
PLEAS OF HILARY TERM, A.D. 1212	59
PLEAS OF EASTER TERM, A.D. 1212	63
PLEAS OF TRINITY TERM, A.D. 1212	65
PLEAS OF TRINITY TERM, A.D. 1214	67
PLEAS FROM SOMERSET AND DORSET BEFORE THE KING AT WELLS	75
PLEAS OF UNCERTAIN DATE	80

III. PLEAS BEFORE THE JUSTICES IN EYRE IN THE REIGN OF HENRY THE THIRD.

PLEAS AT WORCESTER IN THE FIFTH YEAR OF HENRY III. (A.D. 1221)	82
PLEAS OF THE COUNTY OF WARWICK IN THE FIFTH YEAR OF HENRY III. (A.D. 1221)	98
PLEAS AT SHREWSBURY IN THE SIXTH YEAR OF HENRY III. (A.D. 1221)	110
PLEAS AT ILCHESTER IN THE NINTH YEAR OF HENRY III. (A.D. 1225)	115

IV. PLEAS BEFORE THE JUSTICES OF THE BENCH IN THE REIGN OF HENRY THE THIRD.

PLEAS OF HILARY AND EASTER TERMS IN THE FOURTH YEAR OF HENRY III. (A.D. 1220)	120
PLEAS OF TRINITY TERM IN THE FOURTH YEAR OF HENRY III. (A.D. 1220)	135
PLEAS OF MICHAELMAS TERM IN THE FOURTH AND FIFTH YEARS OF HENRY III. (A.D. 1220)	139

GLOSSARY	141
INDEX OF MATTERS	145
INDEX OF PERSONS	151
INDEX OF PLACES	168

INTRODUCTION.

SINCE the aim of the Selden Society is to publish first-hand materials for the history of English law rather than modern dissertations, a few words about the nature of the rolls whence the following extracts have been taken, and the manner in which those extracts have been selected and copied, will be a sufficient preface for this book.

Almost to the extreme limit of legal memory, almost to the coronation day of Richard the First, extends the series of our yet extant Plea Rolls. The oldest of them is a very few years younger than our first classical text-book, the treatise ascribed to Glanvill. In 1835 the work of printing them was begun; Sir Francis Palgrave edited for the Record Commissioners two volumes entitled 'Rotuli Curiae Regis,' the one containing some of the records of Richard's reign, the other those of the first year of John; beyond this point the task was not prosecuted. The earliest roll printed was that for the Michaelmas term of 1194 (6 Ric. I.); but not all of what are now believed to be the rolls of Richard's reign were printed, and it seems probable that we have a few records which are just a little older than the oldest that appear in Palgrave's volumes. From these yet unprinted rolls of Richard's reign no extracts are here given, for it is hoped that those rolls will soon be printed at large, our elder sister, the Pipe Roll Society, having claimed them as her own; thus we begin with the beginning of the thirteenth century. We have good reason, however, for believing that the practice of enrolling the pleas heard in the king's court obtained during the last years of Henry the Second. On one of the rolls of John's reign there is

what seems to be an extract copied from a roll for the Hilary term of 1181, the 27th year of John's father, and very possibly this was one of the first Plea Rolls ever made.[1] The evidence offered by the Feet of Fines (the records, that is, of the solemn compromises of real or simulated actions begun in the king's court) converges with that offered by the yet extant Plea Rolls.[2] In the seventh year of Richard the First there begins a continuous series of these documents; a few of earlier date are still in existence, and we have other evidence which enables us to say that fines were habitually and officially recorded as early as 1178 or thereabouts; beyond that date the practice has not as yet been traced.[3] At present, therefore, it looks as if the enrolment of judicial proceedings was one of the great reforms which we owe to the later years of Henry the Second. In 1178, and again in 1179, he made great changes in the Curia Regis, and in 1180 Glanvill became his chief justiciar. Some measure for the better preservation of records may have marked the year 1194; Hubert Walter, the nephew, pupil, and secretary of Glanvill, had just been raised to the justiciarship. At the beginning of John's reign Hubert became chancellor, and then the Chancery Rolls take up the tale, Close, Patent, Charter, and Fine Rolls; all the affairs of government under his orderly management are punctually registered in black and white.

When once the stream of Plea Rolls begins to flow, it flows abundantly. If the judicial records of the thirteenth century were printed in a hundred volumes, those volumes would be stout; even from John's reign of seventeen years we have still some seventy rolls. But we have not by any means all that we ought to have, not, it may be guessed, so much as half what we ought to have, even had we no right to demand more than a single roll for every term and for every eyre. More than this, however, we might fairly de-

---

[1] See Note A, at the end of this Introduction.

[2] Some of the fines of Richard's and John's reigns were edited by Mr. Hunter for the Record Commissioners. The remaining fines of Richard's reign are to be published by the Pipe Roll Society.

[3] See Note B, at the end of this Introduction.

mand; we might ask for duplicate and triplicate rolls, for duplicate and triplicate rolls we sometimes find; even from John's reign we have duplicates. It seems to have been the regular practice that several independent records should be kept of the court's proceedings, and that these might be used to check or to supplement each other. We are told in 1221, and that by the highest authority, that every justice in eyre has his own roll, and even if this statement applies only to such of the justices as were permanent judges of the king's court, we ought often to find three records of the same eyre.[1] Doubtless some part of our loss we may ascribe to evil chances which befell the rolls after they were deposited in the Treasury, the place appointed for their custody; some of those that exist, despite all that has been done for them of late years, are in evil case; almost or altogether illegible, they tell a mournful story of fire and water and rats and gross human negligence. But there is good reason for thinking that many of their fellows never reached the Treasury. In 1258 an attempt was made to get in those rolls of the last forty years that were in private hands; seemingly the rolls of Stephen Segrave, whose career as a judge had ended in 1234, were still at the Abbey in which he died; Bracton probably had some fifty rolls in his possession.[2] On the same occasion the judges were strictly charged that for the future they must send in their rolls; but the command had to be repeated by statute in 1335 and again in 1409.[3] Naturally it is among the rolls that record the provincial visitations that we find the worst gaps; sometimes we know that there has been an eyre throughout all England and yet we have hardly a roll to show for it.

A Plea Roll, it may be well to explain, is not like one of the Chancery Rolls—for instance, a Patent or a Close Roll—

---

[1] Rot. Cl. vol. i. p. 451: royal letters animadverting severely on the dangerous practice which prevailed in Ireland of having but one justice and one roll: 'in uno solo rotulo periculum imminere possit cui cautius occurritur per plures justiciarios plures rotulos habentes.' See Bracton, f. 352 b; Bracton's Note Book, vol. i. p. 65.

[2] Madox, Hist. Exchequer, vol. ii. p. 257.

[3] 9 Ed. III. st. i. c. 5; 11 Hen. IV. c. 3.

a long continuous strip of parchment made by the sewing of the top of one membrane to the foot of another, but consists of membranes filed together by their tops. It is worth while to observe this, because it must be added that to determine the exact date of an early roll is not always easy, and the possibility must be had in mind that its membranes are not all of the same date, but have been bound together capriciously. Too often the scribe, while careful to note that it is Hilary Term or the Octave of Trinity, has forgotten to say what year it is; too often the first membrane of the roll has perished; the date of every particular membrane then becomes a serious problem. As may well be imagined, there are many signs that a uniform orderly method of making, arranging, and preserving records was only attained by long practice; the earliest rolls are often very untidy and are disfigured by erasures, interlineations, and clerical errors corrected and uncorrected; the work of one clerk differs widely from that of another, and this not only in externals but in substance also: in reporting the business done before justices in eyre this scribe will habitually give details that other scribes will omit. One gay clerk of John's reign, fonder, it would seem, of classical poetry than of legal drudgery, has finished off a list of essoins with *Omnia vincit amor et nos cedamus amori*; such an enrolment would hardly have been ventured in later days. On the whole, however, the art of recording grew apace; a roll from the middle of the thirteenth century is very unlike a roll from the beginning: far neater, fuller, more regular, more mechanical; the rapid development of common law is mirrored on the surface of the rolls.

The Plea Rolls of Richard's reign are consecutively numbered in a single series, and are commonly known as Coram Rege Rolls. Those of John's reign are similarly arranged. Those of Henry the Third's reign are in three different series, known as (1) Coram Rege Rolls, (2) Assize Rolls, (3) Tower Assize Rolls or Tower Coram Rege Rolls. This arrangement is in part due to the fact that some of the rolls were kept in the Chapter House at Westminster,

while others were at the Tower, and one cannot safely infer the nature of a roll from the class in which it is placed: thus one may find what certainly is an Eyre Roll in any one of these three classes. The rolls will, of course, be cited in this book by the names and numbers by means of which they can be found at the Record Office.

To classify the very oldest rolls would be hard, for we know but too little of the judicial arrangements of Richard's and John's reigns, and shall know little until all the rolls and all the fines have been either printed or at least calendared; still a few remarks about this matter must be hazarded, even though we have to stir again the old controversy as to when it was that the several courts of common law became independent entities.

The first line that we have to draw is between the permanent central court or courts and those temporary courts which are held from time to time by justices commissioned to hear the pleas of certain particular counties. To use Glanvill's terms, we have on the one hand *capitalis curia domini Regis*, and on the other *justitiarii itinerantes*.[1] Still even here beneath the obvious distinction we must not fail to notice the essential unity of royal justice. The court held by justices in eyre is *curia Regis*; so it is called in every fine that is levied before it, and though before the end of John's reign such a fine will say that it was levied *in curia domini Regis coram justitiariis itinerantibus*, this distinctive style is not found in the oldest specimens. Also when we find a roll covered with criminal cases all from one county we cannot at once conclude that this is an Eyre Roll, for we have to remember the doctrine of later days, that if the King's Bench comes into a county it becomes a court of oyer and terminer for that county,[2] a doctrine which must have been of great importance at a time when the king still travelled about England with judges in his train. There is a roll of John's reign of pleas of the crown for the two counties of Somerset and Dorset heard at Wells;

---

[1] Glanvill, lib. 8, c. 5.
[2] See Lib. Assis. an. 27, Mich. pl. 1. (f. 133); *Lord Sanchar's Case* 9 Coke Rep. 118 a.

it is very like an Eyre Roll, but we learn from the heading that the pleas were heard *coram domino Rege*.[1] The king himself was making an eyre; the amercements imposed by him were *amerciamenta de Itinere Regis*.[2] What can be done by justices commissioned for the purpose can of course be done by the king and the justices whom he keeps by his side. In 1272 the king left Winchester, we are told, because the justices in eyre were going to sit there;[3] the presence of the king would be incompatible with justice being done by mere commissioners; the moon could not shine until the sun had set.

Turning first to the central court, Glanvill's *capitalis curia domini Regis*, we may ask how it becomes two courts, the King's Bench and the Common Bench or Court of Common Pleas: the history of the Exchequer lies outside our sphere. We have not to ask when a second court other than the *Curia Regis* was instituted, for this never happened. Each of the two courts always asserted its right to the name *Curia Regis*, and that, too, in the most formal records; the King's Bench gave the reasons for its judgments under this form—'and for that it seemeth to the court of the Lord the King now here'; on the other hand, a fine levied in the Common Pleas was 'a final agreement made in the court of our Lord the King at Westminster.'[4] And since of late old things have been passing away very rapidly, one other remark about styles and titles which were still in use but a few years ago may be pardoned. Although in ordinary talk and even in Acts of Parliament the phrase 'the Common Bench' had long given way to 'the Court of Common Pleas,' and a layman might be forgiven for supposing that 'a justice of the Bench' would mean a justice of the King's Bench, still in the most solemn documents this was not its meaning: the Court of Common Pleas was *the* Bench; a judge of that

---

[1] Coram Rege Roll No. 9, memb. 16.
[2] Many examples in Madox, Hist. Exchequer, vol. i. pp. 151-3.
[3] Annales Monastici (Rolls Ser.), vol. ii. p. 111.
[4] In pleading a fine levied in the Common Pleas this was a correct and sufficient description of the court: Plowden, Comment. pp. 481-2.

court was 'one of the justices of our Lord the King of the Bench'; the pleas that it heard were 'Pleas at Westminster [or York or Hertford or elsewhere[1]] before Sir A. B. Knight and his fellows, justices of our Lord the King of the Bench.' On the other hand, the word 'Bench' did not occur in the most formal title of one who was generally called a judge of the King's Bench; he was 'one of the justices of our Lord the King assigned to hold pleas before the King himself.'[2] So again as long as the old writs were in use, a defendant was not told to come before the Court of King's Bench or the Court of Common Pleas; he was told to come 'before us wheresoever we shall be in England,' or 'before our Justices at Westminster.' This, then, is the contrast that demands our attention—'Pleas before the King himself' and 'Pleas before the Justices of the Bench'—'Appear before us wheresoever we shall be in England' and 'Appear before our Justices at such or such a place.' When do we first find this contrast?[3]

Whether it can be traced into Richard's reign, or into his father's, may for the present be left undecided; all the evidence that there is will, we may hope, soon be in print; but certainly it is found in John's reign. Since this statement runs counter to what seems the general belief, it should be proved. Certainly at times during John's reign, there were justices holding court term after term at Westminster or at St. Bride's in London, who were known as the Justices of the Bench, while contemporaneously the king himself with other justices was holding court at divers

---

[1] The Court of Common Pleas sat at York in the reign of Edward III.; see Mr. Pike's Introduction to Year Books of 11 & 12 Edw. III. p. xxviii, and 12 & 13 Edw. III. p. xxxiii; it sat at Hertford under Elizabeth; see 1 Coke Reports, 58 a, 61 a; see also the statute 2 Ed. III. c. 11, against removing the Common Bench without due notice.

[2] In the statutes of the Tudor reigns the titles 'justices of the Common Bench' and 'justices of the Court of Common Pleas' are used promiscuously; but we also find, not very unfrequently, 'the Common Place,' 'the King's Court of his Common Place at Westminster'; *Place* seems connected by sound with *Pleas*, but by sense with *Bench*.

[3] The problem is discussed in Madox, Hist. Exchequer, chap. 19; Foss, Judges of England, vol. ii. pp. 160-186; Stubbs, Introduction to Gesta Henrici (Rolls Ser.), vol. ii. pp. lix-lxxvi; Stubbs, Const. Hist. §§ 163, 233.

places up and down the country. We may be led to suppose that this was so by such entries as the following:—
A. B. owes the king a half-mark for removing *coram Rege* a case *quae est coram Justitiariis de Banco*:[1]—the king greets the Justices of the Bench and bids them put a particular case *coram eo quia illam audire vult*:—the king sends the record of a case to the Justices telling them that it was to have been heard *coram domino Rege*, but that at the prayer of one of the parties it is put before the Justices in London:—the king tells the Justices at Westminster to excuse A. B. for not having been before them on a certain day, because on that day he was *coram nobis in placito*.[2] But for at least one part (the middle part) of the reign a directer proof is given by the yet extant fines. When we have put on one side those which were levied before justices in eyre, those which remain fall into two distinct sets. Fines are levied term after term at Westminster or London before the justiciar, Geoffrey FitzPeter, and three or four justices; other fines are being levied *coram Rege* and another set of justices in all manner of places where, as we can learn from other sources, the king actually was. That in a fine of John's reign the words *coram ipso domino Rege* regularly imply that it was levied at a place where the king was resident, even if he did not always hear the proceedings (peradventure he was hunting), can hardly be doubted; the investigations of Sir Thomas Hardy and of Mr. Hunter seem to have settled this point;[3] though to the general rule there may have been some casual exceptions.[4] It is true, indeed, that in or about 1200, the Abbot of Leicester pleaded to the jurisdiction of the Justices of the Bench on the ground that a royal charter exempted him from being sued except 'before me or my chief justiciar,' and was told that all pleas holden by the Justices of

---

[1] Madox, Hist. Exch. vol. i. p. 790, note *n*: see the other cases on the same page and on p. 99.

[2] Such entries as these may be found on the Plea Rolls; in particular Coram Rege Roll No. 29 (Pasch. 1207), memb. 1, 2, 4 d. I cannot say that they are very common.

[3] Hardy, Introduction to the Patent Rolls, p. xli; Hunter, Introduction to the Fines, p. xxxvi.

[4] Compare the Fines of Hilary Term A. R. 15 (Hunter, vol. i. pp. 85-7) with Hardy's Itinerary.

the Bench were deemed to be holden before the king or his chief justiciar.[1] This may show that a fiction of the king's presence was growing or likely to grow; but as a matter of fact the chief justiciar was at this time so constantly on the Bench, that his absence on the day when the Abbot pleaded may have been a momentary accident. But at any rate the dualism of the king's court can be proved for the 6th, 7th, 9th, and 10th years of the reign. A large part of his 8th year the king spent in France, and during that time no fines, it would seem, were deemed to be levied *coram Rege*. Thus in A. R. 9, the terminal sittings at Westminster were before FitzPeter, Falconberg, Guestling, and Crepping, while the king was journeying about the country with three other judges in his train, Simon Pateshull, Poterne, and Pont Audemer. We can even see that when the king happened to be at Westminster the two bodies of judges did not necessarily coalesce; fines of even date are levied at Westminster before the king and his party and before the justiciar and his party.[2] This seems the normal state of affairs at least from the summer of 1204 to the summer of 1208. As regards the earlier years we have to remember that John spent about half his time in France; from these years we do not get fines *coram Rege*, though we do get other evidence which shows that justice was done before him when he was in England.[3] From the last seven years of the reign we have comparatively few fines; most of them are levied *coram Rege*, and it becomes very difficult to trace any regular terminal sittings at Westminster. The king now seems to have almost all the judges in his train; but not the justiciar. It may be that

[1] Placit. Abbrev. p. 82.
[2] What is here said is the result of a tabulation of the fines printed by Mr. Hunter and of some of those many hundred fines which have not been printed. Until all have been examined details must be insecure and are hardly worth giving; but take the Easter term of A. R. 9: fines are levied at Westminster before FitzPeter, Falconberg, Guestling and Crepping in the third, fourth and fifth weeks after Easter; fines are levied before the King, Pateshull, Poterne, and Pont Audemer at Hereford in the second week, at Woodstock in the third, at Westminster in the fourth.
[3] Madox, vol. i. p. 790, note *k*, and see below, Cases 82, 83, and Note 4 on p. 75.

as John's troubles thickened around him, less and less justice was done, and that a larger fraction of what was done was done under his own eye. Perhaps he did not trust his justiciar; we know how glad he was when, in October 1213, Geoffrey FitzPeter at length (as the king himself put it) followed Hubert Walter to hell.[1] All that can at present be said is, that the existence during these years of two parties of judges who simultaneously do justice, the one with the king, the other at Westminster, has neither been proved nor disproved. In the spring of 1213, Fitz-Peter presided over a court at Westminster; but the judges who sat with him had lately been accompanying the king. In 1214, his successor, Peter Des Roches, was holding plea at Westminster; but John was then in France.[2]

The Plea Rolls, then, of our *capitalis curia*, should already allow themselves to be arranged in two classes: there should already be 'Coram Rege Rolls' and 'De Banco Rolls.' And so there are pretty plainly, though the task of putting a given roll in its proper class may be hard or impossible. They seldom bear any more precise heading than *Placita* of such a date or *Placita apud Westmonasterium* of such a date. For the more part they seem to record the doings of a tribunal that remains stationary. There are just a few, however, which expressly profess to give us *Placita coram Rege*, and there are some which chronicle the movements of the tribunal as it journeys from Winchester to Newton, Beer, Ilchester, Exeter, Bristol, or elsewhere. It has seemed best not to attempt in such a book as the present the task of separating the Pleas before the King from the Pleas before the Justices of the Bench, not merely because this task would be both long and hazardous, but also because an attempt to perform it might do harm unless the editor gave his reasons at very great length. And although we are compelled by cogent facts and dates to

---

[1] Mat. Par. Chron. Maj. (Rolls Ser.), vol. ii. p. 559; Stubbs, Const. Hist. § 154.

[2] We may be led to believe by Case 115 that in Jan. 1213 the king was doing justice at Scarborough while judges were sitting at Westminster; but this does not seem quite certain.

hold that already in John's reign the court sometimes assumed a dual form, that it could be in two places at once, and that the two distinctive forms of summons were already in use, still we may hardly say that there were already two courts. In the first place, we can see from the rolls that whichever of its two forms the court assumed, it was equally competent to hear all manner of business; common pleas may well follow the king, pleas of the crown may well be heard by the Justices of the Bench. Secondly, the two 'divisions of the High Court' (this phrase, though very modern, is perhaps the aptest) seem at times to coalesce. If the king goes to France, the judges who have been attending him join their fellows at Westminster; sometimes when the king comes to London the whole judicial staff sits with him.[1] Thirdly, a particular judge is not permanently assigned to one or to the other division. The justiciar usually presides at Westminster, but occasionally he is with the king; Simon Pateshull is generally the first amongst the king's attendants, but sometimes he is sitting below the justiciar at Westminster. The term *Justitiarii de Banco* was in common use; apparently it served to describe those judges who for the time being were holding the terminal court at Westminster or London; but it was a description rather than a title, and we may doubt whether as yet it was ever used in the singular number. Fourthly, we may also doubt whether a litigant had any reason to expect that an action begun before one division of the court would always continue to be before that division; on the contrary, there are entries which seem to show that the Justices of the Bench might give the parties a day before the king, and that the king might give them a day before the Justices. In short, all judicial arrangements were subject to the king's will, and his will was but gradually becoming fettered by a routine which would stiffen into law: the king's court of John's reign shows no cleft, though it does show a well-marked line of cleavage.

[1] Thus shortly after Easter 1205 the king sits at the Old Temple with FitzPeter, Pateshull, Falconberg, Poterne, Stokes, G. de l'Isle, Fitz-Harvey and Crepping.

Now when Henry the Third came to the throne two great changes had happened: the Charter had provided that common pleas should no longer follow the king;[1] the king was an infant incapable of holding plea. The Justices of the Bench sat at Westminster term after term and heard cases of all kinds, criminal as well as civil. On the other hand, no trace has been found of any pleas that followed the king; the Justices of the Bench seem to be the only permanent, professional justices that there are. The King's Council, however, which was just becoming a definite, organised body, and was acting as a council of regency, exercised what we may perhaps call a supervisory control over all justice.[2] It seems to have usually met at Westminster; those who are summoned before it are generally told to appear *coram consilio nostro, coram H. de Burgo justiciario nostro et consilio nostro,* or *coram nobis et consilio nostro,* but a simple *coram nobis* is occasionally found.[3] That the Council had Plea Rolls of its own may be doubted; if so, they are not to be found; and although it interfered in many ways with judicial matters, it seems hardly to have held itself out to be an ordinary court of law; its work was rather to superintend the course of justice than to hear and determine causes. Hubert de Burgh, the new justiciar, did not, like Geoffrey FitzPeter, preside at the Bench; he was seldom there; his place was at the council board. Then when Henry came of age he began to do justice in person; already in 1224 the assizes of three counties are to be heard *coram Rege* at the shire towns.[4] Some years afterwards (in or about 1234, it would seem) he began to follow the example of his forefathers, to habitually make progresses through the country with judges in his train, and those judges habitually heard cases, their sessions being often afforced by the presence of other

---

[1] Charters of 1215, art. 17; 1216, art. 12; 1217, art. 12.

[2] Hardy, Introduction to the Close Rolls (folio ed.), pp. xxv-xxviii; Stubbs, Const. Hist. § 230.

[3] An instance in Rot. Cl. vol. i. p. 353 (Hibernia).

[4] Rot. Cl. vol. i. p. 631. In April 1223 Henry, who was then not sixteen years old, was declared by the Pope to be old enough to govern. In the following winter the formula of the royal writs was changed from *Teste Huberto* to *Teste Meipso.*

members of the king's council.[1] Thenceforward there are two distinct sets of Plea Rolls, the Coram Rege and the De Banco Rolls; a few years afterwards Bracton tells us that the king has several courts.[2] The arrangement of the judges into two permanently distinct groups may have been a work of time; we can hardly say that it is fully accomplished until there are two chief justices; but at latest from 1234 onwards there are parallel streams of *Placita coram Rege* and *Placita de Banco*. Whether the Justices of the Bench continued to hear pleas of the crown after Henry began to journey through the land with judges in his suit, is a point that has not been yet ascertained; they heard such pleas throughout the period covered by this book.[3] But one distinction as to the competence of the two courts was firmly established: common pleas could no longer follow the king. The Bench then was already the court for common pleas, though perhaps we ought not to say the Court of Common Pleas. Then in King Edward's day as the functions of the judges who followed the king became disentangled from the functions of the royal council,[4] they also were spoken of as forming a 'bench,' the King's Bench; there were thenceforth two benches; but the court which heard common pleas, though the lower of the two benches, continued to the last moment of its existence to be peculiarly and emphatically *the* Bench.

Turning from the central to what we may call the visitatorial courts, their rolls, at least in later days, might be classified according to the various commissions with which the justices were equipped: thus there are Assize Rolls and Gaol Delivery Rolls, and rolls which in a preeminent sense must be called Eyre Rolls. But it was only in course of time that several distinct forms of commission came into habitual use. At the beginning of Henry the

---

[1] Bracton's Note Book, vol. i. pp. 57-60.
[2] Bracton, f. 105 b; 'habet enim [Rex] plures curias': cf. f. 108.
[3] Apparently even when Bracton wrote, criminal cases might still come before the Bench; Bracton, f. 149, § 3, 4.
[4] As to this process, see Hale, Jurisdiction of the House of Lords, ch. 7.

Third's reign it became the practice to enrol the commissions which were issued, and from that date onwards there is little difficulty in discovering from the Patent and Close Rolls what justices there were travelling about the country and with what powers they were armed. During John's reign and part of Richard's we have the Plea Rolls to guide us, and can conjecture what the justices could do from what they did; Roger Hoveden also has handed down to us the articles for the eyres of 1194 and 1198.[1] For information as to yet earlier times we are dependent on the entries of fines and amercements upon the Pipe Rolls and upon documents enshrined in the chronicles or otherwise casually preserved. It seems probable that the *justitiarii errantes* even in Henry the First's time had full power to hear all the then recognised pleas of the crown, a list of which may be found in the Leges Henrici Primi.[2] As to common pleas the tendency seems to have been towards widening the scope of their commissions. In 1176 they were specially charged to take the then very new possessory assizes of mort d'ancestor and novel disseisin.[3] In 1194 they were to take grand assizes also if only a hundred shillingsworth of land or less was in dispute.[4] In 1218 they are competent to take all assizes and all pleas; the whole litigation of the county stands adjourned before them.[5] There are rolls which suggest that already in John's reign the commissions sometimes took this most comprehensive form; but of this we cannot be very certain. Nor can we be very certain whether more restricted commissions were not sometimes issued. We may sometimes find membranes covered entirely with possessory assizes and it is very possible that mere commissions of assize were in use; but these possessory actions had become so much the most common of all forms of litigation, that we

---

[1] Hoveden (Rolls Ser.), vol. iii. p. 263, vol. iv. p. 61.
[2] Leges Hen. Prim. c. 10. As to the date of these Leges, see Forschungen zur deutschen Geschichte, vol. xvi. p. 582, a paper by Dr. Liebermann.
[3] Assize of Northampton, art. 4, 5.
[4] Articles of 1194; Hoveden, vol. iii. pp. 262-7; Stubbs, Select Charters.
[5] Rot. Cl. vol. i. p. 380.

may not be entitled to this inference. How splendid a success had attended their institution may be learned from the Charter of 1215, which ordained that they should be taken four times a year in every county.[1] Perhaps the demand for justice that was thus conceded was a little extravagant; in 1217 once a year was substituted for four times.[2] Thenceforward, therefore, besides the commissions for what were more specifically known as eyres (*itinera ad omnia placita*), there were commissions of assize. The common practice was to issue a commission for each separate possessory action. During the first years of Henry's reign the commissioners were generally four knights of the shire. A little later it became usual to commission one of the royal judges and allow him to choose his own associates. From the same time, from the beginning of Henry's reign, it is that we get the first commissions of gaol delivery, and this work also was commonly entrusted to laymen. We have, therefore, in the first place, Eyre Rolls, the rolls of justices who at irregular intervals—five, six, seven years—are sent to hold all manner of pleas; we have also Assize Rolls and Gaol Delivery Rolls, though these come to us but rarely from the time with which we are now dealing. It may well be doubted whether when laymen were sent as commissioners they kept any written account of their doings; there are many recorded cases which seem to imply that they did not;[3] the usage of keeping plea rolls was but new, and the county courts, which were still important tribunals, had no rolls. The commissions of assize and gaol-delivery seem to have steadily grown in favour, while the general eyres which required the presence of all the freeholders of the county and the representation of every hundred and township, became very burdensome and hateful.[4]

[1] Charter of 1215, art. 18, 19.
[2] Charter 1217, art. 13, 14, 15.
[3] Bracton's Note Book, Cases 281, 367, 431, 512, 530, 564 etc.
[4] The Somersetshire Gaol Delivery Roll of 1225, extracts from which will be found below (p. 115) is the only Gaol Delivery Roll that I have found coming from the period covered by this book. The gaol delivery that it records was of an unusual kind; it was conducted by one of the king's judges and three knights, and all the townships had to send representatives. The writ will be found in Rot. Cl. vol. ii. p. 76.

The justices in eyre, besides receiving commissions, were entrusted with Articles of the Eyre (*Capitula Itineris*): that is, with lists of the interrogatories to be administered to the jurors of the various hundreds. These Articles are not enrolled; they seem to have been settled from time to time by the king or his council, and they grow more detailed and minute as time goes on. Hoveden has chronicled those of 1194 and of 1198. From various sources we get several sets of Articles which belong to the middle of Henry the Third's reign and a set of 1227, for an eyre in the Cinque Ports happens to have been put upon the Close Roll.[1] In reading the cases here selected from the Eyre Rolls, it should not be forgotten that the jurors are making sworn answers to a set of interrogatories with which the justices have been armed. For this among other reasons it has seemed well to separate the cases from the Eyre Rolls from the cases before the court at Westminster, even though chronological order was thus violated. The hearing of crown cases by justices in eyre was in truth a proceeding very unlike any to which we are accustomed. The juries for the several hundreds come up one by one with their answers, but every township in the shire is present by its representatives, and the whole county, the full county court (*totus comitatus*), is there in what we can hardly but call its corporate capacity. The justices can turn from the jurors who are making the presentments to another jury, to the townships, to the whole county; they can weigh the conflicting testimonies which come to them from these different bodies, and amerce those who tell falsehoods or make mistakes. Somehow or another under the Assize of Clarendon

---

[1] Rot. Cl. vol. ii. p. 213. This set is found in Bracton, f. 117 b. On f. 116 Bracton gives another set which has not yet been accurately dated. It is very like the set of 1254 given in the Annals of Burton, p. 330, which again is very like an undated set found in the Gloucester Cartulary (Rolls Ser.), vol. ii. p. 276. The set in Bracton may belong to 1254 it alludes to an assize made 'anno praeterito' against receiving strangers for more than one night. This prohibition was as ancient as 1166, but in 1253 it had been once more promulgated by a writ which is printed in Stubbs, Select Charters, part vi. The Articles in the Annals of Burton, however, which belong to 1254, do not contain any similar allusion.

it has become the practice to refer from the testimony of the hundred-jury to that of four townships. The text of the Assize of Clarendon as we have it directs that inquiry shall be made of twelve men of the hundred and four men of every township as to robbers, murderers, and so forth; it does not fix at four the number of the townships which are to be questioned; but so soon as we get records this number seems to be already fixed. The *quatuor villatae proximae* play an important part, therefore, in the drama of the eyre; whether they are entitled to be called the predecessors of the petty jury of after times, is a question which will only be solved when records later than any that are here printed have been examined.

But if on the one hand it seemed well to bring out, so far as was possible in a volume of extracts, the distinctive character of an Eyre Roll, a record of justices before whom stand the whole county, every hundred and every township, on the other it was necessary to draw a line between the reign of John and that of his son. Between the latest cases here printed from the one and the earliest here printed from the other, much more important events took place than a mere demise of the crown; the Great Charter was granted and the ordeal was abolished; the years which follow are critical years in the history of trial by jury.

The work of making selections has not as yet proved so delicate a task as might have been feared; it is hoped that not many valuable cases have been omitted. The whole mass of crown cases upon the rolls of John's reign is not very large; it is very small when compared with the voluminous records of civil litigation. Evidently it was by no means common for the king's central court to have criminal matters before it; they could only come there by some process of evocation, by *certiorari* or the like, unless the court happened to be taking the crown business for the county in which it was sitting; sometimes a whole term seems to have passed without a plea of the crown. The Eyre Rolls, again, of John's reign are but too few; we have certainly lost many. During the first half of the reign some coun-

ties were visited in almost every year; this we know from the extant fines. From the same source, however, we learn to doubt whether during the last half of the reign there were any eyres at all. Almost every Eyre Roll of our period that has been found has been laid under contribution, except the Gloucestershire roll for 1221, which is already in print.[1] In order to illustrate the justice of the central court it has been necessary to copy records of which too many end without a judgment; there were no better to be had; the series of rolls is so broken that we often lose sight of a case before it is decided. The main object kept in view has been the thorough illustration of the normal course of criminal justice. Cases of special interest have been copied, but the editor has not conceived it his duty to hunt for curiosities: the history of law is not a collection of curiosities; therefore many entries have been copied which may fairly be styled 'common form entries.'

The worst of a mere selection of cases is that it cannot entitle its reader to negative conclusions, therefore a few inferences derived from a superficial perusal of all the rolls of John's reign may be acceptable. In the first place, criminal justice was extremely ineffectual; the punishment of a criminal was a rare event; the law may have been cruel, for, in our eyes, it was capricious; it made use of the irrational ordeal; but bloody it was not. In Henry the Third's time some satisfactory hanging was accomplished, but the number of presentments of undiscovered crime is very large. His father's reign may have been a bad time for honest folk; it seems to have been a holiday for robbers and murderers. Secondly, trial by battle in criminal cases had already become uncommon; the justices seem to have delighted in quashing appeals. Thirdly, success at the ordeal seems to have been far commoner than failure; indeed, only one single case of failure has been found. Lastly, the reader may be asked not to approach these records with the belief that criminal procedure necessarily

[1] Published by Macmillan in 1884: Pleas of the Crown for the County of Gloucester.

involves the use of two juries; as yet the jury which presents the crime is, at least as a general rule, the only jury that there is. If an indicted person puts himself upon the jurors, this means that he puts himself upon those who have made the presentment.

In copying the extracts an attempt has been made to expand the contractions; the expedience of this, a very disputable point, cannot be argued here; but it is hoped that by means of foot-notes some of the worst dangers which beset such an attempt have been avoided. The margins of the rolls, especially of the Eyre Rolls, contain notes intended to call attention to the fact that something remains to be done. These it seemed best to print in their abbreviated form, and they could not have been intelligibly translated except in a too verbose style. They shall here be explained:—

    ad jud' = *ad judicium* = this case stands for judgment.
    loq' = *loquendum* = there must be further talk about this matter; sometimes, this matter must be brought before the king.
    cras = *to-morrow* = this case must be resumed to-morrow.
    mīa, mīe = *misericordia, misericordie* = some person or persons is or are to be amerced.
    custod' = *custodiatur* = some person is to be kept in custody.
    cap' = *capiatur* = some person is to be arrested.
exig', interrog', utl' = *exigatur, interrogetur, utlagetur* = some person is to be exacted, 'put in exigent,' and outlawed.
    cat' = *catalla* = some person has forfeited his chattels and there must be inquiry about them.
    murdr' = *murdrum* = a murder fine is due.
    susp' = *suspendatur* = some one is to be hanged.

The following typographical devices have been used:—

Words or letters about which the editor is uncertain, are printed in *italics*.

Words not in the original which have been inserted in the translation to make it clearer, are printed within [ ].

Words through which a pen has been drawn, and which therefore form no part of the record as finally settled, are printed within { }.

Words or passages which appear to have been interpolated or

added by way of postscript after the context was written, are printed within inverted commas, thus:—et ideo in misericordia. 'Misericordia perdonatur.'

It is hoped that the foot-notes will not be considered as impertinences. In translating the names of places, an effort has been made to put map and gazetteer to profitable use; but mistakes are easy, and no editor can know all England thoroughly. It has seemed best to render such technical terms as *considerare, defendere, recognoscere*, by what came to be their technical English equivalents— namely, *to consider, to defend, to recognise*, and it can hardly yet be necessary to explain that, *to consider* meant to adjudge or award, that *to defend* often meant to deny, and that *to recognise* meant to testify, or, if *testify* be a little too definite, to declare, to make known.

Kind help of many different kinds has been given to the editor by Professor Pollock, Professor Skeat, Dr. A. W. Verrall, Mr. H. W. Elphinstone, Mr. Walford Selby, Mr. J. Firmstone King, Mr. James Greenstreet, and the Society's Honorary Secretary, Mr. P. E. Dove.

Note A. *The Earliest Recorded Plea.*

On a plea roll of the year 1207 (Coram Rege Roll No. 38, m. 8), we find without any explanation the heading, *De termino S. Hillarii anno xxvij° regni Regis Henrici patris;* and under this heading there is a brief record of an action between Philip Monk and Reginald Monk. Sir Francis Palgrave who (Rot. Cur. Reg. vol. i. p. ii) has mentioned, and Mr. Bigelow who (History of Procedure, p. 400) has printed, this entry, ascribe it to the *seventh* year of Henry the Second. But though it may seem rash to differ from such authorities, and though a small hole has been made through the figures in the heading, I cannot but believe that those figures are not *vij*, but *xxvij*. But all doubt seems set at rest by what is found on a roll of 1206 (Coram

Rege Roll No. 31, m. 3 d). It appears there that an action was proceeding between Philip Monk and Berenger Monk; Berenger vouched a fine made between Philip and his (Berenger's) father, Reginald, in 27 Henry II. Doubtless it was on account of this voucher that the rolls of Henry's reign were searched, and that an extract from them was copied on the roll of 1207. The figures on the roll of 1206 are quite distinct and were read by Agard as I have read them; see Placit. Abbrev. p. 58. Madox, Form. Angl. p. xv, gives an entry from the Pipe Roll of 9 John showing how Berenger and Philip fined for a recognition as to whether there had been a plea and a fine in the time of Henry II.

NOTE B. *Early Fines.*

The practice of using the forms of litigation for the purpose of effecting a conveyance of land may well be of great antiquity. Abroad it has been traced into very remote times, and not improbably our phrase 'to levy a fine' bears witness to a very archaic solemnity.[1] But if our inquiry be as to the time when the court began to keep written records of the compromises made before it, to keep one 'part' (the 'foot') of the indenture of compromise (*pes chirographi*), then the evidence seems to point to the year 1178 or thereabouts, just, that is, to the time when King Henry was remodelling the Curia Regis. Thenceforward we have traces of a fairly continuous series of fines. The following list of references may be of use; the years mentioned in the first column are the regnal years of Henry II., whose reign began on December 19, 1154.

A.R.
25. Bracton's Note Book, Case 715.
26–8. Hunter, Fines, vol. i. p. xxii (original pes extant).
28. Hunter, Fines, vol. i. p. xxi (original pes extant).
28. Madox, Exchequer, vol. i. p. 118.

---

[1] For the meaning of *levare cartam*, see Brunner, Deutsche Rechtsgeschichte, vol. i. p. 397.

A.R.	
28.	Dugdale, Origines, p. 92.
28.	Bracton's Note Book, Case 802.
29.	Madox, Exchequer, vol. i. p. 218.
30.	Madox, Formulare, p. 217.
30.	Bracton's Note Book, Cases 716, 1800 (two specimens).
31.	Madox, Formulare, p. 217.
33.	Ramsey Cartulary, vol. i. p. 121 (Coram Rege).
33.	Glanvill, lib. 8, cap. 2, 3 (two specimens).
34.	Ramsey Cartulary, vol. ii. p. 888.
35.	Hunter, Fines, vol. i. p. xxiii (two specimens; original pedes extant).

The documents of earlier date which are most akin to fines seem to differ so much from what came to be the settled form, that they encourage the belief that the practice of having the compromise drawn up by a clerk of the court, who retained a *pes* for official keeping, did not yet prevail. Such documents will be found in Dugdale, Origines, p. 50, Bigelow, Placita Anglo-Normannica, pp. 264-6, Bracton's Note Book, Case 1095.

F. W. M.

Postscript.—As the exact date of the roll of Henry II.'s reign, to which reference is made on a roll of 1207, is a matter of some importance, I ought to add that Mr. Walford Selby has kindly given me his opinion as to the mutilated figures of which I have spoken on p. xxvi. He agrees with me in thinking that they certainly were not *vij*, but holds that they probably were *xvij* and not, as I make them, *xxvij*. I must admit that this is doubtful, but still think that the entry on the roll of 1206 makes it likely that they ought to have been *xxvij*, and even that they actually were *xxvij*.

DESCRIPTION OF FRONTISPIECE.

THE picture which has been reproduced as a frontispiece to this volume is found on a fragment of an Assize Roll of Henry III.'s time (year uncertain), still extant in the Public Record Office. It represents a judicial combat between Walter Bloweberme and Hamo le Stare. Walter was an approver (*probator*) : that is to say, he was a criminal who had confessed his crime and received a pardon conditional on his accusing and vanquishing a certain number of his associates. He accused Hamo of complicity in a robbery, and defeated him. Hamo's consequent fate is depicted in the background. Several cases of appeals by approvers will be found in this volume : see e.g. p. 121. The record which explains the picture is as follows :—

> Idem Walterus [sc. Bloweberme, *named a little above*] venit et appellat Hamonem le Stare de Wyntonia per eadem verba [viz. de latrocinio] scilicet quod fuerunt . . . de Cruce apud Wyntoniam, et ibi furati erant pannos et alia bona unde . . . Hamo habuit ad partem suam duas tunicas unam scilicet de panno de Hybernia et unam tunicam partitam de panno de Abendon et de burello Londonie; et quod simul fuit cum eo ad faciendum dictum latrocinium offert disrationare per corpus suum sicut curia consideraverit. Et Hamo venit et defendit totum; [et dicit] quod vult se defendere per corpus suum etc. Ideo consideratum est quod duellum sit inter eos etc. Et [est du]ellum inter eos percussum. Et predictus Hamo succubuit. Ideo ad judicium de eo etc. Nulla habuit catalla.

> [*Translation.*] The same Walter [Bloweberme] comes and appeals Hamo le Stare of Winchester by the same words [as he has used in his other appeals] to wit that they were . . . the Cross at Winchester, and there stole certain clothes and other goods, whereof Hamo had as his share two coats, to wit, one of Irish cloth and another coat half of Abingdon cloth and half of London burell (a kind of coarse cloth); and that he [Hamo] was along

with him [Walter] in committing the said larceny, he [Walter] offers to deraign against him [Hamo] as the court shall consider. And Hamo comes and defends all of it, [and says] that he will defend by his body etc. Therefore it is considered that there be battle between them. And the battle between them is struck. And the said Hamo has been defeated. Therefore to judgment against him etc. He had no chattels.

A rude engraving of the picture is given by Madox in his History of the Exchequer (quarto edition, vol. ii. p. 551), but on account of its great interest it is here more carefully reproduced by the Woodburytype Company.

PLACITA CORONE.

PLEAS OF THE CROWN.

PLACITA CORONE.

I. PLACITA CORAM JUSTICIARIIS ITINERANTIBUS REGNANTE REGE JOHANNE.

[1] PLACITA APUD LANSTAUETONAM ANNO REGNI REGIS JOHANNIS TERTIO.

Hundredus de Kerior.

1. [2] Dionisia que fuit uxor Antonii appellat Nicholaum Kam de morte Antonii viri sui, quod ipse nequiter occidit virum suum, et hoc offert probare versus eum consideracione curie. Et Nicholaus defendit totum. Consideratum est quod Dionisia non habet appellum quia ipsa non apponit appello suo visum. Juratores interrogati dicunt quod malecredunt eum inde, et totus comitatus similiter malecredit eum. Nicholaus purget se per aquam per assisam.[3]

   vad' lege' Vad' legem.[4]

2. [5] Jordanus prepositus Episcopi Exoniensis interfectus fuit apud Wenne, et pro morte ejus fugerunt Reginaldus Blewin' et Edwardus et Philippus et Rollandus et Odo et multi alii, scilicet tota villata. Catalla eorum xiiij. sol. unde Willelmus de Wrotham debet respondere. Et omnes *sunt* utlagati per sectam amicorum Jordani.

   catalla xiiij. sol.

---

[1] Coram Rege Roll No. 9. The justices were Simon Pateshull, Eustace of Falconberg, Ralph Morin, Stephen Clay.

[2] m. 2.

[3] The Assize of Clarendon (1166) reissued with amendments at Northampton (1176). See Stubbs, Select Charters, Part IV., where these ordinances are printed.

[4] *Vadiavit legem.* He has found pledges (sureties) that he will go to the ordeal. As to the use of *lex* to mean *proof* see Brunner, Die Entstehung der Schwurgerichte, p. 177.

[5] m. 2.

PLEAS OF THE CROWN.

I. PLEAS BEFORE THE JUSTICES IN EYRE IN THE REIGN OF KING JOHN.

PLEAS AT LAUNCESTON IN THE THIRD YEAR OF THE REIGN OF KING JOHN (A.D. 1201).

Hundred of Kerrier.

1.   Denise, who was wife of Anthony, appeals Nicholas Kam of the death of Anthony, her husband, for that he wickedly slew her husband; and this she offers to prove against him under award of the court. And Nicholas defends all of it. It is considered that Denise's appeal is null, for in it she does not say that she saw the deed. The jurors being asked, say that they suspect him of it; the whole county likewise suspects him. Let him purge himself by water [ordeal] under the Assize. He has waged his law.

2.   Jordan, the bishop of Exeter's reeve, was slain at St. Wenn, and on account of his death there fled Reginald Blewin, Edward, Philip, Roland, Odo, and many others, in fact, the whole township. Their chattels were worth fourteen shillings, for which William of Wrotham must answer. All are outlawed at the suit of Jordan's friends.

Hundredus de Powrdesir'.

3. [1] Willelmus de Ros appellat Alwardum Bere, Rogerum Calvum, Robertum Mercatorem, et Nicholaum Parmentarium, quod ipsi venerunt ad domum suam et nequiter in pace domini Regis abstulerunt ei quendam nativum suum quem habuit in vinculis eo quod voluit fugere, et illum abduxerunt, et in roberia asportaverunt scrinium uxoris ejus cum j. marca argenti et aliis catallis, et hoc offert probare per Robertum de Ros filium suum qui hoc vidit. Et Alwardus et alii venerunt et defenderunt feloniam et roberiam et pacem Regis infractam, et dicunt quod sicut consuetudo est in Cornubia Rogerus de Pridias [2] per preceptum vicecomitis fecit convenire xij. homines ad faciendum *sacramentum* de predicto nativo utrum ipse esset nativus Regis an ipsius Willelmi, et recognitum fuit quod ipse fuit villanus Regis, unde idem Rogerus serviens petiit eum ut ei redderet, et noluit, et tunc misit ad vicecomitem et ipse misit ad deliberandum eum, et non fuit inventus set evasit, et hoc appellum facit idem Willelmus ut possit retinere catalla ipsius Thome scil. ij. boves et j. vaccam et j. equam et ij. porcos et ix. oves et xj. capras. Et hoc testatur per juratores ita esse. Judicium, Willelmus et {Rob' [3]}

mīa
mīa
catall'

in misericordia pro falso clamore. Misericordia Willelmi dimidia marca. Misericordia {Rob'} dimidia marca. Plegius marce Warinus filius Roberti. Et Rex habeat catalla sua de Willelmo. Plegius de catallis Ricardus filius Hervici.

4. [4] Serlo de *Inneskathan* appellat Osbertum de *Dimok'* et Jordanum filium Walteri quod ipsi in pace domini Regis nequiter insultaverunt eum, et eum verberaverunt, et graviter vulneraverunt ita quod iij. ossa ex capite ejus per illam verberacionem extracta fuerunt, et hoc offert probare versus eum ut homo maamiatus de hoc maamio considera-

---

[1] m. 2 d.
[2] Probably the serjeant of the hundred.
[3] Robert de Ros, who is proffered as champion, is adjudged to be in mercy; but the amercement seems to have been afterwards forgiven, for his name is struck out.
[4] m. 2 d.

Hundred of Powdershire.

3. William de Ros appeals Ailward Bere, Roger Bald, Robert Merchant, and Nicholas Parmenter, for that they came to his house and wickedly in the king's peace took away from him a certain villein of his whom he kept in chains because he wished to run away, and led him off, and in robbery carried away his wife's coffer with one mark of silver and other chattels; and this he offers to prove by his son, Robert de Ros, who saw it. And Ailward and the others have come and defended the felony, robbery, and breach of the king's peace, and say that (as the custom is in Cornwall) Roger of Prideaux, by the sheriff's orders, caused twelve men to come together and make oath about the said villein, whether he was the king's villein or William's, and it was found that he was the king's villein, so the said Roger the serjeant demanded that [William] should surrender him, and he refused, so [Roger] sent to the sheriff, who then sent to deliver [the villein], who, however, had escaped and was not to be found, and William makes this appeal because he wishes to keep the chattels of Thomas [the villein], to wit, two oxen, one cow, one mare, two pigs, nine sheep, eleven goats. And that this is so the jurors testify. Judgment: William and Robert in mercy for the false claim. William's amercement, a half-mark. Robert's amercement, a half-mark. Pledge for the mark, Warin, Robert's son. Let the king have his chattels from William. Pledge for the chattels, Richard, Hervey's son.

4. Serlo of Ennis-Caven appeals Osbert of Dimiliock and Jordan, Walter's son, for that they in the king's peace wickedly assaulted, beat and seriously wounded him, so that by reason of the beating three bones were extracted from his head; and this he offers to prove against him under the court's award as a man maimed by that mayhem.

cione curie. Et testatum est per custodes placitorum corone[1] quod vulnera fuerunt ostensa in comitatu recentia, et hoc factum ita fuisse. Et Osbertus et Jordanus veniunt et defendunt de verbo in verbum. Consideratum est quod *vad' lege'* Osbertus purget se judicio ferri per appellum, quia Serlo primo se cepit ad Osbertum. Et Jordanus custodiatur donec sciatur quid evenerit de Osberto. Et alii appellati de vi[2] illa sint sub plegio donec sciatur etc.

Hundredus de Estwivelesir'.

5. [3]Juratores dicunt quod malecredunt Willelum Fisman de morte Agnetis de Chilleu ita quod die precedente minatus *vadiavit lege'* fuit ei de corpore et catallis suis. Et iiij. villate jurate proxime malecredunt eum inde. Consideratum est quod purget se per aquam per assisam.

6. [4]Willelmus Burnelle et Lucas de la Welle malecreduntur de burgeria domus Ricardi Palmarii per juratores hundredi *vad' lege'* et per iiij. villatas proximas juratas. Purget[5] se per aquam per assisam.

7. [6]Malot Crawe appellat Robertum filium Godefridi de rapo. Ipse venit et defendit. Et testatum fuit quod ipse eam ita rapuit et quod visa fuit sanguinolenta. Concordati sunt per licenciam justiciariorum per sic quod cepit eam in sponsam.[7]

---

[1] This is the usual title of the coroners.

[2] A person who is appealed as principal is said to be appealed *de facto*. His accessories constitute his *vis* and his *forcia*, and are said to be appealed *de vi* or *de forcia*: see Bracton, f. 188–9. Serlo has elected to make Osbert the principal appellee (*primo cepit se ad Osbertum*).

[3] m. 8.

[4] m. 8.

[5] Corr. *purgent*.

[6] m. 8.

[7] See Glanvill, lib. 14. c. 6; Bracton, f. 147 b.

And it is testified by the coroners that the wounds when fresh were shown in the county [court], and that [the bones were broken] as aforesaid. And Osbert and Jordan come and defend word by word. It is considered that Osbert do purge himself by ordeal of iron on account of the appeal, for Serlo betook himself against Osbert in the first instance. And let Jordan be in custody until it be known how Osbert shall fare. And the other persons who are appealed as accessories are to be under pledge until [Osbert's fate] be known.

Hundred of Eastwivelshire.

5. The jurors say that they suspect William Fisman of the death of Agnes of Chilleu, for the day before he had threatened her body and goods. And the four neighbouring townships being sworn, suspect him of it. It is considered that he purge himself by water under the Assize.

6. William Burnell and Luke of the Well are suspected of the burglary at the house of Richard Palmer by the jurors of the hundred, and by the four neighbouring townships, which are sworn. Let them purge themselves by water under the Assize.

7. Malot Crawe appeals Robert, Godfrey's son, of rape. He comes and defends. It is testified that he thus raped her and that she was seen bleeding. By leave of the justices they made concord on the terms of his espousing her.

Hundredus de Pidelsir'.

8. [1]Walterus Wifin fuit burgatus[2] et de catallis suis de burgeria in domo sua facta invente fuerunt calige in domo Leschildi de Ranam, et idem Walterus sequitur caligas illas ut suas. Et Lefchild dixit quod emit eas in foro de Bomini pro ij. den. et ob. set nescit a quo. Et preterea Walterus dicit quod undecim ulne de linea tela de predicta burgeria vendite fuerunt in domo Lefchild, et alia burgeria tota, et quod ipse Lefchildus fuit receptator illorum burgatorum scil. Roberti de Hideford et Alani Forestariorum quos ipse apellaverat inde. Et ipse Lefchildus defendit. Juratores interrogati dicunt quod malecredunt ipsum Lefchildum inde, de receptacione predicta. Et ideo purget se per aquam per

oras assisam.

9. [3]Edmerus de Penwithen appellat Martinum et Robertum et Thomam de Penwithen quod ipse Robertus vulneravit eum in capite ita quod xxviij. ossa extrahuntur, et interim Martinus et Thomas tenuerunt eum, et hoc offert disracionare versus eum[4] Robertum ut homo inde maimatus consideracione curie.

Et Robertus venit et defendit totum de verbo in verbum. Consideratum est quod purget se per judicium ferri. Et ceteri custodiantur donec sciatur quid evenerit de eodem Roberto. Et post venit Edmerus et retraxit

mīa se et posuit se in misericordiam de j. marca. Plegii Reinfridus filius Gill' et Philippus frater suus. Et ceteri appellati quieti.

10. [5]Reginaldus le *Teinus* retatus de recepcione et socie-
vad' legem tate Roberti utlagi venit et defendit. Et juratores dicunt quod malecredunt eum, et iiij. villate proxime jurate dicunt quod malecredunt eum inde. Et ideo purget se per aquam

---

[1] m. 8.
[2] The word *burgulare, burglare, burgare* is very common and can only be rendered by *to burgle*.
[3] m. 8. [4] Corr. *eundem*. [5] m. 8.

Hundred of Pydershire.

8.   Walter Wifin was burgled, and of his chattels taken from his house in the burglary certain boots were found in the house of Lefchild of Ranam, and the said Walter pursues those boots as his. And Lefchild said that he bought them in Bodmin market for 2½ pence, but he knows not from whom. And besides Walter says that eleven ells of linen cloth, part of the stolen goods, were sold in Lefchild's house, and all the other proceeds of the burglary, and that Lefchild was the receiver of the burglars, namely, Robert of Hideford and Alan the Foresters, whom he [Walter] had appealed of that crime. And Lefchild defends. The jurors on being asked, say that they suspect Lefchild of the said receipt. So let him purge himself by water under the Assize.

9.   Eadmer of Penwithen appeals Martin, Robert and Thomas of Penwithen, for that Robert wounded him in the head so that twenty-eight pieces of bone were extracted, and meanwhile Martin and Thomas held him; and this he offers to deraign against the said Robert as a man thereby maimed, under the court's award.

And Robert comes and defends all of it word by word. It is considered that he purge himself by ordeal of iron. Let the others be in custody until it be known how Robert shall fare. Afterwards Eadmer came and withdrew himself, and submitted to an amercement of one mark. Pledges, Reinfrid, Gill's son, and Philip his brother. Let the other appellees go quit.

10.   Reginald le Teinus accused of the receipt and fellowship of Robert the outlaw comes and defends. The jurors say that they suspect him, and the four neighbouring townships say that they suspect him of it. So let him purge

PLACITA CORONE.

loquend' de Ric' Revel

per assisam. Et loquendum de Ricardo Revel tunc [1] vicecomite in cujus tempore ipse Robertus evasit de custodia sua.

11. [2] Osbertus de Riterc appellat Odonem Hay, quod ipse assultavit eum in redditu suo de foro de Bomine, et eum in pace domini Regis et nequiter percussit in manu cum quodam baculo, et postea percussit eum gladio suo in brachio, quod maimatus est, et hoc offert probare ut homo *vad' legem* maimatus. Et Odo defendit totum. Et testatum est quod maimatus est per milites ad eum missos. Judicium, purget se per judicium ferri per appellum.

12. [3] Wulwardus de Ponte Gode burgatus fuit. Et Odo Hay et Laurencius Faber et Osbertus Medicus et Benedictus filius ejus et Willelmus Molendinarius et Robertus de Frokemere Mattilldis soror ejus malecrediti sunt de *vadiaverunt legem* burgeria illa per juratores hundredi et per iiij. villatas proximas juratas. Purgent se masculi per aquam per assisam, Matilldis per judicium ferri. Et Rogerus Morand' fugit pro illa burgeria et fuit manens apud Bomine, ideo in *mia* misericordia.

Hundredus de Lisniwet'.

13. [4] Robertus filius Godefridi appellat Philippum filium Willelmi quod ipse venit super terram Ricardi Fortescu domini sui et nequiter et in pace domini Regis et in roberia cepit viij. boves et j. mantellum et j. capam et j. gladium et ea asportavit, et hoc offert probare versus eum per corpus suum consideracione curie. Et Philippus venit et defendit totum de verbo in verbum. Consideratum est quod non est appellum quia boves illi non fuerunt ipsius Roberti, set Ricardi. Juratores interrogati dicunt quod

---

[1] He seems to have been sheriff of Cornwall throughout Richard's reign.
[2] m. 3.   [3] m. 3.   [4] m. 3 d.

himself by water under the Assize. And there must be inquiry as to Richard Revel, who was sheriff when the said Robert escaped from his custody.

11. Osbert of Reterth appeals Odo Hay, for that he assaulted him as he was returning from Bodmin market, and in the king's peace and wickedly struck him on the hand with a stick, and afterwards struck him on the arm with his sword so that he is maimed; and this he offers to prove as a maimed man. And Odo defends it all. And that [Osbert] is maimed is testified by knights sent to see him. Judgment: let [Odo] purge himself by ordeal of iron because of this appeal.

12. Wulward of Wadebridge was burgled. And Odo Hay, Lawrence Smith, Osbert Mediciner, and Benet his son, William Miller, Robert of Frokemere, and Maud his sister, are suspected of the burglary by the jurors of the hundred and by the four nearest townships, which are sworn. Let the males purge themselves by water under the Assize, and Maud by ordeal of iron. Roger Morand fled for that burglary, and he was living in Bodmin, [which town is] therefore in mercy.

Hundred of Lesnewth.

13. Robert, Godfrey's son, appeals Philip, William's son, for that he came on the land of [Robert's] lord Richard Fortescue, and wickedly and in the king's peace and in robbery took eight oxen and a mantle, cape, and sword, and carried them off; and this he offers to prove against him by his body under award of the court. And Philip comes and defends all of it word by word. It is considered that the appeal is null, for the oxen were not Robert's, but Richard's. The jurors being asked, say that [Philip] did no robbery to

nullam roberiam fecit ei. Ideo Ricardus Fortescu[1] in misericordia pro falso appello et Philippus sit quietus.

Hundredus de Trigesir'.

14.   [2] Petrus Burel appellat Anketillum de Wingeli quod ipse nequiter in pace domini Regis eum insultavit in campo ubi boves suos pascebat, et eum verberavit, et in capite ei iiij. vulnera fecit, et in roberia ei abstulit j. hachiam et j. gladium, et hoc offert probare versus eum, set nullum vulnus ostendit.

Et Anketillus defendit. Et comitatus recordatur quod ipse primo appellavit Rogerum de Tregadec de eadem roberia, et de eisdem vulneribus. Et ideo consideratum est quod nullum est appellum, et ideo Petrus in misericordia pro falso appello. Misericordia, dimidia marca. Plegius Radulfus Giffard.

15.   [3] Juratores in misericordia pro stulta presentacione, quia presentaverunt quoddam appellum in hundredo factum et non presentatum in comitatu.

16.   [4] Lucia de Morwestewa appellat Robertum de Scaccis, et Rollandum de Killio, et Petrum de Lankarf de roberia xx. sol. et viij den. et j. palii precii dim. marc. Et testatum est per juratores quod non robaverunt eam, et quod ipsa est stipendiaria, et quod quidam homo concubuit cum ea sub quodam gardino, et pueri exclamaverunt eam ita quod ipsa reliquid[5] pallium suum et pueri ceperunt illud et posuerunt in vadium pro dimidio sextario[6] vini. Consideratum est quod Robertus reddat ei iij. den. pro illo vino, et eat quietus.[7] Et Rollandus et Petrus non veniunt vel se essoniant. Et pl' eorum fuit [8] Nicholaus frater Aluredi de

---

[1] Possibly this is a mistake and Robert is amerced: more probably it is discovered that Richard set Robert on to make the appeal.
[2] m. 8 d.
[3] m. 8 d.
[4] m. 8 d.
[5] Corr. *reliquit.*

[6] A sextary is four gallons; Fleta, lib. 2, cap. 12, § 11.
[7] Red wine was selling at sixpence the sextary, white wine at eightpence; Hoveden (Rolls Ser.), vol. iv. p. 100.
[8] Corr. *sunt* or *fuerunt.*

[Richard]. So Richard Fortescue is in mercy for a false appeal, and let Philip be quit.

Hundred of Triggshire.

14.   Peter Burel appeals Anketil of Wingely, for that he wickedly in the king's peace assaulted him in the field where he was pasturing his oxen, and beat him, and gave him four wounds in the head, and in robbery took from him an axe and a sword; and this he offers to prove against him; but he shows no wound.

And Anketil defends. And the county records that [Peter] first appealed Roger of Tregadec of the same robbery and of the same wounds. Therefore it is considered that the appeal is null, and let Peter be in mercy for a false appeal. His amercement, a half-mark; pledge for it, Ralph Giffard.

15.   The jurors are in mercy for a silly presentment, for they presented an appeal which was made in the hundred [court] and which was not presented in the county [court].

16.   Lucy of Morwinstow appeals Robert de Scaccis and Roland of Kellio and Peter of Lancarf of robbing her of twenty shillings and eight pence, and of a cloak, price a half-mark. And it is testified by the jurors that they did not rob her, and that she is a hireling, and that a man lay with her in a garden, and the boys hooted her, so that she left her cloak, and the boys took it and pawned it for two gallons of wine. It is considered that Robert do give her three pence in respect of the wine and do go quit. And Roland and Peter neither come nor essoin themselves. And their pledges

PLACITA CORONE.

<small>mĩc mĩc</small>   Bomini et Herebertus prepositus de Bomini, et ideo in misericordia.

17.   ¹ De comitatu Cornubie c. marce de misericordia et pro quietancia carucagii.

18.   ² Martino clerico Domini Symonis de Pateshulla tradatur rotulus iste, et si non inveniatur, tradatur Willelmo clerico Domini Eustachii de Fauchonberge, et si non inveniantur, tradatur uni clericorum justiciariorum de Banco, qui eum salvo custodiat et tradat eidem Martino cum illum viderit ex parte Bartholomei clerici Ricardi Flandrensis.

19.   ³ Osbertus Wnchcht rettatus de morte Rolandi filii
<small>Penw.</small>   Reginaldi de *Kennel* per appellum ipsius Reginaldi detentus fuit in gaolam, defendit de verbo in verbum. Et Reginaldus offert probare per quendam liberum hominem Arkald qui filiam suam habet in uxorem pro eo desicut ipse transivit etatem lx. annorum. Osbertus *Ecclesia* totum illud defendit. Milites hundredi de Penwith' dicunt quod male ⁴ de predicta morte. Milites de Kerior dicunt idem. Milites de Penewith' ⁵ dicunt idem. Milites de Pidersir' dicunt idem. Judicium, purget se per aquam, et Reginaldus in misericordia quia non loquitur de visu neque de auditu et quia retraxit
<small>duo in mĩa</small>   se et alium loco suo posuit qui nec illud vidit nec vidit ⁶ et illud optulit probare, et ideo ipsi scil. Reginaldus et

---

¹ m. 8 d. This entry occurs at the end of the amercements. In the course of an eyre the county usually incurs many amercements, for which it often compounds with a lump sum. Here the carucage also is included.

² m. 6 d. This entry may serve to show how rolls got lost. Simon Pateshull and Eustace of Falconberg are two of the justices who hold this Cornish eyre. Richard Fleming or Flamank is the sheriff. Martin, the clerk of Simon Pateshull, may well be Martin Pateshull who in the next reign became illustrious as a judge.

³ m. 11. This and the next case are found on a very small membrane bound up in the roll. It is not very certain that they belong to the same eyre as the preceding cases. The name of the accused is difficult, but he seems to be called *Osbertus Ecclesia* (Osbert Church) below.

⁴ Supply *credunt eum*.

⁵ Perhaps the name of some other Cornish hundred should be here substituted for Penwith, for the testimony of Penwith appears above.

⁶ Corr. *audivit*.

were Nicholas brother of Alfred of Bodmin and Herbert Reeve of Bodmin, who are therefore in mercy.

17. Due from the county of Cornwall for amercement and for quittance from the carucage, 100 marks.

18. This roll is to be delivered to Martin, clerk of Sir Simon of Pateshull, or, if he be not found, then to William, clerk of Sir Eustace of Falconberg, or, if neither be found, then to one of the clerks of the Justices of the Bench, who is to keep it safe and deliver it to the said Martin when he sees him, on behalf of Bartholomew, clerk of Richard Fleming.

19. Osbert . . . . accused of the death of Roland, son of Reginald of Kennel, on the appeal of the said Reginald, was detained in gaol and defends word by word. And Reginald offers proof by the body of a certain freeman, Arkald, who has his [Reginald's] daughter to wife, who is to prove in his stead, since he has passed the age of sixty. Osbert . . . . defends all of it. The knights of the hundred of Penwith say that they suspect him of the said death. The knights of Kerrier [hundred] say the same. The knights of Penwith [hundred] say the same. The knights of Pyder [hundred] say the same. Judgment: let him purge himself by water, and Reginald is in mercy, for he does not allege sight and hearing, and because he has withdrawn himself, and put another in his place, who neither saw nor heard and yet offered to prove it, and so let both Reginald and

8   PLACITA CORONE.

Arkild in misericordia. Purgatus est per aquam. Plegii Osberti, Henricus Parvus, Henricus de *Penant*, Ossulfus *Niger*, Rogerus de *Trevithov*, Johannes de Glin, Radulfus de Treleuth.

Kerior

20. [1] Rogerus de Wika appellatus de morte Brict*meri* per appellum Hawisie uxoris predicti Brictmeri et captus fuit in fuga ut dicunt Johannes de Winielton' et Radulfus de Mertherin, set fuga non fuit testificata per hundredum. 'Ideo consideratum est quod purget se per aquam.' [2] Kerior dicit idem. Penwith' dicit idem. 'Purgatus est. Plegii Rogeri Radulfus de Trelewith, Ogerus de *Kurnic*, Ricardus filius Symonis, Aluredus Malus Vicinus, Euriwynus de Landa, Johannes de Kewerion, Warinus de Tiwardeni, Baldewinus Tirel, Rogerus de Trevithov, Johannes de Glin, Willelmus de Duneham, Thomas filius Osberti.'

[3] PLACITA APUD LINCOLNIAM ANNO REGNI REGIS JOHANNIS QUARTO.

Wapentac' de Kandelesho.

21. [4] Ricardus filius Willelmi appellavit Lucam filium Ricardi et Willelmum servientem Alani clerici de roberia et ligatura. Et appellati non venerunt vel se essoniaverunt. Et comitatus cum wapentaco dicit quod non fuerunt appellati de pace Regis, set de pace vicecomitis,[5] ita quod loquela fuit et est in comitatu, et ideo non fuerunt attachiati

m̄a jūr   ad esse coram justiciariis. Et ideo juratores in misericordia quia presentaverunt aliud quam presentare debuerunt.

[1] m. 11.
[2] This phrase has been interpolated, and should be read after that which records the testimony of the hundreds of Kerrier and Penwith. It seems likely that at the session at which this and the preceding case were heard, the townships were not represented, and that therefore the opinion of the knights of several hundreds was taken.
[3] Coram Rege Roll No. 56. This roll bears no date upon its face, but seems to belong to an eyre which took place in the summer of A. R. 4. A very large number of fines levied in this eyre are extant. The justices were Simon Pateshull, Eustace Falconberg, Richard Malebisse, Henry of Northampton, Alexander of Pointon.
[4] m. 1.
[5] There are other cases of this time which show that the sheriff's peace was still a considerable reality.

Arkald be in mercy. Osbert is purged by the water. Osbert's pledges: Henry Little, Henry of Penant, Ossulf Black, Roger of Trevithow, John of Glin, Ralph of Trelew.

20. Roger of Wick [was] appealed of the death of Brictmer by the appeal of Hawise, Brictmer's wife, and was captured in flight, as say John of Winielton and Ralph of Mertherin, but the flight is not testified by the hundred. Kerier [hundred] says the same. Penwith [hundred] says the same. So it is considered that he purge himself by water. He is purged. Roger's pledges: Ralph of Trelew, Ogier of Kurnick, Richard, Simon's son, Alfred Malvoisin, Everwin of Lande, John of Kewerion, Warin of Tiwardeni, Baldwin Tirel, Roger of Trevithow, John of Glin, William of Dunham, Thomas, Osbert's son.

Kerrier

PLEAS AT LINCOLN IN THE FOURTH YEAR OF THE REIGN OF KING JOHN [A.D. 1202].

Wapentake of Candleshoe.

21. Richard, William's son, appealed Luke, Richard's son, and William, the servant of Alan Clerk, of robbery and of binding him. The appellees have not come nor essoined themselves. The county together with the wapentake says that they were appealed, not of the king's peace, but of the sheriff's peace, so that the suit was and is in the county [court], and therefore they were not attached to come before the justices. Therefore the jurors are in mercy for presenting what they ought not to have presented.

22. ¹ In villa de Wainflet frequentatur mercatum per alium diem quam per consuetum diem. Et Prior de Kima est dominus ville et mercati. Et concessum est ex parte domini Regis per justiciarios quod mercatum sit per diem Martis ita quod non sit ad nocumentum vicinorum mercatorum.

Wapentac' de Calwat'.

23. ² Willelmus filius Hawisie appellat Ricardum filium Roberti de Sumercot' quod ipse venit in pace domini Regis ad domum suam apud Sumercot' et fregit domum suam, et robavit ei . . . ³ solidos et j. capam et j. surcot' et xxv. gallinas et xx. solidatas bladi, et eum vulneravit in capite vulnere quod ipse ostendit, et hoc offert probare versus eum consideracione curie etc.

Et Ricardus venit et defendit pacem Regis infractam et fractionem domus et vulneracionem et roberiam, set cognoscit quod ipse venit ad domum quamdam quam predictus Willelmus dicit esse suam sicut ad suam propriam, que escactavit in manum suam de Rogero villano suo qui obiit, et ibi cepit quedam catalla que sui villani erant et que sua erant post mortem ejusdem villani, scilicet, v. travas ⁴ avene, et xiij. garbas ordei et xxv. gallinas, et offert domino Regi xx. solidos pro habenda inquisicione utrum ita sit nec ne.

xx. sol.

Et Willemus dicit quod Ricardus injuste hoc dicit quia predictus Rogerus domum illam nunquam habuit nec in ea mansit, nec catalla predicta fuerunt ipsius Rogeri, set ipse tenuit domum illam ut suam et catalla sua erant que ibi capta fuerunt.

Juratores interrogati utrum ipse Rogerus ita tenuit domum predictam in vilenagio de ipso Ricardo, dicunt quod cciam. Et preterea coronatores testantur et totus comitatus quod ipse nunquam ostendit aliquod vulnus usque nunc,⁵ et vulnus quod ipse ostendit recens est. Et ideo consider-

¹ m. 1.
² m. 1.
³ An abrasion.
⁴ The thrave is said to be twelve or twenty-four sheaves. Halliwell, Dict. of Archaic Words.
⁵ As to the necessity of showing the wounds to the coroners, see Bracton, f. 145, § 2.

22.   In the vill of Wainfleet the market is frequented on a day other than the accustomed day. The Prior of Kyme is lord of the vill and the market. It is granted by the justices on the king's behalf, that the market be on Tuesday, but so that it be not to the nuisance of neighbouring markets.

Wapentake of Calceworth.

23.   William, Hawise's son, appeals Richard, son of Robert of Somercotes, for that he came in the king's peace to his house at Somercotes, and broke his house and robbed him of . . . shillings, and a cape and surcoat, and twenty-five fowls, and twenty shillingsworth of corn, and wounded him in the head with the wound that he shows; and this he offers to prove against him as the court shall consider etc.

And Richard comes and defends the breach of the king's peace and the house-breaking, wounding and robbery, but confesses that he came to a certain house, which William asserts to be his [William's], as to his [Richard's] own proper house, which escheated into his hand on the death of Roger his villein, and there he took certain chattels which were his villein's, and which on his villein's death were his [Richard's] own: to wit, five thraves of oats, thirteen sheaves of barley, and twenty-five fowls; and he offers the king twenty shillings for an inquest [to find] whether this be so or no.

And William says that Richard says this unjustly, for the said Roger never had that house nor dwelt therein, nor were those chattels Roger's, but he [William] held that house as his own, and the chattels there seized were his.

The jurors being questioned whether Roger did thus hold the house of Richard in villeinage, say, Yes. Also the coroners and the whole county testify that [William] never showed any wound until now; and the wound that he now shows is of recent date. Therefore it is considered that

atum est quod nullum est appellum, et Ricardus eat quietus, et Willelmus in misericordia pro falso clamore. Plegii de misericordia, Gilebertus filius Roberti et Ricardus filius Haldengi.

Villata de Hornicast'.

24. [1] Astinus de Wispinton appellat Simonem de Edlinton' quod nequiter et in pace domini Regis insultavit eum in pratis suis et ei oculum eruit, ita quod maimatus est illo oculo, et hoc offert probare etc.

Simon venit et defendit totum de verbo in verbum. Et custodes [2] corone et comitatus testantur quod usque huc sufficienter facta est secta appelli primo per uxorem suam, postea per eum.

vad' leg'   Judicium. Fiat lex et in electione appellati sit portare ferrum vel ut Astinus illud portet. Et ipse elegit quod Astinus portet. Vadiavit legem Astinus.[3] Plegii Simonis, Willelmus de Landa *et francus plegius suus* et Radulfus de Stures. Plegii Astini, Rogerus de Torp, Osgotus de Wis-
mīs   pinton' et Willelmus frater Joelis. 'Et post venerunt et posuerunt se *ambo* in misericordiam.'

Wapentac de Well'.

25. [4] Gilebertus de Wiflingham appellat Gilebertum filium Gaufridi quod ipse in pace domini Regis et nequiter posuit ignem in domo sua et illam combussit ita quod post ignem appositum ipse exivit et levavit uthes et clamorem unde vicini ejus et villata de Wivelingham venerunt, et per hoc quod ipse eis ostendit illum fugientem secuti sunt eum cum clamore, et hoc offert etc.

Et Gilebertus appellatus totum defendit de verbo in verbum etc. Et vicini et villata de Wivelingham quesiti

---

[1] m. 1 d.
[2] Probably *placitorum* should be supplied.
[3] Such a judgment as this is seldom found; but on this same roll (m. 6), there are two very similar decisions. In each case the appellee elects that the appellor shall go to the proof, and in each the appellor declines to do this and withdraws from his suit. In the one case the appellee is maimed; in the other he has passed the age for fighting.
[4] m. 2.

the appeal is null, and let Richard go quit, and William be in mercy for his false claim. Pledges for the amercement, Gilbert, Robert's son, and Richard, Haldeng's son.

Township of Horncastle.

24. Astin of Wispington appeals Simon of Edlington, for that he wickedly and in the king's peace assaulted him in his meadows and put out his eye, so that he is maimed of that eye; and this he offers to prove etc.

Simon comes and defends all of it word by word. And the coroners and the county testify that hitherto the appeal has been duly sued, at first by [Astin's] wife, and then by [Astin himself].

Judgment: let law be made, and let it be in the election of the appellee whether he or Astin shall carry the iron. He has chosen that Astin shall carry it. Astin has waged the law. Simon's pledges, William of Land and his frankpledge and Ralph of Stures. Astin's pledges, Roger of Thorpe, Osgot of Wispington, and William, Joel's brother. Afterwards came [the appellor and appellee] and both put themselves in mercy.

Wapentake of Well.

25. Gilbert of Willingham appeals Gilbert, Geoffrey's son, for that he in the king's peace and wickedly set fire to his house and burned it, so that after the setting fire [the appellor] went forth and raised hue and cry so that his neighbours and the township of Willingham came thither, and he showed them [the appellee] in flight and therefore they pursued him with the cry; and this he offers etc.

And the appellee defends all of it word by word etc. And the neighbours and the township of Willingham being

dicunt quod nunquam viderunt ipsum fugientem nec illum eis ostendit. Et similiter juratores dicunt quod appellat eum per attiam ut credunt pocius quam per justam causam. Et ideo consideratum est quod nullum est appellum, et est appellans in misericordia de dimidia marca. Plegius de misericordia, Robertus Walo.

mīa

Lindesle Wapentac.

26. [1] Willelmus Burel appellat Walterum Morcoc quod ipse in pace domini Regis ita verberavit et pulsavit Margeriam uxorem suam quod ipse occidit infantem infra ventrem suum et eam preter hoc verberavit et sanguinolentam fecit. Et Willelmus de Mannebi bedellus testatus est quod vidit vulnus recens et sanguinem in wapentaco. Et serviens tredingi et placitorum corone custodes et xij. milites dicunt quod nunquam viderunt vulnus vel sanguinem. Et ideo consideratum est quod nullum est appellum, quia cassata una parte appelli cassatur per totum, et Willelmus Burel in misericordia. Custodiatur. Et Willelmus de Mannebi propter falsum testimonium in misericordia. Plegii Willelmi de misericordia, Ricardus de Blesebi, Elias de Welleton'.

custodiatur

nulla

27. [2] Gefridus de Hotham appellat Godardum de Witham et Umfridum fratrem ejus quod occiderunt Robertum filium suum, et hoc offert probare ut homo qui preteriit etatem ut de visu suo et auditu, si curia consideraverit quod illud disracionare debeat. Et serviens domini Regis et duo milites qui fecerunt visum de vulnerato, qui vixit per iiij. septimanas et dimidiam postquam vulneratus fuit, testati sunt quod ipse Robertus dixit quod predicti Godardus et Umfridus ita vulneraverunt eum, et si posset convalescere hoc disracionaret versus eos, sinon, dixit se velle ut eis imputaretur mors sua. Et juratores Wapentaci de Wragho ubi interfectus fuit, quesiti dixerunt quod malecredunt

Memorandum de hoc in wapr̄ ı-tar̄' de W'raghog' [3]

[1] m. 2.
[2] m. 2 d.
[3] The report of what was said by the jurors of Wraggoe wapentake must have been recorded by way of postscript.

questioned, say that they never saw him in flight, and that [the appellor] never showed him to them. Likewise the jurors say that in their belief he appeals him out of spite rather than for just cause. Therefore it is considered that the appeal is null, and the appellee is in mercy for a half-mark. Pledge for the amercement, Robert Walo.

Wapentake of Lindsey.

26. William Burel appeals Walter Morcock, for that he in the king's peace so struck and beat Margery, [William's] wife, that he killed the child in her womb, and besides this beat her and drew blood. And William of Manby, the bedell, testifies that he saw the wound while fresh and the blood in the wapentake [court]. And the serjeant of the riding and the coroners and the twelve knights testify that they never saw wound nor blood. And so it is considered that the appeal is null, for one part of the appeal being quashed, it is quashed altogether, and William Burel is in mercy. Let him be in custody. And William Manby is in mercy for false testimony. Pledges for William's amercement, Richard of Bilsby, Elias of Welton.

27. Geoffrey of Hougham appeals Godard of Witham and Humfrey his brother for slaying Robert, [Geoffrey's] son; and this he offers to prove as one who is past [fighting] age and as of his own sight and hearing, if the court shall consider that he may deraign it. And the king's serjeant and the two knights who made view of the wounded man (who lived four weeks and a half after the wounding), testify that Robert said that Godard and Humphrey thus wounded him, and that should he get well, he would deraign this against them, and should he not, then he wished that his death might be imputed to them. And the jurors of the wapentake of Wraggoe where he was slain, on being asked,

ipsos de morte predicta. 'Post venit Gaufridus et retraxit se et posuit se in misericordiam. Misericordia ejus j. marca. Plegius ejus Robertus de Rasene.'

Wraghog' Wapentac'.

28. [1] Willelmus Marescallus fugit pro morte Sigerid matris Denis unde ipse Dinis eum appellat, et fuit in franco plegio de Sixle Prioris de Sixle, et est in misericordia, et catalla ejus fuerunt ij. vacce et j.. bovett'.

Post venit Prior de Sixle et cepit in manum habendi eundem Willelmum coram justiciariis ad rectum. Qui venit, et tunc Dionis filius predicte Sigerid venit et appellavit eum de morte matris sue. Et testatum fuit quod ipse habuit fratrem primogenitum [2] et quod ix. anni sunt transacti postquam ipsa obiit et quod vixit fere per unum annum postquam vulnerata fuit, et quod ipse Dionis nunquam appellaverat eum *antea*. Et ideo consideratum est quod nullum est appellum et Dionisius in misericordia. Plegius de misericordia, Radulfus filius Dinisii pater ejus.

Nesse Wapentac.

29. [3] Walterus filius Radulfi appellat Widonem Wake quod ipse in pace domini Regis nequiter occidit Willelmum Guberant fratrem suum, et hoc offert probare prout curia consideraverit sicut ille qui non vidit hoc set per alios habet eum suspectum. Nullum est appellum, et ideo in misericordia, et Wido quietus qui totum defendit. Plegii de misericordia, Hugo filius Alani et Willelmus de Morton'.

---

[1] m. 8.

[2] Apparently the rule that in an appeal of homicide the appellor must be the nearest kinsman of the slain man, was growing into law, but was not yet well established. Glanvill (lib. 14, c. 3) requires that the appellor shall be related to the slain by blood or feudal bond, and adds that the nearest kinsman excludes the more remote from the suit. This, however, is not equivalent to saying that the appellee can object that the appellor is not the nearest kinsman, but seems to mean no more than that the nearest of kin may, if he please, insist that the privilege of vengeance belongs to him. Compare Bracton, f. 125, Britton, vol. i. p. 109, and the note by Mr. Nichols.

[3] m. 8.

said that they suspect them of the said death. Afterwards came Geoffrey and withdrew himself and put himself in mercy. His amercement is one mark, for which Robert of Rasen is pledge.

Wapentake of Wraggoe.

28.   William Marshall fled for the death of Sigerid, Denis's mother, whereof Denis appeals him; and he was in the Prior of Sixhills' frank-pledge of Sixhills, which is in mercy, and his chattels were two cows and one bullock.

Afterwards came the Prior of Sixhills and undertook to have William to right before the justices. And he came, and then Denis, Sigerid's son, came and appealed him of his mother's death. And it was testified that [Denis] had an elder brother, and that nine years are past since [Sigerid] died, and that she lived almost a year after she was wounded, and that Denis never appealed [William] before now. Therefore it is considered that the appeal is null and that Denis be in mercy. Pledge for the amercement, his father, Ralph, son of Denis.

Wapentake of Ness.

29.   Walter, Ralph's son, appeals Guy Wake, for that he in the king's peace wickedly slew William Guberant his brother; and this he offers to prove as the court shall consider, as one who did not see the deed but suspects him on the testimony of others. The appeal is null; so let him be in mercy, and Guy (who defends all of it) be quit. Pledges for the amercement, Hugh, Alan's son, and William of Morton.

30. ¹ Alicia uxor Gaufridi de Karlebi appellavit Willelmum filium Rogeri et Willelmum filium suum et Rogerum filium suum de morte Willelmi fratris sui. Et Alicia non est prosecuta. Et ideo in misericordia et capiatur.

capiatur

Ad judicium de vicecomite qui non incarceravit attachiatos predictos cum sint appellati de morte hominis,² et similiter de brevi quod debet ostendere.

Bobi Wapentac.

31. ³ Petrus Pollard' appellavit Simonem de Wadinton' de pace Regis et alios de vi. Et Petrus venit et dixit quod non appellavit eos nisi de pace vicecomitis. Et juratores et custodes placitorum corone testantur quod appellum fecit de pace Regis. Et ideo Petrus in misericordia. Plegius de misericordia Adam de Niweton'.

mīa

Wapentac de Manlei.

32. ⁴ Hawisia filia Turstani appellat Walterum de Croxebi et Willelmum Molindinarium de morte patris sui et de propria plaga sua. Et ipsa habet virum, scilicet, Robertum Franccenat' qui nichil vult inde dicere. Et ideo consideratum est quod nullum est appellum eo quod femina non habet appellum versus aliquem nisi de morte viri sui vel de rapo.⁵ Et Robertus pro uxore sua in misericordia de dimidia marca, et appellati quieti. Plegius Roberti de misericordia, Ricardus Decanus de Marham, et habet laicum feodum.⁶

mīa
dim. marc.

Wapentac de Trehow.

33. ⁷ Willelmus Trig appellat Robertum de Wellebi quod ipse in pace domini Regis et in roberia abstulit ei xxxix.

---

¹ m. 3.
² Accused persons are usually replevied except in cases of homicide; Glanvill, lib. 14, c. 1.
³ m. 3.
⁴ m. 3 d.
⁵ This rule is confirmed by Magna Carta; Charter of 1215, Art. 54. But it was already law; see Glanvill, lib. 14, c. 1. s. 6.
⁶ A clerk would not be an acceptable surety if he had no property subject to the process of the temporal courts.
⁷ m. 4.

80. Alice, wife of Geoffrey of Carlby, appealed William, Roger's son, and William his son and Roger his son of the death of William her brother. And Alice does not prosecute. Therefore let her be in mercy and let her be arrested.

To judgment against the sheriff who did not imprison the said persons who were attached, whereas they are appealed of homicide, and to judgment also as to a writ which he ought to produce.

Wapentake of Boothby.

81. Peter Pollard appealed Simon of Waddington of [a breach of] the king's peace, and others as accessories. And Peter came and said that he only appealed them of the sheriff's peace. And the jurors and coroners testify that he made his appeal of the king's peace. Therefore be Peter in mercy. Pledge for the amercement, Adam of Newton.

Wapentake of Manley.

82. Hawise, Thurstan's daughter, appeals Walter of Croxby and William Miller of the death of her father and of a wound given to herself. And she has a husband, Robert Franchenay, who will not stir in the matter. Therefore it is considered that the appeal is null, for a woman has no appeal against anyone save for the death of her husband or for rape. And let Robert be in mercy on his wife's account, for a half-mark, and let the appellees be quit. Pledge for Robert's amercement, Richard, Dean of Mareham, who has lay property.

Wapentake of Threo.

83. William Trig appeals Robert of Welby, for that he in the king's peace and in robbery took from him 39 shillings

sol. et x. den. ob. et j. aureum anulum de catallis domini sui, et hoc offert etc. Et Robertus defendit totum etc. Consideratum est quod nullum est appellum eo quod in appello suo non facit mencionem de proprio catallo suo sibi robato set tantum de alieno. Et ideo in misericordia Willelmus.

mī

Wapentac' de Asewardechirn'.

84. [1] Juliana de Cretton' appellat Adam de Merle de verberacione et roberia. Et Adam non venit set essoniat se de servicio domini Regis ultra mare. Et quia non licet alicui appellato de pace Regis exire de terra sine waranto antequam fuerit coram justiciariis juriperitis,[2] plegii sui sunt in misericordia, scilicet, Segerus de Arceles, Alanus de Reninton', Robertus de Seuerebi, et ipsemet Adam [3] salvatur de placito per essonium quod fecit.

85. [4] Hugo de Ruperes appellat Johannem de Hasceby quod ipse in pace domini Regis et nequiter venit in prata sua et illa per averia sua pavit, et hoc offert etc. Et Johannes venit et totum defendit. Et quum testatum fuit per vicecomitem et per custodes placitorum corone quod ipse prius appellaverat ipsum Johannem de pratis suis pastis et de verberacione hominum suorum et nunc non vult prosequi appellum suum de hominibus suis set de pratis tantum, et preterea appellum de pratis pastis non pertinet ad coronam Regis,[5] consideratum est quod nullum est appellum, et ideo in misericordia Hugo, et Johannes quietus. Custoditur Hugo quia non potest invenire plegios.

custodiatur
mī

[1] m. 4 d.
[2] This seems a very early official mention of justices learned in the law.
[3] A word is here expunged, and the proper punctuation of this clause may be uncertain; but apparently Adam is quit of the appeal until his return, though his pledges are amerced.
[4] m. 4 d.
[5] The writ of trespass, if already devised, was certainly not in common use. Litigants seem to have tried hard to use the appeal of felony for all manner of purposes.

and 10¼ pence and a gold ring of the chattels of his lord, and this he offers etc. And Robert defends all etc. It is considered that the appeal is null, for that in his appeal he makes no mention of his own proper chattels robbed from him, but only of another's chattels. And so be William in mercy.

Wapentake of Aswardhurn.

84. Juliana of Creeton appeals Adam of Merle of battery and robbery. And Adam does not come, but essoins himself as being in the king's service beyond seas. And for that it is not allowed to anyone appealed of the king's peace to leave the land without a warrant before he has been before justices learned in the law, his pledges are in mercy: to wit, Segar of Arceles, Alan of Renington, and Robert of Searby. Adam himself is excused from the plea by the essoin that he has cast.

85. Hugh of Ruperes appeals John of Ashby, for that he in the king's peace and wickedly came into his meadows and depastured them with his cattle, and this he offers etc. And John comes and defends all of it. And whereas it was testified by the sheriff and the coroners, that in the first instance [Hugh] had appealed John of depasturing his meadows and of beating his men, and now wishes to pursue his appeal, not as regards his men, but only as regards his meadows, and whereas an appeal for depasturing meadows does not appertain to the crown of our lord the king, it is considered that the appeal is null, and so let Hugh be in mercy and John be quit. Hugh is in custody, for he cannot find pledges.

86. ¹Andreas de Estretenton' qui appellavit Robertum Pilate de pace domini Regis, scilicet, de vulnere ei facto, non est prosecutus. Et Andreas in misericordia et plegius ejus similiter, Ricardus Norensis. Et Pilate et alii appellati de vi sine die eant.

Ad judicium de Michaele serviente de Merstona qui ivit ad consilium xij. juratorum qui quesiti fuerunt utrum in wapentaco tenebatur placitum de eo quod francum plegium Theobaldi Hautein levavit clamorem et huthes super predictum Robertum Pilate et si francum plegium suum summonitum fuit veniendi in wapentacum inde respondendi, unde ipsi juratores quesiti dixerunt quod ita summonitum fuit, et ita tenebatur placitum.²

87. ³Thomas filius Lefwini appellat Alanum Messarium quod ipse in pace domini Regis assultavit eum in chimino euntem, et ipse cum vi sua portavit eum in domum ipsius Alani et percussit eum in brachio ita quod fregit quoddam parvum os brachii sui, unde ipse maimatus est, et robavit ei capam suam et cultellum suum et eum tenuit dum Emma uxor ejus abscidit ei unum testiculorum suorum et Radulfus Pilate alterum, et postquam ita demembratus fuit et taliter tractatus, predictus Alanus cum vi sua reportavit eum in viam, ita quod quam cicius potuit levavit clamorem per quem vicini venerunt ad clamorem et viderunt eum taliter attornatum.⁴ Postea statim misit ad servientem domini Regis qui venit et invenit ut dicit roberiam predictam in domo ipsius Alani, et post quam cicius potuit ivit ad wapentacum et comitatum et hoc ostendit.

Serviens ergo Regis quesitus, testatus est quod venit ad domum ipsius Alani et ibi invenit cultellum et testiculos in quodam ciphulo et non capam. Comitatus eciam totus

*Alanus dat domino Regi iij. m. pro habendo judicio suo. plegius Hugo Scotus*⁵

¹ m. 4 d.
² The jurors had been asked a question which affected Michael the serjeant: Had he done his duty? They gave an answer favourable to him; but while they were in consultation, he was guilty of speaking to them, and for this he will be amerced.
³ m. 4 d.
⁴ As to *attornare*, see Glossary.
⁵ Payments to the king for hastening judgment are not uncommon.

86.   Andrew of East Retington, who appealed Robert Pilate of the king's peace, to wit of a wound given him, does not prosecute. Let Andrew be in mercy, and his pledge likewise: to wit, Richard Norris. And let Pilate and those charged as accessories go without day.

To judgment against Michael, the serjeant of Marston, for going to the consultation of the twelve jurors, who were asked whether any plea had been holden in the wapentake touching the levying of hue and cry after the said Robert Pilate by the frank-pledge of Theobald Hautein, and whether his frank-pledge was summoned to the wapentake to answer touching this matter, and thereupon said that [the frank-pledge] was summoned and that the plea was holden in manner aforesaid.

87   Thomas, Leofwin's son, appeals Alan Harvester, for that he in the king's peace assaulted him as he went on the highway, and with his force carried him into Alan's house, and struck him on the arm so that he broke a small bone of his arm, whereby he is maimed, and robbed him of his cape and his knife, and held him while Emma, [Alan's] wife, cut off one of his testicles and Ralph Pilate the other, and when he was thus dismembered and ill-treated, the said Alan with his force carried him back into the road, whereupon as soon as might be he raised the cry, and the neighbours came to the cry, and saw him thus ill-treated, and then at once he sent to the king's serjeant, who came and found, so [Thomas] says, the robbed things in Alan's house, and then as soon as might be [Thomas] went to the wapentake [court] and to the county [court] and showed all this.

So inquiry is made of the king's sergeant, who testifies that he came to Alan's house and there found the knife and the testicles in a little cup, but found not the cape. Also

testatur quod nunquam antea appellavit eundem Alanum de predicta fractura ossis. Et ideo[1] consideratum est quod nullum est appellum, et ideo in misericordia, et alii appellati quieti.

[2] Idem Thomas appellat Emmam uxorem ipsius Alani quod ips... in pace predicta postquam ipse sic positus fuit in domo domini sui abscidit alterum testiculorum suorum.

Idem appellat Radulfum Pilate quod ipse abscidit ei alterum testiculorum.

Wapentac' de Grafhow'.

88. [3] Duodecim juratores in veredicto suo presentaverunt quod Augustinus filius Rumfar' appellavit Radulfum Gille de morte fratris sui, ita quod fugit, et quod Willemus filius Rumfar' appellavit Benedictum Caretarium de eadem morte, et Rannulfus filius Radulfi appellavit Hugonem de Hicha' de eadem morte et Baldewinum de Helesha' et Radulfum Hoth et Collegrim de vi. Et custodes placitorum corone per rotulos suos idem testantur. Set comitatus recordatur aliter, scilicet, quod omnes predicti Radulfus Gille et Benedictus et Hugo et Baldewinus et Radulfus et Colegrim appellati fuerunt a predicto Rannulfo filio Radulfi et non ab alio, ita quod per sectam ipsius Rannulfi utlagati fuerunt iiij. ex illis, scilicet, predicti Radulfus Gille et Hugo et Benedictus et Colegrim, et quod predicti non fuerunt appellati per alium quam per ipsum Rannulfum. Et quia non potuit comitatus contradicere coronatoribus et predictis juratoribus qui super sacramentum suum dictum suum dixerunt, consideratum est etc. Postea comitatus prevenit judicium et finem fecit ante judicium pro cc. lib. exceptis libertatibus.[4]

---

[1] See Bracton, f. 140 b.

[2] What follows must have been written before the clauses which record how the appeal against Alan was quashed.

[3] m. 5 d. There is an abstract of this case in Placitorum Abbreviatio, p. 71.

[4] There are many franchises (*libertates*) the dwellers within which are exempt from contributing to fines imposed on the county. A murder fine, e. g., is said to be paid by the hundred '*exceptis libertatibus*.' The fine imposed in this case seems very heavy. For modern learning as to untraversable presentments, see Hale, Pleas of the Crown, vol. ii. pp. 153–5.

the whole county testifies that [Thomas] never before now appealed Alan of breaking a bone. And so it is considered that the appeal is null, and that [Thomas] be in mercy, and that the other appellees be quit.

Thomas also appeals Emma, Alan's wife, for that she in the peace aforesaid after he was placed in her lord's house cut off one of his testicles.

He also appeals Ralph Pilate, for that he cut off the other of his testicles.

Wapentake of Graffoe.

88   The twelve jurors presented in their verdict that Austin, Rumfar's son, appealed Ralph Gille of the death of his brother, so that [Ralph] fled, and that William, Rumfar's son, appealed Benet Carter of the same death, and Ranulf, Ralph's son, appealed Hugh of Hyckham of the same death and Baldwin of Elsham and Ralph Hoth and Colegrim as accessories. And the coroners by their rolls testify this also. But the county records otherwise, namely, that the said Ralph Gille, Benet, Hugh, Baldwin, Ralph [Hoth] and Colegrim were all appealed by Ranulf, Ralph's son, and by no one else, so that four of them, to wit, Ralph Gille, Hugh, Benet and Colegrim, were outlawed at the suit of the said Ranulf, and that the said persons were not appealed by anyone other than the said Ranulf. And for that the county could not [be heard to] contradict the coroners and the said jurors who have said their say upon oath, it is considered etc. Thereupon the county forestalled the judgment and before judgment was pronounced made fine with 200 pounds [to be collected throughout the county], franchises excepted.

Walecrotf Walpentac.

89   [1] Rannulfus filius Ricardi de Saxelebi appellat Alanum filium Audani quod ipse in pace domini Regis et nequiter occidit patrem suum Ricardum, et hoc offert disracionare etc. set non apponit visum. Et quesitus quantum temporis transiit postquam pater suus occisus fuit, dicit quod xviij. anni jam transierunt et quod tunc fuit infra etatem ita quod eum appellavit primo coram Hugone Bard'.[2] Et xij. juratores quesiti si malecredunt Alanum de morte predicta, dicunt quod non. Et Alanus venit et totum defendit etc., et petit quod ei allocetur quod sepius fuerunt justiciarii in partibus Lincolnie postquam ipse Ricardus occisus fuit, et coram quibus ipse nunquam eum appellavit.[3] Consideratum est quod nullum est appellum. Et ideo Alanus quietus et Rannulfus in misericordia. Plegii de misericordia Robertus de Ounebi et Simon de Saxebi.

cras
mīa

Kirketon Wapent'.

40.   [4] Cristiana que fuit uxor Willelmi filii Johannis appellavit Radulfum filium Aggi et Ricardum fratrem suum de morte viri sui ita quod Radulfus captus fuit et in gaola positus et ibi obiit, ut vicecomes dicit. Set juratores dicunt quod postquam positus fuit in gaola viderunt eum errantem per patriam.

Et Ricardus venit et dicit quod alia vice coram G. filio Petri[5] retraxit se Cristiana inde et relaxavit eundem Ricardum. Et totus comitatus recordatur hoc ita quod ipsa posita fuit in gaola quia noluit sequi et post finem fecit de misericordia sua per j. marcam, et jam redditur ad scaccarium. Set Cristiana dicit quod nunquam retraxit se. Et ideo consideratum est quod tam ipse Ricardus quam ipsa Cristiana sint sub bonis plegiis quousque consilium domini G. filii Petri super hoc habeatur.

[1] m. 5 d.
[2] Geoffrey FitzPeter, Hugh Bardolf and others held a session at Lincoln in the autumn of 1200.
[3] As to this plea see Bracton, f. 116 b., 140 b, § 5, and Bracton's Note Book, case 1691.
[4] m. 7.
[5] Chief Justiciar 1198–1213.

Wapentake of Walshcroft.

39 Ranulf, son of Richard of Saxelby, appeals Alan, Aldane's son, for that he in the king's peace and wickedly slew [Ranulf's] father Richard, and this he offers to deraign etc., but he does not assert that he saw the deed. And being asked how long has elapsed since his father was slain, he says eighteen years, but he was then within age and he made his appeal for the first time before Hugh Bardolf. And the twelve jurors being asked if they suspect Alan of the said death, say that they do not. And Alan comes and defends all of it etc., and craves that it be allowed in his favour that the justices have been in the parts of Lincoln several times since Richard was slain, and [Ranulf] never made his appeal before them. It is considered that the appeal is null. So let Alan be quit and Ranulf in mercy. Pledges for the amercement Robert of Owmby and Simon of Saxby.

Wapentake of Kirton.

40. Cristiana, who was the wife of William, John's son, appealed Ralph, Agge's son, and Richard his brother of the death of her husband, so that Ralph was taken and put in gaol, and there (so the sheriff says) he died. But the jurors say that after he was put in gaol they saw him going about the country.

And Richard comes and says that on a former occasion before Geoffrey FitzPeter, Cristiana withdrew from her suit and released him, Richard. And the whole county records that this was so and that she was put in gaol because she would not prosecute and afterwards made fine for her amercement with one mark, which is already paid at the Exchequer. But Cristiana says that she never withdrew from her suit. Therefore it is considered that both Richard and Cristiana be under good pledges until the counsel of Sir Geoffrey FitzPeter be had upon this matter.

41. ¹Herewardus filius Willelmi appellat Walterum filium Hugonis quod ipse in pace Regis assultavit eum et vulneravit eum in brachio quadam furca ferrea et aliam plagam in capite,² et hoc offert probare per consideracionem curie per corpus suum. Et Walterus totum defendit per corpus suum. Et testatum est per coronatores et per totum comitatum quod idem Herewardus ostendit vulnera sua ad horam et terminum et sufficienter secutus est. Et ideo consideratum est quod duellum fiat. Plegii Walteri, Petrus de Goseberchurch' et Ricardus filius Herewardi. Plegii Herewardi, Willelmus pater ejus, et Prior de Pincebec. Veniant armati a crastino S. Swithini in xv. dies apud Leic'.³

Schirbec Wapentac.

42. ⁴Willelmus Gering appellat Willelmum Cocum de imprisonamento scilicet quod ipse cum vi sua in pace domin Regis et nequiter cum esset in servicio domini sui Widonis apud forgiam cepit eum et duxit eum apud Freston' ad domum Willelmi de Longo Campo, et ibi eum tenuit in prisona ita quod dominus ejus non potuit eum habere per vadium et plegios, et hoc offert probare sicut curia consideraverit.

Et Willelmus Cocus venit et defendit feloniam et imprisonamentum, set cognoscit quod cum misisset servientes domini sui ad capiendum averia predicti Widonis pro quadam misericordia in quam cecidit in curia domini sui et quam sepius summonitus reddere noluit, predictus Willelmus Gering venit et recussit averia capta et servientem domini sui vulneravit missum ad capiendum averia, ita quod ipse arestavit eum donec inveniret plegios standi recto et de vulneracione et recussione, et quando dominus suus venit pro eo, optulit ei eum per plegios, et noluit, et post

---

¹ m. 7 d.
² Supply *ei fecit* or the like.
³ The justices are going on to Leicester. This has been selected as one of the rare cases in which an appeal really leads to what is theoretically its natural conclusion —namely, wager of battle.
⁴ m. 8

41.   Hereward, William's son, appeals Walter, Hugh's son, for that he in the king's peace assaulted him and wounded him in the arm with an iron fork and gave him another wound in the head; and this he offers to prove by his body as the court shall consider. And Walter defends all of it by his body. And it is testified by the coroners and by the whole county that Hereward showed his wounds at the proper time and has made sufficient suit. Therefore it is considered that there be battle. Walter's pledges, Peter of Gosberton church, and Richard Hereward's son. Hereward's pledges, William his father and the Prior of Pinchbeck. Let them come armed in the quindene of St. Swithin at Leicester.

Wapentake of Skirbeck.

42.   William Gering appeals William Cook of imprisonment, to wit, that he with his force in the king's peace and wickedly, while [Gering] was in the service of his lord Guy at the forge, took him and led him to Freiston to the house of William Longchamp, and there kept him in prison so that his lord could not get him replevied; and this he offers to prove as the court shall consider.

And William Cook comes and defends the felony and imprisonment, but confesses that whereas he had sent his lord's servants to seize the beasts of the said Guy on account of a certain amercement which [Guy] had incurred in the court of [Cook's] lord [Longchamp], and which though often summoned he had refused to pay, [Gering] came and rescued the beasts that had been seized and wounded a servant of [Cook's] lord, who had been sent to seize them, whereupon [Cook] arrested [Gering] until he should find pledges to stand to right touching both the wounding and the rescue, and when [Gering's] lord [Guy] came for him, [Cook] offered to let him be replevied, but this [Guy] refused, and afterwards he repeated the offer

optulit eum eidem coram serviente domini Regis, qui [1] eciam tunc noluit eum recipere, et tunc dimisit eum liberatum sine plevina.

Et Wido [2] dicit quod ponit se super wapentacum utrum predicto modo imprisonatum fuit sicut dictum est et si hoc statim ostendit servienti Regis an non. Et Willelmus Cocus similiter. Et wapentacus dicit quod illud factum debuit factum fuisse in Quadragesima, et Wido non ostendit hoc in wapentaco donec ad xv. dies ante festum S. Botulfi.[3] Et comitatus dicit cum coronatoribus quod nunquam audierunt loquelam illam coram se. Et ideo consideratum est quod nullum est appellum set [4] Wido in misericordia. Et Willelmus et alii appellati de vi quieti.

mīa

43.   [5] Sefridus filius Reginaldi Cote arestatus fuit eo quod dictum fuit quod ipse tensavit [6] naves transeuntes per mariscum, et dimissus fuit per plegios, scilicet, Ricardum Bacun et Johannem filium Jordani et Reginaldum Cote. Et post eorum plevinam coronam sibi fecit et totondit se ad modum clerici. Set non fuit in tali statu quando dimissus fuit plegiis ut Ricardus de Camvilla [7] qui eum dimisit et alii testantur. Et post venerunt plegii et cognoverunt quod in plevina sua sic fuit tonsus et corona rasus, et ponunt se in misericordia.

cras

mīa

---

[1] Seemingly *qui* means Guy, not the king's serjeant.

[2] It was evidently a common practice for lords to get their battles fought for them by their men; this will appear in other cases. Of course in civil actions this practice was recognised by law; the demandant offered battle 'by the body of a certain free man of his,' who professed himself a witness. There are many signs that to some extent, difficult to define, a similar practice was permissible in criminal cases, which often enough were really disputes about proprietary rights.

[3] St. Botulph's day is June 17. Freiston is near Boston, where St. Botulph is well known.

[4] It is not the appellor who is amerced, but his lord. The use of *set* instead of *et* seems to draw attention to this.

[5] m. 8.

[6] For *tensare* see Glossary.

[7] Gerard of Camville was sheriff, and Richard may have been one of his serjeants.

before the king's serjeant, but even then it was refused, and then [Cook] let [Gering] go without taking security.

And Guy says that he puts himself upon the wapentake, whether the imprisonment took place in manner aforesaid, and whether he [Guy] at once showed the matter to the king's serjeant, or no. And William Cook does the same. And the wapentake says that the alleged [imprisonment] took place in Lent, and Guy did not show the matter to the wapentake until a fortnight before St. Botulph's day. And the county together with the coroners says that they never heard the suit in their court. Therefore it is considered that the appeal is null, and Guy is in mercy. And let William and those who are appealed as accessories go quit.

48.   Sefrid, son of Reginald Cote, was arrested because it was said of him that he tallaged ships which came through the marsh, and he was replevied by Richard Bacun, John, Jordan's son, and Reginald Cote. And after his replevin he shaved his crown and made him a tonsure like a clerk's. But this was not his condition when he was delivered to his pledges, as is testified by Richard of Camville who delivered him [to his pledges] and by others. Afterwards his pledges came and confessed that while he was in their plevin he had his crown shaved, and they put themselves in mercy.

[1] PLACITA APUD NORHAMTONAM ANNO REGNI REGIS JOHANNIS QUARTO.

44. [2] Mercatum de Undele est remotum de die dominica usque diem Sabbati. Et mercatum est Abbatis de Burgo. Ideo in misericordia.

m̅i̅a̅ apud Westm'

Juratores dicunt quod mercatum de Rowell' est remotum a die dominica usque in diem Sabbati. Et mercatum est Comitis de Clara. Ideo in misericordia. 'Et sit per diem Lune mercatum.' [3]

m̅i̅a̅ apud Westm'

Hundredus de Wimeresle.

45. [4] Juratores dicunt quod Andreas filius Sureman appellavit Petrum filium Lefwini et Thomam Armigerum et Willelmum Oildene de roberia. Et non est prosecutus. Et ideo in misericordia, et Steph' de Spina et Baldewinus Longus,[5] et appellati sine die.

m̅i̅a̅ m̅i̅a̅

Et post venit Andreas predictus et dicit quod ipsi imprisonaverunt eum per preceptum Willelmi Malesoures in domo ipsius Willelmi, ita quod ipse misit ad vicecomitem ut vicecomes deliberaret eum, ita quod vicecomes misit servientem suum illuc et alios qui cum eo venerunt, qui eum invenerunt in prisona et eum deliberaverunt, et producit testes, scilicet, Nicholaum Portehors et Hugonem filium Turkilli, qui testantur quod eum imprisonatum invenerunt, et inde vocat vicecomitem. Et vicecomes quesitus dicit quod revera misit iiij. legales homines cum serviente illuc per querelam Nicholai Portehors ex parte Andree. Qui missi illuc ex parte vicecomitis testantur quod eum invenerunt

m̅i̅a̅

m̅i̅a̅

m̅i̅a̅ m̅i̅a̅ m̅i̅a̅

---

[1] Coram Rege Roll No. 17. This eyre took place in the autumn of 1202. The justices were Simon Pateshull, Eustace of Falconberg, Richard Malebisse, Henry of Northampton, Alexander of Pointon.

[2] m. 1.

[3] Presentments to the effect that market-day has been changed are very frequent. These two are selected because the marginal notes seem to show that Abbots and Earls are to be amerced, not in the ordinary way, but at Westminster, by their peers. See Charter of 1215, art. 21; Bracton, f. 116 b; Madox, Hist. Exchequer, vol. i. p. 528.

[4] m. 1 d.

[5] Probably some words are missing. Stephen and Baldwin are Andrew's pledges for prosecution and are amerced.

PLEAS AT NORTHAMPTON IN THE FOURTH YEAR OF THE REIGN OF KING JOHN [A.D. 1202].

44. The market of Oundle is removed from Sunday to Saturday. The market belongs to the Abbot of Peterborough. Therefore he is in mercy.

The jurors say that the market of Rothwell is removed from Sunday to Saturday. The market belongs to the Earl of Clare. Therefore he is in mercy. And let the market be on Monday.

Hundred of Wymersley.

45. The jurors say that Andrew, Sureman's son, appealed Peter, Leofwin's son, Thomas Squire and William Oildene of robbery. And he does not prosecute. So he and Stephen Despine and Baldwin Long are in mercy, and the appellees go without day.

Afterwards comes Andrew and says that [the appellees] imprisoned him by the order of William Malesoures in the said William's house, so that he sent to the sheriff that the sheriff might deliver him, whereupon the sheriff sent his serjeant and others thither, who on coming there found him imprisoned and delivered him, and he produces witnesses, to wit, Nicholas Portehors and Hugh, Thurkill's son, who testify that they found him imprisoned, and he vouches the sheriff to warrant this. And the sheriff, on being questioned, says that in truth he sent thither four lawful men with the serjeant on a complaint made by Nicholas Portehors on Andrew's behalf. And those who were sent thither by the sheriff testify that they found him at liberty

liberum et jocantem in domo ipsius Willelmi. Et ideo consideratum est quod nullum est appellum[1] pro falso clamore, et appellati quieti, et Nicholaus Portehors et Hugo filius Turkilli in misericordia pro falso testimonio. 'Andreas et Hugo custodiantur donec habuerint plegios.'

Hundredus de Hecham.

46. [2] Juratores dicunt quod Galfridus Cardun levavit novas consuetudines aliter quam debet et quam esse consueverunt, scilicet, capiendo de careta per terram suam transeunte in Winewich' cum anguillis stikam[3] anguillarum, et de careta mulvellorum j. mulvellum[4] et de careta salmonum dimidium salmonem, et de careta hallecium v. allecia, ubi nullam consuetudinem capere debet de aliquo nisi de sale transeunte per terram suam, scilicet, de careta j. bollam salis et tunc debet ipse salnarius habere unum panem pro sale illo, et preterea si careta salinarii fracta fuerit, sine calumpnia habebunt equi salinarii pasturam in terra ipsius Gaufridi dum ipse facit caretam suam parare.

Et Gaufridus venit et cognoscit quod ipse capit predictas consuetudines et capere debet, quia ipse et antecessores sui illas ceperunt a conquestu Anglie, et ponit se in magnam assisam domini Regis, et petit recognicionem fieri utrum illas consuetudines capere debeat, nec ne. Et post obtulit domino Regi xx. solidos ut illa loquela ponatur coram domino G.[5] Plegius de xx. solidis, Ricardus de Hinton'.

Hundredus de Claile.

47. [6] Juratores dicunt quod Hugo filius Walteri presbiteri utlagatus fuit pro morte Rogeri Rombaud per sectam

---

[1] Perhaps *et ideo Andreas in misericordia* should be supplied.
m. 2. This case is abstracted in Placit. Abbrev. p. 41.
[2] Twenty-five eels make a stick; Fleta, lib. 2. cap. 12, § 7.
[4] As to the *mulvellus* see Glossary.
[5] *Dominus G.* is the Justiciar, Geoffrey FitzPeter; he is often referred to on the rolls in this manner.
[6] m. 2 d. This case is abstracted in Placit. Abbrev. p. 41.

and disporting himself in William's house. Therefore it is considered that the appeal is null [and Andrew is in mercy] for his false complaint and Nicholas Portehors and Hugh, Thurkill's son, are in mercy for false testimony. Andrew and Hugh are to be in custody until they have found pledges [for their amercement].

Hundred of Higham.

46. The jurors say that Geoffrey Cardun has levied new customs other than he ought and other than have been usual, to wit, in taking from every cart crossing his land at Winwick with eels, one stick of eels, and from a cart with greenfish, one greenfish, and from a cart with salmon, half a salmon, and from a cart with herrings, five herrings, whereas he ought to take no custom for anything save for salt crossing his land, to wit, for a cart-load, one bole of salt, and in that case the salter ought to have a loaf in return for the salt, and also if the salter's cart breaks down, the salter's horses ought to have pasture on Geoffrey's land without challenge while he repairs his cart.

And Geoffrey comes and confesses that he takes the said customs, and he ought to take them, for he and his ancestors have taken them from the conquest of England, and he puts himself on the grand assize of our lord the king, and craves that a recognition be made whether he ought to take those customs or no. And afterwards he offers the king twenty shillings that this action may be put before Sir Geoffrey [the Justiciar]. Pledge for the twenty shillings, Richard of Hinton.

Hundred of Cleley.

47. The jurors say that Hugh, son of Walter Priest, was outlawed for the death of Roger Rombald at the suit of

Roberti Rumbaud et post rediit per breve domini Regis et postea utlagatus fuit per appellum Gaufridi filii Turstani pro eadem morte. Comitatus ergo quesitus quo waranto ipsi utlagaverunt bis unum hominem pro eadem morte, dicit quod revera tempore Regis Ricardi predictus Hugo utlagatus fuit per sectam cujusdam Lucie sororis ipsius Rogeri, ita quod diu post subtraxit se, et tandem venit in comitatum et protulit literas domini G. filii Petri in hac forma, G. filius Petri etc. vicecomiti Norhantone salutem, Scias quod dominus Rex perdonavit Hugoni filio sacerdotis de Grafton' fugam et utlagariam ei adjudicatam pro morte cujusdam hominis interfecti et literis suis nobis significavit quod simus ipsi Hugoni in auxilium ad pacem reformandam inter ipsum et parentes interfecti, et ideo tibi precipimus quod sis ipsi Hugoni in auxilium ad pacem illam faciendam, et nobis scire facias literis tuis sigillatis quid super hoc feceris, quum tenemur illud domino Regi significare, Teste &c. per breve domini Regis de ultra mare.[1] Lectis ergo literis predictis in pleno comitatu, dixit eidem Hugoni comitatus quod ipse Hugo inveniret plegios ad esse ad pacem domini Regis, et ivit querere plegios, et postea non comparuit. Audientes autem parentes predicti interfecti quod ipse Hugo rediit post utlagariam, venerunt ad proximum comitatum, ita quod Robertus Rumbaud produxit Gaufridum filium Turstani, qui dixit quod si videret predictum Hugonem sequeretur versus eum mortem predicti Rogeri qui fuit   [2] Et comitatus ei ostendit qualiter ipse tulit breve Justiciarii de fuga et utlagaria eidem Hugoni perdonata, et quod deberet querere plegios standi ad pacem Regis, et postea non venit. Unde preceptum fuit servienti domini Regis quod eum quereret et adduceret ad alium comitatum. Ad alium comitatum optulit se idem Gaufridus versus predictum Hugonem, et ipse non comparuit, unde serviens domini Regis quesitus dixit quod non

---

[1] The king's writ from foreign parts was the justiciar's warrant for issuing the letters patent. As to these writs *de ultra mare* see Madox, Hist. Exchequer, vol. i. p. 85.

[2] A space is here left; probably Geoffrey said that Roger was his kinsman in such or such a degree.

Robert Rombald, and afterwards returned under the [protection of the] king's writ, and afterwards was outlawed for the same death on the appeal of Geoffrey, Thurstan's son. The county therefore is asked by what warrant they outlawed the same man twice for the same death, and says that of a truth in King Richard's time the said Hugh was outlawed at the suit of one Lucy, sister of the said Roger, so that for a long time afterwards he hid himself; and at length he came into the county [court] and produced letters of Sir Geoffrey FitzPeter in the form following: 'G. FitzPeter etc. to the sheriff of Northamptonshire, greeting, Know thou that the king hath pardoned to Hugh, son of the priest of Grafton, his flight and the outlawry adjudged to him for the death of a certain slain man, and hath signified to us by his letters that we be aiding to the said Hugh in re-establishing the peace between him and the kinsfolk of the slain; wherefore we command thee that thou be aiding to the said Hugh in making the peace aforesaid, and do us to wit by thy letters under seal what thou hast done in this matter, since we are bound to signify the same to the king. In witness etc. by the king's writ from beyond seas.' And the said letters being read in full county [court] the county told the said Hugh that he must find pledges that he would be in the king's peace, and he went away to find pledges, and afterwards did not appear. But the kinsfolk of the slain, having heard that Hugh had returned after his outlawry, came to the next county [court] and Robert Rombald produced Geoffrey, Thurstan's son, who said that if he saw the said Hugh he would sue against him the death of the said Roger, who was [his kinsman]. And the county showed him how Hugh had brought the Justiciar's letters pardoning him the flight and outlawry, and that he was to find pledges to stand to the king's peace, but had not returned. Whereupon the king's serjeant was ordered to seek Hugh and bring him to a later county [court]. And at a later county [court] Geoffrey offered himself against Hugh, and Hugh did not appear; whereupon the king's

invenit eum, et comitatus ei consuluit ut veniret ad alium comitatum quia si ipse Hugo interim posset inveniri, adduceretur comitatui. Ad tercium vero comitatum optulit se predictus Gaufridus, et testatum fuit a serviente quod Hugo postea non fuit inventus, unde dictum fuit a comitatu quod ex quo Hugo noluit comparere ad pacem Regis, quod gereret lupinum capud¹ sicut prius fecit.

Ad judicium de coronatoribus et de xij. juratoribus.²

³ PLACITA APUD BEDEFORDIAM ANNO REGNI REGIS JOHANNIS QUARTO.

Hundredus de Flitte.

48. ⁴ Juratores dicunt quod Elias filius Stanard' occidit Rogerum filium Gaufridi, et fugit in ecclesiam cognoscens mortem et abjuravit regnum, et nulla habuit catalla.

m͞ia Ad judicium de Roberto de Marisco serviente, qui non fecit convenire hundr' et villat' super mortuum.

m͞ia Stanard de Eia in misericordia quia non levavit clamorem filio suo invento mortuo et occiso.

49. ⁵ Henricus Buscel et Osbertus frater ejus appellaverunt Robertum Flecherum et Petrum filium ejus et Gillebertum de Flitte et Willelmum Maugis de morte Johannis Buscell'. Et Robertus et Petrus sunt utlagati per sectam illorum

---

¹ Bracton, f. 125 b, uses this picturesque phrase; it occurs also in Leg. Edw. Conf. 6, § 2 (Schmid), and is occasionally found on the early Plea Rolls. See Brunner, Deutsche Rechtsgeschichte, vol. i. p. 167.

² This sentence is in the margin. It looks as if the jurors did wrong in making the presentment and the county had acted rightly. The coroners may have been guilty of some irregularity apparent on their rolls.

³ Coram Rege Roll No. 14. The justices were Simon Pateshull, Eustace of Falconberg, Richard Malebisse, Henry of Northampton, Alexander of Pointon.

⁴ m. 5. All the presentments for the hundreds of Flitt and Redbornstoke and the town of Luton are printed here, in order that the reader may form an idea of the amount of business coming from each hundred. These specimens are chosen as fair samples.

⁵ m. 5.

serjeant being questioned said that he had not found him, and the county advised [Geoffrey] to come to another county [court], because if in the meantime Hugh could be found, he would be brought to the county [court]. Then at the third county [court] the said Geoffrey offered himself, and it was testified by the serjeant that Hugh had not yet been found, wherefore the county said that as Hugh would not appear to the king's peace, he must bear the wolf's head as he had done before.

To judgment against the coroners and the twelve jurors.

PLEAS AT BEDFORD IN THE FOURTH YEAR OF THE REIGN OF KING JOHN [A.D. 1202].

Hundred of Flitt.

48. The jurors say that Elias, Stanard's son, slew Roger, Geoffrey's son, and fled to church, confessed the death and abjured the realm, and he had no chattels.

To judgment against Robert of Marsh, the serjeant, for not summoning the hundred and the townships to sit upon the dead man.

Stanard of Eye is in mercy for not raising the hue when his son was found dead and slain.

49. Henry Bussel and Osbert his brother appealed Robert Fletcher and Peter his son and Gilbert of Flitton and William Maugis for the death of John Bussell. And Robert and Peter are outlawed by their suit for the said death, and

pro illa morte, et fuerunt in franco plegio Roberti Pudras in Flitte, et ideo in misericordia, et nulla habuerunt catalla. Et Willelmus fugit in ecclesiam et abjuravit regnum, et catalla ejus fuerunt iij. sol. unde Robertus de Braibroc tunc vicecomes debet respondere.[1]

mia
iij. sol.

Et Henricus Buscell' venit et appellavit Gillebertum predictum quod ipse in pace domini Regis et nequiter occidit ipsum Johannem fratrem ejus, ita quod ipse Gillebertus cognovit ei quod eum occidit, et hoc offert probare versus eum etc. Et Robertus Decanus de Bedeford peciit inde curiam cristianitatis quia Gillebertus est clericus et subdiaconus.

Walkelinus Buscell' appellans et Henricus Bunum appellatus de verberacione ponunt se in misericordia pro habenda licencia concordandi. Plegius Walkelini, Henricus Buscell. Plegius Henrici Bonum, Pirot Bunum frater ejus.

mia
mia

50. [2] Mercatum de L*ui*ton' remotum est de die dominica ad diem Lune, et mercatum est Comitis de Alba Mara, et ideo in misericordia, et sit per diem Lune.

mia

51. [3] De aliis capitulis nichil.

Villa de Luiton.

52. [4] Juratores dicunt quod Petrus Vinitor de Dunstapel' et Willelmus homo Jordani et Henricus filius Henrici vendiderunt vinum contra assisam apud Dunestapell'. Et ideo in misericordia.

mia mia
mia

53. De omnibus aliis capitulis nichil.

Hundredus de Redburnestok'.

54. [5] Juratores dicunt quod Simon filius Simonis de Aunestowe appellat Willelmum fratrem Roberti de Aubeni et

---

[1] For some years past the Justiciar, Geoffrey FitzPeter, has been sheriff, with Robert of Braybrook as his custos.

[2] m. 5.

[3] See note to Case 48.

[4] m. 5. For John's assize of wine see Hoveden (Rolls Ser.), vol. iv. p. 99. Presentments to the effect that it is not kept are very common.

[5] m. 5.

were in the frank-pledge of Robert Pudras in Flitton, which therefore is amerced, and they had no chattels. And William fled to church and abjured the realm; his chattels were worth three shillings, for which Robert of Braybrook, the then sheriff, must account.

And Henry Bussel came and appealed the said Gilbert, for that he in the king's peace and wickedly slew the said John his brother, so that Gilbert confessed to [Henry] that he slew [John]; and this he offers to prove against him etc. And Robert the Dean of Bedford craved [cognizance for] court christian, for Gilbert is a clerk and a subdeacon.

Walklin Bussell appellor and Henry Bunum appellee in an appeal of battery put themselves in mercy that they may have leave to compromise. Walklin's pledge, Henry Bussell; Henry Bunum's pledge, Pirot Bunum his brother.

50. The market of Luton is removed from Sunday to Monday. It belongs to the Earl of Albemarle, who is therefore in mercy. Let it be held on Monday.

51. To the other articles, [the jurors say] nothing.

Town of Luton.

52. The jurors say that Peter Vintner of Dunstaple, William, Jordan's man, and Henry, Henry's son, have sold wine at Dunstaple contrary to the Assize. So they are in mercy.

53. To all the other articles, [the jurors say] nothing.

Hundred of Redbornstoke.

54. The jurors say that Simon son of Simon of Elstow, appeals William, brother of Robert Daubeny, and Simon of

Simonem de Amethull' quod ipsi assultaverunt eum ad carucam suam et ei absciderunt pollicem suum et hoc fecerunt per consilium et voluntatem Willelmi Bunum.

Et Willelmus de Aubeni non fuit inventus set profectus in Jerosolymam nec umquam secutus est versus eum idem Simon, et ideo expectat donec reddierit. Et Simon de Amethull' clericus est de quo Robertus Decanus [1] peciit curiam cristianitatis. Et habuit. Et Willelmus venit et defendit quod per ejus consilium nunquam hoc ei fecerunt. Et Simon quesitus quomodo hoc scivit quod per ejus consilium hoc fecerunt, dixit quod hoc scivit eo quod ei voluit malum quia non potuit eum abastardare. Et quia non locutus fuit de visu et auditu nec aliquam racionem dixit unde appellum debuit fieri, consideratum est quod nullum est appellum, et quod Willelmus eat quietus et Simon in misericordia pro falso appello.

55.   [2] Willelmus de Morton' et Simon Carpentarius utlagati sunt pro morte Walteri de Lega per sectam Juliane uxoris ejus, et nulla habuerunt catalla, et nusquam fuerunt in franco plegio, set fuerunt servientes Abbatis de Wuburn'.

jud'   Post presentator Englescherie Walteri obiit, et nullus loco ejus fuit presentatus nisi coram justiciariis et ideo ad judi-

murdr'   cium de murdro. Consideratum est quod sit murdrum.[3]

56.   [4] Albrea uxor Petri Crawe appellavit Oliverum et Rollandum fratres persone de Cranfeld' quod ipsi vulneraverunt Petrum virum ejus. Et ipsa non est prosecuta. Et quia ipse Petrus obiit inquisitum a juratoribus utrum ipse obierit de illis vulneribus. Dicunt quod non obiit illis vulneribus. Et Oliverus et Rollandus eant quieti.

---

[1] Dean of Bedford: see Case 49.
[2] m. 5.
[3] Englishry is presented in the first instance in the local courts by the kinsfolk of the slain. Then at the eyre the jurors present the presenters. Here the original presenter died; another ought to have been at once found, so that testimony might be kept alive in the local courts; but this was not done, therefore the murder fine must be paid.
[1] m. 5.

Ampthill, for that they assaulted him while at his plough and cut off his thumb, and this they did by the counsel and advice of William Bunum.

And William Daubeny was not found, but had gone to Jerusalem, and Simon [Simon's son] never made suit against him, and therefore awaits his return. And Simon of Ampthill is a clerk and Robert the Dean has claimed [cognizance] of him [for] court christian: and this has been granted. And William [Bunum] comes and denies that they did this by his counsel. And Simon [Simon's son] on being asked how he knew that they did this by [William's] counsel, said that he knew this because [William] wished him ill because he had not been able to bastardise him. And for that he does not allege sight and hearing and alleges no ground for an appeal, it is considered that the appeal is null, and that William do go quit and Simon be in mercy for a false appeal.

55. William of Morton and Simon Carpenter are outlawed for the death of Walter of Leigh at the suit of Juliana his wife, and they had no chattels, and they were nowhere in frank-pledge but were servants of the Abbot of Woburn. The presenter of Walter's Englishry afterwards died, and no one was presented in his place until the case came before the justices. Therefore to judgment whether this be a murder. It is considered that this is a murder.

56. Aubrey, wife of Peter Crawe, appealed Oliver and Roland, brothers of the parson of Cranfield, for that they wounded Peter her husband. And she has not prosecuted her appeal. And because Peter died, the jurors are asked whether he died of those wounds. They say that he did not die of those wounds. Let Oliver and Roland go quit thereof.

57. ¹Domus cujusdam mulieris de Selton' fuit burgata de nocte. Et Robertus Fale malecreditur inde et ab² aliis male*ficiis* per juratores et iiij. villatas proximas. Purget se aqua.³

58. De aliis capitulis nichil.⁴

Hundredus de Clipton'.

59. ⁵Robertus de Sutton' appellat Bonefand Judeum de Bedeford' quod ipse in pace domini Regis et nequiter fecit ementulare Ricardum nepotem suum, unde ipse obiit, ita quod ipse fecit portare eum usque ad terram suam de Hacton' quam ipse habet in vadio et ibi obiit, et hoc offert probare etc. Et Bonefand venit et defendit totum et offert domino Regi j. marcam pro habenda inquisicione utrum sit inde culpabilis vel non. Et juratores inquisiti dicunt quod non est culpabilis inde. Et ideo Bonefand sit quietus et *custodiatur* Robertus in misericordia pro falso appello.⁶

Hundredus de Wristanestre.

60. ⁷Ailbricus de Wiliton' appellavit Willelmum Russell' et Adam fratrem ejus et Gaufridum Prepositum et Nicholaum filium Gervasii et Godwinum Gardinarium, David Espeke, Robertum de Hawenes quod ipsi in pace domini Regis et nequiter noctu venerunt ad domum suam, et portas suas et haias fregerunt, et fregerunt hostia domus sue in hamsoka, et intraverunt et pecuniam ejus ceperunt scil. gallinas, et asportaverunt, et ipsum voluerunt interficere nisi fugisset. Et ipsi venerunt et defendunt totum. Et vicecomes quem Ailbricus vocavit ad warantum quod hoc ei in crastino monstravit, dicit quod non venit ad eum set ad quendam comitatum, set ad quem nescit, et audita querela sua in

---

¹ m. 5.
² Corr. *de*.
³ This sentence is in the margin.
⁴ See note to Case 48.
⁵ m 5 d. An abstract of this case is found in Placitor. Abbrev. p. 36.
⁶ See John's charter to the Jews, dated April 10, 1201, in Rot. Cart. p. 93; also the letters in which he declares that the Jews are in his peace, Rot. Pat. p. 33: 'and if I give my peace to a dog, it must be kept inviolate.'
⁷ m. 6.

57. The house of a certain woman at Shelton was burgled by night. Robert Fale is suspected of this and other crimes by the jurors and the four neighbouring townships. Let him purge himself by water.

58. As to the other articles, [the jurors say] nothing.

Hundred of Clifton.

59. Robert of Sutton appeals Bonefand the Jew of Bedford, for that he in the king's peace and wickedly procured the shameful mutilation of Richard, [Robert's] nephew, whereof he died, so that [Bonefand] had him carried to [Bonefand's] land at Acton which he holds in gage, and there he died; and this he offers to prove etc. And Bonefand comes and defends the whole and offers the king a mark for an inquest whether he is guilty thereof or no. The jurors being questioned, say that he is not guilty thereof. So let Bonefand be quit and Robert in mercy for his false appeal.

Hundred of Wixamtree.

60. Aubrey of Willington appealed William Russel, Adam his brother, Geoffrey Reeve, Nicholas, Gervase's son, Godwin Gardener, David Espeke, and Robert of Hawnes, for that they in the king's peace and wickedly by night came to his house, and broke his gates and fences, and broke his house doors in hamsoken, and entered and took his goods, to wit, fowls, and carried them off, and would have killed him, had he not fled. And they have come and defend all of it. And the sheriff, whom Aubrey vouched to warrant that he showed him this the next day, says that he came not to him, but to a county [court], but to which [session of the] county [court] he cannot say, and his complaint being heard in the county [court], the

comitatu per consideracionem comitatus misit vicecomes legales homines ad domum suam ad illud factum,[1] qui dixerunt ad alium comitatum quod nullam fracturam portarum vel haiarum invenerunt, nec aliquid catall' fuit inde asportatum. Et propter illud testimonium et quia nulla catalla vel precium nominavit, consideratum est quod nullum est appellum, et quod Ailbrict sit in misericordia pro falso appello, et appellati quieti. Plegii Albrici de misericordia, Humfridus de Huntedun', Wimundus Prepositus.

Burgus de Bedef'.

61. [2]Matillis uxor Hugonis capta fuit cum una falsa galona per quam ipsa vendidit cervisiam ita quod custodes mensurarum testantur quod ceperunt eam vendentem inde cervisiam, et *quia* ipsa non potest hoc defendere[3] consideratum est quod ipsa sit in misericordia. Finem fecit per ij. marc. per plegium Willelmi filii Ascelin', Willelmi de Solario, Osberti filii Willelmi, Radulfi Clerici.

Lambertus Molendinarius queritur quod Claricia uxor Laurencii filii Walteri vendidit ei cervisiam per falsam galonam et inde producit sectam, que testatur quod ipsa interfuit ubi ipsa ita vendidit per illam galonam, scil. ad denarium tres galonas. Et Claricia venit et defendit quod non vendidit per falsam galonam nec vendidit per illam galonam quam ipse dicit esse suam ut per galonam integram, set ut per dimidiam galonam. Defendat se xij. manu in adventu justiciariorum. Vadiavit legem. Plegius de lege, Willelmus filius Ascelini. Plegii Lamberti de prosequendo, Willelmus Sanguinel, Ricardus filius Gaufridi, Dionisius, filius Lamberti, Walterus Molendinarius.

---

[1] Probably some word has been omitted; perhaps *videndum*.
[2] m. 6.
[3] There is official testimony that she was taken in the act, so she is not allowed to deny her guilt. Contrast her case with that of Clarice.

sheriff under its judgment sent lawful men to his house [to see] what had happened, and they at a later court said that they found no breakage of gates or fences, nor were any of the chattels carried away. And because of this testimony and because [Aubrey] named no chattels and no price, it is considered that the appeal is null, that Aubrey be in mercy for his false appeal, and the appellees be quit. Pledges for Aubrey's amercement: Humphry of Huntingdon and Wimund Reeve.

Borough of Bedford.

61.   Maud, wife of Hugh, was taken with a false gallon with which she sold beer, so that the keepers of the measures testify that they took her selling beer with it. And since she cannot defend this, it is considered that she be in mercy. She made fine with two marks, for which the pledges are William, son of Ascelin, William de Solar, Osbert, William's son, Ralph Clerk.

Lambert Miller complains that Clarice, wife of Lawrence, Walter's son, sold him beer by a false gallon, and thereof produces suit, which testifies that it was present when she sold by that gallon, to wit, three gallons for a penny. And Clarice comes and defends that she sold by a false gallon, nor did she sell by the gallon which he says is hers, as being a gallon, but as being a half-gallon. Let her defend herself twelve-handed [*i.e.* with eleven compurgators] on the [next] coming of the justices. She has waged her law. Pledge for her law: William, Ascelin's son. Lambert's pledges to prosecute: William Sanguinel, Richard, Geoffrey's son, Denis, Lambert's son, Walter Miller.

[1]PLACITA APUD LICHEFELDIAM ANNO REGNI REGIS JOHANNIS QUINTO.

Hundredus de Cuthuluestan'.

62. [2]Simon filius Ricardi de Bertherton' occisus fuit in reditu suo de quadam cervisia, et Simon Pring fugit pro morte ejus, et fuit in franco plegio Osberti de Abeton', et est in misericordia, et catalla Simonis fuerunt xij. den., unde Thomas de Erdint' vicecomes [3] debet respondere. Et xij. juratores dicunt in veredicto suo ut scriptum [4] eorum testatur et ore dicunt quod non fuit utlagatus. Et ideo ad judicium de juratoribus. Comitatus et coronatores recordantur quod non fuit utlagatus et rotuli coronatorum et rotulus vicecomitis testantur quod fuit utlagatus. Et ideo ad judicium de comitatu et de coronatoribus.[5]

murdrum
mīa
Ad judicium de juratoribus et de coronatoribus.

63. [6]Adam filius Baldewini qui permisit uxorem suam venire in comitatum et appellare Thomam filium Godwini de plaga sibi[7] facta in misericordia, eo quod ipse noluit sequi cum uxor ejus affidaret sequi.

mīa

Hundredus de Thatemanneslowe.

64. [8] Robertus filius Roberti de Ferrariis appellat Ranulfum de Tatteswarhte quod ipse venit in gardinum suum et in pace domini Regis et nequiter assultavit Rogerum hominem suum, et eum verberavit et vulneravit ita quod de vita ejus desperabatur, et ei robavit j. pallium et gladium et arcum et sagittas, et idem Rogerus offert hoc probare per corpus suum prout curia consideraverit. Et Ranulfus venit et

---

[1] Coram Rege Roll No. 21. An eyre of Simon Pateshull, William Cantilupe and others. They were at Lichfield in September.
[2] m. 2.
[3] Geoffrey FitzPeter is sheriff, but Thomas of Erdington is his custos.
[4] This seems to show that, at least occasionally, the jurors put in writing their answers to the Articles of the Eyre.
[5] Compare Case 88.
[6] m. 2.
[7] It seems likely that it was the husband who was wounded, not the wife; but this is doubtful.
[8] m. 2.

PLEAS AT LICHFIELD IN THE FIFTH YEAR OF THE REIGN OF KING JOHN [A.D. 1203].

Hundred of Cuttlestone.

62.   Simon, son of Richard of Brereton, was slain as he was returning from an ale. Simon Pring fled on account of his death. He was in the frank-pledge of Osbert of Abton, which is therefore in mercy. Simon's chattels were worth twelve pence, for which Thomas of Erdington, the sheriff, must account. And the twelve jurors say in their verdict as appears from their writing, and also say by word of mouth that [Simon Pring] was not outlawed. Therefore to judgment against the jurors. The county and the coroners record that he was not outlawed. But the coroners' rolls and the sheriff's roll testify that he was outlawed. Therefore to judgment against the county and the coroners.

63.   Adam, son of Baldwin, who allowed his wife to come into the county [court] and appeal Thomas, son of Godwin, of a wound given him, is in mercy, for that he refused to sue, whereas his wife had pledged faith to sue.

Hundred of Totmonslow.

64.   Robert, son of Robert of Ferrers, appeals Ranulf of Tattesworth, for that he came into Robert's garden and wickedly and in the king's peace assaulted Robert's man Roger, and beat and wounded him so that his life was despaired of, and robbed him [Roger ?] of a cloak, a sword, a bow and arrows: and the said Roger offers to prove this by his body as the court shall consider. And Ranulf comes

defendit totum de verbo in verbum, et offert domino Regi j. marcam argenti pro habenda inquisicione per legales milites utrum culpabilis sit inde nec ne, et preterea dicit quod iste Rogerus nunquam ante appellavit eum et petit ut hoc ei allocetur. Oblacio recipitur. Juratores dicunt quod revera contencio fuit inter gardinarium predicti Roberti, Osmundum nomine, et quosdam garciones, set Ranulfus non fuit ibi, nec malecredunt eum de aliqua roberia vel de aliquo delicto facto eidem Roberto vel ipsi Osmundo. Preterea comitatus recordatur quod milites missi per querelam ipsius Roberti ad vidend' vulnera ipsius Osmundi non invenerunt eum vulneratum nec aliquem alium querentem, et quod idem Robertus questus fuit de Osmundo gardinario suo et nunquam de Rogero, et nunquam idem Rogerus venit ad comitatum ad faciendum appellum istud. Et ideo consideratum est quod Ranulfus inde quietus sit, et Robertus et Rogerus in misericordia. Plegius de marca Ranulfi, Philippus de Draicot'. Plegii de misericordia, Henricus de Hugenhull' et Ricardus Meverell'. Plegius Rogeri, idem Robertus.

nīa

marca

Hundredus de Pirhull'.

65. [1] Quedam Lemis malecreditur a juratoribus quod ipsa interfuit ubi Reinild de Henchirche occisa fuit et quod per ejus auxilium et consensum occisa fuit. Et ipsa defendit. Et ideo purget se per judicium ferri, set quia infirmatur ponitur in respectum quousque convaluerit.

In respectum

66. [2] Andreas de Bureweston' malecreditur a juratoribus de morte cujusdam Hervici eo quod subtraxit se pro morte illa. Et ideo purget se per judicium aque.

purget

Hundredus de Offelawe.

67. [3] Juratores dicunt quod Ricardus frater Johannis de Sowe appellat Herbertum servientem Mathei de Gamages

---

[1] m. 2 d. An abstract of this case is in Placit. Abbrev. p. 43.
[2] m. 2 d.   [3] m. 2 d.

and defends the whole of it, word by word, and offers the king one mark of silver that he may have an inquest of lawful knights [to say] whether he be guilty thereof or no. Also he says that Roger has never until now appealed him of this, and prays that this be allowed in his favour. [Ranulf's] offering is accepted. The jurors say that in truth there was some quarrel between Robert's gardener, Osmund, and some foot-boys, but Ranulf was not there, and they do not suspect him of any robbery or any tort done to Robert or to Osmund. Also the county records that the knights who on Robert's complaint were sent to view Osmund's wounds found him unwounded and found no one else complaining, and that Robert in his plaint spoke of Osmund his gardener and never of Roger, and that Roger never came to the county [court] to make this appeal. Therefore it is considered that Ranulf be quit, and Robert and Roger in mercy. Pledge for Ranulf's mark, Philip of Draycot. Pledges for the amercement, Henry of Hungerhill, and Richard Meverell. Pledge for Roger, the said Robert.

Hundred of Pirehill.

65. One L. is suspected by the jurors of being present when Reinild of Hemchurch was slain, and of having aided and counselled her death. And she defends. Therefore let her purge herself by the ordeal of iron; but as she is ill, the ordeal is respited until her recovery.

66. Andrew of Burwarton is suspected by the jurors of the death of one Hervey, for that he concealed himself because of that death. Therefore let him purge himself by ordeal of water.

Hundred of Offlow.

67. The jurors say that Richard, brother of John of Sowe, appeals Herbert, the serjeant of Mathew of Gamages, for

quod ipse in pace Regis interfecit Johannem fratrem suum et hoc offert probare versus eum prout curia consideraverit. Et Herbertus totum defendit de verbo in verbum prout curia consideraverit. Consideratum est quod nullum est appellum eo quod ipse non apposuit in appello suo visum et auditum nec eciam feloniam. Et ideo appellator in misericordia.

68. [1] Goditha que fuit uxor Walteri Palmeri appellat Ricardum de Stonhale quod ipse in pace domini Regis et nequiter de nocte cum vi sua venit in domum suam et ipsam et virum suum ligavit et postea ipsum Walterum virum suum interfecit, et hoc offert probare versus eum sicut sponsa sua prout curia consideraverit. *Et ipse* totum defendit. Et juratores et totum visnetum malecredunt eum de morte illa. Et ideo consideratum est quod ipse purget se per judicium ferri, quia ipse elegit portare ferrum.[2]

69. [3] Juratores de hundredo de Oflawe dicunt ballivi de Thameworth' ceperunt toloneum de militibus comitatus Staffordie [4] utpote de bobus et aliis averiis suis injuste. Et homines de Lichefeld' queruntur similiter quod ceperunt ab eis toloneum injuste et maxime in comitatu Staffordie. Et ballivi defendunt quod non capiunt in comitatu Staffordie de militibus aliquid. Et quia non possunt contradicere juratoribus,[5] ballivi sunt in misericordia. De hominibus de Lichefeld' dicunt quod debuerunt habere et habuerunt 'tempore Henrici Regis' de eis maxime de mercatoribus toloneum tam in comitatu Staffordie quam in comitatu Warrewici. Et burgenses Lichef' offerunt domino Regi dimidiam marcam pro habenda inquisicione inde per

[1] m. 2 d. An abstract of this case is in Placit. Abbrev. p. 43.
[2] He seems to have had the option of going to the water ordeal. The ordeal of iron seems to have been the easier or the less dishonourable; in Glanvill (lib. 14, c. 1.) this is the ordeal for the *liber homo*, while the *rusticus* goes to the water.
[3] m. 3. An abstract of this case is in Placit. Abbrev. p. 43.
[4] Tamworth is a border town, partly in Staffordshire, partly in Warwickshire.
[5] As to untraversable presentments, see Hale, Pleas of the Crown, vol. ii. pp. 153–5.

that he in the king's peace slew John his brother; and this he offers to prove against him as the court shall consider. And Herbert defends the whole word by word as the court shall consider. It is considered that the appeal is null, for in his appeal he made no mention of sight and hearing, nor even of felony. So let the appellor be in mercy.

68. Godith, formerly wife of Walter Palmer, appeals Richard of Stonall, for that he in the king's peace wickedly and by night with his force came to her house and bound her and her husband, and afterwards slew the said Walter her husband; and this she offers to prove against him as wife of the slain as the court shall consider. And he defends all of it. And the jurors and the whole neighbourhood suspect him of that death. And so it is considered that he purge himself by ordeal of iron, for he has elected to bear the iron.

69. The jurors of Oflow hundred say that the bailiffs of Tamworth have unjustly taken toll from the knights of Staffordshire, to wit, for their oxen and other beasts. And the men of Lichfield complain that likewise they have taken toll from them, more especially in Staffordshire. And the bailiffs deny that they take anything from the knights in Staffordshire. And for that they cannot [be heard to] contradict the jurors, the bailiffs are in mercy. As to the men of Lichfield, [the Tamworth bailiffs] say that they ought to have, and in King Henry's time had, toll of them, more especially of the merchants, as well in Staffordshire as in Warwickshire. And the burgesses of Lichfield offer the king a half-mark for an inquest by the county.

comitatum. Et comitatus recordatur quod homines Lichef' tempore Henrici Regis non dederunt toloneum in comitatu Staffordie. Et ideo in misericordia ballivi.

[1] PLACITA APUD SALOPIAM ANNO REGNI REGIS JOHANNIS QUINTO.

Hundredus de Our.

70. [2] Robertus de Herthal' captus pro morte Rogeri filii Swein qui quinque homines occiderat per insaniam se defendendo commissus est vicecomiti ita quod sit in tali custodia qua prius fuit, quia loquendum est inde cum domino [Rege [3]]. Catalla occisoris v. hominum fuerunt ij. sol. unde Ric' etc.[4]

Villata de Ellesmere.

71. [5] Ad judicium de juratoribus qui devocaverunt scriptum suum.

Hundredus de Musselawe.

72. [6] Juratores dicunt quod quidam Ricardus Auceps hospitatus fuit quadam nocte apud Ludelaw' in domo Edeline de Ludelaw', et dictum fuit quod ipse de nocte surrexit et coadunavit pelfram [7] et asportavit et levato clamore villata consecuta est et eum interfecit. Et Walterus de Muscegros appellavit inde Willelmum Clericum, qui venit, et Walterus essoniat se et habet diem apud Wigorniam. 'Juratores

---

[1] Coram Rege Roll No. 19. The justices, Simon Pateshull, William Cantilupe, and others, were at Shrewsbury about Michaelmas.

[2] m. 2.

[3] The margin of the roll is damaged, and this word is conjectured. There seems some uncertainty as to what is to be done with one who has slain another in self-defence.

[4] Richard of Ambresleigh must account for the chattels; he is the custos of the sheriff, Geoffrey Fitz-Peter.

[5] m. 2. What exactly the jurors had done does not appear; but this is evidence of written presentments; see above, Case 62.

[6] m. 2.

[7] The word, if not *pelfram*, is *pelfam*; it is our *pelf*, O. F. *pelfre*, booty; 'connected with our *pilfer*, and possibly with Lat. *pilare*. See Skeat, s.v. *pelf*. It occurs again in Case 77.

And the county records that in King Henry's time the men of Lichfield did not pay toll in Staffordshire. Therefore the bailiffs are in mercy.

PLEAS AT SHREWSBURY IN THE FIFTH YEAR OF THE REIGN OF KING JOHN [A.D. 1203].

Hundred of Overs.

70.   Robert of Herthale, arrested for having in self-defence slain Roger, Swein's son, who had slain five men in a fit of madness, is committed to the sheriff that he may be in custody as before, for the king must be consulted about this matter. The chattels of him who killed the five men were worth two shillings, for which Richard [the sheriff must account].

Township of Ellesmere.

71.   To judgment concerning the jurors who have disavowed their writing.

Hundred of Munslow.

72.   The jurors say that one Richard Fowler lodged for a night at Ludlow in the house of Edelina of Ludlow, and it was said that he arose by night and collected the pelf and carried it off, and the hue was raised, and the township followed and slew him. And Walter de Muscegros appealed William Clerk of this; and William comes; and Walter essoins himself and has a day given him at Worcester.

ceperunt in custodiam Willelmum Clericum.'¹ 'Et tunc venit Walterus et retraxit se. Et juratores testati sunt quod predicto modo surrexit et asportavit catalla, quia Willelmus dedit viij. marcas pro habenda inquisicione inde, et non malecredunt inde Willelmum. Et ideo Willelmus recedat inde quietus.'

viij mar.

73.   ²Sibilla filia Engelardi appellat Radulfum de Samford quod ipse in pace domini Regis et nequiter et super pacem ei datam a vicecomite in comitatu,³ venit ad domum que fuit domini sui, et fregit cistas suas et catalla asportavit et eam ita tractavit quod infantem quem habuit vivum in ventre suo occidit.

Postea venit ipsa et dixit quod concordati sunt, et retraxit se quia concordati sunt quod ipse Radulfus satisfaciet ei de catallis suis per visum et consideracionem legalium hominum et ipse Radulfus hoc concessit.

Hundredus de Brimestr'.

74.   ⁴Willelmus Pipin occidit Willelmum Guldenema' et fugit, nulla habuit catalla, interrogetur. Et Hùgo Fullo captus fuit pro morte illa et in gaola positus eo quod predictus Johannes⁵ occisus fuit in domo sua. Et Hugo dat domino Regi catalla sua que capta fuerunt cum eo pro habenda inquisitione utrum ipse inde esset culpabilis nec ne. Juratores dicunt quod non est inde culpabilis, et ideo eat inde quietus. Et Willelmus Picot⁶ in misericordia quia vendidit catalla ipsius Hugonis cum non esset convictus de morte illa, et quia vendidit ea pro minori precio quam valuerunt, quia ipse vendidit ea ut dicit pro tribus solidis, et

m͞ia

---

¹ This phrase is in the margin. The next must record what happened at Worcester, where these Staffordshire jurors had to produce William. What was the charge against William : that he was Richard's accomplice, or that he slew Richard ? Probably the latter.

² m. 2.

³ Reference is still occasionally made to breach of some special peace, as though this aggravated the breach of the general peace.

⁴ m. 2 d.

⁵ Corr. *Willelmus* (?)

⁶ One of the coroners ; the others are William of Middlehope and Walter Haket.

The jurors took William Clerk into their custody. And [on the said day at Worcester] came Walter and withdrew himself. And, William having offered eight marks for an inquest, the jurors say that [Richard] in manner aforesaid arose and carried off the chattels, and they do not suspect William of it. So let William go quit thereof.

73. Sibil, Engelard's daughter, appeals Ralph of Sandford, for that he in the king's peace and wickedly and in breach of the peace given to her in the county [court] by the sheriff, came to the house of her lord [or husband] and broke her chests and carried off the chattels, and so treated her that he slew the child that was living in her womb.

Afterwards she came and said that they had made a compromise and she withdrew herself, for they have agreed that Ralph shall satisfy her for the loss of the chattels upon the view and by the appraisement of lawful men; and Ralph has assented to this.

Hundred of Brimstree.

74. William Pipin slew William [or John] Guldeneman and fled. He had no chattels. Let him be exacted. And Hugh Fuller was taken for this death and put in gaol because the said John [or William] was slain in his house. And Hugh gives to the king his chattels which were taken with him, that he may have an inquest [to find] whether he be guilty thereof or no. The jurors say that he is not guilty, and so let him go quit thereof. And William Picot is in mercy for having sold Hugh's chattels before he was convicted of the death, and for having sold them at an undervalue, for he sold them, as he says, for three shillings,

juratores dicunt quod valuerunt xvij. sol. unde Willelmus Picot et illi qui fuerunt socii ejus debent respondere.

de catall'

Will' Picot custodiatur

Et Willelmus dicit quod per consilium sociorum suorum vendita fuerunt catalla illa et socii sui dicunt quod non.

75. [1] Robertus Albus occidit Walterum de Hugeford et fugit. Et juratores dicunt quod utlagatus fuit pro morte illa, et comitatus et coronatores dicunt quod non fuit utlagatus quia nullus secutus fuit versus eum. Et quia juratores non possunt contradicere comitatui et coronatoribus [2] ideo sunt in misericordia, et predictus Robertus interrogetur. Et catalla ejus fuerunt [3] xv. sol. unde R. de Ambresleg' vicecomes debet respondere.

Hundredus de Stottesdun'.

76. [4] Radulfus Russiadic appellat Ricardum *Senem* quod occidit Ricardum hominem domini sui in pace domini Regis et hoc offert probare versus eum prout curia consideraverit. Et Ricardus venit et defendit mortem et feloniam, et dicit quod alia vice fuit quidam Robertus filius Aier 'per Adam de Sancta Brigida fratrem Roberti'[5] appellatus in curia domini Regis apud Westmonasterium de morte illa et ipse Ricardus et multi alii cum eo de vi illa, et tunc venit appellans et retraxit se et quietum clamavit ipsum Robertum, ita quod ipse et alii appellati de vi adjudicati fuerunt quieti inde, et petit ut hoc ei allocetur. Et ipse Radulfus hoc non potuit negare, et preterea ipse non apposuit visum vel auditum in appello suo, et ideo consideratum est quod nullum est appellum et sit in misericordia.

A absens est

Gaufridus Dilun appellat Alanum de Petra Ponte de predicta morte. Alanus absens est. Et juratores quesiti ad quem idem Alanus rediit et a quo receptatus fuit post appellum primo factum, dicunt quod ipse receptatus est sepius postea a Willelmo de Petraponte fratre suo, qui hoc

---

[1] m. 2 d.
[2] Compare Cases 38 and 62.
[3] *fuerunt* repeated.
[4] m. 2 d.
[5] Interpolated in the margin. Perhaps *Roberti* is a mistake for *Ricardi*.

and the jurors say that they were worth seventeen shillings, for which William Picot and those who were his fellows ought to account.

And William says that the chattels were sold by the advice of his fellows, and his fellows deny this.

75. Robert White slew Walter of Hugeford and fled. The jurors say that he was outlawed for the death, and the county and the coroners say that he was not outlawed, because no one sued against him. And because the jurors cannot [be heard to] contradict the county and the coroners, therefore they are in mercy, and let Robert be exacted. His chattels were [worth] fifteen shillings, for which R. of Ambresleigh, the sheriff, must account.

Hundred of Stottesden.

76. Ralph Russiadic appeals Richard Old for that in the king's peace he slew Richard the man of [Ralph's] lord; and this he offers to prove against him as the court shall consider. And Richard comes and defends the death and the felony, and says that on a former occasion one Robert, son of Aier, was appealed of that death in the king's court at Westminster by Adam of St. Brides, brother of Robert, and Richard [the present appellee] and many others with him were then appealed as accessories, and the [then] appellor came and withdrew from his suit and quit-claimed Robert, so that [Robert] and those appealed as his accessories were adjudged quit thereof; and [Richard] craves that this be allowed in his favour. And Ralph could not deny this, and besides in his appeal he made no mention of sight or hearing; so it is considered that the appeal is null, and let him be in mercy.

Geoffrey Dilun appeals Alan of Pierpont of the said death. Alan is absent. And the jurors, on being asked to whom Alan returned and who received him after the appeal was first made, say that he was often received after that by William of Pierpont his brother, and William has confessed

idem cognovit. Post venit Willelmus et finem fecit pro illa receptacione per c. sol. per plegium Johannis Extranei. Misericordia Gaufridi,[1] dim. marc. Et Alanus si voluerit redeat quia nullum est appellum racione supradicta.

Hundredus de Bradeford.

77. [2]Elyas de Lilleshill' fugit in ecclesiam pro morte cujusdam femine occise apud Lilleshill' et nulla habuit catalla, et cognoscens mortem abjuravit regnum.

Alec' Crithecrech' et Eva de Lileshull' et Aldit et Mabilia, Gaufridus et Robertus de Lileshull' et Petrus de Hopton' capti fuerunt pro morte predicte femine occise apud Lileshull'. At Alec' statim post mortem ejus fugit in comitatum Staffordie cum quibusdam de catallis occise ut dicitur, et in comitatu illo capta fuit et reducta in comitatum Salopsire et ibi, ut serviens Regis et plures milites et legales homines de comitatu testantur, coram eis dixit quod cum audiret de nocte tumultum in domo predicte occise, ipsa venit ad hostium suum et intus aspexit, et vidit per medium hostii iiij. homines in domo illa qui exeuntes ceperunt eam et minati fuerunt ei quod eam occiderent nisi celaret eos ita quod ei dederunt pelfram[3] quam *ipsa* habuit. Et cum veniret coram justiciariis totum hoc negavit et ideo meruit mortem, set per dispensacionem eruantur ei occuli. Alii non malecreduntur et ideo sint sub plegiis.

78. [4]Ricardus Wigun appellat Willelmum prepositum de Ercalawe quod ipse recettavit utlagos Regis in domo sua, scil. Fulconem filium Warini[5] et socios suos, et hoc offert

---

[1] He is amerced for a false appeal.
[2] m. 2 d.
[3] As to this word see above, Case 72.
[4] m. 2 d.
[5] The outlawry of Fulk Fitz Warin is the foundation of a very curious medieval romance written in French, which is printed in the Rolls Series at the end of the chronicle of Ralph of Coggeshall. Some entries relating to this matter will be found in Rot. Pat. pp. 84. 34 *b*, 86.

this. Afterwards came William and made fine in respect of this receipt [of his brother] with 100 shillings, for which John L'Estrange is pledge. Geoffrey's amercement, a halfmark. And let Alan return if he will, for the appeal is null for the reason aforesaid.

Hundred of Bradford.

77. Elyas of Lilleshall fled to church for the death of a woman slain at Lilleshall. He had no chattels. He confessed the death and abjured the realm.

Alice Crithecreche and Eva of Lilleshall and Aldith and Mabel, Geoffrey and Robert of Lilleshall, and Peter of Hopton were taken for the death of the said woman slain at Lilleshall. And Alice, at once after the death, fled to the county of Stafford with some of the chattels of the slain, so it is said, and was taken in that county and brought back into Shropshire and there, as the king's serjeant and many knights and lawful men of the county testify, in their presence she said, that at night she heard a tumult in the house of the slain; whereupon she came to the door and looked in, and saw through the middle of the doorway four men in the house, and they came out and caught her, and threatened to kill her unless she would conceal them; and so they gave her the pelf that she had. And when she came before the justices [in eyre] she denied all this. Therefore she has deserved death, but by way of dispensation [the sentence is mitigated, so] let her eyes be torn out. The others are not suspected, therefore let them be under pledges.

78. Richard Wigun appeals William the Reeve of Ercall, for that he received in his house outlaws of the king, to wit, Fulk FitzWarin and his companions; and this he offers

probare etc. Et Willelmus venit et defendit totum, et offert domino Regi pro habenda inquisitione j. marc. Et oblacio recipitur. Plegius inde Hugo Pantulf. Juratores dicunt et totus comitatus testatur ipsum non esse culpabilem inde, et quod ipse legalis homo est et quod Ricardus appellat eum inde per attiam et pro habenda quadam terra quam ipse clamat versus eum. Et ideo Willelmus sit inde quietus et Ricardus in misericordia. Et sciendum quod hoc receptamentum debuit fieri tribus annis transactis ut idem Ricardus dixit et nunquam inde fecit mencionem ante festum S. Johannis proximo preteritum.

j. mar.

Burgus Salop'.

79. [1] Jordanus filius Warini apellavit Rein' Ruffum quod ipse in pace domini Regis et nequiter assultavit eum et abscidit ei digitos suos ita quod inde maimatus est, et hoc offert probare versus illum sicut homo maimatus. Et Rein' venit et defendit assultum illum et feloniam et mahemium, et dicit quod aliquando venit appellum illud coram Domino G. filio Petri Comite Essexie,[2] et per licenciam ejus concordatum fuit inter eos, ita quod ipse remisit eum de illo appello per decem marc. quas ei dedit, et offert domino Regi ij. marc. pro habenda inquisicione per comitatum et per legales homines de villa de Salopesbiria 'scil. juratores' utrum per ejus licenciam ita concordati sunt nec ne. Comitatus et homines de villa Salopesbirie 'scil. juratores' recordantur quod ita concordati sunt per licenciam Domini G. filii Petri per illas x. marc. quas ei dedit.

ij. mar.

Hundredus Abbatis de Forieta.[3]

80. [4] Willelmus filius Johannis appellat Walterum filium Radulfi Hose quod cum dominus suus Wido de Siageberi et

---

[1] m. 8.
[2] Geoffrey FitzPeter is chief justiciar and has been so since 1198.
[3] The Foregate was a suburb of Shrewsbury belonging to the abbot.
[4] m. 8.

to prove etc. And William comes and defends all of it and offers the king one mark for an inquest. His offering is accepted; Hugh Pantulf is pledge [for its payment]. The jurors say, and the whole county testifies, that he is not guilty thereof, and that he is a lawful man, and that Richard appeals him out of spite that he may have certain land which he claims against him. So let William be quit thereof and Richard be in mercy. And be it known that this receipt [of outlaws] took place, according to Richard's story, three years ago and he never made mention of it until St. John's day last past.

Borough of Shrewsbury.

79. Jordan, son of Warin, appealed Reiner Read, for that he in the king's peace and wickedly assaulted him and cut off his fingers, so that he is maimed; and this he offers to prove against him as a maimed man. And Reiner comes and defends the assault and the felony and the mayhem, and says that on a former occasion this appeal came before Sir Geoffrey FitzPeter, Earl of Essex, and by his leave a concord was made between them, so that [Jordan] remitted him from that appeal for ten marks which [Reiner] paid him; and he offers the king two marks for an inquest by the county and lawful men of the town of Shrewsbury (to wit, the jurors), to find whether a concord was thus made between them by licence of [the Chief Justiciar] or no. The county and the town of Shrewsbury (to wit, the jurors) record that a concord was thus made by licence of Sir Geoffrey FitzPeter in consideration of the ten marks paid by [Reiner] to [Jordan].

The Abbot's Hundred of Foregate.

80. William, John's son, appeals Walter, son of Ralph Hose, for that when [William's] lord Guy of Shawbury and [Wil-

ipse venissent de placitis domini Regis in com' Salopesire [1] venerunt v. homines in foresta de Hagema' et ibi in pace domini Regis et nequiter assultaverunt dominum suum Widonem ita quod ipse qui fuit quartus ex illis v. vulneravit eundem Widonem et fuit in vi et auxilio simul cum aliis quod idem Wido dominus suus occisus fuit, et post vulnus quod domino suo fecerat venit ad eundem Willelmum et eum tenuit ita quod non potuit auxiliari domino suo, et hoc offert disracionare versus eum prout curia [2] consideraverit. Et Walterus venit et defendit totum de verbo in verbum prout curia etc. Consideratum est quod duellum sit inter eos. Vadiatum est. Dies datus est eis apud Oxoniam in crast. Oct. Omn. Sanct. et tunc veniant armati. Et Rad' [3] domino Regi dim. marc. pro filio suo habendo in custodia, per plegium Johannis de Cnatton', Reineri de Acton' et committitur custodie Radulfi Hose, Reineri de Aketon', Johannis de Cnatton', Reginaldi del Le, Ade de Mukeleston', Willelmi de Bremele, Stephani de Acle, Eudonis de Merc.

dim. marc.

[4] PLACITA APUD LINCOLNIAM.

81. [5] Martinus filius Admeri et Agnes uxor ejus appellant Johannem filium Gudred' quod ipse et Thomas le Paumer et Alanus filius Roberti occiderunt Walterum filium suum in quodam batello in reditu de S. Botulfo, ita quod ipse Johannes primo percussit eum palo et alii *strangulaverunt* eum, et hoc offerunt probare etc. Ipsi defendunt totum de verbo in verbum, et dant domino Regi iij. marcas pro habenda inquisitione utrum appellant eos per attiam an sint

---

[1] Probably *comitatus* here means *the county court*. A man might ride through Haughmond Forest on his way between Shrewsbury and Shawbury.
[2] *curia* repeated.
[3] Supply *dat.*
[4] Coram Rege Roll No 71. The precise date of this roll has not been ascertained. The case here printed has been chosen as a good illustration of the manner in which trial by jury made its way into the system of appeals.
[5] m. 9.

liam] had come from attending the pleas of our lord the king in the county court of Shropshire, there came five men in the forest of Haughmond and there in the king's peace and wickedly assaulted his lord Guy, and so that [Walter], who was the fourth among those five, wounded Guy and was accessory with the others in force and aid so that Guy his lord was killed, and after having wounded his lord he [Walter] came to William and held him so that he could not aid his lord; and this he offers to deraign against him as the court shall consider. And Walter comes and defends all of it word by word as the court etc. It is considered that there be battle between them. The battle is waged. Day is given them, at Oxford on the morrow of the octave of All Saints, and then let them come armed. And Ralph [Walter's father] gives the king a half-mark that he may have the custody of his son, [for which sum] the pledges are John of Knighton and Reiner of Acton, and he is committed to the custody of Ralph Hose, Reiner of Acton, John of Knighton, Reginald of Leigh, Adam of Mucklestone, William of Bromley, Stephen of Ackleton, Eudo of Mark.

PLEAS AT LINCOLN.

81. Martin, Eadmer's son, and Agnes, his wife, appeal John, Gudred's son, for that he and Thomas Palmer and Alan, Robert's son, slew their son Walter in a boat as he was returning from Boston, so that John first struck him with a stake and the others strangled him, and this they offer to prove etc. They defend all of it word by word, and give the king three marks for an inquest [to find] whether they appeal them out of spite, or whether they be guilty, and

culpabiles, et dicunt quod revera ipse fuit cum eis in batello et cecidit foras et submersus est.

'Jurata civitatis Lincolnie dicit quod non sunt culpabiles de morte illa, set per infortunium cecidit extra batellum et submersus est. Plegii Johannis et Thome et Alani de predictis tribus marcis, plegii Johannis de j. marca, Reinerus de *Cimiterio*, Petrus de Bekeringe in Lincolnia, plegius Thome et Alani de duabus marcis, Reinbaldus Dives.' 'Consideratum est quod nullum est appellum eo quod non viderunt ubi hoc factum fuit, et similiter eo quod omnes testati sunt quod non sunt culpabiles.'

they say that [Walter] was indeed with them in the boat and fell out and was drowned.

A jury of the city of Lincoln says that they are not guilty of that death, but that he fell out of the boat by misadventure and was drowned. Pledges of John, Thomas, and Alan for the said three marks: John's pledges for one mark Reiner Churchyard, Peter Beckering of Lincoln; Thomas's and Alan's pledge for two marks, Reinbald Rich. It is considered that the appeal is null, for that [the appellors] did not see the deed, and likewise because all testify that [the appellees] are not guilty.

II. PLACITA CORAM JUSTITIARIIS DE BANCO ET PLACITA CORAM REGE REGNANTE REGE JOHANNE.

[1] PLACITA DE TERMINO S. MICHAELIS ANNO REGNI SECUNDO.

82. [2] Martinus Martel appellat Petrum filium Johannis quod ipse nequiter et in pace Regis fregit januas suas et hostia domus sue et camere in terra sua de Caunwic[3] extra civitatem,[4] et ei robavit lxvij. marcas et cartas de terris suis in roberia asportavit.[5] Petrus venit et totum defendit de verbo in verbum hic et ubi defendere debuerit tanquam liber civis domini Regis.

Gilebertus de[6] Gant appellat Johannem Flandrensem quod ipse hostia domus sue fregit et ipsum ligavit et ligatum duxit in Lincolniam et eum per fidem posuit[7] et robavit ei ij. marcas et dimidiam et vestes uxoris sue. Et Johannes totum defendit sicut alter prius.

Hugo Crapin appellat Toli quod insultavit eum in domo sua in pace Regis et robbavit ei iij. marcas et duo pallia uxoris sue et j. capam de perseco et j. tunicam de perseco. Et Toli totum defendit sicut prior.

Alanus Wiles appellat Nicholaum Morel quod eum insultavit in domo sua in pace Regis et robbavit ei ij. marcas et j. capam de perseco et vestes uxoris sue in pace domini Regis et nequiter. Et ipse defendit sicut prior.

---

[1] Coram Rege Roll No. 7 collated with No. 8; these are here indicated by A and B respectively.
[2] A, m. 1; B, m. 8.
[3] *Canewic'*, B.
[4] Supply *Lincolnie*, B.
[5] Supply *et hoc offert probare versus eum per corpus suum*, B.
[6] Om. *de*, B.
[7] Om. *et eum per fidem posuit*, B. The charge seems to be that John forced Gilbert to take an oath, perhaps to swear that there should be no appeal of robbery. The same phrase occurs in Case 84.

II. PLEAS BEFORE THE JUSTICES OF THE BENCH AND PLEAS BEFORE THE KING DURING THE REIGN OF JOHN.

PLEAS OF MICHAELMAS TERM (A.D. 1200).

82. Martin Martel appeals Peter, John's son, for that he wickedly and in the king's peace broke the outer and inner doors of his house and chamber on his land at Canwick, outside the city of Lincoln, and robbed him of sixty-seven marks, and in robbery carried off the title-deeds of his lands. Peter comes and defends all of it here and where it shall behove him to defend as a free citizen of our lord the king.

Linc. Gilbert of Gaunt appeals John Fleming, for that he broke the doors of his house and bound him and led him bound into Lincoln, and exacted an oath from him, and robbed him of 2½ marks and of his wife's clothes. And John defends all of it in the same way as [Peter].

Linc. Hugh Crapin appeals Toli, for that he assaulted him in his house in the king's peace, and robbed him of three marks, and two cloaks of his wife, and one blue cape, and one blue tunic. And Toli defends all of it in the same way as [Peter].

Linc. Alan Wiles appeals Nicholas Morel, for that he assaulted him in his house in the king's peace and robbed him of two marks and one blue cape and his wife's clothes, in the king's peace and wickedly. And he defends as [Peter] did.

Linc.

Augnes filia Saxi appellat Johannem de Parisius quod ¹ cum ipsa de partu laboraret¹ ipse venit in domum suam et eam per pedes extraxit et percussit ² quodam palo ² ita quod infantem suum perdidit. Et ipse totum defendit sicut alii.

Cives Civitatis ³ venerunt et ostenderunt cartam domini Regis que testatur quod nullus eorum debet placitare extra muros civitatis ⁴ exceptis monetariis et ministris suis⁴, et quod non debent facere duellum pro aliquo appello set disracionare se secundum libertates et leges civitatis Londonie, et ipsi petunt illam libertatem.⁵ Dies datus est eis coram domino Rege ubicunque fuerit in crastino S. Edmundi.⁶

Linc.

⁷ Martinus Martell' appellat Petrum de Parisius ⁸ quod ipse in pace domini Regis et nequiter venit ad domum suam et eum assultavit et robbavit ei lxvij. marcas et homines suos ligavit, et hoc offert probare versus eum per corpus suum etc.

Et Petrus venit et defendit pacem infractam et feloniam et illam roberiam lxvij. marcarum et totum de verbo in verbum ut liber civis Lincolnie, et si non poterit habere defensionem per libertatem ville, offert defendere se per corpus suum si curia consideraverit. Et dicit quod per licenciam domini Regis ipsi concordati fuerunt ita quod quilibet appellatus vadiavit eidem Martino legem se xxxvij. manu⁹ '*et cum venirent parati leges suas facere, ipse quietas clamavit eis leges*' ¹⁰ et cepit homagia eorum et eos osculo pacis osculatus est et perdonavit eis omnem malevolentiam suam quam ipse versus eos habuit.

---

¹⁻¹ *cum esset in partu laborans*, B.
²⁻² *sude quadam*, B.
³ Supply *Lincolnie*, B.
⁴⁻⁴ Omit, B.
⁵ This charter, dated 21 July 1199, will be found in Rot. Cart. p. 5.
⁶ St. Edmund's day is 20 Nov. The king was at Lincoln on the next day in 1200.
⁷ This continuation of the preceding case is found on Coram Rege Roll No. 41, m. 13.
⁸ Apparently the person who above is called Peter son of John.
⁹ This is the Magna Lex of the London custom: a citizen charged with homicide purges himself with thirty-six oath-helpers. See Munimenta Gildhallae (Rolls Ser.), vol. i. pp. 91, 92, 110.
¹⁰ A cramped interlineation.

Linc.

Agnes, Saxe's daughter, appeals John of Paris, for that as she was labouring with child he came into her house, and dragged her out by the feet, and struck her with a stake so that she lost her child. And he defends this as the others have done.

The citizens of Lincoln came and produced the king's charter which witnesses that none of them need plead outside the city walls, except the king's moneyers and servants, and that they need not fight the duel because of any appeal, but may deraign themselves according to the liberties and laws of the city of London; and they crave this their franchise. A day is given them before the king wheresoever he shall be on the morrow of St. Edmund.

Linc.

[1] Martin Martel appeals Peter of Paris, for that he in the king's peace and wickedly came to his house and assaulted him and robbed him of sixty-seven marks and bound his men, and this he offers to prove against him by his body etc.

And Peter comes and denies the breach of the peace, the felony, the robbery of sixty-seven marks and all of it word by word as a free citizen of Lincoln, and if he be not allowed to make his defence according to the franchise of the town, he offers to defend himself by his body if the court shall so consider. And he says that by the king's leave the appeal was compromised, on the terms that he should wage to Martin a law with thirty-six compurgators, and when [the appellees] came prepared to make their laws, [Martin] quitclaimed them their laws and took their homages and kissed them with the kiss of peace and forgave them all the ill will that he had against them.

[1] What follows is a later account of the preceding case.

Et Martinus non defendit quin ita cepit homagia sua et quod ita non vadiaverunt ei legem, set dicit quod ipsi non *deser*vierunt convencionem factam inter eos, et ideo sequitur appellum suum versus eos. Judicium, nullum est appellum, et ideo Martinus in misericordia.

m̄ia

Gilebertus Gant appellat Johannem filium Hugonis [1] quod ipse in pace predicta venit ad domum suam cum vi sua et fregit domum suam et intravit et robbavit de pannis uxoris sue et propriis catallis ipsius Gileberti ad valenciam xl. solidorum et percussit eum quadam mascea ita quod sanguinolentum eum fecit, et hoc offert etc.

Et Johannes totum defendit ut liber civis, et dicit quod concordati fuerunt ut predictum est, et pĕtit ut hoc ei allocetur. Dies datus est eis in adventu justiciariorum, et habent licenciam concordandi. Idem dies datus est Hugoni Gropin et Tholy appellatis [2] de eodem.[3]

83. [4]Dominus Rex mandavit justiciariis de banco[5] quod duella vadiata coram eis inter Rannulfum de Lancell' et Hugonem de Stoddon' et inter Willelmum de Burmesland'[6] et Ricardum de Duneham de roberia coram ipso Rege ponantur, [7]quia ea vult videre.[7]

Devon.

[8]PLACITA DE TERMINO PASCHE ANNO REGNI [SECUNDO.]

84. [9]Ricardus de Lancell' appellat Hugonem de Morton' quod postquam pax domini Regis tunc Ducis Normannie et Domini Anglie fuit jurata[10] ipse Hugo cum Hugone de

Devon.

---

[1] Above he is called *Johannes Flandrensis*.

[2] There seems to be a mistake here; Hugh was an appellor, not an appellee.

[3] There is an extract from this case in Placit. Abbrev. p. 80.

[4] A, m. 3; B, m. 1 d. See below, Case 84.

[5] Omit *de banco*, B.

[6] *Brunesland*, B.

[7-7] Omit, B.

[8] Coram Rege Roll No 41. This roll has been ascribed to A. R. 11, but some at least of its membranes seem to be of earlier date, and the case here printed probably belongs to A. R. 2; for see above, Case 83; Rot. Cur. Reg. vol. ii. p. 244; Rot. Obl. p. 78.

[9] m. 5.

[10] The alleged crime was done in the interregnum between Richard's

And Martin does not deny that he thus took their homages and that they thus waged him their law, but he says that they did not keep the covenant made between them, and so he pursues his appeal against them. Judgment: the appeal is null, and so let Martin be in mercy.

Gilbert Gaunt appeals John, Hugh's son, for that he in the peace aforesaid came with his force to [Gilbert's] house and broke his house and entered and robbed the clothes of [Gilbert's] wife and Gilbert's own chattels to the value of forty shillings and struck him with a mace so that blood was drawn, and this he offers etc.

And John defends all of it as a free citizen and says that they made compromise as aforesaid, and he craves that this be allowed in his favour. A day is given them, on the coming of the justices, and they have leave to compromise. The same day is given to Hugh Grapin and Tholy who are appealed of the same [crime].

83. Our lord the king has commanded the justices of the bench that the duels which have been waged before them between Ranulf of Launcells and Hugh of Stoddon, and between William of Burnsland and Richard of Dunham, [in appeals] of robbery, be put before the king himself, for he wishes to see them.

Devon

PLEAS OF EASTER TERM, A.D. 1201 (?).

84. Richard of Launcells appeals Hugh of Moreton, for that after the peace of our lord the king, then Duke of Normandy and Lord of England, was sworn, the said Hugh with Hugh

Devon

Stoddon' et Ricardo de Dunham et aliis attachiatis proinde, et cum quibusdam utlagatis per sectam suam, venit ad domum ejusdem Ricardi apud Lancell' et eum ibi cepit et per fidem posuit quod se redderet Henrico domino suo filio Willelmi, et postea nequiter et in pace predicta robavit ei loricas suas, galeas, caligas ferreas et ollas suas ereas et vasa sua, et post intravit in cameram suam et fregit archas suas et cepit coclearia sua argentea et aurum et argentum et pannos uxoris sue et anulos et firmacula sua et proprios anulos extraxit de digitis et equos suos abduxit ita quod dampnum ei fecit de catallis ad valenciam c. marcarum, et ipse Hugo de Morton' ei tradidit quendam runcinum suum et distrinxit eum ad illum equitandum et illum equitavit, et si negare voluerit quod ita runcinum illum non equitavit, offert probare versus eum sicut curia consideraverit per corpus suum vel per quendam liberum hominem suum.

Et Hugo venit et defendit pacem infractam, feloniam et roberiam et quod runcinum suum non ita equitavit, et totum de verbo in verbum per corpus suum sicut homo qui etatem preteriit, vel per Willelmum filium suum, qui etc. Et dicit quod ipse Ricardus facit hoc appellum versus eum per attiam et per vetus odium, unde tres causas ostendit. Quarum prima est, quia ipse Hugo *una* cum serviente hundredi quodam tempore ivit ad capiendum fratrem ipsius Ricardi, qui talis fuit quod non potuit nec debuit in patria morari,[1] per quam capcionem ipse supsensus fuit. Alia causa, quia ipse Hugo aliquando protulit quoddam placitum corone coram justic' quod ipse Ricardus tunc serviens hundredi concelaverat unde in misericordia remansit. Tercia causa, quia ipse Ricardus quandam ecclesiam dederat cuidam nepoti ejusdem Hugonis unde post resipiscere voluit, ita quod ipse nepos ejus impetravit litteras domini Pape per quas ipsum Ricardum implacitat. Et pro habenda inquisitione patrie utrum scilicet appellat eum per attiam

---

death and John's coronation. As to the style 'lord of England,' which is here given to Duke John, see Palgrave, Rotuli Curiæ Regis vol. i. pp. lxxxi–xcvii.

[1] Perhaps he had abjured the realm.

of Stoddon, Richard of Dunham and others who have been attached, and with certain persons who have been outlawed at [Richard's] suit, came to Richard's house at Launcells and there seized him, and forced him to swear that he would yield himself to Henry FitzWilliam [Hugh's] lord, and afterwards wickedly and in the said peace robbed him of his breastplates, helmets, iron boots, his brazen pots and vessels, and afterwards entered his chamber and broke his chests and took his silver spoons and gold and silver and his wife's clothes, rings and buckles, and seized [Richard's] own rings from his fingers, and led off his horses so that he damaged him in his goods to the value of one hundred marks, and the said Hugh of Moreton delivered to him a certain rouncey of his, and forced him to ride it and he rode it, and if [Hugh] will deny that he thus rode the rouncey, [Richard] offers to prove this against him as the court shall consider by his body or by a certain freeman of his:

And Hugh comes and defends the breach of the peace, felony and robbery, and that he thus rode his rouncey, and all of it word by word, by his body, as a man who is past [fighting] age, or by William his son, who [offers to prove etc.]. And he says that Richard makes this appeal against him out of spite and because of an old grudge, whereof he shows three causes. The first is, that once on a time he, Hugh, along with the serjeant of the hundred went to arrest Richard's brother, who was one who could not lawfully remain in the country, and who in consequence of this arrest was hanged. The second is, that once on a time Hugh brought to the notice of the justices a certain plea of the crown, which Richard, who then was serjeant of the hundred, had concealed, so that [Richard] was amerced. The third is, that Richard gave a certain church to a nephew of Hugh, and then wanted to think better of it, so that the nephew in question procured letters from the Pope, by virtue whereof he is impleading Richard. And that he may have an inquest of the country whether [Richard]

et per odium sicut dictum est, offert domino Regi de suo.[1]

Dies datus est eis audiendi judicium suum coram domino Rege a die Oct. Omn. Sanct. in iij. septimanas. 'Consideratum quod nullum est appellum, et ideo Hugo quietus et Ricardus in misericordia'.[2]

Idem Ricardus appellat Thomam de Dunham quod ad domum suam venerunt predicti robatores cum roberia predicta et ipse illam roberiam receptavit in domo sua, ita quod ibi erat distributa inter predictos robatores, et hoc offert probare etc.

Et Thomas totum defendit sicut homo maimatus de crure fracto, vel per Ricardum fratrem suum vel per Rogerum de Morton', qui hoc offert etc., et dicit quod die illo quo illud fieri debuisset fuit ipse in castello domini Regis apud Lancaueton', ita quod die illo fecit ipse fidelitatem domino Regi, et inde ponit se super patriam. 'Nullum est appellum, et ideo Ricardus in misericordia et Thomas quietus.'

Idem appellat Willelmum de Dunham, et dicit quod sicut ivit per forestam ipse obviavit duobus forestariis qui dixerunt quod ipse Willelmus et alii predicti robatores eos verberaverunt et robbaverunt, et hoc offert etc.

Et Willelmus defendit verberacionem et roberiam et totum secundum consideracionem curie sicut homo qui etatem preteriit vel per Johannem filium Gaufridi[3]

Ad eundem terminum. 'Consideratum est quod nullum est appellum et ideo Ricardus in misericordia et Willelmus quietus.'

85. 'Thomas de Baskervilla appellat Rogerum filium Willelmi quod ipse in pace domini Regis et nequiter et noctu interfecit patrem suum Radulfum in domo sua, et hoc offert

---

[1] Perhaps some sum of money should be mentioned.

[2] This judgment has been interpolated on the roll so as to precede the phrase which records the adjournment.

[3] A third of a line is here left blank; perhaps William offered an alternative champion.

[4] m. 15. There is no marginal venue; but the case seems to belong to Northampton. For an earlier stage of it, see Rot. Cur. Reg. vol. ii. p. 257.

appeals him out of hate and spite as aforesaid, [Hugh] offers the king of his property.

A day is given to them, before the king three weeks from the octave of All Saints, to hear their judgment. 'It is considered that the appeal is null, and so let Hugh be quit and Richard in mercy.'

The said Richard appeals Thomas of Dunham, for that the said robbers came to [Thomas's] house with the stolen goods, and he received the goods in his house, and there they were distributed among the said robbers, and this he offers to prove etc.

And Thomas defends all of it as a man maimed with a broken leg, either by Richard his brother or by Roger of Moreton, (who offers etc.,) and he says that on the day on which he is alleged to have done the crime he was in the king's castle at Launceston, and on that day he did fealty to the king, and of this he puts himself upon the country. 'The appeal is null, and so let Richard be in mercy and Thomas be quit.'

[Richard] also appeals William of Dunham, and says that as he was going through the forest he met two foresters, who said that William and the other robbers aforesaid had beaten and robbed them, and this he offers etc.

And William defends the battery and robbery and all of it as the court shall consider, as one who has passed [fighting] age, either by John, Geoffrey's son, Adjourned to the day aforesaid. 'It is considered that the appeal is null, and so let Richard be in mercy and William be quit.'

85. Thomas de Baskerville appeals Roger, William's son, for that he in the king's peace, wickedly and by night, slew his father Ralph in his house; and this he offers [to prove] etc.

etc. sicut ille qui hoc vidit dum fuit infra etatem, unde postquam ipse habuit etatem ipse eum incepit appellare.

Et Rogerus venit et defendit feloniam et mortem versus eum sicut versus dominum suum cui ipse fecit homagium.

Et Thomas venit et defendit quod non est homo ejus nec unquam ei homagium fecit postquam habuit etatem, set dicit quod dum fuit infra etatem ipse fuit in custodia matris sue, et nescit quid ipsa tunc eum fecit facere.

Et ipse Rogerus nichil dixit contra.

Consideratum est quod duellum sit inter eos. Rogerus det vadium defendendi se. Vadiavit. Et Thomas similiter. Plegius Rogeri, Rogerus de Mortuo Mari. Dies ̄ tus est in crastino Oct. S. Trin. et tunc veniant armati.[1]

[2]PLACITA DE TERMINO S. MICHAELIS ANNO TERTIO.

86.   [3]Rogerus filius Nicholai appellat Willelmum de Chimilli ' et Leticiam uxorem suam '[4] quod nequiter et in pace domini Regis venit cum manu armata et vi sua et fregit domus suas in hamsoch' et in felonia robavit ei vj marcas argenti in denariis et ij. lincellos et ij. chalones et j. haubergellum et alia catalla sua ad valenciam xl. marcarum, et hoc offert etc. per corpus suum.

Willelmus venit et defendit roberiam et totum de verbo in verbum per corpus suum si debeat, vel per liberum hominem suum Willelmum scil. Trenchefoille, vel per Thomam de Ho etc., et offert domino Regi ij. marcas pro habenda legali inquisicione visneti utrum athia sit vel non, et preterea dicit quod verum cognoscet inde.[5] Audivit dici

---

[1] When homage has been done, there can be no battle between lord and man until the feudal bond is broken by a defiance; see Bracton, f. 141, line 8.

[2] Coram Rege Roll No. 10.

[3] m. 10.

[4] This mention of the wife seems an afterthought.

[5] This phrase serves to introduce the special plea which follows.

as one who saw it while under age and who when he became of age began his appeal.

And Roger comes and defends the felony and death against him as against one who is his lord and to whom he has done homage.

And Thomas comes and denies that [Roger] is his man or has ever done homage to him since he attained full age, but says that he [Thomas] while an infant was in ward to his mother, and what she may have made him do, he cannot say.

And Roger says nothing to the contrary.

It is considered that there be battle between them. Let Roger give gage to defend himself. He has waged. So has Thomas. Roger's pledge, Roger Mortimer. A day is given them, on the morrow of Trinity octave, and then let them come armed.

PLEAS OF MICHAELMAS TERM, A.D. 1201.

Essex

86. Roger, son of Nicholas, appeals William of Chimilli and Letice his wife, for that wickedly and in the king's peace he came with armed hand and with his force, and broke his houses in hamsoken, and in felony robbed him of six marks of silver in coin and two linen sheets and two counterpanes and one hauberk and other chattels of his to the value of forty marks, and this he offers [to prove] by his body.

William comes and defends the robbery and all of it word by word, by his own body if need be, or by a freeman of his, namely William Trenchefoille, or by Thomas of Hoe, and offers the king two marks for a legal inquest of the neighbourhood [to find] whether this be spite or no, and he adds that he is willing to confess the truth, namely that he

quod idem Rogerus disracionavit quandam terram per assisam de morte antecessoris de feodo suo quod ei debuit servitium iiij. marcarum per annum, et cum nullus eum requireret de servicio suo faciendo vel homagio, ipse venit et hospitatus est in domo illa que sita fuit in feodo suo.

'Rogerus postea venit et posuit se in misericordia xx. solidorum et retraxit se.'

[1] PLACITA DE TERMINO S. MICHAELIS ANNO QUARTO.

87. [2] Willelmus de Brienon' homo Osberti de Hou appellat Willelmum Torell' quod nequiter et in pace domini Regis cum vi sua scil. Edwardo et Eilardo et Johanne et David hominibus suis eum insultavit cum ivit in servicio domini sui in via domini Regis, et eum vulneravit cum cnipulo suo in maxilla et brachio, et vulnera illa ostendit, et hoc offert probare versus eum per corpus suum.

Essex

Et Willelmus venit et defendit totum de verbo in verbum, et dicit quod ipse Willelmus appellat eum per odium et athiam quia ipse quesivit versus eum dedecus et dampnum ut de uxore sua, et Willelmus Torelli percipiens prohibuit ei sepissime accessum ad domum suam, et inde producit sectam, et super illam prohibicionem inventus fuit noctu sub pariete talami ad faciendum ei dedecus, et captus fuit et retentus per Willelmum et homines suos, et postea dimissus domino suo Osberto persone per peticionem ipsius Osberti ad standum inde recto, et quod idem Willelmus ita inventus fuit sub pariete illo producit sectam, et propter illam captionem movit versus illos hoc appellum, et utrum ita fuerit an non ponit [3] super juratam visneti, vel offert probare versus eum per quendam liberum hominem suum Eulardum quod predictus Willelmus inventus fuit predicto

---

[1] Coram Rege Roll No. 12.   [2] m. 4.
[3] Perhaps *se* should be supplied.

heard say that Roger had deraigned by assize of mort d'ancestor certain land in [William's] fee, which [fee] owed him a service of four marks a year, and, as no one sought him for the purpose of doing service and homage, he came and put up in the house, which was situate in his fee.

Afterwards came Roger and submitted to an amercement of twenty shillings and withdrew [from his appeal].

PLEAS OF MICHAELMAS TERM, A.D. 1202.

Essex

87. William of Brienon, the man of Osbert of Hoe, appeals William Torell, for that he wickedly and in the king's peace with his force, to wit, Edward, Aylward, John and David his men, assaulted him as he went in his lord's service on the king's highway, and wounded him with his knife in the jaw and the arm, and these wounds he shows, and this he offers to prove against him by his body.

And William [Torell] comes and defends all word by word, and says that William [of Brienon] appeals him out of hate and spite, for he plotted his shame and loss in respect of his wife, and William Torell, seeing this, very often forbade him access to his house, (and of this he produces suit,) and despite the prohibition he was found by night within the walls of his bedroom, intending his shame, and was taken and detained by William [Torell] and his men, and was afterwards delivered to his lord, Osbert the parson, at Osbert's request, that thereof he might stand to right[1]; and that William [of Brienon] was thus found within the said walls, he produces suit; and it is because of this arrest that [William of Brienon] now appeals them; and whether this be so or no, [William Torell] puts upon a jury of the neighbourhood; or he offers to prove against [William of Brienon] by a freeman of his, to wit, Aylward, that the said William [of Brienon] was found in manner

---

[1] Osbert replevied him, undertaking that he would appear in court to answer the charge.

modo, quia Elardus interfuit captioni illi ut dicit, et si hoc non sufficit totum defendit versus eum per liberum hominem suum Radulfum Gule, qui hoc offert defendere pro domino suo quem ipse Willelmus appellat propter parvitatem ejus cum infra etatem sit.[1]

Willelmus de Brieno' defendit dedecus predicti Willelmi et dampnum et inventionem et captionem et . . .[2] et totum de verbo in verbum, et dicit quod hoc crimen ponit super eum ad adnichilandum appellum suum de pace domini Regis.

[3]PLACITA DE TERMINO S. HILLARII ANNO QUARTO.

88.
Lancast.

[4] Radulfus Longus appellat Willelmum de Winewic' quod nequiter et assultu premeditato robavit ei apud Langeshag' xv. marcas argenti quas portavit de firma domini sui, unde ipse iniit solutionem erga dominum suum,[5] et de suo proprio robavit ei j. pallium virid'[7] et tunicam et dimidiam marcam, et hoc offert probare versus eum. Et dixit quod cum evasisset de manibus suis perrexit ad villam de Chippi,' et ibi levavit clamorem, et venit ad coronatores et post ad comitatum et ibi fuit querela sua inbreviata. Et Willelmus defendit totum, et dicit quod non fuit in illo loco quem nominavit nec in patria, et offert domino Regi j. marcam pro habenda inquisitione utrum sit atia vel non.

De itinere[6]

Johannes de Duuekedale appellat Robertum Drueri quod nequiter et in assultu illo venit cum predicto Willemo et fuit in forcia ad roband' predictas xv. marcas de firma domini sui et de suo viij. solidos argenti, et hoc offert probare versus eum etc. Robertus defendit totum, et dicit quod ipse et alii appellati preter Willelmum Cithyaristam

---

[1] As to appeals by and against infants, see Bracton, f. 141 b, line 8.
[2] There is a word here that has not been read.
[3] Coram Rege Roll No. 16.
[4] m. 9. This long series of appeals may represent some dispute as to forestal rights.

[5] As to the value of this phrase, see Bracton, f. 146, line 80.
[6] The case was reserved from the eyre.
[7] Probably *viridis*, not *viride*. See Du Cange, *viridis*; Bracton, f. 146, line 9.

aforesaid, for Aylward was present at the capture (so he says); and if this be not enough, he defends the whole by his freeman Ralph Gule; who offers to defend this for his lord [William Torell], whom William [of Brienon] appeals, because he is an infant under age.

William of Brienon defends the shame of the said William Torell and the damage and the finding and capture and the . . . and all of it word by word, and says that it is to annul his appeal founded on the king's peace that [the appellee] charges him with this crime.

PLEAS OF HILARY TERM, A.D. 1203.

88. Ralph Long appeals William of Winwick, for that he wickedly and in premeditated assault robbed him at Langhaw of fifteen marks of silver which he was carrying as part of his lord's rent, and in respect of which he had become answerable to his lord, and robbed him also of a cloak of vert and a tunic and a half-mark of [Ralph's] own; and this he offers to prove against him. And he added that when he had escaped from [William's] hands he went to the township of Chipping and there raised the cry, and then went to the coroners and afterwards to the county [court], where his complaint was put in writing. And William defends all of it, and says that he was not at the place which [Ralph] has named, nor in the country, and offers the king one mark for an inquest [to find] whether this be spite or no.

Lancast.

John of Dovedale appeals Robert Drury, for that he wickedly and in the said assault came with the said William and was in the force concerned in robbing the said fifteen marks of his lord's rent, and robbing [John himself] of eight silver shillings of his own; and this he offers to prove against him etc. Robert defends all of it, and says that he and the other appellees, save William Harper, were the

fuerunt servientes Tebb' Walteri¹ de foresta sua, et cum invenissent Bernardum et alios appellatores dampnum facientes in foresta illa bersando² et vastando ceperunt vadia sua, scil. j. ensem et arcum et sagittas, et offert iij. marcas ut inquiratur utrum ita sit nec ne.

Bernardus appellat Willelmum le Fleccher quod fuit in eadem forcia cum predicto Willelmo ad roband' firmam domini sui, et de suo proprio xx. solidos et j. pallium de haubergeto³ et j. ensem et unum venabulum, et hoc offert etc. Et sciendum quod in hoc appello apposuit pacem domini Regis versus ipsum Willelmum et alios predictos appellatos.

Jurdanus appellat Hugonem de Witingham quod fuit in eadem vi ad roband' firmam domini sui et de suo proprio j. marcam et j. capam de bluet, et hoc offert etc.

Henricus Wradere appellat Paulinum filium Roberti quod fuit in eodem loco de Langeshag' in eadem forcia et de suo proprio robavit ei vij. solidos et j. tunicam et pallium et camisiam suam, et hoc offert probare etc. Paulinus defendit totum.

Walterus Godspere appellat Willelmum de Witingham quod fuit in forcia illa et de suo proprio robavit ei ij. solidos et j. tunicam et pallium de precio dimidie marce. Et Willelmus defendit totum.

Robertus Feltrarius appellat Hugonem de Witingham quod fuit in forcia illa et robavit de suo proprio vij. solidos et j. capam et j. ensem et unam asciam. Hugo defendit totum.

Willelmus filius Godelr' appellat Willelmum Fletcher quod in forcia illa robavit ij. solidos et j. tunicam et j. arcum et xij. sagittas, et hoc offert etc. Et Willelmus totum defendit.

Dies datus est omnibus predictis a die S. Mich. in j. mensem ad audiendum judicium suum.

---

[1] Theobald Walter holds the hundred of Amounderness (in which is Whittingham, the village from which the appellees came), with the whole forest of Amounderness. See the charter of Richard I., printed in Baines, History of Lancashire, vol. iv. p. 289.

[2] *Bersare*, to hunt beasts by driving them into nets; see Du Cange, s.v. *bersa*.

[3] *Haubergetum* seems here to mean, not a hauberk, but a kind of cloth; as to this and *bluet* see Du Cange, s.v. *bluet*.

forest servants of Theobald Walter, and having found Bernard, and the other appellors damage feasant in the forest, hunting and destroying the beasts, they took distresses from them, to wit, a sword and a bow and arrows, and he offers three marks for an inquest whether this be so or no.

Bernard appeals William Fletcher, for that he was in the same force with the said William to rob the rent of [Bernard's] lord, and twenty shillings and a cloak of habergett and a sword and a hunting spear of [Bernard's] own, and this he offers etc. And note that in this appeal he made mention of the king's peace against William and the other appellees aforesaid.

Jordan appeals Hugh of Whittingham, for that he was in the same force to rob the rent of [Jordan's] lord, and one mark and a cap of blue cloth of [Jordan's] own, and this he offers etc.

Henry Wrader appeals Paulin, Robert's son, for that he was in the same place, viz. Langhaw, in the same force and robbed him of seven shillings and a tunic and a cloak and a shirt of his own proper goods; and this he offers to prove etc. Paulin defends all of it.

Walter Godspere appeals William of Whittingham, for that he was in the said force and robbed him of two shillings and a tunic and a cloak, price a half-mark, of his own proper goods. And William defends all of it.

Robert Feltrer appeals Hugh of Whittingham, for that he was in the said force and robbed seven shillings and a cap and a sword and an axe of his own proper goods. Hugh defends all of it.

William, Godelram's son, appeals William Fletcher, that in that force he robbed him of two shillings and a tunic, bow and twelve arrows, and this he offers etc. And William defends all of it.

A day is given to all the aforesaid, a month after Michaelmas, to hear their judgment.

¹PLACITA DE TERMINO PASCHE ANNO QUARTO.

89. ²Adam Malherbe appellat Willelmum 'de Witham' Aurifabrum de Walengeford' quod nequiter et de nocte venit ad domum Philippi Croc' domini sui in villa de Eston', et firmavit ostia domus sue deforis cum aliis malefactoribus ita quod ipse nec alii servientes domus exire potuerunt, et postea venit cum aliis malefactoribus et fregit ostia thalami et intravit et dominum suum interfecit nequiter et robavit pecuniam domini sui. Dicit eciam quod ipse vidit eundem Willelmum per medium unius fenestre cum aliis malefactoribus ad illud maleficium faciendum, et hoc offert probare versus eum per corpus suum sicut curia consideraverit.

Willelmus venit et defendit totum de verbo in verbum sicut curia consideraverit.

Consideratum est quod duellum vadietur. Plegii Ade de prosequendo, Walterus de Audeley, Gillebertus Banastre.

Dies datus est eis a crastino S. Marie Magdalene ³ in xv. dies, et tunc veniant ceteri appellatores.

Milites de comitatu 'non' malecredunt Adredum fratrem Aluredi qui se tenet in ecclesia 'et abjuravit terram' quod ipse 'non' consensit predicto maleficio. 'Ideo sit sub plegio Gilleberti Banastre.'

Willelmus de Holecumbe Aurifaber po'⁴ in gaol' malecreditus est.

Willelmus filius Andree appellat Willelmum de Holecumbe Aurifabrum de morte predicti Philippi ut de visu suo eodem modo sicut Adam appellat Willelmum de Witham. Et consideratum est quod duellum vadietur. Plegii Willelmi de prosequendo, Walterus de Audely, Gillebertus Banastre. Dies datus est eis in crast. Oct. S. Trin.⁵

---

¹ Coram Rege Roll No. 13.
² m. 2.
³ St. Mary Magdalen is 22 July.
⁴ Mood and tense uncertain; but probably William is already in gaol (*positus in gaola*). The case may have already come before the justices in eyre, who received a presentment of the jurors and reserved the matter for the court at Westminster.
⁵ Trinity Sunday was 1 June.

PLEAS OF EASTER TERM, A.D. 1203.

Hants. **89.** Adam Malherbe appeals William of Witham, goldsmith of Walingford, for that he wickedly and by night came to the house of his lord, Philip Crook, in the township of Easton, and with other evildoers fastened the doors of his house on the outside so that neither he [Adam] nor the other servants of the house could get out, and afterwards came with the other malefactors and broke the doors of the bedroom and entered and slew his [Adam's] lord wickedly, and robbed his lord's money. He says also that through a window he saw the said William with other evildoers engaged in the crime, and this he offers to prove against him by his body as the court shall consider.

William comes and defends all of it word by word as the court shall consider.

It is considered that battle be waged. Adam's pledges to prosecute: Walter of Audley and Gilbert Banastre.

A day is given them, a fortnight from the morrow of St. Mary Magdalen, and then let the other appellors come.

The knights of the county do not suspect Edred, brother of Alfred, who is keeping himself in sanctuary and has abjured the realm, of having consented to the said crime. So let him be under the pledge of Gilbert Banastre.

William of Holecombe, goldsmith, who is in prison, is suspected.

William, Andrew's son, appeals William of Holecombe, goldsmith, of the death of the said Philip, as an eye-witness, in the same way as Adam appeals William of Witham. It is considered that battle be waged. William's pledges to prosecute, Walter of Audley and Gilbert Banastre. A day is given them on the morrow of the Octave of Trinity.

90. ¹Ricardus de Flich' serviens Willelmi de Gisnei apud Bech' appellat Almaricum de Bore quod ipse nequiter et de nocte in pace domini Regis et in latrocinio furatus est iiij. porcos domini sui in bosco de Bech' qui est clausus de haia et serutus precii iiij. solidorum et iij. porcos proprios suos ibidem precii xxvij. denariorum, et inde invenit eum saisitum et adhuc est saisitus, et hoc offert probare versus eum consideracione curie.

Aumaricus venit et defendit totum de verbo in verbum, et dicit quod dominus suus Abbas de Westmonasterio habet boscum quendam vocatum Peenge et illo bosco cepit porcos illos ut in dampno et in panagio et in defenso ² domini sui, et eos racionabiliter imparcavit, et eos obtulit amittere per vadium et plegium predicto Ricardo, et ipse noluit eos ita recipere, et inde vocat dominum suum ad warantum.

Et Ricardus dicit quod ipse Aumaricus furatus est predictos porcos in parco domini sui de Bech' ut predictum est et non alibi, et hoc offert etc. Et Aumaricus defendit.

Dies datus est eis ad habendum warantum suum in iij. sept. post fest. S. Mich. et ad audiendum judicium suum.³

⁴PLACITA DE TERMINO S. MICHAELIS ANNO QUINTO.

91. ⁵Henricus Engaine appellat Robertum de Waltervilla quod ipse nequiter et de nocte armatus venit in campum de Siberton' et robare voluit bladum suum unius acre et

---

¹ m. 8 d.
² The Abbot's wood was *positus in defenso*—that is, it was an enclosed wood; access to it was prohibited; see Du Cange, *defensa* 3. Penge seems to have been a member of the Abbot's manor at Battersea; *Bech'* may be Beckenham.
³ On this follow several other appeals apparently arising out of the same quarrel, but no judgment is found. We may guess that in this, as in many other cases, the appeal of larceny has its origin in a dispute between two landowners as to tenure, or boundaries, or rights of common.
⁴ Coram Rege Roll No. 22.
⁵ m. 11 d.

90. Richard of Flitch, the servant of William de Guines at Beck, appeals Almaric of Bore, for that he wickedly and by night in the king's peace and in larceny, in the wood of Beck, which is enclosed and locked, stole four pigs, price four shillings, of [Richard's] lord, and three pigs, price twenty-seven pence, of [Richard's] own, and thereof [Richard] found [Almaric] seised, and he is still seised, and this [Richard] offers to prove against him under award of the court.

Kent.

Almaric comes and defends all of it word by word, and says that his lord the Abbot of Westminster has a certain wood called Penge, and in that wood he took those pigs damage feasant in the pannage and the enclosed property of his lord, and he duly impounded them, and offered to surrender them to Richard on gage and pledge, and [Richard] would not take them in that manner, and [Almaric] vouches his lord to warrant this.

And Richard says that Almaric stole the said pigs in the park of [Richard's] lord at Beck as aforesaid and not elsewhere, and this he offers [to prove] etc. And Almaric defends this.

A day is given them, three weeks from Michaelmas, that [Almaric] may produce his warrantor, and that they may hear their judgment.

PLEAS OF MICHAELMAS TERM, A.D. 1203.

91. Henry Engaine appeals Robert of Walterville, for that he wickedly and by night came armed to the field of Sibbertoft and wished to rob him of the crop of one acre

Northam.

cum custodes bladi sui levarent clamorem ipse Henricus accessit ad clamorem et invenit ibidem predictum Robertum armatum in felonia cum vi sua[1] armata et gladio suo extracto qui cepit eundem Henricum et ad terram prostravit et robavit ei vij. solidos et gladium suum de precio xij. denariorum et bladum suum unius acre ad valenciam j. marce, ita quod ipse Henricus et servientes sui levaverunt clamorem et[2] . . . utheis patrie et insecuti sunt eum ita quod Robertus de Braibroc[3] venit ad clamorem levatum, et hoc offert probare per corpus suum sicut curia consideraverit.

Robertus venit et defendit totum de verbo in verbum sicut curia consideraverit, et preterea offert domino Regi j. marcam argenti pro habenda legali inquisitione patrie per tales qui non sunt homines Abbatis de Burgo utrum verum sit appellum vel athia. Dies datus est eis in xv. dies post festum S. Yllarii ad audiendum judicium suum.

Idem Henricus appellat plures de forcia quorum nomina sunt in libro mortis.[4] Postea testatum fuit coram iustic' quod non fuit athia.[5]

[6]PLACITA CORAM REGE ANNO SEPTIMO.

92.

[7]Henricus Engaine appellat Robertum de Waltervilla quod nequiter venit in feodum suum de Siberton' et robavit ei bladum suum de precio j. marce, et gladium suum de

---

[1] The roll has *cum vi sita*.
[2] A word which has not been read; but the sense seems perfect without it, and it may be due to a mistake.
[3] A few years afterwards he became the sheriff's deputy and probably he already held some office under the sheriff.
[4] It seems possible that *liber mortis* was the picturesque term, like 'the black book,' for a record containing the names of accused persons, whose names were not to be divulged for the present. In the Gloucestershire roll for 1221, p. 60, we find, *Nomina occisorum in rotulo de privatis*.
[5] See the next two cases, and observe that the determination of the issue of *odium et athia* in the appellor's favour does not establish the appellee's guilt, nor bring the appeal to an end. This is in accordance with the opinion of Dr. Brunner, who has pointed out the very great importance in the history of trial by jury of this special plea (*exceptio*) of *odium et athia*; Entstehung der Schwurgerichte, p. 472.
[6] Coram Rege Roll No. 27. See Cases 91 and 93.
[7] m. 6. Under heading *A die S. Trinit. in iii. septimanas*.

and when those who had charge of the crop on Henry's behalf raised the cry, he, Henry, came to the cry and found there Robert armed in felony, with his armed force and his sword drawn, and Robert took Henry and threw him to the ground and robbed him of seven shillings and his sword, price twelve pence, and his crop from one acre to the value of one mark, so that Henry and his servants raised the hue and cry of the country and pursued him so that Robert of Braybrook came to the cry thus raised, and this he offers to prove by his body, as the court shall consider.

Robert comes and defends all of it word by word as the court shall consider, and also offers to the king one mark of silver for a lawful inquest of the country, [to be made] by such as are not the Abbot of Peterborough's men, [to find] whether this be a true appeal or spite. A day is given them, a fortnight after Hilary, to hear their judgment.

The same Henry appeals several others as accessories, whose names are written in the book of death. Afterwards it was testified before the justices that the appeal was not made out of spite.

PLEAS BEFORE THE KING, A.D. 1205.

92. Henry Engaine appeals Robert of Walterville, for that
Northamp. he wickedly came to his fee of Sibbertoft and robbed him of his crop, price one mark, and his sword, price twelve

precio xij. denariorum et vij. solidos argenti. Et Robertus venit et defendit feloniam, et petit visum terre in qua debuit fecisse roberiam. Habeat. Dies datus est eis in xv. dies post festum S. Michaelis.

[1]PLACITA CORAM REGE DE TERMINO PASCHE ANNO SEPTIMO.

Norf. 93. [2]Henricus Engaine appellat Robertum de Watervilla quod ipse nequiter et de nocte armatus venit in campum de Siberton' [3]

Vadiatum est duellum. Dies datus est eis a die S. Trinitatis in xv. dies, et tunc veniant armati. Plegii Roberti, Gaufridus de Watervilla, Thomas de Hottot, Elias de Amundevilla, Walterus de Hottot. Plegii Henrici, Willelmus de *Baiocis*, Johannes de Stanford', Rogerus de Stanford'.

[4]PLACITA DE TERMINO PASCHE ANNO SEPTIMO INCIPIENTE OCTAVO.

Hertf. 94. [5]Adam filius Ricardi serviens Simonis de Stiuecle appellat Hugonem Hairu' quod ipse nequiter et in insultu premeditato et de nocte venit ad domum Simonis domini sui in villa de Periton' et ostia domus sue fregit, et in cameram domini sui nequiter intrusit, et robavit ei xl. marcas de denariis domini Regis de collecta foreste quos habuit in custodia, et cum levare vellet clamorem, ipse cum vi sua eum cepit et imprisonavit ita quod per duos dies fuit in prisona quod non potuit huthesium levare, et in illa prisona robavit ei v. solidos de proprio catallo suo et j. gladium de precio xij. denariorum, et postea nequiter fregit parietes cujusdam domus ubi bladum suum fuit et triturare fecit et asportavit

---

[1] Coram Rege Roll No. 28. See Cases 91 and 92.
[2] m. 2. The marginal venue should be Northampton, not Norfolk.
[3] Some five inches of parchment are here left blank. Probably the clerk intended to fill up the gap with a statement of the pleadings, but forgot to do so.
[4] Coram Rege Roll No. 29.
[5] m. 7.

pence, and of seven shillings of silver. And Robert comes and defends the felony and craves a view of the land where he is alleged to have done the robbery. Let him have it. A day is given them, a fortnight after Michaelmas.

PLEAS BEFORE THE KING, EASTER TERM, A.D. 1206.

93.
Northam.

Henry Engaine appeals Robert of Walterville, for that he wickedly and by night came armed to the field of Sibbertoft

The battle is waged. A day is given them, a fortnight after Trinity, and then let them come armed. Robert's pledges: Geoffrey of Walterville, Thomas of Hottot, Elias of Amundeville, Walter of Hottot. Henry's pledges: William of Bayeux, John of Stanford, Roger of Stanford.

PLEAS OF EASTER TERM, A.D. 1206.

94.
Hertf.

Adam, Richard's son, the servant of Simon of Stukeley, appeals Hugh Hairun, for that he wickedly and in premeditated assault and by night came to the house of Simon his lord in the township of Pirton, and broke the doors of his house, and wickedly intruded into the chamber of his lord, and robbed him of forty marks, monies of our lord the king which he had in his keeping as collected forest dues, and when he [Adam] was about to raise the cry, [Hugh] with his force took and imprisoned him so that he was two days in his prison so that he could not raise the hue, and in that prison he robbed him of five shillings of his own proper goods and a sword, price twelve pence, and afterwards wickedly broke the walls of a certain house where his corn was, and caused it to be ground and carried

ad valenciam x. marcarum, et hoc offert probare versus eum per corpus suum sicut curia consideraverit.

Idem Simon appellat eundem Hugonem quod cum vellet ad domum suam redire in pace domini Regis, idem Hugo direxit sagittam quandam et percussit eum in manum et fecit plagam quam ostendit recentem ut dicit in comitatu, quam eciam adhuc ostendit, et hoc offert disracionare versus eum sicut curia consideraverit per corpus suum.

Hugo venit et defendit roberiam et totum de verbo in verbum sicut curia consideraverit versus eundem Adam, et versus Simonem, et dicit quod per atiam faciunt appellum illud, et offert j. marcam pro habenda inde inquisitione etc.

Dies [datus] est in xv. dies post fest. S. Trin. ad audiendum judicium suum.[1]

'Postea venerunt Adam et Simon et dixerunt quod ponerent se super sex milites de comitatu Bedefordie[2] et super sex milites de comitatu Hertfordie ad recognoscendum utrum appellum verum sit vel athia.'

[3]PLACITA DE TERMINO S. MICHAELIS ANNO OCTAVO.

95.
Buk.
'Henricus del Estocke appellat Thomam Clericum filium Laurencii decani et Johannem fratrem suum et Walterum de Eton' et Gillebertum de Ake et Gaufridum de Wilekebi quod in pace domini Regis et in felonia ceperunt eum in chimino domini Regis in Eton', et inprisonaverunt eum in domo quadam et robaverunt ei ij. marcas et j. denarium et gladium suum, et hoc offert etc. per corpus suum, et dicit quod ad clamorem quem fecit in domo in qua fuit inprisonatus venerunt quidam de villa de Eton' et fregerunt ostia et deliberaverunt eum et hoc offert etc.

Et Thomas qui clericus est ut dicitur non venit, nec

---

[1] Two persons are appealed as accessories, but do not appear.
[2] Pirton is in Hertfordshire, but close to the border of Bedfordshire.
[3] Coram Rege Roll No. 81.
[4] m. 1.

it off, to the value of ten marks; and this he offers to prove against him by his body as the court shall consider.

The said Simon appeals the same Hugh, for that when he was returning to his house in the king's peace, Hugh aimed an arrow and hit him in the hand and made a wound, which he showed (so he says) in the county [court] while it was fresh, and which he still shows, and this he offers to deraign against him by his body, as the court shall consider.

Hugh comes and defends the robbery and all of it word by word as the court shall consider, against Adam and against Simon, and says that for spite they make this appeal, and offers one mark to have an inquest thereof etc.

A day is given them, a fortnight after Trinity, to hear their judgment.

Afterwards came Adam and Simon and said that they would put themselves upon six knights of Bedfordshire and upon six knights of Hertfordshire, to recognize whether this be a true appeal or spite.

PLEAS OF MICHAELMAS TERM, A.D. 1206.

95. Buck.

Henry of Stoke appeals Thomas Clerk, son of Laurence the dean, and John his brother and Walter of Eton and Gilbert of Ake and Geoffrey of Wilekeby, for that in the king's peace and in felony they took him in the king's highway in Eton, and imprisoned him in a certain house and robbed him of two marks and one penny and his sword; and this he offers [to prove] by his body; and he says that there came to the cry that he raised in the house in which he was imprisoned, certain folk of the vill of Eton, and broke the doors and delivered him; and this he offers etc.

And Thomas, who, it is said, is a clerk, does not come,

Gaufridus, set alii venerunt et defenderunt totum de verbo in verbum, et offerunt domino Regi ij. marcas pro habenda inquisitione utrum verum sit appellum vel athia. Et concessum est eis. Dies datus est eis in crast. Animarum. Plegii predictorum iiij. Walterus Duredent, Willelmus de Buuenie.

'Et inquisitum est per legales homines quod athia est. Et postea ad diem sibi datum comparuit in curia, et postea [1] essoniavit se eo die de malo veniendi, et quum non servavit diem suum rem'[2] in misericordia, et plegii de misericordia Ricardus filius Crestan et Willelmus de *Wiceyst*.'

96. [3] Matillis filia Gaufridi queritur quod Willelmus le Bedell' et Elias Ruffus et Rogerus frater Clementis et Gaufridus Serviens et Robertus le Bacheler in pace domini Regis eam robaverunt, et abstulerunt in felonia j. *chemisiam*[4] et j. tunicam et duas ulnas linee tele et satulares suos, et quod Willelmus Bedell' predictus in rapo eam defloravit et hoc offert etc. Et appellat Clementem de Turroc quod a domo sua exierunt predicti malefactores ad illum maleficium faciendum.

Et appellati defendunt feloniam, et Clemens dicit quod ipse serviens fuit hundredi, et suo tempore exierunt servientes sui et invenerunt predictas vestes et ipsam de nocte fugientem et relinquentem predictas vestes, credentes illam esse malefactricem,[5] et dicit quod ipsa male credita est quia victricus suus malefactor fuit et fugit a patria, et inde suspectam eam habent.

Dies datus est eis in crast. S. Mart. et vicecomes interim inquirat rei veritatem et scire faciat justiciarios per literas suas sigillatas etc.

---

[1] This seems to mean that Henry was seen in court, and afterwards on the same day attempted to cast an essoin, so that his attempt to excuse himself from hearing judgment was obviously false. The essoin '*de malo veniendi*' is an assertion that one is prevented from appearing by difficulties encountered on the road: see Bracton, f. 389 b.
[2] *remanet, remaneat*, or *remansit*.
[3] m. 3 d.
[4] The word looks like *cheins'*.
[5] Some words seem missing, perhaps *ceperunt vestes*.

nor does Geoffrey, but the others have come and defended all of it word by word, and offer the king two marks to have an inquest whether this be a true appeal or spite. And this is granted them. A day is given them, on the morrow of All Souls. Pledges for the said four men, Walter Duredent, William of Boveney.

And it is found by inquest of lawful men that this is spite. And afterwards at the day given him [Henry] appeared in court, and afterwards on the same day cast an essoin *de malo reniendi*, and as he did not keep his day let him remain in mercy. Pledges for the amercement, Richard, Crestan's son, and William of Wiceyst.

96. **Essex** Maud, Geoffrey's daughter, complains that William Bedell, Elias Read, Roger, Clement's brother, Geoffrey Serjeant, and Robert Bachelor in the king's peace robbed her, and in felony carried off a chemise, a gown, two ells of linen cloth and her slippers, and that the said William Bedell in rape deflowered her, and this she offers etc. And she appeals Clement of Thurrock for that the said evildoers started from his house to do that crime.

And the appellees defend the felony, and Clement says that he was the serjeant of the hundred, and in his time of office his serjeants went out and found the raiment aforesaid, and found her flying by night and leaving the raiment, [which they took] believing her a malefactor; and he says that she is suspected because her stepfather was a malefactor and fled the country, and thereof they suspect her.

A day is given, on the morrow of Martinmas, and meanwhile let the sheriff inquire the truth and signify it to the justices by letters under his seal etc.

97. [1] Warinus de Gisorz appellat Edwardum de Aula quod nequiter et cum vi sua interfecit Alanum de Gisorcio et in pace domini Regis, et ipse interfuit ut dicit et vidit ubi ipse Edwardus eum interfecit, et apud Neuha', et hoc offert disracionare versus eum sicut curia consideraverit.

Et Edwardus defendit et feloniam et quod eum non interfecit. Warinus postea interrogatus ubi ipse Alanus obiit dixit quod obiit apud Londoniam. Unde quum prius dixit quod vidit eum interfici apud Neuha', et postea confessus est ipsum obisse apud Londoniam, Edwardus sit quietus, et Warinus in misericordia.

nisi

98. [2] Quidam homines Episcopi Eliensis appellant homines Prioris de Suldham de pace domini Regis, et per cartas suas petiit [3] libertatem et curiam inde. Et habent [4] curiam suam, et preceptum est quod teneat appellantibus rectum in curia sua.

Norf.

99. [5] Robertus de Lurdingestrete appellat Willelmum Tassell' quod ipse nequiter et in pace domini Regis eum assultavit et coxam fregit in pace domini Regis et nequiter. Idem appellat Margariam de Bodiha' de precepto et Willelmum filium ejus qui infra etatem est de vi, et hoc offert.

Susex

Et Willelmus defendit pacem domini Regis fractam et feloniam, et dicit quod idem Robertus appellatus est in comitatu Susexie per Ricardum de Sundiherst de pace domini Regis et de roberia, et antequam idem Robertus moveret appellum istud versus eundem Willelmum, et nondum inde purgavit se, et petit utrum debeat ei respondere quousque inde purgatus sit, et offert dimidiam marcam ut inquiratur utrum ita appellatus sit de roberia et utrum appellum suum precessit necne.[6] 'Et Robertus concedit inquisitionem.' Plegius de dimidia marca Margaria de

dim. m.

---

[1] m. 4 d. Marginal venue uncertain.
[2] m. 5 d.
[3] In all probability it is the bishop, not the prior, who thus claims to hold pleas of the crown. The bishop of Ely had franchises of a very high order.
[4] Corr. *habet.*
[5] m. 14.
[6] As to this plea, see Bracton, f. 141: *cadit appellum propter crimen appellantis.*

97. Warin of Gisors appeals Edward of the Hall, for that wickedly and with his force and in the king's peace he slew Alan of Gisors, and [Warin] was present and an eye-witness when Edward slew him, which was at Newnham, and this he offers to deraign against him as the court shall consider.

And Edward defends the felony, and denies that he slew him. Afterwards Warin, being asked where Alan died, said that he died at London. Wherefore, since he first said that he saw him slain at Newnham, and afterwards confessed that he died at London, let Edward be quit, and Warin in mercy.

Norf.
98. Certain of the Bishop of Ely's men appeal men of the Prior of Shouldham of [a breach of] the king's peace, and [the Bishop] under his charters craved his franchise and cognizance of the case. Cognizance is granted him, and he is ordered to hold right to the appellors in his court.

Sussex
99. Robert of Lordington appeals William Tassell, for that he wickedly and in the king's peace assaulted him and broke his hip-bone in the king's peace and wickedly. He also appeals Margery of Bodiham as having ordered the crime, and William her son, who is within age, as an accessory; and this he offers etc.

And William defends the breach of the king's peace and the felony, and says that Robert was appealed in the county [court] of Sussex by Richard of Sandhurst of the king's peace and robbery, and this before Robert began this appeal against William, and [Robert] has not yet cleared himself of the appeal against him, and [William] demands whether he need answer [Robert] until he be cleared thereof, and offers the king a half-mark that it may be inquired whether [Robert] be appealed of robbery and whether his appeal was the earlier or no. And Robert concedes that an inquest be made. Pledge for the half-

Bodiha'. Dies datus est eis in xv. dies post festum S. Yllarii, et tunc etc.

Et Margaria recedit sine die appellata de vi, et Willelmus filius ejus similiter qui infra etatem est.

[1]PLACITA DE TERMINO S. MICHAELIS ANNO NONO.

100.
orht.

[2]Willelmus filius Ricardi de Clendon' appellat Ricardum de Clendon' quod ipse in pace domini Regis et nequiter occidit Ricardum patrem suum ita quod ipse qui tunc fuit infra etatem hoc vidit, et hoc offert etc.

Et Ricardus venit et defendit totum de verbo in verbum et dicit quod tempore Regis Ricardi appellaverunt Sibilla mater Willelmi que fuit uxor Ricardi occisi et Stephanus frater occisi Rogerum et Wilekinum qui per sectam eorum utlagati fuerunt, et postea ipsi Sibilla et Stephanus appellaverunt eundem Ricardum modo appellatum ita quod captus et in prisona positus fuit per appellum eorum, et Archiepiscopus tunc Justiciarius[3] precepit fieri inquisicionem si ipse culpabilis fuit nec ne, et inquisitum fuit quod non fuit culpabilis ita quod dimissus fuit per plegios standi inde recto in adventu justiciariorum, qui cum ibi essent inquisitum fuit quod non fuit culpabilis coram eis, et posuerunt iterum loquelam illam apud Westmonasterium, et tunc tulerunt [4] Sibilla et Stephanus et tulerunt breve Regis Ricardi de facienda inde inquisicione, et facta inquisicione, que eum acquietavit, posita fuit loquela iterum coram justiciariis itinerantibus in partibus Norhantonie, ita quod quando venerunt, fecerunt fieri inquisicionem de morte illa per sacramentum, que eum acquietavit, et ipsi iterum posuerunt loquelam illam apud Westmonasterium, qua penitus audita, ipse judicatus fuit quietus, et adhuc offert xv. marcas pro habenda adhuc [5] inde inquisicione.[6]

[1] Coram Rege Roll No. 83.
[2] m. 3.
[3] Hubert Walter, now archbishop, was justiciar from Christmas 1193 to the summer of 1198.
[4] Corr. *venerunt*.
[5] One *adhuc* seems superfluous.
[6] The first of the four inquests would merely decide whether Richard was to remain in gaol or to be replevied; but after this, there were three more inquests. Seemingly

mark, Margery of Bodiham. A day is given them, a fortnight from Hilary, and then etc.

And Margery, appealed as accessory, goes hence without day, and so does William her son, who is within age.

PLEAS OF MICHAELMAS TERM, A.D. 1207.

100. William, son of Richard of Clendon, appeals Richard of
Northam. Clendon, for that he in the king's peace and wickedly slew Richard [the appellor's] father so that [the appellor], who was then within age saw this; and this he offers etc.

And Richard comes and defends all of it word by word, and says that in king Richard's time Sibil, William's mother, and wife of Richard the slain, and Stephen, brother of Richard the slain, appealed Roger and Wilkin, who were outlawed at their suit, and afterwards Sibil and Stephen appealed Richard, the now appellee, so that he was taken and put in prison on their appeal, and the now Archbishop, who was then Justiciar, ordered that an inquest should be made, [to find] whether he were guilty or no, and it was found that he was not guilty, so that he was liberated on finding pledges that he would stand to right on the coming of the justices [in eyre], and when they came it was found by inquest taken before them that he was not guilty, so they again adjourned the suit to Westminster, and then came Sibil and Stephen and brought a writ of king Richard ordering an inquest, and the inquest was made and acquitted him, and then the suit was again adjourned before the justices making eyre in the county of Northampton, so that when they came they caused an inquest as to that death to be made upon oath, and this acquitted him, and then they again adjourned the suit to Westminster, and after a full hearing of it, he was adjudged quit, and he still offers fifteen marks that he may have an inquest of this matter.

Dies datus est eis a die S. Martini in xv. dies ad audiendum judicium suum.

101.
Hereford.

[1] Mariona uxor Hugonis Dobin malecreditur per totum visnetum 'de Markel' de morte Hugonis Dobin viri sui '*scilicet quod ejus purkacium*' [2] eo quod sepius fuit melleta et contencio inter eos pro delictis suis, quia plures adulterabantur cum ea, et similiter malecreditur eo quod omnia catalla amota fuerunt de domo. Et ideo purget se per judicium ferri. Vad'.[3]

vad'

Henricus Blundus malecreditur quod ipse consensus fuit de morte illa, eo quod serviens fuit et non venit ad uthes et semper fuit domi quando adulteratores fuerunt in domo Hugonis Dobin. Purget se aqua.

Willelmus de Trilleg' rettatus de eadem morte et malecreditus eo quod solitus fuit adulterari cum predicta Mariona fugit. Et ideo interrogetur.

Willelmus Molendinarius frater Tebelin' malecreditus de eadem morte eadem de causa fugit. Et ideo interrogetur.

Gaufridus de Norf' captus fuit pro eadem morte eo quod venit ad clamorem cum arcu et sagittis ipsius occisi, unde testat' est quod uxor occisi ei tradidit ad levandum *uthes* et sequendum malefactores, non malecreditur. Et ideo sit sub plegiis.[4]

---

the king had a large power of granting inquests as pleased him best, and a verdict of acquittal was inconclusive. Some traces of the earlier proceedings will be found in Rot. Cur. Reg. vol. i. pp. 227, 301, vol. ii. pp. 52, 265, 266. It appears from the Pipe Roll for John's tenth year, that Richard fined fourteen marks and William six marks for leave to compromise: Madox, Hist. Exchequer, vol. i. p. 151 *x*.

[1] m. 6. The foundation of this case must be the presentment of some Herefordshire jurors, probably before justices in eyre.

[2] A very obscure interlineation.

[3] Probably *Vadiavit*.

[4] Part of this case is in Placit. Abbrev. p. 99.

A day is given them, a fortnight from Martinmas, to hear their judgment.

101. Marion, wife of Hugh Dobin, is suspected by the whole
Hereford neighbourhood of Marcle of the death of Hugh Dobin her husband, to wit, that this was her purchase [i.e. done by her procurement], for that there often were quarrels and disputes between them over her offences, for many committed adultery with her, and likewise she is suspected because all the chattels were removed from the house. So let her purge herself by ordeal of iron. She has waged [her law].

Henry Blund is suspected of consenting to that death, because he was [Hugh's] servant and did not come to the hue, and was always in the house of the said Hugh Dobin when the adulterers were there. Let him purge himself by water.

William of Triley, charged with the same death, and suspected because he was wont to commit adultery with the said Marion, has fled. So let him be exacted.

William Miller, Tebelin's brother, suspected of the said death for the same reason, has fled. So let him be exacted.

Geoffrey of Norfolk was arrested for the same death because he came to the hue and cry with the bow and arrows of the slain man. It is testified that the wife of the slain handed these [arms] to him that he might raise the hue and pursue the malefactors. He is not suspected. So let him be under pledge.

¹PLACITA DE TERMINO S. TRINITATIS ANNO DECIMO.

102.
Nort.

²Convenit per licenciam domini Regis inter Johannem Camerarium appellantem et Herebertum de Patesle appellatum de morte Drogonis fratris ipsius Johannis, scilicet, quod idem Herebertus ibit in terram Jerosolimitanam et ibi moram faciet in servicio Dei pro anima occisi cum tempore itineris sui in redeundo et eundo per vij. annos, et si infra terminum illum redierit, fiat de eo justicia tanquam convictus esset de morte predicta, et incipiet movere de domo sua a die Martis proxima ante festum S. Margarete³ in xl. dies anno regni Regis Johannis decimo. Preterea Thomas de Ingaldestorp pro anima ejusdem occisi faciet fieri unum monacum vel unum canonicum de progenie ipsius occisi,⁴ et si debeat esse monacus erit monacus ad unam istarum trium domorum, scilicet, apud Norew' vel apud Acram vel apud Binham, si canonicus apud Tieford' vel apud Kokesford vel apud Walsingham, et debet clericus ille presentari Thome predicto et amicis ejus die dominica proxima post festum S. Marie Magdalene⁵ anno x., '*et recipere habitum citra festum S. Michaelis,*' et preterea idem Thomas dabit parentibus occisi xl. marcas, unde reddet x. marcas die dominica proxima post festum S. Marie Magdalene, et x. marcas ad festum S. Martini, et x. marcas vij. diebus ante Natale, et x. marcas ad Annunciacionem Beate Marie. Et inde sunt plegii Thom' de Ingaldestorp, Rogerus de Weston', Hervicus de Docking', Robertus de Brancestria, Jacobus de Vabadun, Gaufridus de Congham. Et Thomas [concedit⁶] quod curia distringat eum ad perficiendum istam convencionem.

¹ Coram Rege Roll No. 35. There is an abstract of this case in Placit. Abbrev. p. 60.
² m. 9 d.
³ St. Margaret is 20 July.
⁴ The burden of Thomas's obligation probably lies in this, that the religious house will not receive a new inmate unless some provision be made for his support.
⁵ St. Mary Magdalene is 22 July.
⁶ This word is not on the roll, but is supplied conjecturally.

PLEAS OF TRINITY TERM, A.D. 1208.

102.
Norf.

By the king's licence, it is covenanted between John Chamberlain the appellor and Herbert of Pattesley the appellee touching the death of Drogo, John's brother, to wit, that Herbert shall go to the Holy Land and remain there in the service of God for the soul of the slain for seven years, the time spent in journeying there and back being reckoned part of that term, and if within that term he shall return, let justice be done on him as though he were convicted of the said death, and he shall begin to move from his house forty days after the Tuesday next before S. Margaret's day in the tenth year of King John. Also Thomas of Ingoldsthorpe shall for the soul of the slain procure one of the slain man's family to be made either a monk or a canon, and if he is to be a monk, then he shall be a monk in one of these three houses, to wit, Norwich, Castleacre, or Binham, but if a canon, then at Thetford, Coxford or Walsingham, and the said clerk shall be presented to the said Thomas and his friends on the Sunday next after S. Mary Magdalene's day in the tenth year, and shall take the habit before Michaelmas, and further the said Thomas shall give the kinsfolk of the slain forty marks, whereof he shall pay ten marks on the Sunday next after S. Mary Magdalene's day, and ten marks at Martinmas, and ten marks a week before Christmas, and ten marks at Lady Day. And of this the following are Thomas of Ingoldsthorpe's pledges, Roger of Weston, Hervey of Docking, Robert of Brancester, Jacob of Vabadun, Geoffrey of Congham. And Thomas grants that the court may distrain him to perform this covenant.

Et Thomas dat domino Regi xl. marcas pro licencia concordandi per plegium predictorum.

108. [1]'Willelmus Makeblith' et Thomas Aurifaber et Robertus nepos Edmundi capti fuerunt pro morte uxoris Milonis Judei de Eboraco per appellum ejusdem Milonis. Et ipsi non malecreduntur nec a Judeis nec a Cristianis, set ipse Milo malecreditur de eadem morte unde cum Benedictus frater occise eum vellet appellare de morte illa, ipse Milo fugit. Et non prosequitur versus eosdem captos, et ideo sint sub plegiis predicti Willelmus, Thomas et Robertus standi recto si quis versus eos loqui voluerit, et vicecomes habeat nomina plegiorum, et ipsi dant xx. solidos domino Regi scilicet quilibet dimidiam marcam per plegium Walteri Aurifabri, Ade Aurifabri, Clerenbaldi, et plegii Milonis de prosequendo sint in misericordia scilicet Ursell' Medicus et Ysaac *Niger* uterque de dimidia marca per plegium commune [2] Judeorum Eboraci. Et Benedictus filius Ursell' appellavit predictum Milonem quod intellexit per inquisicionem quam fecerat quod Milo interfecit sororem suam et quod per Kelinam Judeam fuit occisa eo quod ipse Milo dicitur habuisse rem cum ea, ita quod ipsa Kelina fuit capta, set non malecreditur, et ideo sit sub plegio, et dat dimidiam marcam per plegium Vinanti Judei. Et ipse Benedictus per cujus appellum quod nullum fuit [3] ipsa fuit capta et inprisonata in misericordia pro falso clamore de dimidia marca per plegium commune Judeorum.

---

[1] m. 11 d. The marginal venue is illegible, but probably it should be Yorkshire. The case seems to have been heard at York.

[2] *commune* is the genitive of *communa*. The Jews of York are an organized commune or community, which can become surety in its corporate character.

[3] He did not assert that he saw the crime; *non locutus est de visu.*

And Thomas gives the king forty marks for the licence to compromise, for which sum the above-named persons are pledges.

103. William Makeblithe and Thomas Goldsmith and Robert, Edmund's nephew, were arrested for the death of the wife of Milo the Jew of York upon the appeal of the said Milo. And they are not suspected; neither by Jews nor by Christians; but Milo himself is suspected of the said death, and when Benedict, brother of the slain woman, was about to appeal Milo, he fled. And [Milo] does not prosecute against those who were arrested, and so let the said William, Thomas and Robert be under pledges to stand to right in case any shall accuse them; let the sheriff take the names of their pledges; and they give twenty shillings to the king, to wit, each of them a half-mark on the pledge of Walter Goldsmith, Adam Goldsmith and Clarenbald; and let Milo's pledges to prosecute be in mercy, to wit, Ursell the Physician and Isaac Black each for a half-mark on the pledge of the commonalty of the Jews of York. And Benedict, Ursell's son, appealed the said Milo, for that he learnt by inquiry which he made that Milo killed [Benedict's] sister [Milo's wife], and that she was slain on account of Kelina the Jewess, for that Milo is said to have had an intrigue with her; and Kelina was arrested, but is not suspected; so let her be under pledge, and she gives a half-mark, for which Vinant the Jew is pledge; and let Benedict upon whose appeal, which is null, she was taken and imprisoned be in mercy for his false appeal in a half-mark, for which the commonalty of the Jews is pledge.

[1]PLACITA DE TERMINO S. MICHAELIS ANNO TERTIO DECIMO.

104. [2]Ricardus de Credewell' appellat Johannem Scotum et dicit quod vigilia Nativitatis Beate Marie [3] tribus annis preteritis venit idem Johannes de Asle ubi fuerat ad quoddam scotale et in via sicut venit de mercato de Cicestr' [4] fecit eum ascendere retro super equum suum, et cum putasset quod eum portaret in bona fide, ipse retro se jactavit manum suam cum cultello et eum percussit inde et fecit ei plagam in humero dextro ita quod cecidit de equo illo, et ipse descendit de equo suo et iterum percussit eum illo cultello et fecit ei aliam plagam in humero *superius*, ita quod prima plaga fuit profunda de iiij. pollicibus et dimidio, et reliquit eum fere mortuum, et preter hoc ipse robavit ei de bursa sua xliij. solidos in denariis et j. anulum aureum precii xv. den., et cum hoc fecisset ipse sicut potuit ivit domum pedibus et manibus et mandavit servientem Regis, scilicet, Robertum de Hal die crastino scilicet die Nativitatis, qui venit et vidit plagas suas et dedit ei pacem domini Regis [5] et recessit, et nocte quinta venit idem Johannes cum vi sua ad domum matris sue in Credewell' et burgavit domum suam et eam ligavit et taliter tractavit quod nunquam postea legalis fuit corpore,[6] set inde suscepit mortem, et post pelfavit domum et asportavit omnia que inventa fuerunt in domo illa, et post illam burgacionem die quinta vel die quarta venit ipse ad matrem suam et invenit eam talem, et ipsa dixit ei quod si ipsa moriretur antequam ipse, ipse sequeretur mortem suam versus predictum Johannem, et hoc totum offert disracionare versus eum prout curia consideraverit.

[1] Coram Rege Roll No 43.
[2] m. 5.
[3] The Nativity is 8 September.
[4] *Sic*; but it is Cirencester, not Chichester, that is meant; Crudwell and Ashley lie between Cirencester and Malmesbury.
[5] See the Leges Henrici Primi, 79, § 4; breach of the king's peace when given by his sheriff or other officer is 'emendable,' if at all, with 100 shillings. The practice of pleading special peaces had not quite disappeared in John's reign.
[6] As to this phrase see the Glossary.

PLEAS OF MICHAELMAS TERM, A.D. 1211.

104. Richard of Crudwell appeals John Scot and says that on the eve of Our Lady's birthday three years ago, the said John came from Ashley where he had been at a scotale and in the way as he came from Cirencester market made [Richard] get up behind him on his horse, and whereas [Richard] had thought that he would give him a lift in good faith, he struck out his hand backwards with a knife in it and struck [Richard] and wounded him in the right shoulder so that he fell off the horse, and [John] dismounted and again struck him with the knife and gave him another wound on the shoulder higher up (and the first wound was four and a half inches deep), and left him nearly dead, and besides this robbed him of forty-three shillings in coin from his purse and of a gold ring price fifteen pence; and when he had done this, [Richard] went home as best he might on all fours; and on the next day, the day of S. Mary's birth, he informed the king's serjeant, Robert of Hale, who came and saw the wounds and granted him the king's peace and went away; and five nights afterwards John came with his force to the house of [Richard's] mother in Crudwell and burgled her house and bound her and so treated her that never afterwards was she leal of body, but got her death thereby; and afterwards he robbed the house and carried off whatever was therein; and on the fourth or fifth day after the burglary [Richard] came to his mother and found her in the said condition, and she bade him, in case of her dying before him, to prosecute her death against the said John; and all this he offers to deraign against him as the court shall consider.

Wilts.

Et Johannes venit et defendit totum de verbo in verbum et offert ij. marcas pro habenda inquisicione per legales homines de visneto utrum faciat hoc appellum per odium et attiam, an justa causa.

Et Johannes[1] quesitus quid fecit [et] si clamor levatus fuit, dicit quod non.

Dies datus est eis in proxima[2] adventu domini Regis apud Divisas, et Johannes remaneat in eadem custodia in qua prius fuit, et Ricardus habeat breve ad vicecomitem quod ipse faciat venire milites de visneto ad testificandum veritatem de appello illo, et vicecomes tunc sit ibi et habeat ibi servientem, scilicet, Robertum de Hal.

[3]PLACITA DE TERMINO S. HILLARII ANNO TERTIO-DECIMO.

105. [4]'Alicia que fuit uxor Haraldi queritur quod cum ipsa vigilia S. Michaelis venisset ad domum Walteri de Couintr' apud Harcha' pro averiis suis replegiandis que idem Walterus ceperat, idem Walterus conviciatus est ei et illam verberavit quodem baculo et jactavit ultra quendam *truncum* ita quod ipsa ita *obstinata* fuit quod non potuit postea per xviij. dies audire, et cum Robertus filius ejus qui foris extitit audisset matrem suam clamantem ipse intravit et cepit matrem suam inter brachia sua, et idem Walterus inter brachia sua[5] eo vidente verberavit ipsam Aliciam et eciam quandam plagam ei[6] fecit cum quadam securi in tibia et eis robavit j. anulum precii xx. sol. cum toto almererio in quo fuit, ' et hoc totum fecit in pace domini Regis et nequiter,' et hoc offert ipsa disracionare versus eum ut femina prout curia consideraverit, et si curia consideraverit quod ipsa disracionare illud non possit, Robertus filius suus hoc offert disracionare versus eum ut ille qui hoc vidit et audivit et

---

[1] Corr. *Ricardus*.
[2] *Sic*.
[3] Coram Rege Roll No. 48.
[4] m. 19. There is an abstract of this case in Placit. Abbrev. p. 84.
[5] An attempt seems made to give Robert a legal interest in his mother's bruises.
[6] *To him* or *to her*; but probably *to him*, for see what Robert says further on.

And John comes and defends all of it word by word, and offers two marks for an inquest by lawful men of the neighbourhood [to find] whether [Richard] makes this appeal out of hate and spite, or for good cause.

And [Richard] on being asked what he did and whether the hue was raised, says that it was not.

A day is given them, on the first coming of the king to Devizes, and let John remain in the same custody as before, and let Richard have a writ to the sheriff ordering him to cause knights of the neighbourhood to come and testify the truth about this appeal, and let the sheriff be there and have with him his serjeant, Robert of Hale.

PLEAS OF HILARY TERM, A.D. 1212.

105. Alice, who was wife of Harold, complains that whereas on the eve of Michaelmas she had come to the house of Walter of Coventry at Househam to replevy her beasts which Walter had taken, Walter reviled her and beat her with a stick and threw her across a log, so that she was so stunned that she lost her hearing for eighteen days; and when Robert her son, who was outside, heard his mother's cries, he entered and took her within his arms, and Walter beat her while she was thus in his arms and in his sight, and also wounded him with an axe on his shin, and robbed them of a ring, price twenty shillings, together with the casket in which it was, and all this he did in the king's peace and wickedly; and this she offers to deraign against him as a woman as the court shall consider, and if the court shall consider that she herself cannot deraign this, Robert her son offers to deraign this against him as one who saw and heard it and was present at it, and within

Linc.

interfuit et inter cujus brachia hoc factum fuit. Dicit eciam[1] Robertus quod idem Walterus eum verberavit cum quodam baculo sine plaga quam ei fecisset nequiter et in pace domini Regis et ei robavit capam suam et capellum suum et gladium suum, et hoc offert disracionare versus eum per corpus suum prout curia consideraverit, et cum hoc factum esset ipsi Alicia et Robertus exiverunt de domo illa sicut potuerunt et statim levaverunt uthesium et clamorem, quod cum Walterus audisset precepit Waltero Monaco, et Eudoni Servienti, et Roberto de *Mentenge*, Hugoni Caue, Gaufrido Emme, Johanni Preposito, et David Servienti quod ipsi sequerentur eos, *et* ipsi secuti fuerunt eos usque ad domum ipsius Alicie apud Kattesdale ubi ipsa intraverat et *per preceptum ipsius Walteri* fregerunt hostia domus et parietes et intraverunt et fregerunt hostium camere et intraverunt et fregerunt archam ipsius Alicie nequiter et in pace domini Regis et in roberia ceperunt scrinium suum in quo fuerunt *quinque* firmacula aurea et tres anuli aurei et quinque pepla serica et quinque solidi in denariis et . . .[2] et alia, et postea fregerunt hostium capelle et intraverunt, et totum hoc non suffecit set ipsi venerunt ad boveriam et fregerunt hostium et abduxerunt xiiij. animalia tam boves quam vaccas et ij. aueros et illa nequiter et in pace domini Regis abduxerunt, et in roberia ceperunt cccc. bidentes et abduxerunt, et omnia ista habuit ipse in custodia per balliam matris sue,[3] et de custodia sua ea robata fuerunt, et hoc offert disracionare versus eum per corpus suum prout curia consideraverit.

Et Walterus venit et defendit pro se pacem domini Regis infractam et feloniam et plagam et roberiam tam anuli quam aliarum rerum et verberacionem et quicquid ad pacem domini Regis infractam pertinet versus eam ut versus feminam et versus ipsum Robertum ut versus eum qui de alterius plaga et alterius dampno faciat appellum, et ut versus eum qui habet fratrem primogenitum qui nullum

---

[1] This is a second appeal distinct from Alice's.

[2] An illegible word is interlined.

[3] As to this allegation, see Bracton, f. 146.

whose arms it was done. Robert also says that Walter beat him with a stick, let alone the wound which he had given him, wickedly and in the king's peace, and robbed him of his cape, hat and sword; and this he offers to deraign against him by his body as the court shall consider; and when this had been done they, Alice and Robert, left the house as best they might and at once raised hue and cry; and when Walter heard this, he ordered Walter Monk, Eudo Serjeant, Robert of Minting, Hugh Cave, Geoffrey, Emma's son, John Reeve and David Serjeant to pursue them, and they pursued them to Alice's house at Cadsdale, into which she had gone, and by Walter's command they broke the doors of the house and the walls and entered and broke the door of the chamber and entered and broke open Alice's chest, wickedly and in the king's peace, and in robbery took her coffer in which were five gold buckles and three gold rings and five silken wimples and five shillings in coin and . . . and other things, and afterwards broke the door of the chapel and entered; and all this did not suffice, for they came to the cattle shed and broke the door and drove off fourteen beasts, both oxen and cows and two work-horses, and these they drove off wickedly and in the king's peace; and in robbery they took 400 sheep and drove them off; and all these things [Robert] had in his charge by bailment from his mother, and from his charge were they robbed; and this he offers to deraign against him by his body as the court shall consider:

And Walter comes and on his own behalf defends the breach of the king's peace, the felony, the wound, the robbery both of the ring and of the other things, and the beating, and all that pertains to a breach of the king's peace, against [Alice] as against one who is a woman, and against Robert as against one who makes an appeal touching a wound given and damage done to someone else, and as against one who has an elder brother who makes no

appellum facit.¹ Defendit eciam versus eundem Robertum pacem domini Regis infractam et feloniam et roberiam et totum de verbo in verbum prout curia consideraverit, set bene cognoscit quod per preceptum domini sui Comitis Cestrie fecit ipse capi xx. animalia tam de equis quam bobus et vaccis, et ccc. bidentes et xxxvj. bidentes pro defectu servicii domini sui quod aretro fuit, quia ipse tenet quoddam tenementum de feodo Comitis de Roberto de Lekeburn' et Robertus tenet de Radulfo de Sulee et Radulfus de eodem Comite, et ipse tenet aliud tenementum de Roberto de Lekeburn' et Robertus de Comite, et pro defectu servicii utriusque tenementi fecit ipse capi predicta averia per preceptum domini sui Comitis. Qui venit et illud warentizat. Et sciendum quod ipse primo capit se ad Walterum Monacum.²

³ Et predictus Walterus Monacus et alii appellati defendunt pacem domini Regis infractam et brusuram domorum et hostiorum et roberiam et feloniam. Set revera dicunt quod ipsi ceperunt averia illa per preceptum domini sui pro arreragio servicii sicut predictum est.

Et Walterus offert domino Regi j. palefridum per sic quod ipse det licenciam excommunicandi per totum comitatum Lincolnie omnes illos qui plagam vel verberacionem vel feloniam vel roberiam aliquam ipsis fecisset,⁴ et per sic quod inquiratur si domino Regi placuerit per legales milites de eodem comitatu qui non sint homines ejusdem Comitis nec in ballia ipsius Walteri manentes nec eum nec ipsos Aliciam et Robertum affinitate attingant si ipse sit inde culpabilis vel non, petit eciam quod Johannes avunculus Gileberti fil' ipsius Alicie⁵ et Adam le Miner homo suus sint in eadem inquisicione.

---

¹ The suggestion seems to be that Alice's eldest son is her proper champion; see above, Case 28.
² As regards Robert's own appeal touching the robbery of the beasts, Walter Monk is the principal appellee, not Walter of Coventry.
³ m. 19 d.
⁴ Corr. *fecissent.* This request seems intended as evidence of innocence; it is just possible that *excommunicare* does not here bear its technical ecclesiastical sense, but refers to temporal outlawry.
⁵ Perhaps the first-born son mentioned above. There may be some dispute about an inheritance at the bottom of this case.

appeal. And against Robert he defends the breach of the king's peace, the felony and robbery and all of it word by word as the court shall consider, but he freely confesses that by command of his lord the Earl of Chester he caused twenty beasts, horses, oxen and cows, and three hundred and thirty-six sheep to be seized for default of the service due to his lord which was in arrear; for [Robert] holds a tenement belonging to the Earl's fee of Robert of Lekeburn, who holds of Ralph of Suley, who holds of the Earl, and [Robert] holds another tenement of Robert of Lekeburn, who holds it of the Earl; and for default of service due from both tenements he caused the said beasts to be seized by command of his lord, the Earl. And the Earl comes and warrants this. And be it noted that [Robert] betakes himself in the first instance against Walter Monk.

And the said Walter Monk and the other appellees defend the breach of the king's peace and the breaking of houses and doors and the robbery and felony. But they say that in truth they took the beasts by command of their lord for arrears of service in manner aforesaid.

And Walter offers the king a palfrey, that the king may give him licence to excommunicate throughout the county of Lincoln all those who have been guilty of the wounding, beating, felony and robbery committed against [Alice and Robert], and that it may be inquired, if the king shall please, by lawful knights of the said county, who are not men of the Earl, nor dwelling in Walter's bailiwick, nor related to him, nor to Alice and Robert, whether he be guilty or no; and he also craves that John, Gilbert's uncle, son of the said Alice, and his man Adam Miner may be upon that inquest.

Et Alicia et Robertus non ponunt se super aliquam inquisitionem set tenent se ad appellum suum.

Dies datus est eis a die Purificacionis in iij. septimanas ad audiendum judicium suum.

106. [1]Willelmus de Tameton', Alanus de Wilton', {Thomas de Wilton'} Walterus de Saureb', Nigellus de *Plunton'*, Robertus de Wiwelestorp, Robertus le Vavassur, Maugerus le Vavassur, omnes illi preter {Thomam de Wilton'} et Nigellum de Plunton' recordantur, quod cum ipsi per preceptum vicecomitis fuerunt ad castellum ad tenendum residua[2] placitorum comitatus, quidam homines duxerunt coram eis de gaola quendam ligatum, scilicet, Willelmum filium Andree. Et venit coram eis Gaufridus de Colethorp et appellavit eum *dicens* quod predictus Willelmus nocte venit in curia sua et nequiter et in latrocinio furatus est ei j. vaccam que ad eum ligata fuit per quendam tier'[3] quem ipse prius furatus fuerat de equo suo, et cum ipse hoc percepisset ipse levavit uthes et clamorem et secutus fuit eum cum clamore et eum cepit, et quod ita furatus fuit vaccam offert[4] disracionare versus eum prout curia consideraverit per corpus suum etc. Et Willelmus defendit feloniam et latrocinium et seisinam vacce et totum de verbo in verbum prout curia consideraverit per corpus suum. 'Et vicecomes quesitus si aliquis summonitus fuit per eum, dicit quod non.'[5] Et quum plures ibi fuerunt qui testati fuerunt quod ita captus fuit cum clamore illo et cum tali seisina, sine interrogacione quam eis facta fuit, ipsi adjudicaverunt duellum inter eos. per emendacionem.[6]

Ebor.

---

[1] m. 20.

[2] Pleas which stood over for want of time to hear them are sometimes designated as *placita residua*.

[3] This seems an English word and perhaps means a halter. The word *tie* seems to be still used to describe a rope which is used for hobbling a cow when she is being milked.—Halliwell. Probably the cow was tied to William in order that Geoffrey might count against him as against a thief in seisin, a thief 'handhaving and backbearing.'

[4] Despite the present tense, this and the following sentences seem part of the record of the county court.

[5] This interpolated sentence seems to state what happened in the king's court; in the English version it is transplanted into what seems its proper place.

[6] Perhaps the words *per emendacionem* should come in the next sentence; I translate them as though that were their place.

And Alice and Robert do not put themselves upon any inquest but hold to their appeal.

A day is given them to hear their judgment, three weeks from Candlemas.

106. William of Tameton, Alan of Wilton, Walter of Sowerby, Nigel of Plumpton, Robert of Wivelsthorpe, Robert Vavassour, Mauger Vavassour, all these except Nigel of Plumpton record, that whereas by the sheriff's precept they were at [York] castle to hold the adjourned pleas of the county, certain men brought before them from the gaol a man in bonds, namely, William, Andrew's son. And Geoffrey of Calthorpe came before them and appealed him, saying that the said William came to his court by night and wickedly and in larceny stole from him a cow (which was bound to him by a tie which he had previously stolen from [Geoffrey's] horse), and when [Geoffrey] saw that, he raised hue and cry and pursued him with cry and caught him, and that he thus stole the cow he offered to deraign against him, as the court should consider, by his body etc. And William defended felony and larceny and seisin of the cow and all of it word by word by his body as the court should consider. And since many were there [in court] who testified that he was thus captured by the hue and cry, seised of the cow as aforesaid without any demand being made for their testimony, [the aforesaid knights] adjudged that there should be battle between them.

York

Consideratum est quod duellum sit devadiatum eo quod nullus testatus fuit quod captus fuit cum vacca nec serviens vicecomitis fuit cum eo quando ductus fuit ad carcerem, nec per vicecomitem aliquis de visneto summonitus fuit, et Gaufridus quia cepit et duxit eum ad carcerem sine visu servientis, sit in misericordia, et capiatur, et milites qui interfuerunt judicio in misericordia.

Isti interfuerunt.[1]

mīc multo

[2]PLACITA DE TERMINO PASCHE ANNO TERTIODECIMO.

107. [3]Wille Brun rettatus de morte cujusdem hominis et purgatus per aquam et qui ejuravit regnum [4] offert j. marcam per sic quod possit redire et invenire plegios standi recto si quis versus eum loqui voluerit.

Suff.

108. [5]Inquisicio de Awelton' de femina mortua quam Ricardus Swel' fecit sepelire sine visu coronatorum et vicecomitis.

Ailwinus Flagellator dicit quod Goda vidua locaverat [6] eum ad fodiendum in orto suo, et ipsa venit die crastina et fodit in orto usque primam, et circa primam venit quedam mulier que vocatur Seild filia Fot et dixit ei quod predicta

---

[1] No names follow. The point of the case seems to be, that the county court could adjudge the duel only if the thief were taken in seisin by hue and cry, and then only if the seisin were duly testified: Bracton, f. 154 b; Britton, vol. i. p. 56.

[2] Coram Rege Roll No. 44.

[3] m. 3.

[4] Under the Assize of Clarendon, one who undergoes the ordeal successfully must none the less abjure the realm.

[5] This fragmentary record is appended to the last membrane of the roll for Easter A. R. 13. It seemed worthy of publication as a rare illustration of the way in which witnesses were summoned and examined when there was an inquest as to royal rights. The point of the case is that if the dead woman was a usurer, her chattels are forfeited to the king. See Glanvill, lib. x. c. 8. The *Awelton* in question seems to be Alton in Hampshire.

[6] A blank space is left; as the words stand they seemingly mean that Goda hired Ailwin.

The sheriff is asked whether anyone was summoned by him, and says No. It is considered by way of amendment that the battle be unwaged, since no one testified that [William] was taken with the cow, and the sheriff's serjeant was not with him when he was led to gaol, nor were any of the neighbours summoned by the sheriff [to testify]; and let Geoffrey be in mercy for having arrested him and taken him to gaol without the view of the serjeant; let [Geoffrey] be arrested; and let the knights who assisted at the judgment be in mercy.

The following were present.

PLEAS OF EASTER TERM, A.D. 1212.

107. Wille Brown, who was charged with slaying a man and who purged himself by water and abjured the realm, offers the king one mark that he may be suffered to return and find pledges to stand to right in case any shall wish to accuse him.

Suff.

108. An inquest of Alton touching a dead woman whom Richard Swell caused to be buried without the view of coroners and sheriff.

Ailwin Thrasher says that Goda the widow hired him to dig in her garden, and next day she came and dug there until prime, and at about prime a woman called Seilda, Fot's daughter, came and told him that the said woman

femina fuit mortua in domo sua, et ipse intravit in domum et invenit eam jacentem mortuam et vestitam super lectum suum. Idem Ailwinus dicit quod predicta Goda fuit infirma antequam per dimidium annum et eo amplius, ita quod una die jacuit in lecto suo et alio die ivit per villam ut sana. Idem Ailwinus dicit quod ipse dixit illud primo Ricardo Beaupeinnie. Et idem Ricardus hoc negat et defendit, et dicit quod ipse monstravit illud prius Waltero Guldene et ipse Walterus eidem Ricardo, qui Ricardus *dixit* eidem Waltero quod ipse intraret in domum ad videndum utrum verum esset, et ipse Walterus respondit quod non ausus fuit.

Johannes de Awelton' et Henricus Wiard' plegiaverunt Ricardum Beaupeinnie.

Walterus Parmentar' et thethinga sua plegiaverunt predictum Ailwinum.

Ricardus Guldene et thethinga sua plegiaverunt Walterum Gulden' qui profectus fuit peregre.

Preceptum est villate quod habeant Seildam coram Rege ad summonicionem suam.

Henricus Wiard' et Laurencius de Heglo' dicunt pro toto hundredo forinseco de Awelton' quod Walterus de la Ber' venit ad eos et dixit quod ipse audivit dici quod quedam femina Goda nomine fodit in orto suo et in intrando domum suam cecidit mortua super limen ostii sui, et quod sepulta fuit eodem die ante prandium . . .[1] nonam post vesperas in quadragesima sine visu vicecomitis et coronatorum. Postea venit predictus Walterus et Gaufridus de . . . et Johannes de Arund' et Johannes de Molendino servientes predicti Walteri ad domum predicte Gode et invenerunt in . . . sua ij. porcos et j. vaccam et unum plumbum et alia plura utensilia, et ea seisiaverunt in manum [domini] Regis, et preterea posuerunt serruram domini Regis super cameram suam in qua erant catalla ad valenciam . . . ut putant, et prohibuerunt ex parte domini Regis quod nemo inde aliquid amoveret antequam adjudicatum esset *quis* catalla habere deberet, et tradiderunt clavem Gaufrido Torberti. Et

---

[1] The margin of the roll has been damaged and some words are illegible.

[Goda] was dead in her house, and he entered the house and found her lying dead on her bed with her clothes on. He also says that the said Goda had been infirm for a half-year and more, so that one day she would lie in bed and another would go about the village apparently in sound health. He also says that in the first place he told this to Richard Beaupeinnie. And Richard denies and contradicts this, and says that [Ailwin] first showed it to Walter Guldene, and Walter told Richard, and Richard bade Walter enter the house to see whether it were true, and Walter answered that he dared not.

John of Alton and Henry Wiard are pledges for Richard Beaupeinnie.

Walter Parmenter and his tithing are pledges for Ailwin.

Richard Guldene and his tithing are pledges for Walter Guldene, who has gone abroad.

The township is ordered to produce Seilda before the king at his summons.

Henry Wiard and Lawrence of Heglo' say for the whole hundred of Alton Forinseca that Walter de la Bere came to them and said that he heard tell that a woman named Goda was digging in her garden and, on entering her house, fell dead on the threshold, and that she was buried on the same day before dinner . . . . . . without the view of the sheriff and the coroners. Afterwards Walter [de la Bere] and Geoffrey of . . . and John of Arundel and John of the Mill, Walter's servants, came to Goda's house and found in her . . . two pigs and one cow and one leaden vessel and many other utensils, and seized them into the king's hand, and also put the king's lock upon her chamber, in which were chattels to the value of . . . as they believe, and in the king's name forbade anyone to remove anything before it should be adjudged who ought to have the chattels, and delivered the key to Geoffrey Torbert. And afterwards

postea venit Ricardus Swele et Alanus Torberti *et intra-verunt* in predictam domum, et amoverunt porcos et vaccam et alia utensilia, et ceperunt clavem camere [de] Gaufr' Torberti et aperuerunt serruram domini Regis que fuit super hostium camere et asportaverunt omnia ibidem inventa ad valenciam xx. marcarum ut superius dictum est. Et postea venit predictus Walterus de Ber' in pleno *hundredo* et conquestus fuit de predicto Ricardo et Alano Torberti, quod ita asportaverunt catalla super defensum *iniuste ut* ei videbatur, et ideo iniuste quia ipse audivit dici quod ipsa Goda fuit usuraria.

Johannes de Arund' dicit quod ipse apposuit serruram propria manu super hostium camere ex parte domini Regis. Et Johannes [de] Lond' et Ricardus Beaupeinnie qui hoc viderunt hoc testantur. Et Gaufridus Torberti testatus fuit in pleno hundredo [quod] *li*beravit clavem predicto Ricardo Swele et Alano Torberti.

Hundredus intrinsecus dicit quod serrura apposita fuit ex parte domini Regis et quod prohibitum fuit ex parte sua [ne] inde amoveretur, et quod predictus Ricardus Swel' et Alanus asportaverunt catalla que fuerunt in camera set nesciunt quantum catallorum.

Ricardus Swel' et Alanus dicunt quod per . . .[1]

[2]PLACITA DE TERMINO S. TRINITATIS ANNO QUARTODECIMO.

109. [3]Herebertus Pudifot appellat Rogerum Lelman quod ipse fuit cum eo apud Coutun' ad brusandum quandam domum et ibi furati fuerunt plura, ita quod Rogerus habuit ad partem suam de latrocinio illo j. pallium de poenacio[4] et quandam penulam, et fuit cum eo ad plura alia latrocinia, et hoc offert.

Ebor.

---

[1] Here the record becomes fragmentary.

[2] Coram Rege Roll No. 45. At the end of this term there seems to have been a session at York at which pleas of the crown were taken; the county, wapentakes and townships were represented. The king was at York at the end of August.

[3] m. 10 d.

[4] As to this word see the Glossary.

came Richard Swell and Alan Torbert and entered the said house, and removed the pigs and cow and utensils and took the key of the chamber from Geoffrey Torbert and opened the king's lock, which was upon the chamber door, and carried off all that was found therein, to the value of twenty marks as aforesaid. And afterwards the said Walter de la Bere came into the full hundred [court] and complained of the said Richard and Alan Torbert, that thus they had carried off the chattels against [the king's] prohibition, and unjustly, as it seemed to him, for he had heard say that Goda was a usurer.

John of Arundel says that he with his own hand put the lock upon the chamber door on the king's behalf. And John of London and Richard Beaupeinnie, who saw this, testify to it. And Geoffrey Torbert testified in full hundred [court] that he delivered the key to the said Richard Swell and Alan Torbert.

The hundred of Alton Intrinseca says that the lock was put there on the king's behalf and that in his name its removal was forbidden, and that the said Richard Swell and Alan carried off the chattels which were in the chamber, but they know not the value thereof.

Richard Swell and Alan say that . . . . . .

PLEAS OF TRINITY TERM, A.D. 1212.

York 109. Herbert Pudifot appeals Roger Lelman, for that he was along with him at Cowton in the breaking of a certain house, and there they stole many things, so that Roger had for his share of the stolen goods a violet cloak and a hood, and he was with him also in many other larcenies, and this he offers [to prove by his body etc.].

j. m.

Et Rogerus defendit brusuram illius domus et latrocinia et receptacionem et societatem et totum de verbo in verbum, et dicit quod ipse homo legalis est et boni testimonii, et offert j. marcam pro habendo testimonio et inquisicione patrie.[1] Et xij. milites de wapentaco veniunt et dicunt quod ipsi bene inquisiverunt quod nunquam auditum fuit de eo nisi quod homo legalis fuit.

Plegii de illa marca et quod ipse staret recto si quis versus eum loqui voluerit Gilebertus filius Horin, Johannes filius Laising, Willelmus filius Radulfi, Johannes Aelker, Gaufridus filius Normanni, Henricus filius Gill', Willelmus filius Win', Rogerus filius Willelmi, Andreas filius Horin, Bruning' filius Hukeman, Albanus filius Willelmi, Rogerus filius Alicie.

110. Ebor.

[2] Robertus filius Bere et Hernaldus filius Gamel' qui appellaverunt Hugonem filium Andree de combustione domorum Johannis de Dreintun' domini sui non sunt prosecuti. Et villate proxime et wapentac non malecredunt eum. Et ideo predicti Robertus et Hernaldus in misericordia, et plegii eorum de prosequendo similiter, scilicet, Johannes de Dreintun' et Robertus de Evereswic, et Hugo eat quietus.

mīa

111. Ebor.

[3] Hynge de Sproufford' et Gamell' Fremantel malecrediti suspendantur, quia servientes vicecomitis et liberi homines [et] iiij. villate proxime testati fuerunt quod recognoverunt roboriam factam homini vicecomitis de xxxiij. denariis.

112. Ebor.

[4] Henricus de Apelton' captus est pro morte Reginaldi filii Hugonis de Etton', et testatum est quod ubi eum occidit cultello suo ipse vulneratus eum retinuit donec per clamorem levatum tota villata eum cepit in ipso facto. Et ideo suspendatur.

113. [5] Loquendum cum Rege de quodam stulto qui est in

[1] Bracton, f. 158 b. [2] m. 14. [3] m. 14. [4] m. 14. [5] m. 14.

And Roger defends the breaking of the house and the larcenies, receipt, companionship, and all word by word, and says that he is a lawful man and of good repute, and offers one mark for the testimony and inquest of the country. And twelve knights of the wapentake come and say that they have well inquired and that nothing was ever heard of him save that he was a lawful man.

Pledges for the mark and that he will stand to right in case any shall accuse him, Gilbert, Horin's son, John, Laising's son, William, Ralph's son, John Aelker, Geoffrey, Norman's son, Henry, Gill's son, William, Win's son, Roger, William's son, Andrew, Horin's son, Bruning, Hukeman's son, Alban, William's son, Roger, Alice's son.

110. Robert, Bere's son, and Arnald, Gamel's son, who appealed Hugh, Andrew's son, of burning the houses of John of Draughton, their lord, do not prosecute. And the neighbouring townships and the wapentake do not suspect him. And therefore let Robert and Arnald be in mercy, and likewise their pledges to prosecute, to wit, John of Draughton and Robert of York, and let Hugh go quit.
York.

111. Hynge of Spofforth and Gamel Fremantle, suspected persons, are to be hanged, for the sheriff's serjeants and the free men and the four neighbouring townships testified that they confessed a robbery of thirty-three pence done to one of the sheriff's men.
York.

112. Henry of Appleton is arrested for the death of Reginald, son of Hugh of Etton, and it is testified that when he killed him with his knife, the wounded man held him until the whole township came to the hue and took him in the very act. So let him be hanged.
York.

113. The king is to be consulted about an insane man who

loquend' prisona eo quod per demenciam cognoscit se esse latronem set non est culpabilis.

114. ¹Rogerus de Steinton' captus fuit eo quod ipse jactando quendam lapidem per infortunium occidit quandam garciam. Et testatum est quod non per feloniam. Et monstratum fuit hoc domino Regi, et dominus Rex motus misericordia perdonavit ei mortem. Et ideo deliberetur.

²PLACITA DE TERMINO S. TRINITATIS ANNO [SEXTODECIMO].

115
Cornub.
³Preceptum fuit vicecomiti quod haberet coram domino Rege corpus Baldewini Tyrell in Oct. S. Hill. anno xiiij° ad respondendum Rannulfo de Devenesbi et Gilliberto de Girmunvilla de appello quod ipsi fecerunt in comitatu versus eum de denuntiatione ⁴mortis domini Regis, et quod summoneret ipsos Rannulfum et Gillibertum quod tunc essent ibi ad prosequendum appellum suum versus eum.

Et ad diem illum habuit eundem Baldewinum vicecomes apud Westmonasterium. Qui Baldewinus expectavit ibi per viij. dies, et Rannulfus et Gillibertus non venerunt. Et quum loquela illa spectabat ad personam domini Regis et propter xx. solidos quos Baldewinus dedit per sic quod recordum de appello quod ipsi inde fecerunt versus eum et recordum de appello quod ipse fecit versus eos et Alanum de Dunstanvilla et Henricum de Pomeria de pace domini Regis infracta venirent coram justiciariis apud Westmonasterium, mandatum fuit vicecomiti quod de utroque appello

---

¹ m. 14.
² Coram Rege Roll No 47. The roll professes to belong to Trinity A. R. 15; but in all probability the scribe forgot that a new regnal year began on Ascension day. This appears from the following case.
³ m. 9 d.
⁴ It is difficult to translate this word, for *threatening* seems too strong. At worst, as will appear below, Baldwin had merely declared that the king was dead; and perhaps *denouncing* here means little more than *announcing*. One is inclined to say that the charge is that of 'imagining the king's death.' Peter of Wakefield was hanged for prophesying that before Ascension day 1213 John would no longer be king. Possibly the charge here made has something to do with this prophecy. Mat. Par. vol ii. pp. 535, 547.

is in prison because in his madness he confesses himself a thief, while really he is not guilty.

114. Roger of Stainton was arrested because in throwing a stone he by misadventure killed a girl. And it is testified that this was not by felony. And this was shown to the king, and the king moved by pity pardoned him the death. So let him be set free.

PLEAS OF TRINITY TERM, A.D. 1214.

115. The sheriff was commanded to have the body of Baldwin
Cornw. Tyrel before the king on the octave of Hilary, A.R. 14, to answer Ranulf of Devonsby and Gilbert of Girmunville touching an appeal they made against him in the county [court] of 'denouncing' the king's death, and to summon the said Ranulf and Gilbert to be there to prosecute their appeal against him.

And on that day the sheriff produced Baldwin at Westminster. And Baldwin there awaited [his adversaries] for eight days, and Ranulf and Gilbert did not come. And because the suit concerned the king's person, and because Baldwin gave twenty shillings in order that the record of the appeal which they made against him and the record of the appeal which he made against them and Alan of Dunstanville and Henry of Pomeroy for a breach of the king's peace, might come before the justices at Westminster, the sheriff was ordered that he should cause to be made in his

fieri faceret recordum in comitatu suo, et quod haberet recordum illud apud Westmonasterium prima dominica quadragesime per quatuor milites qui recordo illi interfuissent et per literas suas sigillatas,[1] et quod haberet ibi corpora Rannulfi et Giliberti predictorum ad prosequendum appellum suum. Et interim venit Alanus de Dunstanvilla coram justiciariis domini Regis et tulit breve domini Regis eis directum, per quod mandavit quod Alanus fuit coram eo in Oct. S. Hillarii apud Scardeburg' cum Rannulfo de Devenesby et Gilleberto de Girmunvilla predictis pro quodam appello quod ipsi Rannulfus et Gilibertus fecerunt versus Baldewinum Tyrel et quod warentizavit eis diem illum.[2] Et tunc idem Alanus cepit in manum habendi eosdem Rannulfum et Gillibertum coram justiciariis prima dominica quadragesime.

Ad diem vero illum misit vicecomes sicut ei preceptum fuit recordum de predictis appellis per literas suas sigillatas et per duos milites qui illi recordo interfuerunt faciendo, scilicet, Gaufridum filium Willelmi et Robertum filium Willelmi de Almath'. Et est recordum tale.

In die Oct. B. Martini[3] apud Triueru Johannes[4] vicecomes Cornubie tenuit hundredum ibidem et coram predicto vicecomite et quodam coronario[5] comitatus et multis militibus et libere tenentibus apparuit ibi Baldewinus Tyrel et proposuit quod Henricus de Pomeria et Alanus de Dunstanvilla et Rannulfus de Deveneb' et Gilibertus de Girmunvilla et quidam alii ceperunt eum apud Tregeny in die S. Leonardi[6] et posuerunt eum in prisonam, scilicet, in firgiis,

---

[1] The county court has no written record. When its proceedings are to be brought before the king's court, those proceedings are solemnly recited in the county court, and are then committed to writing; this writing is brought to Westminster by some of the knights who were present at the 'making of the record,' i.e. at the recital in the county court. In civil cases this procedure is very common.

[2] When a litigant excuses himself for not keeping his day on the ground that he was in the king's service, the king in certifying the truth of the excuse 'warrants him the day.' John was at Scarborough in the middle of January 1213; it certainly seems that a court was being held simultaneously before the king at Scarborough and before the justices at Westminster.

[3] St. Martin is 11 November.

[4] John FitzRichard.

[5] Sic.

[6] St. Leonard is 6 November.

county [court] a record of both appeals, and have that record at Westminster on the first Sunday of Lent by four knights who were present at the record and by his letters under seal, and that he should have there the bodies of Ranulf and Gilbert to prosecute their appeal. And meanwhile came Alan of Dunstanville before the king's justices and produced the king's writ directed to them, whereby he announced that on the octave of Hilary Alan was before him at Scarborough with Ranulf of Devonsby and Gilbert of Girmunville on account of an appeal which they had made against Baldwin Tyrel, and that he warranted them that day. And Alan then undertook to have Ranulf and Gilbert before the justices on the first Sunday of Lent.

And on that day the sheriff, as he was commanded, sent the record of the said appeals by his letters under seal and by two knights who were at the making of the record, namely, Geoffrey Fitzwilliam and Robert Fitzwilliam of Almath. And the record is as follows.

On the octave of St. Martin's day at Truro, John, sheriff of Cornwall held a hundred [court], and before the said sheriff and one of the coroners of the county and many knights and freeholders appeared Baldwin Tyrel and declared that Henry of Pomeroy, Alan of Dunstanville, Ranulf of Devonsby, and Gilbert of Girmunville and certain others on St. Leonard's day at Tregoney took him and put him in prison, to wit, in fetters, and put him in a cellar in the

et posuerunt eum in uno celario in curia Henrici de Pomeria, et illuc ut dixit ipsi miserunt Ricardum clericum de Stokes et Johannem clericum Henrici de Pomerei, et ipsi intimaverunt ei quod illinc non recederet nisi per redemptionem xv. marcarum ut dixit, et quum illis adquiescere noluit predicti Rannulfus et Gilibertus adduxerunt eum a predicto celario infirgiatum usque in vicum de Tregeny, et hoc de media nocte, et tunc cornaverunt hutes,[1] et illuc convenerunt burgenses de predicto burgo, et predicti Rannulfus et Gilibertus et alii duxerunt eum ad domum que fuit Johannis de Goiz, ut dixit, et illuc illum custodiverunt et ceperunt ab eo xiij. solidos et iij. denarios in roberia in pace domini Regis infracta ut dicit, et ipsa nocte ante diem serviens de eodem hundredo, scilicet de Penrethsira venit illuc et invenit eum inprisonatum ut dicit, et predictus Baldewinus conquestus fuit ei quod predicti eum ceperunt et inprisonaverunt et optulit illud probare quod illud ei impie fecerunt. Mane autem post Alanus de Dunstanvilla et Ricardus clericus de Stokes illuc venerunt et posuerunt eum per fidem et per redempcionem c. solidorum, et insuper fecerunt eum affidare quod ipse non appellaret Henricum de Pomeria neque Alanum de Dunstanvilla neque aliquem hominem suorum pro hoc facto ut dicit, et ita permiserunt eum abire.

[2] Postea autem in xv. dies predictus vicecomes Cornubie tenuit hundredum suum apud S. Austellum cum predicto coronario et militibus et libere tenentibus, et illuc venit Alanus de Dunstanvilla et dixit quod misit senescallum suum scilicet Rogerum de Lancuc et Rannulfum de Deveneb' et Gillibertum de Girmunvilla ad domum que fuit Her' de Herigen que de feudo suo est et illuc, ut predicti Rannulfus et Gilibertus dicunt, invenerunt predictam domum castellatam et brittaschiatam,[3] et ibi invenerunt Baldewinum Tyrell, et dixerunt quod voluerunt intrare et facere seisinam [4]

---

[1] The hue and cry was raised by blowing of horns; compare the 'hornying' of Scottish law.

[2] The record of the county continues.

[3] Wedgwood, Dict. Eng. Etym. s. v. *Brattice*, cites from Matthew Paris, 'Duæ testudines quas Gallice *brutesches* appellant.'

[4] They were sent to seize a tenement which had been held of Alan by a tenant who had died.

court of Henry of Pomeroy, and thither (so he said) they sent Richard, the clerk of Stokes, and John, the clerk of Henry of Pomeroy, who intimated to him that he should not come out thence save for a ransom of fifteen marks (so he said), and as he would not yield to their demand, Ranulf and Gilbert drew him forth from the said cellar in fetters to the street of Tregoney, and this at midnight, and then they horned the hue; and thither came the burgesses of the said borough; and Ranulf and Gilbert and the others took him to the house of John Goiz (so he said), and there they kept him prisoner, and in robbery and breach of the king's peace took from him thirteen shillings and three pence (so he says), and on the same night before dawn came the serjeant of the hundred, namely, of Penrithshire, and found him imprisoned (so he says), and he, Baldwin, complained to the serjeant that the said men took and imprisoned him, and he offered to prove that they did this wickedly. On the next morning Alan of Dunstanville and Richard the clerk of Stokes came thither and put him to his oath and to a ransom of one hundred shillings, and besides made him swear that he would not appeal Henry of Pomeroy nor Alan of Dunstanville nor any of their men for this deed (so he says), and so they let him go.

Then a fortnight afterwards the said sheriff of Cornwall held his hundred [court] at St. Austell with the said coroner, knights, and freeholders, and thither came Alan of Dunstanville and said that he sent his steward, Roger of Lancuc by name, and Ranulf of Devonsby and Gilbert of Girmunville to the house of Hervey of Herigen, which is in his fee, and there (as Ranulf and Gilbert say) they found the said house castellated and bratticed, and there they found Baldwin Tyrel, and they said that they wished to enter and make a seisin [i.e. seizure] in their lord's fee, and they

in feudo domini sui, et dixerunt[1] quod non potuerunt habere ingressum, et interrogaverunt quare intrare non potuerunt cum Dominus Rex adhuc esset vivens, et Baldewinus, ut dicunt, respondit quod dominus Rex non erat vivens set murdritus inter inimicos suos in Norwallia.[2] Et Baldewinus hoc totum defendit et optulit ponere se super veredictum visneti. Et illuc remansit Baldewinus in custodia vicecomitis Cornubie, et predicti Rannulfus et Gilebertus remanserunt in custodia Henrici de Pomereia et Alani de Dunstanvilla usque ad proximum comitatum.

Et illuc predicti Rannulfus et Gilibertus renovaverunt appellum suum. Et predictus Baldewinus qui fuit in custodia vicecomitis defendit totum et renovavit appellum suum. Et Rogerus senescallus Alani de Dunstanvilla interrogatus coram comitatu respondit quod non invenit domum castellatam neque brittaschiatam, set barratam, et quod non vidit neque audivit Baldewinum denunciantem mortem domini Regis. Et quia predicti Rannulfus et Gilibertus locuti fuerunt de morte domini Regis, vicecomes Cornubie et coronarii voluerunt retinere predictos Rannulfum et Gilibertum. Tunc responderunt predicti Henricus et Alanus de Dunstanvilla quod illi fuerunt de privata familia domini Regis jurati[3] quod si illi aliquid audirent quod fuisset contra dominum Regem quod domino Regi illud intimarent. Et dixerunt quod caperent predictos Rannulfum et Gilibertum in custodia et irent et ducerent predictos Rannulfum et Gilibertum ad hoc ostendendum domino Regi cum festinatione. Et tunc vicecomes et coronarii in pleno comitatu liberaverunt Henrico de Pomereia et Alano de Dunstanvilla predictos Rannulfum et Gilibertum in custodiam et ipsi receperunt eos in custo-

[1] The people who were in the house *dixerunt*.

[2] In 1212 John summoned an army for a Welsh war; 'but, warned of the existence of a conspiracy, he did not venture to lead it into Wales. In panic fear he dismissed his host and shut himself up in Nottingham Castle' (Stubbs, Const. Hist. § 153). Probably this record alludes to the supposed conspiracy and to the king's horror of death.

[3] This looks like a very early trace of the privy councillor's oath. Henry of Pomeroy seems to have taken John's side in 1215, and to have been trusted with a command in the west. See Rot. Pat. pp. 128 b, 135 b, 136; Rot. Cl. vol. i, pp. 199 b, 243 b, 244 b, 250 b.

were told that they could not enter, and they asked why not, since the king was still alive, and Baldwin (so they say) answered that the king was not alive but was murdered among his enemies in North Wales. And Baldwin defended all this, and offered to put himself on the verdict of the neighbourhood. And Baldwin remained there in the custody of the sheriff of Cornwall, and Ranulf and Gilbert remained in the custody of Henry of Pomeroy and Alan of Dunstanville until the next county [court].

And [at the next county court] Ranulf and Gilbert renewed their appeal. And Baldwin, who was in the sheriff's custody, defended all of it and renewed his appeal. And Roger the steward of Alan of Dunstanville on being asked in the county [court] answered that he did not find the house castellated and bratticed, but merely barred, and that he did not see nor hear Baldwin proclaiming the king's death. And for that Ranulf and Gilbert made mention of the king's death in their appeal, the sheriff of Cornwall and the coroners wished to detain them. Then Henry of Pomeroy and Alan of Dunstanville answered that they belonged to the king's private household and were sworn that in case they heard anything that was against the king, they would report it to the king. And they said that they would take Ranulf and Gilbert into their custody and would go and take them with all speed to show this matter to the king. Then the sheriff and coroners in full county [court] delivered Ranulf and Gilbert into the keeping of Henry and Alan, and they took them into their

diam super corpora eorum et super terras et tenementa eorum.[1]

Ad eundem vero diem, scilicet prima dominica quadragesime venerunt Alanus de Dunstanvilla, Henricus de Pomereya et Rannulfus et Gillibertus et hoc modo fecerunt appella sua. Alanus de Dunstanvilla ostendit quod quidam tenens suus, scilicet, Henricus[2] de Heligan obiit, quo audito, ipse voluit seisire in manum suam, sicut consuetudo est, feudum quod de eo tenuit quousque inde fieret quod fieri deberet,[3] et dictum fuit ei quod homines armati tenuerunt se in feudo illo et ei necare[4] voluerunt ingressum, ita quod ipse misit illuc Rannulfum de Devenesbi et Gilibertum de Girmunvilla et Rogerum de Lancuc senescallum ejus et alios plures de hominibus suis ad domum quam predictus Henricus de eo tenuit, et cum intrare vellent, viderunt in ea plures armatos, ita quod Baldewinus Tyrel fuit in ea armatus lorica et purpuinto et capello ferreo in capite, et tenuit unam magnam hachiam in manu sua, et dixit quod non intrarent. Et ipsi responderunt quod voluerunt intrare in feudum domini sui et intrarent secundum quod deberent quia pax domini Regis erat et dominus Rex erat vivus.[5] Et ipse Baldewinus respondit quod hoc ei non valeret, quia dominus Rex fuit murdritus vel in tali loco inter inimicos suos quod non exiret. Et ibi fuerunt predicti Rannulfus et Gilibertus qui hoc viderunt et audiverunt, et Rannulfus hoc offert disracionare versus eum per corpus suum prout curia consideraverit, ut ille qui hoc vidit et audivit, et si de eo male contingeret,[6] Gilibertus predictus hoc offert disracionare etc.

Et Baldewinus Tirel venit et defendit pacem Regis infractam et feloniam et denuntiationem mortis Regis et

---

[1] Here ends the record of the county.
[2] Called *Hervicus* below.
[3] Until relief should be paid and homage be done.
[4] Corr. *negare*.
[5] The suggestion of course is, that the king's peace dies with him. When there is no king in England, every man does that which is right in his own eyes.
[6] For this formula, see Bracton, f. 138. It was sometimes used in writs of right. It is well to have two champions, so that if one dies or falls ill before the day of battle, the other can fight.

custody, engaging their bodies, lands and tenements [for their production].

On the same day, to wit, the first Sunday of Lent came Alan of Dunstanville, Henry Pomeroy, Ranulf and Gilbert and made their appeals in manner following. Alan shows that a certain tenant of his, Hervey of Heligan died, and, hearing this, Alan wished to seize into his hand, as the custom is, the fee which [Hervey] held of him until there should be done in respect thereof what by rights ought to be done; and he was told that armed men were occupying the tenement and would oppose his entry, so he sent Ranulf and Gilbert and his steward Roger of Lancuc and many other of his men to the house which Hervey held of him, and when they would have entered they saw within many armed men, and Baldwin Tyrel was within, armed with breastplate and purpoint and with an iron cap upon his head and in his hand he held a great axe, and said that they should not enter. And they said that they wished to enter their lord's fee, and would enter as of right they should, for it was the king's peace and the king was alive. And Baldwin answered that this would not do for him, for the king was either murdered or so hemmed in by his enemies that he would never escape. And Ranulf and Gilbert were there and saw and heard this; and Ranulf offers to deraign it by his body as one who saw and heard it, and in case any mischance should befall him, then Gilbert offers to deraign it etc.

And Baldwin Tyrel comes and defends the breach of the king's peace and the felony and the denouncing of the

quicquid est contra pacem domini Regis et dictum et factum et velle et cogitatum de denuntiatione mortis domini Regis, et hoc offert defendere prout curia consideraverit. Et dicit quod Alanus de Dunstanvilla et Henricus de Pomerya et predicti faciunt illud appellum versus ipsum pro adnichilando et impediendo appello suo quod ipse prius fecit versus eos de imprisonamento et pace Regis infracta quod monstraverat alias justiciariis, et offert xl. solidos pro habenda inquisitione utrum illud appellum faciant per athiam et pro appello suo adnichilando, nec ne.

Henricus de Pomeria autem ostendit quod ipse et Alanus de Dunstanvilla et sui fuerunt simul in domo sua apud Tregenni die S. Leonardi et sicut fuerunt hillares simul sero venit quidam serviens suus, scilicet, Gaufridus Cofin, et dixit ei quod vidit in curia quendam hominem cum arcu et sagittis et dixit quod provideret sibi quia non credidit quod pro bono suo illuc veniret. Et ipse respondit quod per auxilium Dei nullum malum ei faceret, et quesivit candelam ut iret cubitum, et sicut fuit in eundo versus lectum et quidam serviens ferret candelam coram eo, venit quedam sagitta subito juxta ipsum Henricum, ita quod illa volavit juxta manum illius qui portaverat candelam, et quod cum factum esset, ipsi exiverunt et viderunt ipsum Baldewinum fugientem cum arcu in manu sua, et hoc vidit serviens Regis quem mandaverat, scilicet Rogerus Calvus de Tiberestr', et ibi fuit predictus Gaufridus Cofin qui vidit qualiter predicta sagitta voluit occidere dominum suum, Henricum, in pace domini Regis et nequiter, et hoc offert etc.[1]

Et Baldewinus defendit pacem Regis infractam et feloniam et quod nunquam sagittam traxit nec arcum habuit nec cum arcu captus fuit.

Dies datus fuit omnibus a die Pasche in xv. dies[2] apud Westmonasterium et Baldewinus remansit in custodia vicecomitis sicut prius fecit, et predicti Alanus et Henricus

---

[1] It appears below that it is Geoffrey Coffin, not Henry, who thus offers proof by his body.
[2] Easter 1218.

king's death and all that is against the king's peace, and any word, deed, will, or thought of denouncing the king's death, and this he offers to defend as the court shall consider. And he says that Alan of Dunstanville and Henry of Pomeroy and the others aforesaid make this appeal against him in order to impede and annul the earlier appeal which he made against them for an imprisonment and breach of the king's peace, which appeal he had already laid before the justices, and he offers forty shillings for an inquest whether they make their appeal out of spite and to annul his appeal, or no.

Then Henry of Pomeroy shows that he and Alan of Dunstanville and their friends were together in his house at Tregoney on St. Leonard's day, and when they were merry together in the evening, there came a servant of his, Geoffrey Coffin, and told him that he saw in the courtyard a certain man with bow and arrows, and told him [Henry] to have a care for himself, for seemingly that man had not come thither meaning him any good. And [Henry] answered that by God's help the man would do him no harm, and he asked for a candle to light him to bed; and as he was going to his bed and a servant was carrying the candle before him, suddenly their came an arrow close by him, and it flew close to the hand of him who had carried the candle; whereupon they went out and saw Baldwin fleeing, bow in hand; and the king's serjeant, whom he [Henry] had summoned, saw this, namely, Roger Bald of Tybesta; and there was present there the said Geoffrey Coffin who saw how the arrow was like to kill his lord, in the king's peace and wickedly; and this he [Geoffrey] offers [to prove by his body etc.]

And Baldwin defends the breach of the king's peace and the felony, and denies that he ever drew the arrow or had the bow or that he had a bow with him when he was arrested.

A day was given to all of them, at Westminster on Easter quindene, and Baldwin remained in the sheriff's custody as before, and Alan and Henry undertook to have

ceperunt in manum habendi homines suos tunc apud Westmonasterium, et Alanus similiter cepit in manum habendi tunc senescallum suum, et mandatum fuit vicecomiti quod ipse esset in propria persona tunc apud Westmonasterium et haberet secum xij. milites de comitatu et servientem Regis ad certificandum justiciarios de recordo quod fecerunt.

Ad diem illum remansit loquela illa sicut alie loquele pro exercitu Kantie.[1] Et iterum resummonita fuit loquela ita quod Baldewinus et Alanus et Gillibertus et Rannulfus fuerunt apud Westmonasterium a die Pasche in tres septimanas anno xv°, et datus fuit eis dies a die S. Trinitatis in tres septimanas anno Regis xvj° pro defectu militum qui debuerunt ferre recordum,[2] et preceptum fuit vicecomiti quod tunc haberet ibi illos milites, et dictum fuit Alano quod tunc haberet ibi homines suos sicut fuerunt in custodia sua. Nulla mencio facta fuit tunc de Henrico quia fuit in servicio domini Regis in Pictavia.[3]

Ad diem autem illum venit ibi vicecomes Cornubie in propria persona et xij. milites cum eo sicut preceptum fuit, scilicet Willemus de Tikenbret, Serlo de Pempol, Juelus de Vautort, Ricardus de Kylgath, Willemus de Cruitur, Ricardus filius Hervici, Rollandus de Penwur', Ricardus de Cerysaus, Drogo de Trethach, Rogerus de Kaul, Drogo de Meisac, Euerwinus de Landa, qui recordum de predictis appellis faciunt eodem modo et per eadem verba per que illud venit per litteras vicecomitis et per predictos duos milites. Rogerus eciam serviens Regis venit et testatus fuit quod in festo S. Leonardi de nocte circa mediam noctem venit ipse apud Tregenni per mandatum Henrici de Pomereya qui misit propter eum per quendam servientem suum, scilicet, Rogerum Cumine, et cum veniret in villa ipse audivit tumultum in villa, et ipse Rogerus duxit eum ad domum cujusdam Johannis le Goiz ubi ipse invenit

---

[1] John had planned an invasion of France; but the barons refused to follow him. On the quindene of Easter (28 April) 1213, he was at Winchelsea: he remained in Kent some six weeks.

[2] The case was adjourned from Easter 1213 to Easter 1214, and then to Trinity 1214. The break in the regnal years occurs on Ascension Day.

[3] In 1214 an expedition against France kept John out of England from February until October.

their men at Westminster on that day, and Alan likewise undertook to have his steward there on that day, and the sheriff was commanded to be then at Westminster in his proper person, and to have with him twelve knights of the shire and the king's serjeant to certify the justices as to the record which they had made.

At that day the case stood over along with all other cases because the army was out in Kent. And it was again resummoned, so that Baldwin, Alan, Gilbert, and Ranulf were at Westminster on Easter three weeks A.R. 15, and a day was given them, on Trinity three weeks A.R. 16, for default of the knights [of the shire] who were to bring the record, and the sheriff was commanded to have those knights on the day so given, and Alan was told to have his men there on that day as they were in his custody. No mention was then made of Henry, for he was in the king's service in Poitou.

Then at that day there came thither the sheriff of Cornwall in his proper person and twelve knights with him, as was commanded, to wit, William of Tikenbret, Serlo of Penpol, Joel of Vautort, Richard of Kilgarth, William of Cruitur, Richard, Hervey's son, Roland of Penwur, Richard of Cereseaux, Drogo of Trethake, Roger of Call, Drogo of Meisac, Everwin of Lande, who made record of the said appeals in the same manner and the same words in which the record had been brought [on a former day] by the sheriff's letters and by the two knights. Also Roger, the king's serjeant [of the hundred], came and testified that on St. Leonard's feast by night, about midnight, he came to Tregoney at the instance of Henry of Pomeroy who sent for him by a servant of his, namely, Roger Cumine, and when he came to the town he heard a tumult therein, and Roger [Henry's servant] brought him to the house of one John le Goiz, and there he found Baldwin in fetters and

Baldewinum in firgiis et circa eum predictos Rannulfum et Gilibertum et multos alios de villa, et ipse quesivit quare ipse fuit arestatus et ipsi qui fuerunt cum eo dixerunt quod quia ipse Baldewinus voluit occidere dominum suum et Baldewinus petiit eum ut deliberaret eum, et ipse Rogerus serviens petiit vadium et plegios, et ipse respondit quod non potuit ibi plegios invenire, set ipse obtulit ei corpus suum in obside quousque inveniret plegios, et ipse precepit eis ex parte domini Regis quod eum deliberarent, set noluerunt, et ipse venit in crastino et assumpsit secum legales homines et voluit eum deliberare, set non invenit eum, et fuit deliberatus set nescit quomodo. Et testatur quod non vidit Baldewinum fugientem, nec vidit quod ipsi ceperunt eum cum arcu in manu nec aliquem hutheisium audivit post eum.

Et Rogerus senescallus testatus fuit quod non invenit domum predictam castellatam nec bretaschiatam set barratam, nec invenit ipsum Baldewinum armatum lorica nec purpuinto nec capello ferreo in capite, set tantummodo ipse habuit quandam hachiam in manu sua, et fuit extra domum illam, et nichil locutus fuit de Rege nec de morte Regis, nec alio modo, nec aliquid superfactum ibi fecit, set Herevicus dominus feudi illius tenuit se in domo predicta et dixit quod ipse intellexit quod ipsi non debuerunt facere nisi simplicem seisinam [1] eo quod etatem habuit et putavit quod aliter facere voluerunt et ideo tenuit se in predicta domo.

Ad diem vero illum essoniaverunt se Alanus de Dunstanvilla et Gilibertus de Girmunvilla et Rannulfus de Devonby, et quum ipsi Gillibertus et Rannulfus fuerunt in custodia, consideratum fuit quod nullum essonium ibi

---

[1] The rights of a lord whose tenant has died leaving an heir of full age are in John's reign a matter about which lords and tenants have very different notions. The lord is apt to think that he may seize the tenement and hold it until a relief of indefinite amount is paid. In this case, Hervey, the dead tenant's heir, states what came to be the common law: namely, that the lord is only entitled 'to make a simple seisin,' i.e. a barely formal seizure of the land, sufficient to serve as evidence of title. As to this 'simple seisin,' see Bracton, f. 252 b, line 8, and Stat. Marlb. cap. 16. Probably this difference of opinion between Alan and Hervey is the origin of all the elaborate disputes here chronicled.

around him were Ranulf, Gilbert and many others of the town, and he asked why [Baldwin] was arrested, and those who were with him said because he wished to kill their lord; and Baldwin begged him to deliver him, and he (Roger the serjeant) demanded gage and pledge, and [Baldwin] said that he could not find pledges there, but offered [Roger] his body as a hostage until he should find pledges; and [Roger] in the king's name bade them deliver [Baldwin], but they would not: and [Roger] returned on the morrow and took with him lawful men meaning to deliver [Baldwin] but could not find him; he had been delivered, but [Roger] knows not how. And he testifies that he did not see Baldwin fleeing, nor did he see that Baldwin had a bow in his hand when they took him, nor did he hear that any hue was made after him.

And Roger [Alan's] steward testified that he did not find the said house castellated and bratticed, but merely barred, and he did not find Baldwin armed with breastplate and purpoint, nor with an iron cap on his head, but he merely had an axe in his hand, and he was outside the house, and he said nothing about the king, nor the king's death, nor anything of the kind, and was guilty of no excess; but Hervey, the owner of the tenement, was keeping himself in the house, and said that in his opinion [Alan's men] were only entitled to make a simple seisin since he [Hervey] was of full age, and that he thought that they were going to do more than this, and so kept house.

But on that day Alan of Dunstanville, Gilbert of Girmunville, and Ranulf of Devonsby essoined themselves. And since Gilbert and Ranulf were in custody, it was considered that no essoin lay. And therefore the sheriff was

jacuit. Et ideo preceptum fuit vicecomiti in banco et per breve quod ipse haberet corpora eorum, scilicet, Gilliberti et Rannulfi apud Westmonasterium a die S. Joh. Bapt. in tres septimanas, et similiter preceptum est vicecomiti quod habeat corpus Gaufridi Cofin ad predictum terminum ad audiendum judicium suum de appello quod fecit versus eundem Baldewinum. Et judicium de Henrico de Pomerya et Alano de Dunstanvilla est in respectu *quia* Henricus est in Pictavia et Alanus in eundo versus Pictaviam.[1]

116.
Midd.

[2] Walterus Trenchebof de quo dictum fuit quod ipse tradidit Ingero de Faudingestorp' cultellum unde ipse occidit Widonem Foliot, et malecreditus inde, purget se aqua quod non fuit consenciens. Periit[3] et suspensus est.

Simon filius Roberti qui captus fuit cum latronibus et detentus in prisona eo quod fuit infra etatem similiter purget se aqua. Purgavit se et ejuravit regnum.

[4] PLACITA APUD WELLES DE COMITATIBUS SUMERSETIE ET DORSETIE CORAM REGE.

117.
Dorset.

[5] Juliana de Holeworth' appellat Willelmum Pech quod cum Willelmus filius ejus veniret in domum predicti Willelmi Pech et ab eo exigeret debitum quod ipse ei debuit,

---

[1] An entry on a subsequent membrane of the same roll (22 d.) shows that the appellees did not keep their day. The case is again adjourned to Michaelmas three weeks: I have found no later trace of it.

[2] m. 21.

[3] This is the only record of a failure at the ordeal that I have found; success seems common.

[4] The date of these cases is somewhat uncertain. They occur at the end of a Cornish Eyre Roll of A. R. 3 (Coram Rege Roll No. 9) and are said to have been heard Coram Rege on Thursday next after St. George's day. It does not appear from Hardy's Itinerary that John was ever at Wells soon after St. George's day (23 April). In A. R. 14 he was there on the Thursday next after St. Gregory's day, and to write *Georgii* in mistake for *Gregorii* would be easy; but these cases apparently belong to an earlier time, for Hubert de Burgh seems sheriff of Somerset and Dorset, and Ralph Morin of Devon. Perhaps they belong to A. R. 2; in that year John was at Exeter on the 22nd and at Tewkesbury on the 30th of April, and his way between those places would take him through Wells.

[5] m. 16.

ordered at the Bench [by word of mouth] and also by writ to have the bodies of Gilbert and Ranulf at Westminster three weeks from Midsummer, and was likewise ordered to have the body of Geoffrey Coffin at the said term to hear judgment of the appeal which he made against Baldwin. And as to Henry of Pomeroy and Alan of Dunstanville judgment is respited, for Henry is in Poitou and Alan is on his way thither.

116. William Trenchebof was said to have handed to Inger
dd. of Faldingthorpe the knife wherewith [Inger] slew Wido Foliot. He is suspected thereof [by jurors]. Let him purge himself by the water that he was not consenting [to the death]. He has failed and is hanged.

Simon, Robert's son, was arrested in company with robbers and was detained in prison, because he was under age. Let him likewise purge himself by the water. He has purged himself and abjured the realm.

PLEAS FROM SOMERSET AND DORSET BEFORE THE KING AT WELLS.

117. Juliana of Holwell appeals William Pech, for that when
ract. her son William came to William Pech's house and demanded from him a debt that he owed him, he ordered his

ipse precepit filiis suis Rogero et Henrico, qui utlagati sunt
pro inde, et Hugoni tercio filio suo qui clericus est, quod
ipsi eum interficerent, ita quod ipsi per preceptum suum
in pace domini Regis et nequiter ipsum occiderunt in domo
ipsius Willelmi Pech cum securibus et aliis armis et hoc
offert etc. Et Willelmus venit et defendit totum de verbo
in verbum. Et Hugo venit et defendit totum sicut clericus
'subdiaconus' et defendet ubi et quando debuerit. Et
Archidiaconus petit curiam cristianitatis. Habeat. Et ibi
sequatur Juliana si voluerit. Et similiter consideratum
est quod nullum est appellum versus patrem, eo quod ipsa
habet virum qui non comparet, et preterea non potest
appellum facere nisi de morte viri sui, vel de rapo sibi
facto.[1] Et ideo Willelmus sit inde quietus. Et Hugo et
Rogerus qui utlagati sunt fuerunt in thedinga de *Chaunedon'*, et est in misericordia, et nulla habuerunt catalla.

118.
Dorset.

[2]Edelina mater Petri appellat eundem [3] Willelmum Pech
quod per preceptum suum predicti filii sui interfecerunt
super limitem domus ipsius Willelmi Petrum filium suum
in pace domini Regis et nequiter et hoc offert etc. ut de
auditu et visu suo. Et Willelmus defendit totum de verbo
in verbum. Sequatur versus clericos in curia cristianitatis,
et versus Willelmum non habet appellum supradicta causa.

119.
Dorset.

[4] Sibilla que fuit uxor Reginaldi de Brochamton' appellat
Willelmum Wither et Robertum et Walterum et Petrum
filios suos et Richoldam uxorem suam et Matillidem filiam
suam quod ipsi in pace domini Regis et nequiter occiderunt
Reginaldum virum suum, et hoc offert probare versus eum [5]
sicut curia consideraverit ut de visu et auditu suo. Willelmus appellatus pater obiit et Robertus filius et Richolda
mater similiter obierunt, et Walterus et Petrus et Matillis
soror eorum veniunt et defendunt totum de verbo in verbum

---

[1] This rule was sanctioned by Magna Carta: see above, Case 82.
[2] m. 16. [3] See the last case. [4] m. 16. [5] *Sic.*

sons Roger and Henry, who are outlawed for this, and Hugh his third son, who is a clerk, to kill him, whereupon they by his command in the king's peace and wickedly slew him in the house of the said William Pech with axes and other arms, and this she offers [to prove etc.]. And William comes and defends all of it word by word. And Hugh comes and defends all of it as a clerk, a subdeacon, and will defend where and when it shall behove him. And the Archdeacon craves [cognizance of the case for] Court Christian. This is granted him. Let Juliana prosecute there if she wishes. Likewise it is considered that the appeal is null against the father, because she has a husband who does not appear; also she can make no appeal save for a husband's death or for rape done to her. Therefore let William be quit thereof. And Hugh and Roger, who are outlawed, were in the tithing of Chaldon; it is in mercy; they had no chattels.

118.
Dorset.

Edelina, mother of Peter, appeals the same William Pech, for that by his command his said sons, on the threshold of the house of the said William, killed her son Peter, in the king's peace and wickedly; and this she offers [to prove] etc. as of her own sight and hearing. And William defends all of it word by word. Let her prosecute the clerks in Court Christian, and against William her appeal is null for the cause aforesaid.

119.
Dorset.

Sibil, who was wife of Reginald of Brochampton, appeals William Wither, Robert, Walter, and Peter, his sons, Richolda, his wife, and Maud, his daughter, for that they in the king's peace and wickedly killed Reginald, her husband; and this she offers to prove against him, as the court shall consider, as of her sight and hearing. William the father, the appellee, is dead; so are Robert the son and Richolda the mother. Walter and Peter and Maud, their sister, come and defend all of it word by word as the court shall con-

sicut curia consideraverit. Et Ricardus '*Francus*' serviens hundredi 'cum hundredo' testatur quod Petrus predictus in hundredo propter hoc convocato coram eo et hundredo cognovit quod ipsi fecerunt plagam unde idem Reginaldus obiit, et quod dixit quod tribus diebus vellet se suspensum esse per sic quod posset mori de plaga illa.[1] Assisa,[2] suspendatur Petrus propter cognicionem suam, et Walterus et Matillis purgent se judicio ferri. Vadiaverunt.

120. Sumerset.
[3] Editha de Molton' que appellavit in comitatu Randulfum de Chiewer et Willelmum Iberniensem qui obiit in gaola de morte 'Matill' ux' ' Osb' de Depeford' venit coram justiciariis et dixit quod de nocte venerunt malefactores ad domum ipsius Osberti cui serviebat et eum ceperunt et verberaverunt et uxorem suam occiderunt set nescit utrum hoc fecerunt predicti nec ne. Et xij. milites jurati de eodem hundredo non malecredunt eum inde nec de alio malo retto. Ideo sit sub plegiis.

121. Sumerset.
[4] Willelmus de Caune appellat Willelmum Tropinel et Robertum Molendinarium et Gaufridum et Hugonem et Walterum et Jordanum et Henricum filios ipsius Roberti et Rogerum de Ponte et Willelmum filium Prioris, et Rogerum filium Chaut et Ricardum Cophin et Ricardum filium Botild' qui fuerunt de manupastu Prioris de Tanton', quod ipsi super pacem quam ipsi affidaverunt et vadiaverunt ei in comitatu exierunt de molendino quodam ubi fuerunt in abscondito, et venerunt in assultu premeditato ad Walterum de Wik' quem ipse *miserat* in nuncium suum, et eum vulneraverunt ita quod unus illorum vulneravit eum in capite j. hascia et alius fecit ei aliam plagam similiter in capite et ita ibi attornaverunt eum quod ipse obiit per vulnera ei data, et tunc vulneraverunt Serlonem hominem ipsius Willelmi ita quod maimatus est.

---

[1] Perhaps Reginald was not yet dead when Peter made this remark.
[2] *Assisa* seems here used to mean *Judgment*.   [3] m. 16.   [4] m. 16.

sider. And Richard Frank, serjeant of the hundred, along with the hundred testifies that in a hundred [court] convoked for this purpose before him and the hundred Peter confessed that they gave the wound of which Reginald died, and that Peter said that he would gladly be hanged on three days [i.e. three times over] if thereby [Reginald] might die of that wound. Judgment: let Peter be hanged because of his confession, and let Walter and Maud purge themselves by ordeal of iron. They have waged [their law].

120.
Somerset.

Edith of Molton, who in the county [court] appealed Randolph of Chew and William the Irishman (who died in gaol) of the death of Maud, wife of Osbert of Deepford, came before the justices and said that malefactors came by night to the house of Osbert, whose servant she was, and took him and beat him, and killed his wife, but she knows not whether [Randolph and William] did this or no. And twelve knights of the same hundred, being sworn, do not suspect [Randolph] of this or of other ill-fame. So let him be under pledges.

121.
Somerset.

William of Calne appeals William Tropinel, and Robert Miller, and Geoffrey, Hugh, Walter, Jordan, and Henry, Robert's sons, and Roger of the Bridge, and William, Prior's son, and Roger, Chaut's son, and Richard Coffin, and Richard, Botild's son, who were of the mainpast of the Prior of Taunton, for that they against the peace which they had sworn and gaged to him in the county [court], came out of a mill in which they had lain concealed, and in premeditated assault came upon Walter of Wick, whom [the appellor] had sent on a message, and wounded him, so that one of them wounded him on the head with an axe, and another gave him another wound likewise on the head, and they so maltreated him that he died of the wounds given him, and then they wounded Serlo, one of the appellor's men, so that he is maimed.

Qui appellat Willelmum filium Prioris quod ipse in pace domini Regis et nequiter assultavit eum et fecit ei j. vulnus in sinistra scapula ita quod mahemiatus est, et appellat Hugonem predictum quod ipse fecit ei quoddam vulnus in capite et fixit eum cum quodam cultello in brachiis et in tibiis ita quod xiiij. vulnera ei fecerunt, et in illa vi fuerunt omnes predicti, et similiter ad occisionem predicti Walteri Wik', et ipse hoc vidit et audivit et hoc offert probare versus predictos Willelmum et Hugonem de mahemio suo sicut curia consideraverit, et quod predicti fuerunt in illa vi.

Et omnes predicti, preter Ricardum Cophin et Ricardum filium Botild' qui utlagati sunt, veniunt et defendunt totum de verbo in verbum, et appellati dicunt quod antequam predictus Walterus obiit venit ipse coram serviente hundredi et aliis recognovit quod nullus eum interfecit nec aliquem inde rettavit nisi Ricardum Cophin et Ricardum filium Botild,' et petunt ut hoc eis allocetur. Preterea petunt quod eis allocetur quod nunquam Serlo predictus fecit appellum versus eos in comitatu nec alibi nec vulnera recentia ostendit nec mahemium nisi post utlagacionem predictorum, scilicet, post quintum comitatum, et inde vocant comitatum. Qui hoc eis warentizat. Dicunt eciam Molindinarius et filii quod antequam hoc appellum fuit, appellaverunt ipsi quosdam de nepotibus Willelmi de Caune et pro suo appello extinguendo factum est hoc appellum.

Et comitatus quesitus utrum appellum prius factum fuit, dicunt quod appellum Roberti Molindinarii et filiorum ejus.

Judicium, nullum est appellum supradicta causa. Et ideo Serlo in misericordia et alii sint quieti. Et Willelmus de Caune qui questus fuit quod vicecomes noluit attachiare predictos appellatos per appellum ipsius Serlonis in misericordia pro falso clamore suo, quia totus comitatus testatur ipsum eos attachiasse. Et in adventu justiciariorum procedat appellum prius factum.

---

[1] William vouches the county to warrant an assertion of his as to the sheriff's neglect of duty, and the county 'fails him,' i.e. does not support his assertion.

And Serlo appeals William, Prior's son, for that he in the king's peace and wickedly assaulted him and gave him a wound on his left shoulder, so that he is maimed, and he appeals the said Hugh, for that he gave him a wound on the head, and stabbed him with a knife in his arms and legs, so that they gave him fourteen wounds, and all the aforesaid were [accessories] in that force, and were also at the death of the said Walter Wick; and this he saw and heard, and offers to prove it against William and Hugh as to his mayhem as the court shall consider, and also as to all the aforesaid being [accessories] in the force.

And all the aforesaid, save Richard Coffin and Richard, Botild's son, who are outlawed, come and defend all of it word by word; and the appellees say that the said Walter before his death came before the serjeant of the hundred and others, and declared that no one had slain him, and he accused no one, save Richard Coffin and Richard, Botild's son, and they crave that this be allowed in their favour. Also they crave that it be allowed in their favour that Serlo never appealed them in the county [court] nor elsewhere, nor showed fresh wounds nor mayhem, until after the outlawry [of the two Richards], to wit, after the fifth county [court], and they vouch the county to warranty. And the county warrants this. And the Miller and his sons say also that before this appeal was made, they [the speakers] had appealed some nephews of William of Calne, and it is for the purpose of extinguishing that appeal that the present appeal is made.

And the county being asked which appeal was first made, says the appeal of Robert Miller and his sons.

Judgment: the appeal is null for the cause aforesaid. And let Serlo be in mercy and the others be quit. And let William of Calne, who complained that the sheriff would not attach those whom Serlo appealed, be in mercy for his false complaint, for the whole county testifies that the sheriff did attach them. And let the earlier appeal [i.e. the Miller's] proceed on the next coming of the justices.

122.
Sumerset.

[1] Gervasius de Pedewell' appellat Stephanum Forestarium quod ipse simul cum aliis quos non cognoscit venit noctu ad domum suam in pace domini Regis et nequiter, et fregerunt domum suam in burgeria et ut catalla sua ei robarent, et eum voluerunt occidere cum gladio quodam quem ipse eis abstulit et retinuit cum quodam scapulari et hoc offert etc. Et filia ejusdem Gervasii similiter que hoc vidit. Et ipse Stephanus hoc defendit. Preterea totus comitatus testatur quod ipse et amici sui per eum tulerunt breve justic' in comitatu de facienda inquisicione utrum verum esset nec ne, et cum audiret quod comitatus testatus fuit contra eum quod fuit de malo retto et quod malecredebat eum inde sicut adhuc testatur.[2] Judicium, purget se aqua. Vad'.

123.
Sumerset.

[3] Swanilda que fuit uxor Hugonis appellat Robertum Clericum de morte viri. Qui venit et dicit quod ipse subdiaconus est et bene defendit mortem et defendet ubi defendere debebit. Et Magister Alanus Officialis Episcopi Bathoniensis dicit quod subdiaconus est et ordinatus a Domino Cantuariensi[4] qui hoc ei dixit ut dicit et petit curiam domini sui. Et quia inde non habuit sufficiens testimonium Archiepiscopi non dimittitur ei quietus, set ei committitur ita quod illum habeat in adventum justiciariorum, et tunc habeat literas Archiepiscopi de testimonio ordinacionis ejus.

124.
Sumerset.

[5] Rogerus Corbin quesitus quomodo ipse venit ad quoddam pallium et j. napam que Willelmus le Burguunin dicit sibi furto fuisse sublata simul cum aliis rebus suis quando domus sua fuit fracta et burgata, venit et dicit quod ipse

---

[1] m. 16 d.
[2] Something seems missing. Perhaps Stephen fled when he heard the testimony of the county.
[3] m. 16 d.
[4] As between July 1205 and the spring of 1213, there was no Archbishop of Canterbury acknowledged as such by the king, it seems probable that these cases belong to the first years of the reign.
[5] m. 16 d.

122. Somerset. Gervase of Pedwell appeals Stephen Forester for that he with others, whom [Gervase] does not know, came by night to his house in the king's peace and wickedly, and broke his house in burglary and to rob him of his goods, and wished to kill him with a certain sword which he snatched from them and retained along with a scapulary; and this he offers [to prove etc.]. And Gervase's daughter who saw this, does the same. And Stephen defends this. Also the whole county testifies that he [Stephen?] and his friends brought a writ from the justiciar into the county [court], ordering an inquest whether the facts were as alleged or no, and when he heard that the county testified against him that he was of ill-fame, and suspected him thereof as it still testifies. . . . Judgment: let him purge himself by water. He has waged [his law].

123. Somerset. Swanild, who was wife of Hugh, appeals Robert Clerk of her husband's death. He comes and says that he is a subdeacon and fully defends the death, and will defend where he ought to defend. And Master Alan, Official of the Bishop of Bath, says that [Hugh] is a subdeacon and ordained by the Archbishop of Canterbury, who told [Alan] this (as he says), and he claims [cognizance for] his lord's court. And because he had no sufficient testimony from the Archbishop, [Hugh] is not handed over to him quit, but is committed to him for production on the [next] coming of the justices, and then let him produce the Archbishop's letters testifying the ordination.

124. Somerset. Roger Corbin, questioned how he came by a certain cloak and a napkin which William le Burguinin says were taken from him in theft with other things of his when his house was broken into and robbed, comes and says that he bought

emit predictum pallium et napam de Roberto *Turz* qui misit propter eum per Robertum Brun, et eum vocat ad warantum, et si non vult esse warantus ejus inde offert probare versus eum sicut curia consideraverit.¹ Et Robertus venit et defendit totum quod ipse nunquam vendidit ei pallium illud vel napam, et dicit quod alia vice in pleno comitatu appellaverat eum inde, et postea remisit eum inde et vocavit alium ad warantum Willelmum filium Ricardi. Et hoc testatur totus comitatus. Et quia ipse Rogerus inventus est seisitus de roberia illa et variavit in narracione sua et vocando warantos suos, consideratum est quod ipse suspendatur, et Robertus *Turz* sit inde quietus. Et Willelmus filius Ricardi utlagatus proinde fuit in thedinga de Acford' Johannis Eskellings',² et est in misericordia. Et catalla ejus fuerunt iiij. sol. unde H. de Burgo³ etc.

mīa

de catall'

125.
Somerset.

⁴ Gaufridus de Malecumb' occisus fuit in reditu suo de taberna in campis de Aili et Willelmus Sutor captus fuit pro morte ejus, et inventus fuit seisitus cappa mortui et cultello unde occisus fuit mortuus. Et totus comitatus testatur hoc, et Willelmus totum defendit. Judicium, purget se aqua. Vadiavit.

⁵ PLACITA INCERTI TEMPORIS.

126.
Glouc.

⁶ Willelmus de Parco, Henricus de Praeriis, Willelmus de Eston, Robertus Achard missi per comitatum Gloucestrie ad faciendum recordum de duello vadiato inter Radulfum Russodic appellantem et Eliam de Dumberton' in comitatu

---

¹ As to warranty of chattels, see Glanvill, lib. x. cap. 15, Bracton, f. 151.

² As to 'Shillingston, vulgarly Ockford Shilling, more truly Ockford Eskelling, or Acford Skyllings,' see Hutchens, Hist. Dorset, vol. iii. p. 93.

³ The future justiciar accounted as sheriff of Dorset and Somerset for the third, fourth, fifth, and sixth years of John's reign.

⁴ m. 17.

⁵ Coram Rege Roll No. 70. The date of this roll has not been ascertained, but the following case seemed worthy of publication, regard being had to the common law of later days as to larceny by bailees, servants, and so forth.

⁶ m. 8 d.

the cloak and napkin of Robert Turz who sent for him by Robert Brown, and [Roger] vouches [Robert Turz] to warranty, and if he will not warrant him then he offers to prove against him [Robert Turz] as the court shall consider. And Robert comes and defends all of it, that he never sold him the cloak or napkin, and says that on another occasion [Roger] in full county [court] had appealed him of this, but afterwards discharged him and vouched another warrantor, William, Richard's son. And this the whole county testifies. And for that Roger is found seised of that robbery and has varied in his pleading and in his voucher of warrantors, it is considered that he be hanged, and let Robert Turz be quit thereof. William, Richard's son, who was outlawed for this [theft], was in the tithing of John Eskelling's Ockford, which is therefore in mercy. His chattels were four shillings, for which Hubert de Burgh [must account].

125. Geoffrey of Melcombe was slain as he was returning from
Somerset. the tavern in the fields of Isle and William Cobbler was taken for that death and was found seised of the dead man's cap and the knife wherewith he was slain. And the whole county testifies this, and William defends it. Judgment: let him purge himself by the water. He has waged [his law].

PLEAS OF UNCERTAIN DATE.

126. William of Park, Henry of Praeres, William of Easton,
Glouc. Robert Achard, sent by the county of Gloucester to make record of the battle waged between Ralph Rusdike appellor and Elias of Dumbleton in the county [court] of Gloucester,

Gloucestrie recordantur quod Willelmus de Mara questus fuit de predicto Elia quod ipse asportaverat ei catalla sua ita quod per querelam ejusdem Willelmi attachiatus fuit idem Elias quod veniret ad comitatum, et venit, et tunc venit Willelmus et appellavit ipsum Eliam et dixit quod ipse fuit cum eo per aliquantum tempus et habuit in custodia omnia sua et postea recessit ab eo et nequiter et in latrocinio asportavit de catallis suis ad valenciam x. marcarum. Et Elias venit et defendit versus eum ut versus dominum suum[1] feloniam et latrocinium et totum etc. Quo audito predictus Radulfus surrexit et appellavit eum et dixit quod ipse injuste hoc defendit quia ipse asportavit nequiter et in latrocinio predicta catalla domini sui[2] ita quod ipse furatus est ei et asportavit j. firmaculum aureum et j. anulum precii xl. solidorum quos dominus suus ei[3] commiserat custodiendum, et hoc obtulit etc. Et Elias defendit totum versus eum ut versus campionem conducticium et villanum. Et ipse Radulfus defendit vilenagium et quod non est conducticius, set est homo ejus ita quod ipse intravit in solucionem versus dominum suum pro predicto firmaculo et anulo.[4] Et tunc consideratum fuit hiis auditis quod duellum *fuit* inter eos.

'Dies datus est eis a die Mercurii proxima post festum Omnium Sanctorum in iij. septimanas.' 'Willelmus de Parco, Radulfus de Rulesdon', Willelmus de Eston', Philippus de Bello Monte plegii Willelmi de Mara standi ad judicium.'

---

[1] There can be no appeal between lord and tenant while the bond of homage subsists, nor between lord and servant (*servus*); Bracton, f. 141.

[2] *sui* is ambiguous, but it seems that William is lord both of Elias and of Ralph.

[3] *ei* must mean Ralph, for see what follows.

[4] Ralph was answerable to William for the safety of these goods, therefore (so runs the argument) he has a sufficient interest in them to ground an appeal against Elias; see Bracton, f. 146, where the phrase *intrare in solutionem* occurs in just the same context: apparently 'to enter into payment' means to make oneself liable to pay.

record that William de la Mare complained against the said Elias for that he had carried off his chattels, whereupon, upon the complaint of William, Elias was attached to come to the county [court], and he came, and then came William and appealed Elias and said that [Elias] was with him [William, i.e. was in William's service] for a certain time and had charge of all his property and afterwards left him and wickedly and in larceny carried off chattels of his to the value of ten marks. And Elias comes and defends against him, as against one who is his lord, felony and larceny and all of it etc. And, upon hearing this, the said Ralph arose and appealed [Elias] and said that unjustly did he defend this, for he carried off wickedly and in larceny the said chattels of his lord, namely, that he stole a golden buckle and a ring, price forty shillings, which his lord had committed to his [Ralph's] keeping; and this [Ralph] offered [to prove etc.]. And Elias defended all of it against him as against a hireling champion and a villein. And Ralph defended the villeinage and says that he is no hireling, but says that he is [William's] man and had become answerable to his lord [William] for the said buckle and ring. And thereupon these things having been heard it was considered [by the county court] that battle lay between them.

A day is given them, three weeks from Wednesday next after All Saints. William of Park, Ralph of Rulesdon, William of Easton, Philip of Beaumont are pledges that William de la Mare will stand to judgment.

III. PLACITA CORAM JUSTICIARIIS ITINERANTIBUS REGNANTE HENRICO FILIO JOHANNIS.

[1] PLACITA APUD WIGORNIAM ANNO REGNI REGIS HENRICI QUINTO.

Hundredus de Persor'.

127. [2] Emma que fuit uxor Rogeri de Cumbrinton' submersa fuit in Afna. Postea testatum est per alios quod Rogerus vir suus eam occidit quodam lapide et fugit et postea suspensus fuit per judicium coram militibus missis a domino Rege ad gaolam deliberandam. Et juratores hoc cognoverunt. Et ideo ad judicium de eis qui dixerunt quod submersa fuit. {Griffinus [3] pater suus eam invenit et non venit nec habuimus plegios et ideo loquendum, 'et attachiatus fuit per David de Dugingehal' et Ricardum de Duginehal' et ideo in misericordia.'} Villata de Cumbrinton' nichil sciuit [4] in cujus decenna idem Rogerus fuit in plegio, et ideo villata in misericordia. Englescheria non fuit presentata. Judicium murdrum. Rogerus nulla catalla habuit.

mīe
ad judm̄.

mīa
murdr'

128. [5] Gilibertus filius Holdewini inventus fuit occisus in foresta Malvernie. Nescitur quis eum occidit. Inventus fuit in chemino inter Parvam Malverniam et Magnam Malverniam. Et quia inventus fuit in cooperto foreste Malvernie, nullum est ibi murdrum per antiquam consuetudinem.[6]

---

[1] Assize Roll 6, 81. The commission for this Eyre is in Rot. Cl. vol. i. p. 476.

[2] m. 7.

[3] *obiit* is written above Griffin's name, and the words which follow are struck out. As Griffin is dead, his pledges will not be amerced.

[4] Or *sciunt*.

[5] m. 7.

[6] That part of Gloucestershire which lies west of the Severn enjoyed a similar immunity from murder fines. See Pleas of the Crown, Gloucestershire, 1221, p. 30.

III. PLEAS BEFORE THE JUSTICES IN EYRE IN THE REIGN OF HENRY THE THIRD.

PLEAS AT WORCESTER IN THE FIFTH YEAR OF HENRY III. (A.D. 1221).

Hundred of Pershore.

127. Emma, wife of Roger of Comberton, was drowned in the Avon. Afterwards it was testified by others [than the jurors] that Roger her husband slew her with a stone and fled and was afterwards hanged under a judgment of the knights sent by the king to deliver the gaol. And the jurors confessed this. And so to judgment against them, for they said that she was drowned. {Griffin her father found her [body] and does not come, and we have not his pledges; this must be discussed; he was attached by David of Duginghall and Richard of Duginghall; so [they are] in mercy.} The township of Comberton, in whose tithing [Roger] was in pledge, knew nothing [*i.e.* said nothing of the matter], so it is in mercy. Englishry was not presented. Judgment: a murder. Roger had no chattels.

128. Gilbert, Holdwin's son, was found slain in the forest of Malvern. It is not known who slew him. He was found in the highway between Little Malvern and Great Malvern. And because he was found in the covert of Malvern forest, there is no murder [fine], and this by ancient custom.

129. ¹Johannes le Waller' occidit Willelmum le Clodder' et fugit. Nullus alius malecreditur. Fuit in franco plegio Ricardi Barat de Hull' Chaddeleg', et ideo in misericordia, et Johannes ²interrogetur et utlagetur.² Nulla catalla habuit. Postea recordatur comitatus quod utlagatus fuit per sectam Johannis fratris Willelmi ad quintum comitatum desicut racionabiliter facta fuit secta per ipsum Johannem. Et ideo ad judicium de comitatu qui debuerunt utlagasse ad quartum comitatum.³

130. ⁴ Agnes que fuit uxor Willelmi Neuna' appellat Willelmum Walensem {et Godardum forestarium} quod occidit Willelmum virum suum quadam hachia. Et Willelmus fugit. Et Agnes dicit quod idem Willelmus et Godardus forestarius magister suus comederunt *eo die* ad domum Walteri Haket et de domo illa exivit ad hoc faciendum et ad domum illam de facto rediit, et hoc *fecit* per preceptum uxoris Walteri et filii sui et 'Lucie' filie sue {et per preceptum ipsius Godardi}. Et Walterus filius Walteri et idem Walterus veniunt et defendunt totum et ponunt se super patriam et de bono et de malo. Post venerunt Margeria uxor Walteri et *Lucia* filia ejus, et defendunt preceptum et consensum et totum de [verbo in⁵] verbum sicut curia consideraverit, et Walterus pro eis et pro se offert domino Regi xv. marcas⁶ pro habendo inde veredicto jur'. Recipiuntur. Et juratores dicunt quod nullus eorum est inde culpabilis. Et ideo *inde* quieti. Et loquendum de juratoribus qui heri⁷ dixerunt quod habuerunt filium et feminas inde suspectos. {Plegius de v. marcis Robertus Marmiun.} Plegii de denariis Rogerus le Poher de j. marca, Hugo le

---

¹ m. 7.

²⁻² Substituted for *utlagatus est per sectam*.

³ See Bracton, f. 125 b, § 6. The outlawry should take place at the fifth, or, according to another mode of reckoning, the fourth, county court. It is the fourth if you do not include the day on which the complaint is first made, on which day the culprit is not exacted, but is merely called upon to appear.

⁴ m. 7. The margin of the roll is damaged, and some words are uncertain.

⁵ These words are not on the roll, but are wanted.

⁶ Substituted for *v. marcas*; but how much he had to pay is not very clear.

⁷ The *cras* in the margin shows that the case took two days.

129.   John Waller slew William Clothier and fled. No one else is suspected. He was in the frank pledge of Richard Barat of Hill Chaddesley, which is therefore in mercy, and let him be exacted and outlawed. He had no chattels. Afterwards the county records that he was outlawed at the suit of John, William's brother, at the fifth county [court], as suit was duly made by the said John. So to judgment against the county who ought to have outlawed him at the fourth county [court].

130.   Agnes, formerly wife of William Neunam, appeals William Welsh {and Godard Forester}, for that he slew William her husband with an axe. And William [Welsh] fled. And Agnes says that the said William and Godard Forester his master dined on that day at the house of Walter Haket, and from that house [William] went out to do the deed, and to it he returned when the deed was done, and this he did by the command of Walter's wife and son and of Lucy his daughter {and by the command of the said Godard}. And Walter, son of Walter, and the said Walter [Haket] come and defend all of it and put themselves upon their country for good and ill. Afterwards came Margery, Walter's wife, and Lucy, his daughter, and defend the command and consent and all of it word by word, as the court shall consider. And Walter on their behalf and his own offers the king fifteen marks to have a verdict of the jurors about this. The marks are accepted. And the jurors say that none of them is guilty thereof. Therefore be they quit thereof. And [the conduct of] the jurors must be discussed, for yesterday they said that they suspected the younger Walter and the women. {Pledge for the five marks, Robert Marmion.} Pledges for the money, Roger le Poer for one mark, Hugh le Poer for one mark, B . . .

Poher de j. marca, B. . . . de j. marca, Willelmus filius War' de dimidia marca, Walterus de Gratteshull' de dimidia marca, Radulfus Haket de j. marca.

Postea *venit* Godardus foristarius et posuit se super veredictum xij. juratorum si ipse culpabilis sit de morte predicta sive de [*precepto sive*[1]] de consensu. Qui dicunt quod non est aliquo modo culpabilis et ideo Godefr'[2] eat inde quietus.

Villata de Haunleg'.

131. [3] Juratores dicunt quod Henricus filius Podrich' occidit Lithulfum de Bisseleg' sicut venerunt de Theokesbiria de cervisia, et fugit [et fuit] in franco plegio villate de Bisseleg' et ideo villata in misericordia. Englescheria non est presentata et ideo murdrum. Et sciendum quod comitatus recordatur quod murdrum si evenerit dandum est ubique in manerio de Haunleg' excepto in coverto foreste Malvernie,[4] in quo si quis occisus fuerit inventus, non est presentanda Englescheria nec jacet ibi murdrum ex antiqua consuetudine.[5]

132. [6] Johannes filius Suain percussus fuit ad gurgitem de Theokesbury quodam palo in capite sicut fuit in quadam navi ascendendo versus Haunleg'. Et juratores dicunt quod nullum inde malecredunt. Judicium infortunium.

Et coronatores dicunt quod ballivi Comitis non permiserunt eos attachiare navem nec illos qui in navi fuerunt. Et Martinus ballivus presens est et hoc non dedicit quia talis est libertas Comitis. Et recordatum est quod non, immo ad vicecomitem et ad coronatores pertinet facere hujusmodi attachiamenta. Et ideo dictum est ballivo quod decetero permittat vicecomitem et ballivos domini Regis facere attachiamenta sicut ad eos pertinet.

---

[1] These words are conjectured.   [2] Corr. *Godardus*.
[3] m. 7 d.   [4] As to this immunity, see above, Case 128.
[5] Substituted for *libertate*.   [6] m. 7 d.

for one mark, William FitzWarin for a half-mark, Walter of Gratteshull for a half-mark, Ralph Haket for one mark.

Afterwards came Godard the forester and put himself upon the verdict of the twelve jurors whether he be guilty of the said death, by commanding or consenting to it. They say that he is not in any way guilty, so let him go quit thereof.

Township of Castle Hanley.

131. The jurors say that Henry, Podrick's son, slew Lithulf of Bushley as they came from an ale at Tewkesbury, and fled. He was in the frank-pledge of the township of Bushley, so the township is in mercy. Englishry was not presented, so it is a murder. And note that the county records that if a murder [fine] arises it must be collected in all parts of the manor of Hanley, save within the covert of Malvern forest, in which if any be found slain, Englishry need not be presented, and no murder [fine] lies there, and this by ancient custom.

132. John, Swain's son, was struck on the head by a stake at the Tewkesbury dam as he was in a ship going up towards Hanley. The jurors say that they suspect nobody of this. Judgment: misadventure.

The coroners say that the Earl [of Gloucester's] bailiffs would not suffer them to attach the ship nor those who were in it. And Martin the bailiff is present and does not deny this, for the Earl has this franchise. And it is recorded that this is not so, and that it belongs to the sheriff and coroners to make attachments of this kind. Therefore the bailiff is told that in future he must suffer the sheriff and the king's bailiffs to make the attachments which it is their duty to make.

Hundr' Dimid' Com'.

133. ¹ Leoninus filius Philippi et Jacobus serviens ejus occiderunt Johannem de Middelton' in foresta de Kenefar et fugerunt et fuerunt manentes in Staff' in villa de Kenefar'.

ap' Staff

Et ideo inde loquendum apud Stafford'. Interrogentur et utlagentur. Inquiratur de catallis eorum apud Staff'. Englescheria est presentata.

'Post venerunt Johannes filius Philippi, Robertus de Stapelton', Adam de Peissi et ceperunt in manum ² habendi ipsos Leoninum et Jacobum coram justiciariis apud Stafford' standi ibi recto. Et ideo mandatum est vicecomiti quod interrogacio et utlagacio ponatur in respectum quousque aliud mandatum habuerit.'

³ 'Apud Lich' venerunt Leoninus et Jacobus et ponunt se super veredictum suum de quo tempore et loco et a quo hoc factum fuit. Juratores hundredi de Seysten' dicunt quod tempore guerre venit Johannes cum aliis pluribus in foresta domini Regis sicut ille qui solitus fuit malefacere in foresta, et inventus fuit tunc seisitus de una bissia integra, et servientes domini Regis et forestarii non potuerunt eum capere vivum et *ipse* defendidit se ⁴ contra dominum Regem ⁴ et abscidit cuidam forestario digitum, et tali modo occisus. Et ideo consideratum est quod ipsi sint inde quieti.'

134. ⁵ Ricardus filius Walteri inventus fuit occisus in cimiterio de Walton' et Hubertus Balistarius ut dicitur eum occidit 'in domo Huberti' pro uxore ejus Alienora que amavit

m̅ïs

ipsum Ricardum. Et Alienora attachiata fuit per Willelmum Shine et Thomam cum barba, et non venit, et ideo

cap'

plegii in misericordia et ipsa capiatur, et est uxor Walteri Toki. Et Willelmus de Sukebergh' tunc serviens nescit respondere de pl' ⁶ eorum qui fuerunt in domo Huberti, et

---

¹ m. 8.
² *in manum* repeated.
³ What follows is obviously a postscript. The justices who were at Worcester visited Lichfield later in the same year. Kinfare is in the hundred of Seisdon.
⁴⁻⁴ The place at which these words should come is not quite certain; on the roll they are interlined.
⁵ m. 8.
⁶ Probably *plegiis*. All those who were present at the death should have been attached.

Hundred of Halfshire.

133.   Leonin, Philip's son, and Jacob his servant slew John of Middleton in the forest of Kinfare and fled and were dwelling in Staffordshire in the township of Kinfare. And therefore this must be discussed at Stafford. Let them be exacted and outlawed. Inquiry as to their chattels must be made at Stafford. Englishry is presented.

Afterwards came John, Philip's son, Robert of Stapleton and Adam of Peissi and undertook to produce Leonin and Jacob before the justices at Stafford to abide judgment. So the sheriff is ordered that the exacting and outlawing be respited until he shall have another order.

At Lichfield came Leonin and Jacob and put themselves upon their verdict as to when, where, and by whom the deed was done. The jurors of the hundred of Seisdon say that in the time of the war John came with many others into the king's forest to offend in the forest, as was his wont, and was found seised of the whole body of a doe, and the king's servants and foresters could not take him alive, and he defended himself against our lord the king and cut off a forester's finger, and thus it was that he was slain. And so it is considered that [Leonin and Jacob] be quit thereof.

134.   Richard, Walter's son, was found slain in the churchyard of Walton, and it is said that Hubert Crossbowman killed him in Hubert's house because of his [Hubert's] wife Eleanor, who loved the said Richard. And Eleanor was attached by William Shine and Thomas with the Beard, and she does not come, and so let her pledges be in mercy and let her be arrested; she is Walter Toki's wife. And William of Shuckburgh, the then serjeant of the hundred, has no answer to make touching the pledges of those who were in Hubert's house; therefore this must be

ideo inde loquendum. Englescheria non est presentata et ideo murdrum. Hubertus habuit pacem per dominum Regem Johannem per breve suum et interim obiit.

'Post venit Alienora et offert domino Regi v. marcas pro habenda inquisicione si ipsa culpabilis sit de morte predicta vel non. Et juratores dicunt quod ipsa non est culpabilis inde. Et ideo consideratum est quod ipsa eat inde quieta. Plegii de *illis denariis* Ricardus frater ipsius Alienore et Robertus de Morton' et Ricardus de Lond' et Johannes de London'.'

135. ¹Willelmus de Stanes captus fuit in domo sua a malefactoribus et ductus ad boscum de Chaddesleg' ubi ipsi occiderunt eum. Et Willelmus Brasey qui fuit in domo ipsius Willelmi quando occisus ² et qui fuit rettatus de morte Philippi de Herwinton', fugit in ecclesiam apud Stanes, et ibi se tenuit, et serviens domini Regis commisit custodiam ipsius ne evaderet villate ³ de Stanes et de Hethe et de Dunclent, et ⁴ in eorum custodia venit Abbas de Bordesl' cum monachis suis et ipsum Willelmum inductum capa unius monachi abduxit. Et villate hoc cognoscunt, et ideo in misericordia. Et ad judicium de Abbate qui illum recepit in monachum. Consideratum est quod Abbas in misericordia.

Et Isabella uxor ejusdem Willelmi appellat de morte illa Henricum de Herwinton' et Robertum fratrem ejus, Robertum Painell' et Johannem Painell' fratrem ejus. Et ipsi non venerunt etc. et ideo ipsa sequatur in comitatu quousque utlagentur et vicecomes capiat terras et catalla eorum in manum domini Regis.

'Post venerunt predicti Henricus de Herwintona et Robertus Painel in reditu justiciariorum apud Wigorniam ⁵ et predicta Isabella presens fuit, et dixit quod nec ipsi nec eorum fratres culpabiles fuerunt de morte predicta sicut

---

¹ m. 8.
² Supply *fuit*.
³ Stone, Dunclent, Hethy Mill, Chaddesley and Harvington lie close together between Bromsgrove and Kidderminster.
⁴ Supply *dum fuit*.
⁵ It appears from other entries that the justices began their eyre at Worcester and revisited it on their return journey.

discussed. Englishry is not presented: so it is a murder. Hubert had peace granted to him by writ of King John, and has died in the meanwhile.

Afterwards comes Eleanor and gives the king five marks for an inquest [to find] if she be guilty of the said death or no. The jurors say that she is not guilty thereof. Therefore it is considered that she go quit thereof. Pledges for the money, Richard her brother, Robert of Morton, Richard of London, John of London.

135. William of Stone was captured in his house by evildoers and taken off to Chaddesley wood, where they slew him. And William Brasey, who was in that house when he was killed and who is charged with the death of Philip of Harvington, fled into the church at Stone, and kept himself there; and the king's serjeant committed the duty of seeing that he did not escape to the townships of Stone, Heath, and Dunclent; and while they had him in charge, the Abbot of Bordesly came with his monks and carried him off clad in the cowl of one of the monks. And the townships confess this, and therefore are in mercy. And to judgment as to the Abbot who received him as a monk. It is considered that the Abbot be in mercy.

And Isabella, William [of Stone's] wife, appeals of that death Henry of Harvington and Robert his brother, Robert Painel and John Painel his brother. And they do not come etc. Therefore let her sue in the county [court] until they be outlawed, and let the sheriff take their lands and chattels into the king's hand.

Afterwards when the justices came to Worcester on their return journey, came the said Henry of Harvington and Robert Painel, and Isabella was present and said that neither they nor their brothers were guilty of that death, as she had

ipsa bene inquisivit, et remisit eos de appello predicto. Et ideo ipsa custodiatur.'

'Post venerunt predicti Henricus et Robertus et dant domino Regi xx. marcas ne occasionentur eo quod ipsi subtraxerunt se in primo adventu justiciariorum, per plegium Willelmi de Parles, Ricardi de Sullee, Willelmi de Sumeri, Ricardi de Ambresleg', Willelmi de Belne le Brun, Hugonis de Belne, Walteri filii *Thenard'*, Radulfi de . . . diford', Rogeri de Whiteford', Rogeri de Bremesgrave, Willelmi de Betecote.

'Plegii Henrici, Osbertus de Abetot, Willelmus de Parles, Stephanus de Wareslete, Thomas de D*uue*dale, Ricardus de *Shenere*, Willelmus de Sukeberge.

'Plegii Roberti Painel, Rogerus de Br*imes*grave, Thomas de Stokes, Ricardus filius Osberti, Willelmus de Sukeberge, Radulfus Painel, Matheus de Bosco.

'Villata de Chaddeleg' malecredit predictos iiij. homines de morte illa, et ea racione quia Philippus frater predicti Henrici occisus fuit.'[1]

136. [2]Thomas Marescallus appellat Hugonem Wery quod sicut Walterus Marescallus frater suus fuit in servicio domini sui Ricardi Pauencefort' ad boscum suum custodiendum et blada sua, venit idem Hugo cum Osberto filio suo et nequiter et in felonia occidit ipsum Walterum in bosco de Benetleg' in pace domini Regis, et hoc offert probare per corpus suum sicut curia consideraverit.

Ricardus Marescallus appellat predictum Osbertum filium Hugonis eodem modo et per eadem verba quod occidit Walterum predictum fratrem suum cum ipso Hugone, et hoc offert probare per corpus suum.

Et Hugo et Osbertus veniunt et defendunt feloniam et mortem et totum de verbo in verbum et ponunt se super visnetum.

Et Hobbe Kittere rettatus de eadem morte captus fuit

---

[1] The suggestion is, that the death of William of Stone was a reprisal for the death of Philip of Harvington. The accused persons are not acquitted; they may yet hear more of the charge.

[2] m. 8 d.

fully ascertained, and she released them from her appeal. Therefore let her be in custody.

Afterwards came the said Henry and Robert, and they give the king twenty marks that advantage be not taken of them for having withdrawn themselves on the first coming of the justices; pledges for the money, William of Parles, Richard of Sulley, William of Sumery, Richard of Ambresleigh, William of Belne the Brown, Hugh of Belne, Walter, Thenard's son, Ralph of . . ., Roger of Whiteford, Roger of Bromsgrove, William of Betecote.

Henry's pledges, Osbert D'Abitot, William of Parles, Stephen of Warslow, Thomas of Doverdale, Richard of Shenere, William of Shuckburgh.

Robert Painel's pledges, Roger of Bromsgrove, Thomas of Stoke, Richard, Osbert's son, William of Shuckburgh, Ralph Painel, Matthew of Wood.

The township of Chaddesley suspects the said four men of the said death, and [that they caused it] because Philip, Henry's brother, had been slain.

186. Thomas Marshall appeals Hugh Wery, for that, whereas his brother Walter Marshall was in the service of his lord Richard Pauncefot in charge of his wood and crops, the said Hugh came with Osbert his son and wickedly and in felony slew Walter in Bentley wood in the king's peace; and this he offers to prove by his body as the court shall consider.

Richard Marshall appeals the said Osbert, Hugh's son, of the same death by the same words, for that along with Hugh he slew Walter [Richard's] brother; and this he offers to prove by his body.

And Hugh and Osbert come and defend the felony, death, and all of it word by word and put themselves upon the neighbourhood.

And Hobbe Kitter, accused of the same death, was arrested

et inprisonatus, et commissus Rogero de Bremesgrave, et Rogerus illum non habuit et ideo in misericordia. Et juratores malecredunt Hobbe et ideo interrogetur et utlagetur. Et juratores non malecredunt ipsos Hugonem vel Osbertum, et appellantes non locuntur in appello suo de visu vel auditu, immo dixerunt quod tunc temporis fuerunt in comitatu Gloucestrie. Et ideo consideratum est quod duellum non jacet inter eos et ideo Hugo et Osbertus inde quieti, {et alii custodiantur [1]} pro falso appello. 'Ricardus Pauncefot est plegius eorum de misericordia sua et ideo ipsi committantur ei.'

Et comitatus et coronatores recordantur quod primo in comitatu appellaverunt eos de visu et auditu, et invenerunt plegios de prosequendo.[2] Et quia nunc retrahunt se de visu, sunt in misericordia et plegii de prosequendo similiter, scilicet, Alardus de Benetleg', Johannes Samson, Gaufridus de Wreneford', Ricardus de la Hulle, Nicholaus filius Sibille, Ricardus de Benetleg', Ricardus Gamel, Adam Faber, Gerardus Burgeis, Henricus de Mora. 'Perdon' quia pauperes.'[3]

Ad judicium de comitatu quod recordantur quod allocaverunt essonium cujusdam Edelwini qui ad quartum comitatum super utlag'[4] cepit in manum habendi predictos Hugonem et Osbertum ad quintum comitatum, ad quem allocaverunt essonium.[5]

Villata de Wich'.

137. [6]Burgenses de Wichio queruntur quod cives Wigornie vexant eos contra libertatem qua usi sunt *et* contra tenorem carte domini Regis 'Johannis' quam proferunt et que testatur [7] quod concessit eis ut emant et vendant *per* totam

---

[1] As they find a pledge for an amercement they are discharged from custody; therefore a pen is drawn through these words.

[2] This seems the case cited by Bracton on f. 141.

[3] Amercements are often forgiven because of the poverty of the offenders.

[4] *utlagacioniem* or *utlagariam*.

[5] Seemingly this is the case to which Bracton refers on f. 128, § 12; compare f. 125 b, § 6.

[6] m. 8 d.

[7] This charter, dated 1 Aug. 1215. is in Rot. Cart. p. 216 b. It frees the burgesses from pontage, passage, stallage and toll throughout all England.

and imprisoned, and committed to Roger of Bromsgrove, and Roger has not produced him, and is therefore in mercy. And the jurors suspect Hobbe, so let him be exacted and outlawed. And the jurors do not suspect Hugh and Osbert. And the appellors in their appeal do not say that they saw or heard [the deed], but said that at that time they were in Gloucestershire. Therefore it is considered that battle does not lie between them and so let Hugh and Osbert be quit. And let the others be in custody for their false appeal. Richard Pauncefot is pledge for their amercement, and so let them be committed to him.

And the county and the coroners record that in the first instance in the county court the appellors alleged sight and hearing, and found pledges to prosecute. And because they now withdraw [this allegation], they are in mercy, and likewise their pledges to prosecute, to wit, Ailward of Bentley, John Samson, Geoffrey of Wreneford, Richard of Hull, Nicholas, Sibill's son, Richard of Bentley, Richard Gamel, Adam Smith, Gerard Burgess, Henry of the Moor. They are pardoned, for they are poor.

To judgment against the county, for they record that they allowed the essoin of one Ethelwin, who at the fourth county [court], when Hugh and Osbert were exacted, undertook to produce them at the fifth court, and was then allowed the essoin.

Township of Droitwich.

137.   The burgesses of Droitwich complain that the citizens of Worcester vex them contrary to their accustomed franchises and contrary to the tenor of the charter of King John which they produce, and which witnesses that he

Angliam in civitatem et extra omnia genera marchidise etc., unde queruntur quod contra libertatem illam non *permittunt* eos in villa sua Wigornie emere vel vendere secundum concessionem domini Regis, et preterea mercatores *sui* salsarii qui vendunt salem cum bussellis non possunt habere stallagium in villa sua nisi dent stallagium desicut quieti sunt de stallagio per cartam predictam, unde ceperunt ab eis injuste xxiij. denarios de stallagio etc., et preterea per diem Sabbati quo dominus Rex per cartam illam concessit eis mercatum in villa sua ipsi cives non permittunt eis habere illud mercatum sicut habere debent per cartam illam [1] et preterea burgenses de villa sua cum fuerint Wigornie non possunt emere cibum suum ante horam terciam, et petunt hoc sibi emendari.

Et cives veniunt et defendunt quod in nullo venerunt contra cartam domini Regis, quia bene concedunt quod emant et vendant in grosso sicut facere debent et solent per alios dies quam in die mercati, set ipsi nunquam vendere solebant ut regratarii nec debent eo quod nunquam fuerunt inde in seisina per cartam illam et *bene* concedunt quod habeant eandem super hoc libertatem quam habent cives Londonie. Bene autem concedunt quod *emant* cibum suum mane et sero et omni hora diei, set regratarii sui solebant emere privatim dum *cives* fuerunt apud monasterium ut venderent ad lucrandum, ita quod milites de comitatu et ipsi de Wigornia non potuerunt aliquid invenire ad vendendum circa horam primam, et ideo provisum fuit quod hujusmodi regratarii non potuerunt ita emere, nec eciam illi de Wigornia eodem modo.

ad jud'

Dies datus est eis de audiendo judicio suo in reditu justiciariorum apud Wigorniam.[2]

---

[1] The charter as printed from the Charter Roll contains a grant of a yearly fair, but no grant of a weekly market.

[2] The roll does not seem to record the proceedings before the justices on their return journey: see above, p. 86.

granted them that they might buy and sell throughout all England, within cities and without, all kinds of merchandise etc., and they complain that contrary to this franchise [the citizens] do not permit them to buy or sell in their town of Worcester according to the king's grant, and moreover their [Droitwich] salt-merchants who sell salt by the bushel cannot have stall-room in their town [of Worcester] without paying stallage, whereas they are quit of stallage under the said charter, so that [the citizens] have taken from them unjustly the sum of twenty-three pence for stallage etc., and also on Saturdays, on which the king by his said charter has granted them a market in their town, the citizens do not permit them to have that market as they ought to have under that charter, and moreover the burgesses of [Droitwich] when at Worcester cannot buy victuals before the hour of terce [9 A.M.]: and they pray that these their grievances be rectified.

And the citizens come and deny that in any point they have gone against the king's charter, for they freely grant that [the Droitwich folk] may buy and sell in gross as they are wont and ought to do, on days other than market days, but they have not hitherto been wont to buy as regraters nor ought they so to do, for of such franchise they were never seised under their charter, and [the citizens] freely grant that [the burgesses] may have in this respect as much liberty as the citizens of London. They also grant that they may buy their victuals at all hours early and late, but their regraters have been buying privately while the citizens were at church in order to sell at a profit, so that the knights of the shire and the Worcester folk have not been able to find anything for sale after the hour of prime [6 A.M.], and so it was provided that regraters of this kind should not buy thus, and no more should the Worcester folk.

A day is given them to hear their judgment, on the return of the justices to Worcester.

Villata de Brimesgrave.

188. [1] Willelmus Not appellat Rogerum Dunger' quod ipse nequiter et in pace domini Regis cepit averia 'sua et aliorum hominum ejusdem ville' in communi pastura de Norton' ad valenciam lx. solidorum et in roberia abduxit etc. et ea detinuit contra vadium et plegium ita quod serviens hundredi quandam partem eis deliberavit de catallis illis et quedam mortua fuerunt in parco ejusdem Rogeri, et hoc offert etc.

Et Rogerus defendit vim et injuriam et pacem domini Regis infractam et roberiam et totum de verbo in verbum, set veritatem vult cognoscere. Ipse fuit villanus et consuetudinarius Roberti de Roppelle, cujus villa de Norton' fuit, et per preceptum ejusdem Roberti, cujus communa illa fuit, cepit averia illa, et dicit quod ipse appellat eum per odium et atiam et offert ponere se super patriam. Set quum ipse appellat eum de alienis averiis, et preterea cognovit quod ipsi receperunt quandam partem averiorum ipsorum, consideratum est quod nullum est appellum, et Rogerus eat inde sine die et Willemus in misericordia per plegium Walteri de Catteshull'.

mia

189. [2] Juratores dicunt quod homines de Wichebaud', scilicet, Hugo le Tolnur ejusdem ville 'qui per feodum habet teloneum' levavit novas consuetudines in villa de Wichebaud 'de theloneo' scilicet si quedam caretta cum peregrinis [3] transitum fecerit per medium ville sue dabit unum obolum si fuerit de comitatu, et si de alio comitatu j. denarium, et de caretta honerata de bosco ubi solebant capere unam astelam [4] capiunt majus lignum et similiter de petris quas ipsi deferri fecerunt ad *astrium* [5] quoddam faciendum

---

[1] m. 9.
[2] m. 9. Wichbold is a manor in the parish of Dodderhill, a parish partly within the borough of Droitwich; see Nash, Hist. Worcestershire, vol. i. p. 845.
[3] The *peregrini* are *foreigners*, thereby being meant all men who are not of Wichbold.

[4] *Astela* seems to be connected with *hasta*; see Du Cange.
[5] *Ipsi* seems to mean the people of Bromsgrove, whose jurors are making the complaint. The word *astrum* with the meaning of *hearth* is not very uncommon in the law books; see the Glossary.

Township of Bromsgrove.

138.   William Not appeals Roger Dunger, for that he wickedly and in the king's peace took his beasts and those of others of the same vill in the common pasture of Norton, to the value of sixty shillings, and in robbery led them away etc., and detained them against gage and pledge, so that the serjeant of the hundred delivered some of those chattels to [the owners] and other part died in Roger's pound; and this he offers etc.

And Roger defends tort and force and breach of the king's peace and robbery and all word by word, but he will confess the truth. He was the villain and customary tenant of Robert of Ropesley, whose the vill of Norton was, and by command of the said Robert, whose that common was, he took those beasts; and he says he is appealed out of hate and spite and offers to put himself upon the country. But whereas the appellor appeals of beasts that were not his own, and moreover has confessed that [the owners] have received back part of their beasts, it is considered that the appeal is null, and that Roger go thence without day and William be in mercy; pledge for the amercement, Walter of Catshill.

139.   The jurors say that the men of Wichbold, to wit, Hugh the Toller of the said vill, who holds the toll in fee, have levied new customs in the vill of Wichbold as regards toll, to wit, that if any cart with foreigners in it go through their town it shall pay a halfpenny if it belong to this county, and if to another county, a penny; and from a cart loaded with wood from which they used to take one staff, they now take the largest log, and so as to the stone which they [the Bromsgrove folk] caused to be brought there for making a pavement, they took a halfpenny [per cart-load];

ceperunt j. obolum, et de duabus carettis que detulerunt libros Ricardi Decani de Wigornia[1] 'dicunt ipsi quod ipsi' ceperunt illas duas carettas et noluerunt illas deliberare absque teloneo ita quod illas detinuerunt per sex septimanas ita quod ipse deterioratus est ad valenciam centum solidorum. Preterea ceperunt de quadam femina peregrina que militavit[2] in quadam caretta duos solidos.

Et Hugo le Tolnur et ballivi domini Willelmi de Stutevilla defendunt quod nullam novam consuetudinem levaverunt.

Et milites de comitatu recordantur quod non debent de jure teloneum capere de caretis novis nisi sint venales vel ferant merkandisam, nec eciam de rotis nisi sint venales. De carettis ducentibus peregrinos nullum teloneum capere possunt, nec eciam de carettis archiepiscoporum et episcoporum comitum baronum abbatum militum de visneto corredia sua ferentibus. De omnibus istis dicit comitatus quod ipsi teloneum de novo et contra racionem [capiunt[3]]. De caretis autem que de jure dare debent teloneum dicunt quod si caretta fuerit de comitatu dabit j. obolum, si de alio comitatu j. denarium. De carettis autem ligna focalia ferentibus consueverunt capere unam astelam ad electionem illorum quorum fuerunt ligna, et modo capiunt ad electionem ballivi de Winchebaud, et si ipse cujus fuerint ligna astelam fregerit,[4] remanebit in misericordia per consuetudinem illorum de novo contra racionem statutam.

[5]'Dies datus est eis de audiendo judicio suo in Oct. Omn. Sanct. apud Westmonasterium.'

---

[1] Richard the parson of St. Martin's church became dean in 1219 and died in 1225. Ann. Monast. (Rolls Ser.), vol. iv. pp. 411, 418.

[2] As a woman would not be going to the wars, it seems necessary to take *militare* to mean either *to fight, to scuffle*, or else simply *to journey*. Du Cange has 'militare, iter habere, maxime cum difficile et asperum est.' But the two shillings seem a large sum to be taken for mere toll; it looks like a fine for disorderly conduct.

[3] This word is supplied by conjecture.

[4] The value of the right to take 'a staff' would be diminished if the owner might break up the wood as small as he pleased.

[5] In the margin. Search has been made for a judgment, but unsuccessfully.

and as to two carts which were carrying the books of Richard the Dean of Worcester, they took (say the jurors) those carts and would not deliver them without toll, and so kept them six weeks, so that [the Dean] suffered damage to the amount of one hundred shillings; moreover, they took from a foreign woman who was fighting in a cart two shillings.

And Hugh the Toller and the bailiffs of Sir William Stuteville deny that they have levied any new custom.

And the knights of the county record that by rights they ought not to take toll of new carts,[1] unless they be for sale or are bearing merchandise, nor of wheels unless they be for sale. From carts carrying foreigners they can take no toll, nor from the carts of archbishops and bishops, earls, barons, abbots or knights of the neighbourhood which are carrying their victuals. As to all these the county says that they have lately and wrongfully begun to take toll. But as to those carts which by rights ought to give toll, they say that if the cart belongs to this county it shall pay a halfpenny, if to another county, a penny. As to carts carrying firewood they were wont to take one staff chosen for them by the owners of the wood, but now they insist that the bailiff of Wichbold may make the choice, and if the owner of the wood breaks the staff he is amerced under a custom which they have newly and wrongfully established.

A day is given them to hear their judgment, on the octave of All Saints at Westminster.

---

[1] The 'new carts' seem to be carts newly made, which are being taken home to their owners.

Villata de Kideministr'.

140. ¹Robertus filius Patric captus fuit apud Kideministr' fugiendo in societate latronum qui postea cognoverunt se esse latrones et suspensi fuerunt et dicebant ipsum esse socium eorum. Et prepositus ville de Kideministr' et alii liberi homines ejusdem ville testati fuerunt quod ipse cognovit coram eis quod ipse fuit socius eorum et latro, et preterea cognovit quod equus quem ipse equitavit 'quando captus fuit,' fuit unius ipsorum latronum. Et ipse hoc non potuit defendere. Postea vero cognovit idem Robertus quod ipse latro est et non est diaconus nec subdiaconus sicut ipse prius se fecit. Et devenit probator ad faciendum quinque duella.²

Villa de Fekeham.

141. ³Willelmus de Littlingeton' cepit Aliciam filiam Walteri Stanchard' 'in domo patris sui apud Fekeham' et eam abduxit usque ad curiam de Fekeham et voluit jacere cum ea, set clamor supervenit, ita quod idem Willelmus fugit priusquam eam rapuisset. 'Postea vero cognovit ipsa quod nullam sectam fecit versus eum que racionabilis esset, et preterea cognovit quod Thomas filius Simonis cepit in manum versus eam emendandi illud. Et quum ipsa hoc cognovit, et preterea postea cepit virum qui presens non fuit, sine quo ipsa non potest sequi, consideratum est quod nullum est appellum et ideo appellatus eat inde quietus.'

142. ⁴Petrus Judas cepit quendam hominem et tenuit in prisona quousque obiit et post mortem ejus suspendit eum per pedes. Et idem Petrus venit et cognovit quod cepit quendam hominem qui abjuravit regnum pro foresta domini Regis, et obiit in prisona sua per infirmitatem, preterquam fregerat gaolam domini Regis, et bene defendit quod nunquam suspendit eum. Et villata hoc cognovit, et ideo

¹ m. d.
² An approver receives pardon on condition of his accusing, fighting, and vanquishing a certain number, in this case five, of his accomplices; Bracton, f. 152.
³ m. 9 d.
⁴ m. 9 d.

Township of Kidderminster.

140.   Robert, Patrick's son, was captured at Kidderminster fleeing in company with thieves, who afterwards confessed themselves thieves and were hanged, and said that he was their fellow. And the reeve of the vill of Kidderminster and other free men of the same vill testified that in their presence he confessed himself the fellow of [the said thieves] and a thief, and also confessed that the horse he was riding when arrested belonged to one of those thieves. And he could not [be heard to] defend this. Afterwards he confessed that he is a thief and is not a deacon or subdeacon as he at one time pretended. And he turns an approver to fight five battles.

Vill of Feckenham.

141.   William of Littlington took Alice, daughter of Walter Stanchard, in her father's house at Feckenham, and led her off to Feckenham court and would have lain with her, but the cry was raised, so that he fled without having committed rape. Afterwards, however, she confessed that she made no suit in due form against him, and also that Thomas, Simon's son, had undertaken to make amends to her for it. And since she has confessed this and also has since [the attempted rape] taken a husband, who is not present and without whom she cannot make suit, it is considered that the appeal is null, and so let the appellee go quit thereof.

142.   Peter Judas took a man and kept him in prison until he died, and when dead hanged him up by the heels. And Peter came and confessed that he did arrest a man and that he died of illness in [Peter's] prison, but he was one who had abjured the realm on account of [some offence in] the king's forest, and had also broken the king's gaol, and he fully denies that he hanged him. And the township con-

villata in misericordia et Petrus inde quietus. Et juratores non malecredunt eum de aliis maleficiis et ideo quietus.

Hundredus de Oswaldeslauwe.

148.   [1]Juratores dicunt quod Nicholaus de Hagel' et Stephanus Ruffus fuerunt socii de latrocinio, ita quod pro quodam facto fugit idem Stephanus in ecclesiam. Postea vero cum idem Nicholaus vellet deliberare ipsum Stephanum de ecclesia accessit ad Osbertum Alfolc de Almthechierche et peciit eum quod ipse iret cum eo ad eum deliberandum, et noluit ita quod contencio mota fuit inter eos et Osbertus occidit ipsum Nicholaum.

Et sciendum quod Osbertus invenit plegios, scilicet, Adam de la Wederake et Willelmum filium Ernwici, Gilebertum Wischard, Willelmum Schirreve, Reginaldum de la Wederake, Rogerum Kade et totam decennam ejusdem Osberti.[2]

'Post venit Osbertus {et offert domino Regi j. marcam pro habenda inquisicione[3]} si ipse culpabilis sit de latrocinio et de societate predicti Stephani nec ne per plegium Willelmi Eghe. Juratores dicunt quod ipse Osbertus latro est et receptator latronum et nominatim predictorum, et quod occidit ipsum Nicholaum ut sic celaret iniquitatem suam. Et ideo consideratum est quod Osbertus suspendatur.'

suspendatur

'Et Johannes Alfolc frater ipsius Osberti captus pro malo retto, venit et non est in franco plegio nec vult ponere se super patriam, nec habet dominum qui velit eum replegiare. Et ideo abjuret regnum et vacuet terram infra diem Sabbati proximam post Oct. S. Joh. Bapt., et elegit ire apud Dovoriam. Catalla Osberti v. solidi unde vicecomes respondeat.'

abjuravit regnum

v. sol.

[1] m. 10.
[2] In the margin, which is defaced, there were words which are now illegible.
[3] These words are struck out, probably because Osbert is hanged, and therefore all his chattels are forfeited; besides, he was not worth a mark.

fessed that this was so, and is therefore in mercy, and let Peter be quit thereof. And the jurors do not suspect him of other misdeeds and so let him be quit.

Hundred of Oswaldslow.

143. The jurors say that Nicholas of Hagley and Stephen Read were companions in larceny, so that Stephen fled to church because of what they had done. Afterwards Nicholas wished to deliver Stephen from the church, and went to Osbert Alfolk of Alvechurch and asked him to go with him to deliver [Stephen], and [Osbert] would not, so a quarrel ensued between them and Osbert killed Nicholas.

And note that Osbert found pledges, to wit, Adam of Weathereak, William, Ernwic's son, Gilbert Wischard, William Sheriff, Reginald of Weathereak, Roger Kade, and the whole of Osbert's tithing.

Afterwards comes Osbert and offers the king one mark for an inquest [to find] if he be guilty of larceny and fellowship with Stephen or no, for which sum William Eghe is pledge. The jurors say that Osbert is a thief, and receiver of thieves, in particular of [Nicholas and Stephen], and slew Nicholas in order to conceal his crimes. And so it is considered that Osbert be hanged.

And John Alfolk, Osbert's brother, arrested for ill-fame, comes, and he is not in frank-pledge and will not put himself upon the country, and has no lord who will replevy him. Therefore let him abjure the realm and vacate the country before Saturday next after the octave of John Baptist; and he has chosen Dover as his port. Osbert's chattels, five shillings, for which the sheriff must answer.

144. ¹Walterus le Pleidur latro 'et utlaga' captus fuit in domo Franke in Cnihteton' de nocte sicut jacuit in lecto, et idem Franke attachiatus fuit veniendi coram justiciariis. Et venit et defendit societatem ejusdem et latrocinium et consensum, set revera ipse scivit quod jacuit in domo sua 'et cognovit quod scivit ipsum esse utlagam,' et bene ponit se super xij. juratores et de bono et de malo.

{viij. sol.} Juratores dicunt super sacramentum suum quod intelligunt ipsum esse culpabilem de consensu et de societate et
{susp'} de pluribus maleficiis. Et ideo suspendatur. Catalla ejus
loq' de cat' viij. solidi unde vicecomes respondeat.² Comes Marescallus³
x. sol. finem fecit pro terra habenda x. sol. scilicet de dimidia hida terre per plegium Johannis de la Harlatriee, Roberti de Motton', Ricardi de Lond' . . . .

145. ⁴Howel le Marchis quidam latro itinerans et socii sui assultaverunt quendam Caretarium et voluerunt eum robare, ita quod Caretarius occidit ipsum Howell' et versus alios se defendit et evasit de eis. Et quum testatum est quod idem Howel fuit latro, ideo Caretarius est inde quietus. Et sciendum quod ipse est in partes Jerosolyme, set securus reveniat et quietus de morte illa.

Manerium de Suckeleg'.

146. ⁵Juratores dicunt quod Warn' Constabularius de Hanleg' per Rogerum de Clifford' et servientes sui ceperunt Johannem clericum de Suckeleg' tempore pacis dum manerium fuit in manu domini Regis et fregerunt domum suam et catalla sua asportaverunt, et ipsum ligatum abduxerunt in Walliam, et in prisona tenuerunt per unum mensem, et ibi redemptus fuit per octo marcas. Et tres ex illis qui fuerunt in forcia illa capti fuerunt postea in domo ejusdem Johannis, scilicet, Robertus de Stokes, Hugo Place, Nicholaus Forestarius, et inprisonati fuerunt apud Wigorniam. Postea vero misit idem Rogerus apud Suckeleg' Thomam

---

¹ m. 10 d.
² Three or four words are interlined here; the first is *dantur*; the others have not been read.
³ The lord of the fee buys in the king's right to year, day and waste.
⁴ m. 10 d.
⁵ m. 11.

144. Walter Pleader, thief and outlaw, was captured in the house of Frank at Knighton by night as he lay in bed, and Frank was attached to come before the justices. And he comes and defends fellowship with [Walter] and larceny and consent, but confesses that he knew that Walter lay in his house, and that he was an outlaw, and he freely puts himself upon the twelve jurors for good and ill.

The jurors say upon their oath that they think him guilty of the consent and fellowship and of many other crimes. And therefore let him be hanged. His chattels, eight shillings, for which the sheriff must answer. The Earl Marshall made fine with ten shillings for having his land, to wit, one half-hide; pledges for the money, John of . . . Robert of Motton, Richard of London, . . .

145. Howel the Markman, a wandering robber, and his fellows, assaulted a carter, and would have robbed him, but the carter slew Howel and defended himself against the others and escaped. And whereas it is testified that Howel was a robber, let the carter go quit thereof. And note that he is in the parts of Jerusalem, but let him come back safely, quit of that death.

Manor of Suckley.

146. The jurors say that Warner, the constable of Hanley [Castle, put there] by Roger Clifford, and his servants, took John, the clerk of Suckley, in time of peace when the manor was in the king's hands, broke his house, carried off his chattels, and led him away bound into Wales, and kept him a month in prison, whence he was ransomed for eight marks; and three of those who were in that foray were afterwards captured in the house of the said John, to wit, Robert of Stoke, Hugh Place, Nicholas Forester, and were imprisoned at Worcester. Afterwards the said Roger [Clifford] sent Thomas of Kenetton, Hugh of Kinnersley,

de Kenetton', Hugonem de Kinardesleg' et Ricardum Foke, qui attachiaverunt xxiiij. homines de eadem villa ut venirent apud Herefordiam coram domino suo, qui illuc venerunt et retenti fuerunt et non potuerunt deliberari antequam pacassent xlv. marcas in denariis exceptis aliis donis factis militibus suis.

Et Nicholaus, Robertus de Stokes non venerunt et dimissi fuerunt per hos plegios, Willelmum le Curteis, Robertum Ernlly de Savernestoc' et Robertum de Blake, et Ricardum de Cruce, Simonem le Waleis et Osbertum de la *Plested*. Et ideo omnes in misericordia, et Hugo Place suspensus est.

nīe

Et Ricardus Foke et Hugo de Kynardesleg' veniunt et dicunt quod de facto Warneri non possunt ipsi nec volunt respondere. De hoc quod dicunt versus eos, respondent quod revera manerium fuit tunc in manu Rogeri domini sui,[1] et quia homines illi multis modis deliquerunt versus dominum suum, consuluerunt eis ut accederent ad dominum suum apud Hanleg' et impetrarent amorem domini sui, et ipsi tunc venerunt apud Hanleg' et finem fecerunt per xlv. marcas cum domino suo vel plus vel minus, quia nolunt pro domino suo respondere nec de facto suo, set bene defendunt quod ipsi nichil ceperunt.

ad jud'

Et juratores dicunt quod coacti fuerunt venire apud Herefordiam per unum annum post coronationem domini Regis[2] et ibi detenti quousque finem fecerunt.

Dies datus est eis de audiendo judicio suo apud Westmonasterium in Oct. Omn. Sanct. et tunc habeant Hugo et Ricardus warantum suum et unus eorum veniat tantum.

ap. Westm.

Villa Wigornie.

147. [3] De purpresturis dicunt quod Magister Radulfus de Wykewau' edificavit quandam domum super terram domini Regis juxta pottaur de Suthbir'.[4]

---

[1] See Rot. Cl. vol. i. p. 337; on 29 Oct. 1217 the manor of Suckley, which has been seized into the king's hand, is restored to Roger Clifford.

[2] Therefore this was done after the civil war was at an end.

[3] m. 11.

[4] 'The present porcelain works are near to the part of Worcester known as Sidbury, and a Roman

and Richard Foke to Suckley, who attached twenty-four men of the said vill to go to Hereford to their lord's presence, and they came thither and were detained, and could not be delivered until they had paid forty-five marks in coin, let alone other gifts to [Roger's] knights.

And Nicholas and Robert of Stokes have not come, and were bailed to these pledges, namely, William Curteis, Robert Ernly of Severnstoke, Robert Blake, Richard Cross, Simon Welsh, Osbert of Plestead, all of whom are therefore in mercy. And Hugh Place has been hanged.

And Richard Foke and Hugh of Kinnersley come and say that they cannot and will not answer for Warner's acts. But to what is said against themselves, they answer that really the manor was then in the hands of Roger their lord, and because the men [thereof] had offended against their lord in many ways, they counselled them to seek their lord at Hanley and beg his favour, and they came to Hanley and made fine with their lord for forty-five marks, more or less. And [these defendants] will not answer for their lord nor for his acts, but they fully deny that they themselves took anything.

And the jurors say that they were forced to go to Hereford a year after the king's coronation, and were detained there until they made fine.

A day is given them to hear their judgment at Westminster, on the octave of All Saints, and then let Hugh and Richard produce their warrantor, and one only of [the men of Suckley] need come.

Vill of Worcester.

147. As to purprestures [the jurors] say that Master Ralph of Wickwar built a house upon the king's land near the pottery of Sidbury.

Johannes Ruffus eodem modo juxta eandem domum levavit unam domum. Et xij. milites de comitatu et xij. homines infra burgum et xij. de suburbio missi ad domos illas unde testatum est quod levate sunt super feodum Episcopi et non ad nocumentum Burgi.

Postea testatum est quod domus Johannis levata est prope murum ad nocumentum defensionis ville. Et ideo purprestura et Johannes in misericordia et adrecietur [1] sicut debet et solet.

'Postea venerunt milites et alii et dicunt quod uterque domus levata est ad nocumentum ville. Et ideo adrec' sicut esse debet et solet.'

Persona ecclesie S. Suithini fecit purpresturam super dominum Regem juxta ecclesiam {et ideo in misericordia} et videatur.

Persona ecclesie S. Martini eodem modo juxta ecclesiam suam.

'Cives dicunt quod non sunt ad nocumentum ville, et ideo pro anima Regis Johannis [2] remaneant purpresture.'

Item Willelmus de Bruges fecit purpresturam super dominum Regem versus aquam, et ideo in misericordia. [Et est [3]] ad nocumentum ville, et ideo adrecietur per legales homines sicut esse debet et solet. 'Nichil habet.' [4]

Item Robertus *Pride* ultra Sabrinam fecit purpresturam super dominum Regem supra viam, et ideo in misericordia. Eodem modo adrecietur. 'Nichil habet.'

Item Willelmus Ferrator eodem modo ultra viam, et ideo in misericordia. Eodem modo adrecietur. 'Nichil habet.'

Item Adam filius Roberti Wene eodem modo, et ideo in misericordia. Eodem modo adrecietur. Postea dictum est quod pater suus fecit purpresturam et non Adam et ideo misericordia perdonatur.

---

pottery kiln was found there in 1860 ... near the old castle in Sidbury, which with its approaches would belong to the king.' (Information kindly supplied by Mr. H. Firmstone King.)

[1] As to *adreciare* see Glossary.
[2] King John lies buried in the cathedral.
[3] These words are not on the roll.
[4] It is no good amercing those who have nothing.

John Read in the same way built a house next the aforesaid house. And twelve knights of the county and twelve men from within the borough and twelve from the suburb were sent to see the houses, concerning which it is testified that they are built upon the bishop's fee and not to the nuisance of the borough.

Afterwards it is testified that John's house is built against the town wall to the prejudice of the defence of the town. Therefore it is a purpresture and John is in mercy and let it be set to rights as it ought to be and formerly was.

Afterwards come the knights and others and say that both houses are built to the nuisance of the town. And so let it be set to rights as it ought to be and formerly was.

The parson of St. Swithin's has made a purpresture upon the king, near his church, {let him be in mercy} and let it be viewed.

The parson of St. Martin's in the same manner near his church.

The citizens say that these are not to the nuisance of the town, so let the purprestures remain, for the good of King John's soul.

Also William of Bridge has made a purpresture upon the king near the water. So let him be in mercy. And it is to the nuisance of the town, so let it be set to rights by lawful men as it ought to be and formerly was. [William] has no property.

Also Robert Pride across the Severn has made a purpresture upon the king, upon the highway. Therefore be he in mercy and be it set to rights in manner aforesaid. He has no property.

Also William Ironer in the same manner across the road. Therefore be he in mercy and be it set to rights in manner aforesaid. He has nothing.

Also Adam, son of Robert Wene, in the same way. Therefore be he in mercy and be it set to rights in manner aforesaid. Afterwards it was said that it was not Adam, but his father, who made the purpresture, so the amercement is forgiven.

148.   ¹Juratores dicunt quod assisa de latitudine pannorum non est servata sicut provisum fuit. Et ideo loquendum. Misericordia eorum ponitur in respectum usque provisum fuerit quid inde faciendum sit per consilium.

loq'

149.   ²De novis consuetudinibus levatis dicunt quod Prior Hospitalis Jerosolyme in Anglia habet tenentes in villa sua qui ad taillagia domini Regis nolunt auxiliari sicut solent et debent. Et preterea ipsi qui faciunt panem et cervisiam non permittunt se justificari secundum consuetudinem ville quando delinquunt nec eciam volunt vigilare sicut alii ad villam custodiendam. Et ideo preceptum est quod salvo eidem Priori quodam libero hospite³ suo, faciant sicut facere consueverunt et debent et de tallagio et de pane et de cervisia et de aliis rebus.

150.   ⁴Relaxatio hominum de Wich' Priorisse et Conventui de Westwod', scilicet quod burgenses de Wich' relaxaverunt demand' panis et cervisie, ita quod prepositi nec baillivi habebunt aliud mercatum panis aut cervisie quam alius vicinus, ubi prepositi solebant capere v. panes et v. galones cervisie pro j. denario ubi alii solebant capere iiij. illud relaxant. Relaxaverunt similiter dicte Priorisse et hominibus suis quod non capient nec ement piscem nec bladum nec aliam mercandisam ab eis ad levius precium quam alii vicini nisi sit de propria voluntate venditorum. Preterea temptares⁵ cervisie non temptabunt cervisiam super terram Priorisse nisi per unum solum ciphum semel impletum, et si amplius voluerint potare ement de bursa sua propria, et si cervisia sit contra rationem Priorissa habebit emendas. Preterea prepositi nec balliti nec alii de

---

¹ m. 11 d. Entries to the effect that the assize of cloth is not observed are very common.
² m. 11 d.
³ The word is *hospite*, but *hospitio* would be more intelligible.
⁴ m. 11 d. The priory of Westwood was about three miles from Droitwich.
⁵ Corr. *temptatores*.

148. The jurors say that the assize of the breadth of cloths is not observed as has been provided. This must be discussed. Their amercement is respited until what is to be done in this matter shall be provided by the [king's] council.

149. As to the levying of new customs: [the jurors] say that the Prior of the Hospital of St. John in England has tenants in their town, who refuse to give aid towards the king's tallages as they are used and of right ought to do. Moreover, those [of them] who make bread and beer will not suffer themselves to be brought to justice according to the custom of the town when they offend. Nor will [these tenants] take their turn with others in the watch and ward of the town. Therefore it is commanded that as regards tallage and bread and beer and all other matters they do what is due by law and what they have used to do, saving to the Prior a certain free [hospice] of his.

150. This is a release granted by the men of Droitwich to the Prioress and Convent of Westwood, to wit, the burgesses of Droitwich have released the demand for bread and beer, so that the reeves and bailiffs shall have no other right of buying bread and beer than any other neighbour has, whereas the reeves have been wont to take five loaves of bread and five gallons of beer for one penny while other people have had only four; this they release. They have released also to the said Prioress and her men any right of buying fish, corn, or other merchandise from them at a less price than other neighbours pay, unless it be by consent of the vendors. Moreover, their ale-tasters shall not taste beer upon the land of the Prioress save one mug once filled, and if they want to drink more they must buy it out of their own purse; and if the beer be not of the proper quality, the Prioress is to have the mulcts [due from the brewers]. Moreover the reeves, bailiffs, and others of the

villa removebunt stalla ex quo posita fuerint in loco competenti cum mercandisis suis. Preterea homines Priorisse sine licencia alicujus debent cariare compostum suum ubicunque voluerint super terras suas vel super terras aliorum utrum habeant illud de domo sive de emptione. Preterea si dicti homines emerint bladum aut aliam mercandisam ubi ernes dederint nullus inde eos perturbabit, nec a mercandisa sua eos elongabit.[1] Burgenses eciam de Wich' in omnibus concedunt quicquid continetur in carta domini Regis quam Priorissa et Conventus de Westwode penes se habent, que lecta fuit coram justiciariis domini Regis.

151. [2]Isti sunt facti custodes ad placita corone custodienda in villa Wigornie Johannes *Cumin* et Walterus Wilibbye. Et preceptum est eis quod similiter custodiant assisam vini, ita quod si quis vendat vinum contra assisam, scilicet ultra octo[3] denarios de sextaria tam albi quam rubei, quod coronatores illi capiant vinum illud in manum domini Regis et per assisam illud vendant et denarios salvo custodiant in manum suam ad opus domini Regis.

[4]PLACITA DE COMITATU WARREWICI ANNO REGNI REGIS HENRICI QUINTO.

Hundredus de Balrichweie.

152. [5]In hoc comitatu debet Englescheria presentari per duos homines, unum ex parte patris et alium ex parte matris.

---

[1] To eloign (*elongare*) a person from his merchandise means to deprive him of it; to eloign a person from life means to slay him or compass his death.

[2] m. 11 d.

[3] John had attempted to fix the price of the sextary at fourpence for red wine, sixpence for white; but had been obliged to allow the sale of red at sixpence, and white at eightpence. Hoveden, vol iv. p. 99.

[4] Assize Roll 6 M/16 }1.

[5] m. 1. The custom of Gloucestershire required two kinsmen on the father's, one on the mother's side. Pleas of the Crown for Gloucester, p. 1.

town shall not remove the stalls [of the Westwood folk] with their merchandise when they have been erected in a suitable spot. Also the men of the Prioress without licence from anyone may carry their manure whither they shall please, on to either their own lands or the lands of others, and whether it comes from their own houses or has been purchased. Moreover, if the said men shall have bought corn or other merchandise and shall have given earnest, none shall deprive them of their bargain. And the burgesses of Droitwich grant in all points all that is contained in the king's charter which the Prioress and Convent of Westwood have in their possession, and which charter was read before the king's justices.

151. These are appointed keepers of the pleas of the crown in the town of Worcester, namely, John Cumin and William Wiliby. And they are further commanded to keep the assize of wine, so that if anyone sells wine against the assize, to wit, by taking more than eightpence for the sextary whether of white wine or of red, the said coroners shall seize that wine into the king's hand and sell it under the assize and hold the money in their hands to the king's use.

PLEAS OF THE COUNTY OF WARWICK IN THE FIFTH YEAR OF HENRY III. [A.D. 1221].

Hundred of Barlichway.

152. In this county Englishry ought to be presented by two men, one on the side of the father and the other on the side of the mother [of the slain].

158.

{cras}
loq' de catall.

susp'

xxxiiij. sol.
et vj. den.

[1] Agnes que fuit uxor Roberti de Bosco appellat Thomam filium Huberti de morte Roberti viri sui. Et Thomas venit. Et quia ipsa habet virum Robertum de Verdun nomine qui nullum facit appellum, ipsa non habet vocem appellandi, et ideo inquiratur veritas per patriam. Et Thomas defendit mortem set non vult ponere se super patriam. Et xij. juratores dicunt quod culpabilis est de morte illa, et xxiiij. milites alii a predictis xij. ad hoc electi idem dicunt, et ideo suspendatur. Catalla Thome xxxiiij. sol. et vj. den. unde vicecomes resp'.[2]

{ad jud'}

mia

Et juratores testantur quod idem Thomas semper post factum illud venit et rediit ad domum suam et terram suam coluit, et non fuit captus, nec terra sua capta fuit in manum domini Regis nisi pridie contra adventum justiciariorum. Et ideo ad judicium de vicecomite. 'Et villanus fuit et ideo non cap' terra.' Et villata de Spernour' non venit, et ideo in misericordia pro defalta et veniat cras.

ad jud'

Eadem appellavit de vi Henricum filium Huberti, Michaelem prepositum de Spernour', Simonem filium Sacerdotis et Patecoc' filium Simonis de Spernour' et Robertum de Shortenhal'. Et nullus venit, et ipsa secuta fuit ad plures comitatus post mortem viri sui, et non sunt utlagati nec attachiati, et ideo ad judicium de comitatu.

mia

{cras}

xiiij. sol.

Post venit villata de Spernour' et cognovit quod omnes predicti fuerunt manentes in villa sua 'post mortem Roberti' et eos non ceperunt, et ideo in misericordia. Et ipsi omnes appellati de vi fugerunt et fuerunt in franco plegio villate de Spernour', et ideo in misericordia. Catalla Henrici, nulla. Catalla Michaelis xiiij.[3] sol. unde vicecomes resp'. 'Post venit Michael et dat domino Regi j. marcam per sic quod possit invenire plegios standi recto si quis etc. per plegium Johannis Duruassal.'

---

[1] m. 1.
[2] Part of this case has long been known, having been printed together with Case 157 in the notes to Hale's Pleas of the Crown, vol. ii. p. 322. They seem clear instances of a man being tried and hanged though he refused trial. No other cases to the same effect have as yet been found.
[3] This seems the sum fixed after some negotiations represented by corrections on the roll.

153. Agnes, formerly wife of Robert at Wood, appeals Thomas, Hubert's son, of the death of Robert her husband. And Thomas comes. And because she has a husband, Robert of Verdun by name, who makes no appeal, she cannot be heard to make an appeal, so let the truth be inquired by the country. And Thomas defends the death, but will not put himself upon the country. And the twelve jurors say that he is guilty of that death, and twenty-four knights (other than the twelve) chosen for this purpose say the same. Therefore let him be hanged. Thomas's chattels are worth thirty-four shillings and sixpence, for which the sheriff must account.

And the jurors testify that Thomas, after the said deed, constantly went in and out of his house and cultivated his land, and was not arrested, nor was his land taken into the king's hand until just the day before the coming of the justices. Therefore to judgment against the sheriff. Thomas was a villain, so his land is not to be seized.[1] And the township of Spernal does not come, therefore it is in mercy for the default, and let it come to-morrow.

Agnes also appealed as accessories Henry, Hubert's son, Michael, the reeve of Spernal, Simon, the priest's son, Patecoc, son of Simon of Spernal, and Robert of Shortenhall. None of them comes. And she sued at several county courts after her husband's death, and they are not outlawed nor attached. Therefore to judgment against the county.

Afterwards comes the township of Spernal and confesses that all the aforesaid were dwelling in its town after Robert's death, and they did not arrest them. Therefore [the township is] in mercy. All those appealed as accessories fled and were in the frank-pledge of the township of Spernal, therefore [the township is] in mercy. Chattels of Henry: none. Chattels of Michael: fourteen shillings, for which the sheriff must account. Afterwards Michael comes and gives the king one mark that he may find pledges that he will stand to right should any [accuse him]. Pledge [for the mark] John Durvassal.

[1] This clause is a postscript. The sheriff has an excuse for not having seized the land.

154. ¹Alditha de Ippeleg' occidit Sirias virum suum, et capta fuit et imprisonata apud Warrewicum, et evasit de gaola tempore W. de Cantalupo vicecomitis. Et ideo ad judicium de eo. Et fiat de ea sicut de convicta.²

<small>ad jud'</small>

155. ³Robertus de Hal appellavit Hugonem filium Roberti Rodenicht de pace domini Regis et plag', et Hugo captus fuit et liberatus gaole de Warewico tempore W. de Cantilupo vicecomitis, et evasit de gaola et fregit gaolam et fugit. Et ideo ad judicium de evasione, et fiat de Hugone sicut de convicto. Et Robertus appellavit de forcia Gilebertum avunculum ipsius Hugonis et Thomam filium Sweyn, et Edwardum de Fulebroc. Et Thomas obiit et Gilebertus venit, et Robertus non vult sequi versus eum. Et ideo custodiatur. Et similiter retrahit se versus Edwardum. Et juratores non malecredunt eos, et ideo quieti.

<small>ad jud'</small>

<small>custod'</small>

156. ⁴Simon de Cochtan' cecidit mortuus de equo suo in villa de Alencestr' per ebrietatem. Et Simon filius ejus fuit cum eo, et non venit nec fuit attachiatus, et non malecreditur. Et villata de Alencestr' cognovit quod non presentaverunt mortem ejus ad comitatum nec coronatoribus. Et ideo villata in misericordia. Nullus malecreditur. Judicium, infortunium. Et villata de Cochtan' cognovit quod corpus asportatum fuit in villam suam et quod sepultum fuit sine visu servientis vel coronatorum et nichil presentaverunt ad comitatum. Et ideo in misericordia. Precium equi⁵ j. marca unde vicecomes respond'.

<small>mīa</small>

<small>mīa</small>

<small>deo dand'
j. m.</small>

157. ⁶Thomas de la Hethe captus per indictamentum pro furtis et aliis nequitiis 'et pro receptamento' venit et non vult ponere se super patriam.⁷ Et juratores dicunt super

---

¹ m. 1.
² This means that she is to be hanged. Prison breach is treated as equivalent to a confession of guilt. See Bracton, f. 124; Hale, P. C. vol. i. p. 607.
³ m. 1.   ⁴ m. 1 d.   ⁵ The horse is deodand.   ⁶ m. 1 d.
⁷ See above, Case 153.

154. Aldith of Ipsley killed Sirias her husband and was arrested and imprisoned at Warwick and escaped from the gaol when William of Cantilupe was sheriff. Therefore to judgment against him, and let her be treated as one convicted.

155. Robert of Hale appealed Hugh, son of Robert Rodeknight, of the king's peace and of wounds. Hugh was arrested and delivered to the gaol of Warwick when William of Cantilupe was sheriff, and he escaped and broke the gaol and fled; therefore to judgment for the escape, and let Hugh be treated as one convicted. And Robert appealed as accessories Gilbert, Hugh's uncle, and Thomas, Sweyn's son, and Edward of Fulbrook. Thomas is dead. Gilbert comes and Robert will not sue against him; so let [Robert] be in custody; and he likewise withdraws from his suit against Edward. The jurors do not suspect [Gilbert and Edward], so let them go quit.

156. Simon of Coughton fell dead from his horse in the town of Alcester through drunkenness. And Simon his son was with him, and does not come and was not attached and is not suspected. The township of Alcester confesses that they did not present his death at the county [court] nor to the coroners. Therefore the township is in mercy. None is suspected. Judgment: misadventure. The township of Coughton confesses that the body was brought into their town and was buried without the view of the serjeant or the coroners, and they made no presentment at the county [court]. Therefore they are in mercy. The horse's price is one mark, for which the sheriff must account.

157. Thomas of the Heath, taken on an indictment for thefts and other misdeeds and for receipt [of felons], comes and will not put himself upon his country. The jurors say

<small>loq' de catallis</small>

sacramentum suum quod malecredunt eum de receptamento Hobbe Golichtly qui fuit latro cognitus, et postea suspensus fuit apud Caumpeden'. Et de hoc et de aliis furtis ipsum malecredunt. Et xxiiij. milites ad hoc electi dicunt idem quod predicti xij. juratores et quod latro est de omnibus et

<small>susp'</small>

de averiis et de aliis rebus. Et ideo suspendatur.

Hundredus de Kintan'.

158.   [1]Rogerus de Wulward et Engelr' de Berton' occiderunt

<small>utl.</small>

Simonem de Berton'. Et Rogerus fugit, et utlagatus est

<small>cap'</small>

per sectam uxoris Simonis. Et Engelr' captus fuit et imprisonatus, et deliberatus fuit postea.

Et Sibilla que fuit uxor Simonis appellat de forcia illa Engelr' de Berton' quod ipse in pace domini Regis nequiter fuit cum ipso Rogero quando vir suus fuit occisus, ita quod quando Rogerus eum percusserat quadam hachia ita quod cecidit idem Engelr' cepit palefridum suum et abiit super eum, et ipsa hoc vidit et audivit quod per preceptum suum et consilium occisus fuit vir suus, et hoc parata est probare

<small>inferius plegii quinque marc'[2]</small>

sicut curia consideraverit.

Et Elger' venit et defendit pacem domini Regis et feloniam et mortem et consensum et preceptum etc., et dicit quod ipse captus fuit propter mortem illam per appellum ipsius Sibille et imprisonatus, et postea in comitatu Leircestrie coram capitali justiciario per judicium curie domini Regis remansit ipse quietus, et ipsa tunc fuit vidua et remansit in prisona pro falso appello suo, et petit hoc sibi

<small>ad jud'</small>

allocari, et quod ipsa nunc habet virum Robertum de Eselington'. Et ipsa hoc cognoscit, et vir suus non offert probare desicut ipsa non habet vocem appellandi etc. et ideo sine die. Et Engelr' dat v. marc. pro habendo auxilio,[3] et ideo sine die usque ad aliam summonicionem. 'Isti fuerunt plegii Engelr' de v. marcis Willelmus de Parles,

---

[1] m. 2 d.

[2] The names of the pledges for the five marks are written at the bottom of the roll. They are here printed at the end of the case.

[3] Engelram, it seems, buys a respite. The appeal has failed, but he is not acquitted.

upon their oath that they suspect him of the receipt of Hobbe Golightly, who was a known thief and was afterwards hanged at Campden, and of this and of other thefts they suspect him. And twenty-four knights chosen for the purpose say the same as the said twelve jurors, and that he is a thief of all [sorts of] things, both cattle and other things. Therefore let him be hanged.

Hundred of Kington.

158.   Roger of Wulward and Engelram of Barton slew Simon of Barton, and Roger fled and was outlawed at the suit of Simon's wife, and Engelram was taken and imprisoned, and was afterwards delivered.

And Sibil, who was Simon's wife, appeals as accessory to that crime Engelram of Barton, for that he in the king's peace wickedly was with the said Roger when her husband was slain, so that when Roger had struck him [Simon] with an axe so that he fell, the said Engelram took his [Simon's] palfrey and rode off upon it, and she saw this and heard how by his [Engelram's] command and counsel her husband was slain, and this she is ready to prove as the court shall consider.

And Engelram comes and defends the king's peace and the felony, and the death and the consent and the command etc., and says that he was arrested because of that death on the appeal of the said Sibil, and afterwards in the county of Leicester before the chief justiciar by judgment of the king's court he was acquitted, and she (then a widow) was imprisoned for her false appeal, and he craves that this be allowed in his favour, also that she now has a husband, Robert of Eslington. And she admits this and her husband does not offer to prove [the crime]. And whereas she herself cannot be heard as an appellor, therefore let her go without day. And Engelram gives five marks that he may have aid, and so let him go without day until he is again summoned. These are Engelram's pledges for the five marks:

Gaufridus de Cherlecot, H. . . le Notte, Rat' de Berdeston, et Alanus de Berdeston'.'

159. 'Willelmus de Pilardinton', Rogerus et Ricardus de Pilardinton et Iveta uxor ejusdem Ricardi queruntur quod Hugo persona de Pilardinton' et Henricus et Rogerus et Simon fratres sui, et Radulfus de Fonte, et Robertus Carucarius fregerunt domum ipsius [2] et abduxerunt predictam Ivetam et catalla sua asportaverunt ad valenciam c. solidorum, et quod hoc fecerunt nequiter et in pace domini Regis offerunt probare sicut curia consideraverit.

Et Hugo venit et defendit totum sicut clericus, et non vult hic placitare set sine placito vult dicere veritatem. Ipsi Ricardus et Iveta tulerunt breve de assisa nove disseisine versus [eum [3]] coram S. de Segrave [4] et sociis suis, ita quod ipsi per assisam illam recuperaverunt versus eum et reddidit eis duas marcas de dampno, et de hoc eodem facto modo eum appellant.

Et alii appellati non veniunt, et attachiati fuerunt, scilicet, Henricus per Gilebertum et Hugonem de Pilardinton', et Simon [5] per Gaufridum de Pilardinton' et Radulfum Hobbe, et Radulfus per Robertum Hobbe et Willelmum Hobbe, et Robertus per Willelmum filium Tholy de Cumpton' Murdac' et Robertum filium Tholy fratrem ejus. Et ideo omnes in misericordia, et Simon [6] non fuit inventus.

Et villate de Magna Pilardinton' et de alia Pilardinton' [7] et de Merston' et de Etindon' testantur quod Ricardus fuit prepositus et custos per duos annos et eo amplius. Et juratores dicunt quod non fuit ballivus ejus nec custos rerum, et inde convicti sunt, et ideo in misericordia.

Et Hugo cognoscit quod quia noluit reddere compotum suum et quia convicit eum de falsitate et de latrocinio, ideo

---

[1] m. 8.
[2] *ipsius* seems to refer to Richard.
[3] This word is not on the roll.
[4] Afterwards chief justiciar.
[5] Sic.
[6] Sic. But probably instead of *Simon* in one of the two places in which this name occurs in this paragraph we should read *Rogerus*.
[7] These seem the villages now known as Pillerton Hercy and Pillerton Priors. Butler's Marston and Eatington lie near at hand.

William of Parles, Geoffrey of Charlecot, H . . . la Notte, R. of Barston, Alan of Barston.

159. William of Pillerton, Roger and Richard of Pillerton and Iveta, Richard's wife, complain that Hugh the parson of Pillerton and Henry, Roger and Simon his brothers, and Ralph at Well and Robert Ploughman broke his house and abducted the said Iveta and carried off their chattels to the value of 100 shillings; and that they did this wickedly and in the king's peace, they offer to prove as the court shall consider.

And Hugh comes and defends the whole as a clerk, and declines to plead before this court, but without pleading is willing to tell the truth, namely, that Richard and Iveta brought against him a writ for an assize of novel disseisin before S[tephen] of Segrave and his companions and recovered against him in the assize, and he paid them two marks for damages, and it is in respect of the same facts that they now appeal him.

And the other appellees do not come, and they were attached, to wit, Henry by Gilbert and Hugh of Pillerton, and Simon by Geoffrey of Pillerton and Ralph Hobbe, and Ralph by Robert Hobbe and William Hobbe, and Robert by William son of Tholy of Compton Murdaker and Robert son of Tholy his brother. Therefore all are in mercy, and Simon [Roger?] was not found.

And the townships of Great Pillerton, the other Pillerton, Marston and Eatington testify that Richard was [Hugh's] reeve and caretaker for two years and more. And the jurors say that he was not his bailiff nor the caretaker of his property, and [the jurors] are convicted of this [false statement] and therefore in mercy.

And Hugh confesses that because [Richard] would not render his account and because [Hugh] convicted [Richard] of falsehood and larceny, therefore he distrained them

distrinxit eos per domum suam et per catalla sua, sine
hoc quod aliquid inde caperent.

    ¹ 'Et quia iiij. villate subscripte testantur quod Ricardus
fuit custos rerum ipsius Hugonis, et quod noluit reddere
compotum suum, et preterea dicunt quod idem Hugo vel
custod'   alii appellati nichil ceperunt de catallis predictis, et preterea
nīc   de eodem facto fuit assisa capta et dampnum datum, consideratum est quod nullum est appellum inter eos. Et
nichil habuit ideo Hugo et alii inde quieti et Willelmus et alii appellantes in misericordia pro falso appello.'

160.   ²Beatricia que fuit uxor Henrici de Cumpton' appellavit Nicholaum le Bigot de morte Henrici viri sui. Et
Nicholaus captus fuit et liberatus Roberto de Wighelby
Officiali Archidiaconi Convintrensis et Abbati Leircestrie ex
parte Episcopi Convintrensis ut eum haberent coram justiciariis etc. Et coronatores et comitatus recordantur quod
idem Abbas cepit in manum coram pleno comitatu habendi
eum coram justiciariis sub pena centum marcarum. Et
eum non habuit, et ideo ad judicium de Abbate. Et similiter
ad jud'   recordantur quod Officiales Episcopi tunc presentes fuerunt
quando ita liberatus fuit et eum petierunt ex parte Episcopi.
{oras}   'Post venit Nicholaus et Ricardus de Staunleg' Decanus
Archidiaconi Convintrensis petiit curiam cristianitatis loco
Episcopi, et habet, et commissus est ei ut purget se etc.'
Et juratores testantur quod occidit eum in hostio ecclesie
quodam cnipulo.

    Villata de Warewico.

161.   ³Willelmus Mayn' occidit Jacobum le Marchaunt et
abjur'   fugit in ecclesiam, et cognovit mortem, et abjuravit regnum.

---

¹ This is a postscript inserted in the middle of the matter which is here printed before it, so that the *villate subscripte* are the four townships which are here named *above*.
² m. 8.
³ m. 8.

[the appellors] by their house and their chattels, but without taking anything thence.

And because the four townships mentioned above testify that Richard was the caretaker of Hugh's property, and would not render his account, and also say that Hugh and the other appellees carried off none of the said chattels, and besides an assize was taken, and damages were given, it is considered that the appeal between them is null. Therefore Hugh and the other [appellees] are acquitted, and William and the other appellors are in mercy for a false appeal.

160. Beatrice, formerly wife of Henry of Compton, appealed Nicholas the Bigot of the death of Henry, her husband. Nicholas was taken and delivered to Robert of Wighelby, the Archdeacon of Coventry's Official, and the Abbot of Leicester on behalf of the Bishop of Coventry, that they might produce him before the justices etc. The coroners and the county record that the Abbot undertook in full county [court] to have him before the justices under penalty of 100 marks. And he has not produced him. Therefore to judgment against the Abbot. They likewise record that the Bishop's Officials were then present when he was so delivered, and claimed him on the Bishop's behalf. Afterwards Nicholas comes, and Richard of Stanley, the Archdeacon of Coventry's Dean, has demanded [cognizance of the case for] the Court Christian on the Bishop's behalf. And this is granted him, and [Nicholas] is committed to him that he may make his purgation etc. And the jurors testify that [Nicholas] killed [Henry] in the church porch with a knife.

Township of Warwick.

161. William Maynard killed Jacob the Merchant and fled to church, confessed the death, and abjured the realm. His

Catalla ejus v. sol. unde vicecomes resp', et similiter de xvij. sol. de precio terre ejusdem Willelmi de termino domini Regis, et reddatur Comiti feodum suum. Et Willelmus non fuit in franco plegio, immo manens in suburbio Warewici extra francum plegium, et ideo in misericordia.

Editha uxor ejusdem Jacobi appellat de morte ejusdem Jacobi viri sui Ketellum de Warewico quod ipse cum vi sua et mainpastu suo fregit domum suam et ipsum Jacobum virum suum cepit de nocte et abduxit eum ad domum Johannis Coci et ibi tenuit eum in prisona 'et in pace domini Regis et in felonia,' et ita eum 'percussit cum pede suo'[1] quod in prisona illa obiit, et hoc offert probare versus eum prout curia consideraverit.

Et Ketellus venit et defendit pacem domini Regis etc. et feloniam et mortem et totum etc., et petit sibi allocari quod predictus Willelmus Maynard per fugam suam in ecclesiam et per appellum et per sectam ipsius Edithe cognovit mortem et abjuravit regnum, et quod ipsa nullum clamorem de eo fecit quando hoc factum fuit, nisi ad secundum vel tercium comitatum, et ponit se super patriam, et dat v. marcas pro habendo veredicto.

Et omnes juratores tam de villa quam de hundredo dicunt precise quod Ketellus non est culpabilis, nec percussit eum, nec aliquis ex parte sua, nec aliquod malum ei fecit, nisi tantum quod precepit eum *prius* attachiari pro quadam melleta que fuit inter eum et predictum Willelmum qui eum occidit. Et comitatus recordatur quod ad secundum comitatum post factum fecit ipsa appellum suum, set nichil dixit de ictu cum pede. Et ideo consideratum est quod nullum est appellum, et ideo ipse inde quietus et Editha custodiatur.

Villata de Tamewurthe per septem juratores.

162. [2]Willelmus Goman de Munewurth' et Ricardus Prepositus de Sutton' rettati de latrocinio et receptamento

---

[1] Substituted for *rerberavit*.   [2] m. 4 d.

chattels were five shillings, for which the sheriff must account, as also for seventeen shillings, the price of William's land for the king's term [year and day], and let the fief be given back to the Earl [of Warwick, William's lord]. William was not in frank-pledge, but dwelt in the suburb of Warwick out of frank-pledge, so [the township is] in mercy.

Edith, Jacob's wife, appeals of the death of Jacob, her husband, Ketel of Warwick, for that he with his force and his mainpast [retainers] broke her house, and took off Jacob her husband by night, and led him to the house of John Cook and there held him in prison, and in the king's peace and in felony, and so struck him with his foot that he died in the said prison; and this she offers to prove against him as the court shall consider.

And Ketel comes and defends the king's peace etc., felony, death, and all etc., and craves that it be allowed in his favour that the said William Maynard by his flight to church and on the appeal and suit of Edith confessed the death and abjured the realm, and that she raised no cry against him [Ketel] when this was done, or not until the second or third county [court]; and he puts himself on his country and gives five marks to have a verdict.

All the jurors both of the town and of the hundred say in so many words that Ketel is not guilty, and did not strike him, nor did anyone on his behalf, nor do him any harm, save only that on a former occasion [Ketel] ordered [Jacob] to be attached because of a squabble between [Jacob] and William who slew him [Jacob]. And the county records that at the second county [court] after the deed, she [Edith] made her appeal and said nought of the kick. Therefore, it is considered that the appeal is null, so let him be quit of it, and Edith be in custody.

Township of Tamworth [represented] by seven jurors.

162. William Goman of Moneyworth and Richard the Reeve of Sutton, accused of larceny and receipt [of felons], come

veniunt et defendunt totum et ponunt se super patriam. Juratores dicunt quod non malecredunt Willelmum Goma' de aliquo malo. Et ideo ipse sit sub plegiis. Vicecomes capiat plegios. De Ricardo dicunt quod ipse receptavit Herebertum fratrem suum et Thomam filium Hereberti qui fugitivi sunt pro depredacione carete robate. Et quia non sunt utlagati et adhuc poterunt venire ad pacem Regis, nec malecreditus est de aliis latrociniis, vicecomes capiat ab eo salvos plegios standi recto.

vic' cap' pl'

Johannes Kynebaut rettatus de eodem venit et ponit se super patriam. Juratores dicunt quod culpabilis est, scilicet, de receptamento Willelmi de Hanekesford' qui latro est de comitatu Leircestrie, ita quod idem Willelmus ducit boves et latrocinia et equos et hujusmodi de comitatu Leircestrie ad domum Johannis, et Johannes eodem modo ad domum Willelmi.

Villata de Scistok'
Villata de Withacr' Jordani
Villata de Baxterleye
Villata de Withacr' Radulfi
} dicunt quod nichil sciunt de eo nisi bonum neque de receptamento Willelmi de Hanekesford' nec de aliquo latrocinio.

Et ideo sit sub plegiis et vicecomes capiat plegios ab eo.

Hundredus de Knichtelawe.

163. [1]Radulfus de Suham appellavit Rogerum Heyrun et Willelmum fratrem ejus et Adam Sumon*o*nitorem[2] de pace etc. et de combustione domus et averiorum Prioris de Coventria etc. Et Radulfus non est prosecutus. Et ideo plegii sui de prosequendo in misericordia, scilicet, Henricus de Sakebrich'.[3] 'Et Willelmus et Adam malecreduntur et ideo exigantur et utlagentur etc.'

mīa

exig'
{jam}

Et Willelmus de Lutreworthe appellavit eosdem de roberia et de eadem combustione etc., et non venit. Et ideo plegii sui de prosequendo in misericordia, scilicet,

mīe

[1] m. 4 d. [2] Corr. *Summonitorem.*
[3] The name of some other pledge seems missing.

and defend all of it, and put themselves on their country. The jurors say that they do not suspect William Goman of any ill. So let him be under pledges; the sheriff is to take the pledges. Of Richard they say that he received Herbert his brother, and Thomas, Herbert's son, who are in flight for depredating from a cart which was robbed. And since they are not outlawed, and may yet come in to the king's peace, and Richard is not suspected of other thefts, let the sheriff take safe pledges from him that he will stand to right.

John Kynebaut, accused of the same, comes and puts himself on his country. The jurors say that he is guilty, to wit, of receiving William of Hanksford, a known robber of Leicestershire, so that William brings oxen and horses, and other stolen things of that sort, from Leicestershire to John's house, and John in the same way to William's house.

The township of Shustoke			say that they know nought of him but good, neither as to the receipt of William of Hanksford nor of any larceny.
,,	,,	,, Whitacre Jordan	
,,	,,	,, Baxterley	
,,	,,	,, Whitacre Ralph	

So let him be under pledges, and let the sheriff take pledges from him.

Hundred of Knightlow.

163.   Ralph of Southam appealed Roger Heyrun and William, his brother, and Adam Summoner, of the peace etc., and the burning of the house and cattle of the Prior of Coventry etc. And Ralph does not prosecute, and so his pledges to prosecute are in mercy, namely, Henry of Sawbridge. And William and Adam are suspected, so let them be exacted and outlawed.

And William of Lutterworth appealed the same men of robbery and the said arson, &c., and does not come; so his pledges to prosecute are in mercy, namely, Henry of Southam

Henricus de Suham et Robertus de Fougeres. Et Rogerus Heirun venit et defendit totum et ponit se super patriam, et alii non fuerunt inventi.

'Juratores dicunt quod Rogerus non est culpabilis de facto, et ideo inde quietus,[1] et alii duo malecreduntur et ideo exigantur.'

Villata de Suham[2]

Villata de Neunham dicit quod Rogerus Heyrun pacem fecit cum Radulfo de Suham appellatore qui eum appellavit, et bene sciunt quod predicti Willelmus et Adam istam combustionem fecerunt, et malecredunt eos quia retraxerunt se, et melius credunt quod Rogerus fuit cum eis ad hoc factum faciendum quam non.

Villata de Stratton' idem in eodem dicunt quod superius dictum est.

Villata de Wlericheston'

Villata de Longa Lalleford' dicit quod non malecredunt ipsum Rogerum, set malecredunt ipsos Willelmum et Adam.

'Postea dixerunt omnes quod ipsum Rogerum credunt esse culpabilem de facto illo simul cum aliis.'

Rogerus dat xxx. marcas pro habendo auxilio per plegium Henrici de Rockeby, Rogeri de Craft, Roberti filii Odonis, Rogeri de Waur, Willelmi filii Josce, Johannis Hairun, Willelmi de Waur de Lalleford', Joie de Lalleford', et Willelmi Paumeri de Lalleford'.

164. [3]Ricardus filius Johannis appellat Gaufridum de Shireford' quod ipse cum vi sua die Sabbati in vigilia S. Crucis sicut jacuit in domo sua apud Sowe languore qui ei adjudicatus fuit per iiij. milites de comitatu ad eum missos [4]

---

[1] This case has so many postscripts that it is rather hard to see what happened; but apparently, the jurors having spoken in Roger's favour, he was at first acquitted; afterwards, however, the townships were consulted and declared him guilty, and perhaps the jurors also declared him guilty (notice the word *omnes* below); in the end he purchased 'aid,' which seems to mean a respite, time to consult with his friends and prepare a defence.

[2] Perhaps the townships of Southam and Woolston knew nothing and said nothing.

[3] m. 5.

[4] When a person excuses his non-appearance in court on the ground that he is ill in bed, four knights are

and Robert of Fougeres. And Roger Heyrun comes and defends the whole, and puts himself on the country, and the other [appellees] have not been found.

The jurors say that Roger is not guilty of the deed, and therefore he is acquitted of it, and the other two are suspected, so let them be exacted.

The township of Southam

The township of Newnham says that Roger Heyrun made a compromise with Ralph of Southam, the appellor who appealed him, and they well know that the said William and Adam committed this arson, and suspect them because they withdrew themselves, and they are inclined to believe that Roger was with them at the doing of the deed, rather than that he was not.

The township of Stretton says the same as is said above in the same words.

The township of Woolston

The township of Long Lawford says that they do not suspect Roger, but suspect William and Adam.

Afterwards all said that they believe that Roger was guilty of the deed along with the others.

Roger gives thirty marks that he may have aid, on the pledge of Henry of Rokeby, Roger of Craft, Robert, Odo's son, Roger of Waure, William, son of Josce, John Heyrun, William of Waure of Lawford, Joias of Lawford, and William Palmer of Lawford.

164. Richard, John's son, appeals Geoffrey of Shireford, for that on Saturday, the eve of Holy Cross, as [Richard] lay in his house at Sowe in a sickness, which was adjudged to him [as an essoin] in an action, by four knights of the

per judicium comitatus pro quodam placito, venit ipse et intrusit domum suam super eum et nequiter et in felonia et in assultu premeditato eum assultavit et verberavit et turpiter tractavit, et cum Emma uxor sua audiret tumultum, venit de orto suo et invenit ipsum Gaufridum cum vi sua ita verberantem dominum suum, et statim exivit et levavit clamorem et uthesium. Quo audito, idem Gaufridus exivit et in felonia vulneravit ipsam Emmam uxorem suam in capite 'sicut ipsa ei auxiliari et succurrere voluit,' et in roberia ei abstulit de denariis suis dimidiam marcam, et quod hoc fecit nequiter et in felonia et in pace domini Regis, offert disracionare per corpus suum prout curia consideraverit.

Et Gaufridus venit et defendit pacem etc. et feloniam et roberiam et totum etc., set verum vult dicere. Dicit quod revera idem Ricardus habuit languorem per judicium comitatus per iiij. milites sicut idem Ricardus dicit, et quia[1] dictum fuit ei quod idem Ricardus exivit cotidie de domo sua et ivit ad carucam suam et ad alia negotia sua facienda, ipse per consilium amicorum suorum venit in campis et invenit eum in bladis suis in campis, et levavit clamorem super eum et voluit eum capere, set homines Prioris de Covintria de eadem villa ipsum Ricardum ei abstulerunt, et predicta Emma supervenit et levavit clamorem, et quidam
{ad jud'} Alexander Capellanus qui interfuit impulsit eam quod cecidit super unam petram et ibi recepit plagam etc.[2] Et ideo
{custod'} custod'. 'Et quesitus si plus dicere velit, dicit quod defendit plagam et feloniam et roberiam dimidie marce et totum sicut curia consideraverit.'

'Et quia comitatus et coronatores testantur quod secta rationabiliter facta est, et idem Gaufridus non cognovit pla-
{cras} gam nec roberiam,[3] consideratum est quod duellum sit

---

sent to see whether he is really ill, and if so, they report that he is entitled to his essoin, and the case is adjourned for year and day.

[1] A person who has essoined himself as being ill in bed is bound to remain in bed. As to Geoffrey's proceedings, see Bracton, f. 858.

[2] No stop in MS. Geoffrey is to be kept in custody while the court is deliberating on his plea.

[3] It seems hardly too technical to say that since Geoffrey does not confess anything, his special plea is overruled as being tantamount to the general issue.

county sent to him by judgment of the county [court], Geoffrey with his force came and intruded into his house against him, and wickedly and in felony and premeditated assault, assaulted, and beat, and ill-treated him; and when Emma his wife heard the tumult, she came from her garden and found Geoffrey with his force thus beating her lord, and at once went out and raised hue and cry; hearing which, Geoffrey went out, and in felony wounded Emma his [Richard's] wife in the head as she was endeavouring to aid and succour him, and in robbery took from him a half-mark of his money; and that this he did wickedly and in felony and in the king's peace, he offers to deraign by his body as the court shall consider.

And Geoffrey comes and defends the peace etc. and the felony and robbery and all of it etc., but desires to speak the truth. He says that in truth Richard was adjudged sick by the judgment of the county by the four knights, as Richard says, and because it was told to [Geoffrey] that Richard was daily leaving his house and going to his plough and his other business, he, by his friends' counsel, came to the fields, and found Richard among his crops in the fields, and raised the cry against him and would have captured him, but the Prior of Coventry's men of that township took Richard from him, and then Emma came up and raised the cry, and one Alexander the Chaplain who was there gave her a push so that she fell upon a stone and thus got the wound etc. Therefore let [Geoffrey] be in custody. And being asked whether he will say more, he says that he defends the wound and the felony and the robbery of the half-mark and all of it as the court shall consider.

And because the county and coroners testify that the suit is duly made, and Geoffrey does not confess the wound nor the robbery, it is considered that there be battle between

inter eos, et Gaufridus det vadium defendendi se et Ricardus probandi.'

Simon frater Alexandri Capellani appellatus de vi venit. Et vicecomes capiat plegios de eo.

Et Thomas de Burbech' et Johannes filius *Gama'* appellati de forcia illa non venerunt.

{duellum} Plegii¹ Gaufridi, Thomas de Shireford', Wakelinus de Shireford', Radulfus Araby, Simon filius Unfridi de Burchton', Robertus filius Godrici de Burton', Robertus prepositus de Burton', Gaufridus de Staverton' de Burton' et Robertus de Shireford'.

Plegii Ricardi, Rogerus Bagot, Jollanus de Sowe, Willelmus Forestar' de Sowe, Reginaldus prepositus de Sowe, Simon de Sowe, et Willelmus filius Gervasii.

{ap' Lich'} Dies datus est eis apud Lichefeld' die Martis in crastino S. Luce Evangeliste,² et tunc veniant armati.

'Ad diem illum percussum est duellum, et Ricardus victus est, et ideo Gaufridus inde quietus et Ricardus custodiatur.'

165.   ³Ricardus Rodknicht de Ichinton' appella Ricardum filium Widonis quod nequiter et in pace domini Regis per denarios suos et per purchacium suum fecit comburere domus suas, et hoc offert probare versus eum sicut homo majoris etatis prout curia consideraverit.

Et Ricardus venit et defendit feloniam et combustionem et totum de verbo in verbum et dicit quod idem Ricardus Rodcnicht apposuit ignem, et inde ponit se super jur'.⁴ 'Et juratores dicunt quod domus combusta fuit de igne proprio per filium suum et non per Ricardum filium Guidonis. Et quia in comitatu appellavit eum quod ipse combussit domum etc. et nunc appellat eum quod fecit eam comburere, consideratum est quod nullum est appellum {et ideo custod' {custod'} pro falso⁵ et Ric' custod'}.'
perdon'

¹ Pledges that the parties will fight.
² St. Luke is Oct. 18.
³ m. 5 d.
⁴ Probably *juratores*; perhaps *juratam*.
⁵ Supply *appello*. But this phrase is struck out, and the margin shows that the appellor was pardoned.

them, and let Geoffrey give gage for defence, and Richard for proof.

Simon, brother of Alexander the Chaplain, appealed as an accessory, comes. Let the sheriff take pledges from him.

And Thomas of Burbeck and John Gaman's son, appealed as accessories, do not come.

Geoffrey's pledges, Thomas of Shireford, Wakelin of Shireford, Ralph Araby, Simon, son of Humfrey of Bourton, Robert, son of Godric of Bourton, Robert the Reeve of Bourton, Geoffrey Staverton of Bourton, and Robert of Shireford.

Richard's pledges, Roger Bagot, Jollan of Sowe, William Forester of Sowe, Reginald the Reeve of Sowe, Simon of Sowe, and William, son of Gervase.

A day is given them at Lichfield, on Tuesday the morrow of St. Luke the Evangelist, and then let them come armed.

On that day the duel is fought and Richard is vanquished, and so let Geoffrey be quit thereof, and Richard be in custody.

165. Richard Rodeknight of Itchington, appeals Richard, Guy's son, that wickedly and in the king's peace, by his money and procurement, he caused the burning of his house; and this he offers to prove against him as one who is past fighting age, as the court shall consider.

And Richard comes and defends the felony and burning, and all of it word by word, and says that Richard Rodeknight set fire to his own house, and of this puts himself on the jurors. The jurors say that the house was burnt by [the appellor's] own fire by his son, and not by Richard, Guy's son. And because in the county [court] the appellor appealed the appellee of having himself burnt the house, and now appeals him of having procured the burning, it is considered that the appeal is null.

Idem Ricardus appellat Willelmum le Noreis quod ipse in pace domini Regis nequiter et in felonia et in hamsokne venit in domum suam et eum verberavit et turpiter tractavit quod noluit ita verberari pro centum solidis, et eum cepit et imprisonavit et in prisona tenuit in ferro et in ceppo per duos dies, et hoc offert etc. sicut prius.

Et Willelmus venit et defendit feloniam et pacem domini Regis etc. et totum de verbo in verbum, et dicit quod idem Ricardus inventus fuit metens bladum Episcopi[1] de nocte, et servientes sui eum ceperunt cum toto blado et adduxerunt ad curiam Episcopi, et quam cito ipse venit domi eum statim deliberavit per pleg', et inde se ponit super jur'.

Et dicit predictus Ricardus quod idem Willelmus injuste cepit oves suas et fecit eas tondere dum illas tenuit in namio.

xx. sol. Et vicecomes testatur quod hoc verum est, et quod idem Willelmus reddidit lanam illam servienti suo qui illam adhuc habet. Et Willelmus non potuit hoc dedicere. Willelmus convictus est similiter de predicto imprisonamento, et quod

{custod'} idem Ricardus fuit in firgiis et in ceppo. Et ideo custodiatur. Finem fecit per xx. sol. per plegium Willelmi Bal*raue*' et Nicholai Bel*raie*' et Petri filii Johannis.

Villata de Covintria.

166.   [2]Margeria filia Ailrici appellat Reginaldum filium Aunfridi de Covintria quod ipse in pace domini Regis in vigilia S. Pauli eam rapuit, et hoc offert disracionare versus eum sicut curia consideraverit.

j. marc. Et Reginaldus venit et defendit pacem domini Regis et rapum et totum sicut curia consideraverit, et ponit se super veredictum et de bono et de malo et dat domino Regi j. marcam pro habendo inde veredictum per plegium Walteri de Covintria. Juratores dicunt quod ipse non est culpabilis de rapo quia ipse eam prius habuit per magnum tempus ad

---

[1] Apparently William is the steward or bailiff of the bishop of Coventry.
[2] m. 6.

The same Richard appeals William le Noreis, that he in the king's peace wickedly and in felony and in hamsoken came to his house and beat him and ill-treated him, so that he would not willingly have been so beaten for a hundred shillings, and took and imprisoned and in prison held him for two days in irons and in the stocks; and this he offers to prove etc. as above.

And William comes and defends the felony and the king's peace etc. and all of it word by word, and says that Richard was found reaping the Bishop's crops by night, and his [William's?] servants took him with all the corn, and brought him to the Bishop's court, and so soon as he [William] came home he straightway set him free on bail, and of this he puts himself upon the jurors.

And Richard says that William unjustly took his sheep and caused them to be sheared while he held them in distress. And the sheriff testifies that this is true and that William handed over the wool to his [the sheriff's] serjeant, who still has it. And William could not deny this. William is also convicted of the aforesaid imprisonment, and of having kept Richard in fetters and in the stocks. Therefore let him be in custody. He made fine with twenty shillings, for which William Balraven, Nicholas Balraven, and Peter, John's son, are pledges.

Township of Coventry.

166. Margery, daughter of Ælfric, appeals Reginald, son of Aunfrey of Coventry, for that in the king's peace on the vigil of St. Paul he raped her; and this she offers to deraign against him as the court shall consider.

And Reginald comes and defends the king's peace and the rape and all of it as the court shall consider, and puts himself upon a verdict for good and ill, and gives the king one mark that he may have a verdict, for which mark Walter of Coventry is pledge. The jurors says that he is not guilty of rape, because a long time before this he had

voluntatem suam, et postea per duos annos [1] in domo patris sui, et dicunt quod nullus clamor levatus fuit. Et ideo consideratum est quod ipse eat inde quietus, et ipsa in misericordia pro falso appello. Custodiatur.

{custod'}

[2] PLACITA APUD SALOPIAM ANNO REGNI REGIS HENRICI SEXTO.

Hundredus de Pehenhull'.

167. [3] Thomas Wabode serviens cepit mercedem a quibusdam pro vaccis eorum dimittendis ne caperentur ad opus domini Regis. Et ideo in misericordia.

mīa

Idem Thomas et alii bedelli faciunt tabernas et distringunt homines ad veniendum ad cervisiam suam. Et ideo in misericordia, et prohibitum est eis ne de cetero ita faciant cervisiam.[4]

mīa

168. [5] Item de consuetudinibus levatis dicunt quod Hugo Puintulf[6] posuit servientes ad voluntatem suam pro patria custodienda, et adhuc sunt in comitatu xij. vel plus qui penitus vivunt de hominibus patrie. Et milites de comitatu dicunt quod comitatus emendaretur ad opus domini Regis si amoverentur. Et testatum est quod Hugo primo apposuit eos pro terra sua custodienda, et postea attornavit ad comitatum custodiendum.

loq'

---

[1] Apparently this means, not *and afterwards for two years*, but *and two years afterwards*; such a use of *per* is not uncommon.

[2] Assize roll, 5 M⎫
         8 ⎬ 1.
            ⎭

[3] m. 8.

[4] Local officers seem to have indulged in the practice of making 'scot-ales,' i.e. of brewing beer and compelling the neighbours to come and drink, or at least pay for, it. See Bracton, f. 117 b; the learning as to scot-ales will be found in Stubbs, Const. Hist. § 165, and Hale, Doomsday of St. Pauls, p. cvii.

[5] m. 8.

[6] Hugh Pauntulf was sheriff at the end of Henry II.'s reign; so this is an old grievance.

[7] It appears from Rot. Cl. vol. i. pp. 422, 589 b, that in 1220 the men of Staffordshire paid 200 marks to be rid of these serjeants: the king's council, however, refused the demand; but in 1224 their removal was at last ordered. The *loquendum* in the margin means that this matter must be brought before the royal council.

her of her own free will, and again two years afterwards in the house of her father, and they say that no cry was raised. And so it is considered that he go thence quit, and she be in mercy for her false appeal. Let her be in custody.

PLEAS AT SHREWSBURY IN THE SIXTH YEAR OF HENRY III. [A.D. 1221].

Hundred of Pimhill.

167. Thomas Wabode the serjeant took money from certain persons for excusing them from having their cows taken to the king's use. Therefore he is in mercy.

The said Thomas and other bedells set up taverns and distrain people to come to their ale. Therefore they are in mercy and they are enjoined not to make such ales for the future.

168. Also as to customs levied, [the jurors] say that Hugh Pauntulf instituted serjeants to guard the country under his orders, and there are still twelve or more such serjeants in the county, who just live on the men of the country. And the knights of the county say that the [state of the] county would be bettered to the king's profit, if these serjeants were removed. And it is testified that Hugh in the first instance appointed them to guard his own land and afterwards set them to guard the county.

Hundredus de Bradeford'.

169.   [1] Osbertus Brun et Petrus le Nedler' et Alicia de Harstan capti cum panno veniunt. Et testatum est quod Alicia et Petrus abjuraverunt terram in comitatu Gloucestrie coram Radulfo Musard' [2] vicecomite qui hoc idem recordatur, et plures alii hoc idem dicunt. Et ballivi domini Regis et milites et alii testantur quod Osbertus inventus fuit seisitus de panno furato, et Petrus cum eo et quidam Flentarius qui abjuravit terram, et ideo [3]

Hundredus de Cunedour'.

170.   [4] Willelmus filius Odonis de Kenleia et Henricus filius Rogeri le Hare capti per indictamentum xij. veniunt. Et Willelmus de quo dictum fuit quod caro unius vacce furate inventa fuit in domo sua forinseca, dicit quod apposita fuit in domo sua in odium ejus, et per Warnerum de Wililega dominum suum qui captat terram suam quam tenet de eo libere.

Et juratores [5] dicunt precise quod Willelmus legalis homo est, et quod non est culpabilis de vacca illa, set posita fuit in odium ejus in domo sua et ad exheredationem ejus pro quadam terra sua quam tenet de predicto Warnero, et quod per uxorem ejusdem Warneri captus fuit. Et hoc idem dicit serviens domini Regis qui eum cepit, et dicit quod uxor Warneri mandavit eum, et quod ipsa ei dixit qualiter invenire potuit carnem in domo illa scil. in grangia exteriori longe a curia ipsius Willelmi, et monstravit ei ubi et quando ipsum Willelmum capere potuit. Et ideo consideratum est quod Willelmus eat inde quietus et Warnerus

---

[1] m. 8 d.

[2] He is sheriff of Gloucestershire, and also is one of the justices commissioned for this Shropshire eyre.

[3] Doubtless Osbert is to be hanged. Other cases have been noticed in which the fatal word *suspendatur* is left unwritten. Perhaps the scribe was an ordained clerk, and therefore bound by canon law not to take any part in a judgment of blood.

[4] m. 8 d.

[5] Probably the same jurors who indicted William. They were seemingly bound to indict if an accusation had been made, even though they disbelieved the charge.

Hundred of Bradford.

169.   Osbert Brown and Peter the Needler and Alice of Harston, who were taken with [stolen] cloth, come. And it is testified that Alice and Peter abjured the realm in the county of Gloucester before Ralph Musard the Sheriff, who records the same fact; and many others say the same. And the king's bailiffs and the knights and others testify that Osbert was found seised of stolen cloth, and Peter with him, and one Flentar, who has abjured the realm; and therefore [let them be hanged].

Hundred of Condover.

170.   William, son of Odo of Kenley, and Henry, son of Roger Hare, taken on the indictment of [the] twelve [jurors], come. And William, of whom it was said that the flesh of a stolen cow was found in his outhouse, says that it was put in his house to spite him by Warner of Willey his lord, who is grasping at [William's] land which he holds freely of [Warner].

And the jurors say in so many words that William is a lawful man, and is not guilty of the cow, but it was put in his house to spite him and to disinherit him because of certain land, which he holds of Warner, and that he was taken at the instance of Warner's wife. And the king's serjeant who took him, says the same, and says that Warner's wife sent for him and told him how he would find the flesh in the said house, in an outer barn far from William's court-yard, and showed him where and when he might take William. And so it is considered that William do go quit thereof, and that Warner be taken; he is com-

{custod'} capiatur et committitur gaole. Et Henricus non male creditur, et ideo quietus.

{custod'} Et Mauricius de Alrigg' serviens cepit averia ipsius Willelmi et ea vendidit et *vastavit* et ideo custodiatur in gaola. 'Postea commissus est Willelmo de Bassecherche', Willelmo Burnel, J. . . . de Eton'.' 'Warnerus finem fecit per v. marcas.'

Hundredus de Musselawe.

171. [1]Rogerus de Prestehop' occidit Johannem de Patinton'. Et Rogerus venit et profert literas J. Regis patentes in quibus continetur quod ipse perdonavit ei mortem ejusdem Johannis unde Juliana uxor ejusdem Johannis et Herebertus frater ejus eum appellaverunt, unde vult quod firmam pacem inde habeat, ita quod stet recto si quis versus eum loqui voluerit, et in hujus rei etc. Et quia nullus sequitur versus eum, eat inde sine die et quietus quantum ad dominum Regem pertinet. Et sciendum quod non fuit utlagatus.

Villata de Bruges cum Hundredo.

172. [2]Andreas filius Willelmi appellavit Willelmum de Ingwarthi' de roberia, et ambo mortui sunt, et juratores dicunt quod duellum vadiatum fuit inter eos de roberia in comitatu per judicium comitatus. Et ideo comitatus faciat recordum.

{cras} 'Et comitatus recordatur quod revera idem Andreas aliquando appellavit in comitatu predictum Willelmum in comitatu, et cum mencio fieret de pace domini Regis, attachiata fuit loquela usque in adventum justiciariorum, set bene defendunt quod nunquam fuit duellum vadiatum.

{ad jud'} Et ideo ad judicium.' 'Juratores in misericordia.'[3]

---

[1] m. 9.
[2] m. 9 d.
[3] The jurors have falsely charged the county court with having taken on itself to award trial by battle in a case which was beyond its competence, since the king's peace had been mentioned; whereas really the county court did its duty and attached the parties to appear before the king's justices.

mitted to gaol. And Henry is not suspected and therefore is quit.

And Maurice of Aldridge, the serjeant, took William's beasts and sold and wasted them, and so let him be kept in gaol. Afterwards he is committed to William of Baschurch, William Burnel, J . . . . . of Eaton. Warner made fine with five marks.

Hundred of Munslow.

171.   Roger of Presthope killed John of Patinton. And Roger came and proffered letters patent of King John, wherein is contained that he has pardoned the death of the said John, whereof Juliana, John's wife, and Herbert his brother have appealed him, wherefore he [the king] wills that he should have sure peace thereof, so that he may abide judgment if any shall wish to accuse him of it, In [witness] whereof etc. And for that no one sues against him, let him go without day and quit so far as concerns the king. And be it known that he was not outlawed.

Township of Bridgnorth with the Hundred.

172.   Andrew, William's son, appealed William of Ingwarthin of robbery, and both are dead and the jurors say that battle was waged between them for the robbery in the county [court] by its judgment. So let the county make a record. And the county records that in truth Andrew did appeal William in the county [court], and when mention was made of the king's peace, the suit was attached to the coming of the justices, but they fully deny that the duel was waged. Therefore to judgment. The jurors are in mercy.

173.   ¹De novis consuetudinibus dicunt quod ballivi vicecomitis et homines de patria committunt eis traceam sequendam, et nullam sequi poterunt per mediam villam suam, et dicunt quod Robertus de Shireford' cepit nuper ab eis xl. sol. ea occasione quod non potuerunt sequi hujusmodi traceam. Et ideo ad judicium.²

ad jud'

174.   ³Burgenses de Bruges queruntur quod burgenses Salopie injuste et contra libertatem suam deforciant eis quod non possunt in villa de Salopia emere coria recencia et pannos crudos sicut solent.

Veredictum Burgensium de Salopia cum Hundredo.

175.   ⁴Juratores dicunt quod Abbas de Salopia fecit purpresturam super dominum Regem in aqua de Sauern', scil. opturavit quandam guletam per quam naves solent transire per gurgitem suum quem ipse ibi levavit. Et xxiiij. milites ad hoc electi, missi fuerunt ad videndum gurgitem. Veniunt et dicunt quod viderunt gurgitem ut credunt in eodem statu in quo fuit quando justiciarii ultimo itineraverunt, set due brecee aliquando fuerunt juxta terram, set nesciunt quomodo vel quando obstructe fuerunt, set bene dicunt quod post iter justiciariorum nullam fecit ibi purpresturam. Et ideo remaneat ita sicut fuit.

Idem dicunt de quodam gurgite quem Stephanus Punbelee levavit.

---

¹ m. 9 d.
² As to the duty incumbent on the township of following the trail of stolen cattle within its boundaries, see Laws of Edgar, 1. cap. 5, (Schmid).
³ m. 9 d. On m. 10 there is a long plea between Bridgnorth and Shrewsbury arising out of this presentment. The former relies on charters of Henry II, and 16 John, the latter on a charter of 11 John. At length they take issue on the question of seisin; but the record goes no further. The oldest charter pleaded by Bridgnorth is tested by Thomas the Chancellor, i.e. by Becket, and confirms in general terms the liberties enjoyed by the burgesses under Henry I.
⁴ m. 10.

173. As to new customs, [the jurors] say that the sheriff's bailiffs and the men of the country commit to [the men of Bridgnorth] the duty of following the trail [of stolen cattle] through their town, and they cannot follow [a trail] through the middle of the town; and they say that Robert of Shireford lately took from them forty shillings because they could not follow a trail of this kind. Therefore to judgment.

174. The burgesses of Bridgnorth complain that the burgesses of Shrewsbury unjustly and against their franchise deforce them so that they cannot buy untanned hides and undyed cloth in the town of Shrewsbury as they were wont.

Verdict of the Burgesses of Shrewsbury along with the Hundred.

175. The jurors say that the Abbot of Shrewsbury has made a purpresture upon our lord the king in the river Severn, to wit, that he has stopped up a certain gulley, through which ships were wont to pass through his dam which he has set up. And twenty-four knights chosen for the purpose were sent to view the dam. They come and say that they saw the dam, as they believe, in the same state in which it was when the justices last came in eyre, but at one time there were two breaches [in the dam] near the land, and they know not how or when they were stopped up; but they say for certain that [the Abbot] has made no purpresture there since the last eyre. So let it remain as it was before.

They say the same of a dam which Stephen Punbclee has raised.

176. ¹Abbas de Lilleshull' levavit quandam novam consuetudinem ad pontem de Attingeham ² quia capit de qualibet careta honerata transeunte j. den. Et Abbas venit et defendit quod ipse nullam novam consuetudinem levavit, set revera tempore predecessoris sui non fuit ibi aliquis pons, ita quod Abbas ille tunc habuit ibi duos batellos ad transducendum homines transeuntes qui ei solebant reddere duas marcas per annum. Postea per commune consilium Domini Willelmi filii Alani ³ et aliorum magnatum provisum fuit quod ipse Abbas faceret ibi pontem quendam et caperet de qualibet careta de Salopia honerata j. den. et de alia j. ob. et pons ille jam peractus est preter quandam arcam. Hoc modo capit ipse consuetudinem illam.

Et juratores dicunt quod ipse Abbas et ejus predecessores ceperunt consuetudinem illam jam per xx. annos et nullam emendacionem apposuerunt.⁴

177. ⁵Burgenses queruntur quod Abbas Salopie injuste deforciat eis vigiliam Sancti Petri advincula scil. mercatum de hora nona usque ad vesperas quod pertinet ad villam domini Regis, et unde semper fuerunt seisiti.

Et Abbas venit et dicit quod domus sua semper fuit inde seisita et non villa Salopie, et inde ponit se super juratam de toto comitatu. Et Burgenses quesiti si inde se ponere velint super comitatum, dicunt quod non. Et ideo loquendum ad magnam curiam,⁶ et similiter de ma*num*ulis ⁷ unde queruntur.

ad jud' ap'
Westm'

¹ m. 10.
² Atcham bridge over the Severn, a few miles south of Shrewsbury. There are some remarks on this case in Eyton, Hist. Staffordshire, vol. viii. p. 242.
³ He was sheriff during the whole of Richard's and the first two years of John's reign.
⁴ No judgment is found.
⁵ m. 10.
⁶ The Great Court seems to be the Bench at Westminster; Bracton, f. 1 b, 332 b, uses this term. Search has been made for subsequent proceedings, but in vain.
⁷ This word is not very plainly written, but it seems certainly to mean *hand-mills*. The Abbey of Shrewsbury had a fair of three days at the feast of St. Peter ad Vincula (1 Aug.), also a monopoly for its mill. A few years after this case, Henry III. confirms to it a fishery below the bridge at Shrewsbury and the whole multure of the said city, and that none do make a mill in the Severn in the territory of the said town save by licence of the monks; also a fair to last for three days at the feast of St. Peter: see Monasticon, vol. iii. pp. 517-523. A suit between the abbey of Peterborough and some of its tenants

176. The Abbot of Lilleshall has levied a new custom at the bridge of Atcham, for he takes for every loaded cart which goes across one penny. And the Abbot comes and denies that he has raised any new custom, but in truth in his predecessor's day there was no bridge there, and the then Abbot had two boats there to carry over those who would cross, and they used to pay him two marks a year; then afterwards by the common counsel of Sir William FitzAlan and the other magnates [of the county] it was provided that the Abbot should build a bridge and take from every cart of Shrewsbury if loaded one penny, and from any other cart, one halfpenny, and the bridge is already finished except one arch; and it is thus that he takes the said custom.

The jurors say that the Abbot and his predecessors have taken that custom already for twenty years and have never made any improvement.

177. The burgesses complain that the Abbot of Shrewsbury unjustly deforces them of the vigil of St. Peter at Chains, to wit, of a market from the hour of noon to vespers which belongs to the town of our lord the king, and whereof they were always seised.

And the Abbot comes and says that his house was seised thereof and not the town of Shrewsbury, and of this he puts himself on a jury of the whole county. And the burgesses, being asked whether they will put themselves upon the county, say that they will not. And therefore this must be discussed at the Great Court, and so too as to the handmills whereof they complain.

178. Abbas de Lilleshull' queritur quod ballivi de Salopia contra libertatem suam plures injurias ei faciunt et quod ipsi clamari fecerunt in villa quod non esset ita audax aliquis qui ipsi Abbati vel hominibus suis aliquam mercandisam venderet super forisfacturam x. sol., ita quod Ricardus Pecche bedellus ejusdem ville hoc clamavit per preceptum eorum. Et ballivi defendunt totum, et Ricardus similiter defendit totum et quod hoc nunquam clamari audivit ab aliquo. Consideratum est quod ipse defendat se duodecima

Sabbat' manu, et veniat die Sabbati cum lege. Plegii Ricardi Peche bedelli de lege sua Robertus de Brai et Petrus Pin. 'Post venit Abbas et per licenciam justiciariorum remisit legem.'

[1] PLACITA APUD IVELCESTRIAM ANNO REGNI REGIS HENRICI NONO.

Hundredus de Milvertone.

179. [2] Ricardus Pistor et Stephanus Prepositus de Sanford' et Ricardus Cape et Johannes filius ejus Rogerus de B . . . et Jacobus ad capud ville de Sanford' et Ricardus de Paiseie capti pro morte Nicholai de Arundel domini sui qui occisus fuit et combustus in domo sua veniunt et deffendunt mortem illam. Et quesiti ubi fuerunt quando domus illa accensa fuit, dicunt quod jacuerunt in villa et non in curia, set revera venerunt ibi antequam esset combusta dicta domus, et *bene* cognoscunt quod viderunt dominum suum combustum in domo sua circa horam primam, et non ausi fuerunt *extrahere corpus* sine visu coronatorum. Et testatum est per milites de comitatu quod idem prepositus ante combustionem domus asportavit omnia catalla domini sui de curia domini, et quod idem Ricardus Pistor in crastino ivit in

---

touching certain *molae manuales* will be found in Chronicon Petroburgense, Camd. Soc., p. 67.

[1] Tower Roll No. 4. The commission is in Rot. Cl. vol. ii. p. 76;

Martin Pateshull and three knights of the shire are to take the assises of novel disseisin and deliver the gaols.

[2] m. 1.

178. The Abbot of Lilleshall complains that the bailiffs of Shrewsbury do him many injuries against his liberty, and that they have caused proclamation to be made in the town that none be so bold as to sell any merchandise to the Abbot or his men upon pain of forfeiting ten shillings, so that Richard Peche, the bedell of the said town, made this proclamation by their orders. And the bailiffs defend all of it, and Richard likewise defends all of it and that he never heard such proclamation made by anyone. It is considered that he do defend himself twelve-handed [with eleven compurgators], and do come on Saturday with his law. Pledges for the law of Richard Peche the bedell: Robert of Bray and Peter Pin. Afterwards came the Abbot and by leave of the justices remitted the law.

PLEAS AT ILCHESTER IN THE NINTH YEAR OF HENRY III. [A.D. 1225].

Hundred of Milverton.

179. Richard Baker and Stephen Reeve of Sampford [Arundel], Richard Cape and John his son, Roger of . . ., James Townsend of Sampford and Richard of Peashays, arrested for the death of Nicholas of Arundel their lord, who was slain and burnt in his house, come and defend the death. And being asked where they were when the house was set on fire, say that they slept in the vill and not in the court, but in truth they came thither before the house was burnt down, and they fully admit that they saw their lord burnt in his house about the hour of prime [6 A.M.] and dared not carry out the body without the view of the coroners. And it is testified by the knights of the county that the said reeve, before the house was burnt, carried off all his lord's chattels from his lord's court, and that on the morrow Richard Baker went to his lord's land

Devoniam ad terram domini sui et j. equum abduxit et ibi catalla domini sui cepit et asportavit. Et ipsi omnes ponunt se super patriam. Et milites de hundredo et milites de hundredo de Tanton' et alii et villate veniunt et dicunt super sacramentum suum *quod male*credunt eos et totam villatam preter iiij. homines, scil. Ricardum de Bosco, Willelmum Brekeherte, Stephanum Prepositum *seniorem* et Warinum le Tailur ' et Ric' Monoculus,'[1] et bene dicunt quod cum ipsi persequerentur dominum suum ut ipsum interficerent idem Nicholaus fugit in ecclesiam et voluit ingredi, et capellanus clausit hostium et non ausus fuit ingredi, et tunc eum occiderunt et posuerunt eum in domum suam et tunc illam incendebant. Et ideo detrahantur et tunc suspendantur, et alii homines de Sanford' capiantur. Inquirendum de catallis.

Et Rogerus Akerman et Hugo filius Hugonis Cape rettati de eadem morte fugierunt et malecreduntur, ideo exigantur et utlagentur. Inquirendum de catallis.

Aylbriht de Hulecumbe, Ricardus filius Ricardi de Holecumbe, Walterus de Pasheie et alius Walterus de Pasheie et . . . Atetonesande et Radulfus frater ejus et Ricardus de Holecumbe senex et Editha filia Johannis de B . . . cumbe *capti pro* eadem morte veniunt et deffendunt mortem illam. Et predicti juratores et villate veniunt et dicunt super sacramentum suum *quod* omnes isti preter Ric' de Holecumbe monoculo[2] quem prius aquietaverunt sunt culpabiles de felonia illa. Et ideo suspendantur.

Jordanus de Hallere, Robertus de Diggelford', Hugo filius . . . et Edwardus de Sanford' rettati sunt de eadem felonia et ipsi preter Edwardum qui infirmus est fugierunt et malecreduntur. Et ideo exigantur et utlagentur. Inquirendum de catallis.

---

[1] *Sic.* This name has been interpolated, so that there are five persons not suspected.
[2] *Sic.*

in Devon and led away a horse and there took and carried away the chattels of his lord. And all of them put themselves upon the country. And the knights of this hundred and those of Taunton hundred and others and the townships come and say upon their oaths that they suspect these men, and indeed the whole township [of Sampford] except four men, to wit, Richard of the Wood, William Brekeherte, Stephen Reeve the elder, Warin Tailor, and Richard One-eye, and say positively that when they were pursuing their lord to slay him, he fled to the church and would have entered it, but the chaplain shut the door, and he dared not enter, and then they slew him and put him in his house and set fire to it. And therefore let them be drawn and afterwards hanged. And let the rest of the men of Sampford be arrested. Let inquiry be made as to their chattels.

And Roger Akerman and Hugh, son of Hugh Cape, accused of the same death, have fled and are suspected. Let them be exacted and outlawed, and let inquiry be made as to their chattels.

Ailbert of Holecombe, Richard, son of Richard of Holecombe, Walter of Peashays and a second Walter of Peashays and . . . Atetonesande and Ralph his brother and Richard of Holecombe the elder and Edith, daughter of John of . . ., arrested for the said death, come and defend that death. And the said jurors and the townships come and say upon their oath that all of these, except Richard of Holecombe the one-eyed, whom they have already acquitted, are guilty of that felony. Therefore let them be hanged.

Jordan of Haller, Robert of Diggelsford, Hugh, son of . . ., and Edward of Sampford, are accused of the same felony, and they (save Edward, who is infirm) have fled and are suspected. Therefore let them be exacted and outlawed, and let inquiry be made as to their chattels.

Hundredus de Kantinton'.

180. ¹ Quidam extraneus et nescitur quis occidit Ricardum de Kantinton' cocum. Nullus alius malecreditur. Englisheria ponitur in respectum usque in adventum justiciariorum ad omnia placita.²

in adv' justic'

Hundredus de Norhtperiton.

181. ³ Ricardus Goky rettatus de morte Henrici Lihtfot occisi in Leng' venit et deffendit totum et ponit se super patriam. Et villate de Northcury, Bruges, Kriz et de Niwenton' et xij. juratores dicunt super sacramentum suum quod neminem malecredunt de morte illa nisi eundem Ricardum, et bene dicunt quod eum occidit. Et ideo suspendatur. Inquirendum de catallis.

susp'

Et villata de Leng' et xij. juratores primo presentaverunt quod quidam Robertus Juvenis eum debuit occidisse. Et postea veniunt et cognoscunt quod hoc fecerunt per Rogerum Baryl servientem hundredi. Et ideo cust', et xij. juratores et villata de Leng' in misericordia pro falso dicto suo. Misericordia juratorum perdonatur.

custod'

Et coronatores recordantur quod ballivi Abbatis de Alegenny non permittunt eos hundr' ducere apud Leng' ut inquisiciones faciant nec aliquam inquisicionem facere, et nullum inde warantum habent. Et ideo capiatur libertas in manum domini Regis.⁴

182. ⁵ Gocelinus Hnokel de Norhtperiton' captus pro receptamento latronum venit et deffendit totum et ponit se super patriam. Et xij. juratores et villate de Newentone, Hunteworth', Norhtperiton' et de Hamme veniunt et dicunt super sacramentum suum quod malecredunt eum de receptamento latronum et societate latronum. Et ideo suspendatur. Inquirendum de catallis.

---

¹ m. 2.
² The justices now present are only empowered to deliver the gaol.
³ m. 2.
⁴ In the margin, which is damaged, stands *libertas* preceded by some other word.
⁵ m. 2.

Hundred of Cannington.

180. A certain stranger, but it is not known who he was, killed Richard Cook of Cannington. No other is suspected. [Presentment of] Englishry is respited unto the coming of justices empowered to hear pleas of all kinds.

Hundred of North Petherton.

181. Richard Goky, accused of the death of Henry Lightfoot slain at Ling, comes and defends all of it and puts himself on the country. And the townships of North Curry, Bridgewater, Creech and Newton and the twelve jurors say upon their oath that they suspect no one of that death save Richard, and they say positively that he slew [Henry]. Therefore let him be hanged. Inquire as to his chattels.

And the township of Ling and the jurors presented at the outset that one Robert Young slew [Henry]. Afterwards they come and confess that they did this at the instance of Roger Baryl, the serjeant of the hundred. Therefore let him be in custody and the twelve jurors and the township of Ling in mercy for their false statement. The jurors' amercement is pardoned.

And the coroners record that the bailiffs of the Abbot of Athelney do not suffer them to convene the hundred at Ling for the making of inquests or to make any inquests. And [the bailiffs] have no warrant for this. Therefore let the [Abbot's] franchise be seized into the king's hand.

182. Joscelin Hnokel of North Petherton, arrested for receipt of thieves, comes and defends all of it and puts himself upon the country. And the twelve jurors and the townships of Newton, Huntworth, North Petherton and Ham come and say upon their oath that they suspect him of receiving and consorting with thieves. Therefore let him be hanged. Inquire as to his chattels.

Hundredus de Wileton'.

183. ¹Duo latrones fugati fuerunt cum duobus equis furatis, ita quod dimiserunt equos coram domo Johannis de Reigni et equi capti fuerunt et nullus secutus fuit eos. Et ideo sint domino Regi. Precium eorum viij. sol . . .² unde vicecomes respondeat.

viij. s.

Hundredus de Cruk.

184. ³Simon de Shiteroc captus pro morte Johannis de Cruk venit et defendit totum. Et ballivus domini Regis de hundredo dicit quod quando cepit eum in crastino facti mane cognovit coram eo et coram pluribus hominibus mortem illam, et producit unam tethingam integram que hoc testatur. Et Simon postea testatur quod interfuit ubi occisus fuit et quod Elias frater . . . occidit eum et quod hoc vidit. Et interrogatus quid tunc fecit dicit quod nichil, nec alicui monstravit nec utesium levavit. Et xij. juratores precise dicunt quod Simon occidit eum et nullus alius. Et quia ballivus Regis habet sectam quod cognovit coram eo, ideo suspendatur.

{ad jud'}

susp'

inquir' de catall'

Hundredus de Kareinton.

185. ⁴Robertus de Ar occidit Walterum Capellanum de Ar, et captus est et venit et defendit totum sicut clericus. Et juratores precise dicunt quod ipse occidit eum et quod ipse vulneravit Gervasium filium Capellani, qui presens est et hoc idem dicit. Et quia clericus est judicium ponatur in respectum. Custodiatur. Nullus eum petit.

ad jud'

Hundredus de Whitstan.

186. ⁵Ricardus le Franceys captus fuit pro morte Roberti filii Goldine, et serviens Abbatis Glastonie ipsum recepit captum.

loquend'

⁶Postea captus est et deffendit totum et ponit se super

¹ m. 2 d.   ² There is a small hole in the roll.
³ m. 3.   ⁴ m. 3.   ⁵ m. 3.

Hundred of Williton.

183.   Two thieves with two stolen horses were being chased, and left those horses before the house of John of Reigny, and the horses were taken and no one pursued the thieves. Therefore [the horses] are the king's. Their price is eight shillings for which the sheriff must account.

Hundred of Crewkerne.

184.   Simon of Shedricks, arrested for the death of John of Crewkerne, comes and defends all of it. And the king's bailiff of the hundred says that when he arrested him on the next morning after the crime was done, [Simon] confessed the death before him and before many others, and he produces a whole tithing which testifies the same. And Simon afterwards testifies that he was present when [John] was slain, and that Elias, brother of . . . , slew him, and that [Simon] saw this. And being asked what he did then, he says, Nothing, he did not tell anyone nor raise the hue. And the twelve jurors say in so many words that Simon, and no other, slew him. And because the king's bailiff produces suit to prove the confession made before him, let [Simon] be hanged.

Hundred of Carhampton.

185.   Robert of Oare slew Walter Chaplain of Oare and was taken, and comes and defends all of it as a clerk. The jurors say in so many words that he slew him and wounded Gervase, the chaplain's son, who is present and says the same. Since he is a clerk, judgment is respited, and let him be in custody. No [ordinary] claims him.

Hundred of Whitestone.

186.   Richard French was taken for the death of Robert, Goldin's son, and the serjeant of the Abbot of Glastonbury took him into his custody. This must be discussed.

Afterwards [Richard] is arrested and defends all of it,

patriam. Et ideo mandatum est vicecomiti Sumersetie quod in pleno comitatu coram eo et Jordano Oliver et Johanne de Reyny et Radulfo de Lidiard convenire faciat iiij. hundreda propinquiora etc. et per eorum sacramentum diligenter faciant inquisicionem, et secundum inquisicionem quam facerent ei habere faciant judicium suum etc.'[1]

Hundredus de Witheleg'.

187. [2]Ricardus de Brente filius Ade Thurbern rettatus de latrocinio venit et defendit totum et ponit se super patriam. Et xij. juratores et villate Brente, Suthbrente, Limpelesham, Burneham dicunt quod non malecredunt eum nisi de uno pullo quem cepit in furore tempore quo fuit lunaticus. Et ideo sit sub plegiis quousque plus sciatur.

Hundredus de Stanes.

188. [3]Mabilia filia Derwin' lusit cum quodam lapide in Giuele et cecidit lapis super capud Walteri Critele, set nullum malum habuit per ictum illum, et obiit postea per infirmitatem post unum mensem, et ipsa pre timore fugit in ecclesiam, set precise dicunt quod non obiit de ictu illo. Et ideo sit in custodia usque loquatur cum domino Rege. Willelmus Derwin, Henricus Derwin', Ricardus de Stanes, Nicholaus Derwin', Hugo Derwin', Edwardus Sutor, Norman filius Paie, Herbertus filius Ricardi.

---

[1] Jordan Oliver, John Reigny and Ralph Lydiard were the three knights commissioned along with Martin Pateshull for this gaol delivery. It seems probable that Richard was not arrested until the hundredors had been dismissed, and Pateshull was on the point of leaving the county.

[2] m. 4.

[3] m. 4 d.

and puts himself upon the country. Therefore the sheriff of Somerset is commanded that in full county [court] before him, Jordan Oliver, John of Reigny, and Ralph of Lydiard, he do convene the four neighbouring hundreds etc. and diligently make inquest by their oath, and according to the result of the inquest do let [Richard] have his judgment etc.

Hundred of Whitley.

187. Richard of Brent, son of Adam Thurbern, accused of larceny, comes and defends all of it and puts himself upon the country. And the twelve jurors and the townships of Brent, South Brent, Limpsham, and Burnham say that they do not suspect him, save of a fowl which he took in his madness at a time when he was lunatic. Therefore let him be under pledges until more be known.

Hundred of Stone.

188. Mabel, Derwin's daughter, was playing with a stone at Yeovil, and the stone fell on the head of Walter Critele, but he had no harm from the blow, and a month after this he died of an infirmity, and she fled to church for fear, but [the jurors] say positively that he did not die of the blow. Therefore let her be in custody until the king be consulted. [Her pledges are] William Derwin, Henry Derwin, Richard of Stone, Nicholas Derwin, Hugh Derwin, Edward Cobbler, Norman, Paie's son, Herbert, Richard's son.

IV. PLACITA CORAM JUSTICIARIIS DE BANCO REGNANTE HENRICO FILIO JOHANNIS.

[1] PLACITA DE TERMINIS S. HILLARII ET PASCHE ANNO REGNI REGIS HENRICI QUARTO.

189.
Sussex

[2] Hugo Hoppeouerhumbr' appellat Thomam de Dene quod die S. Egidii 'inter primam horam et terciam' [3] anno regni Regis secundo sicut ipse una cum Willelmo de Legh' 'cognato suo' fuerunt in parco de Cukefeld' Comitis Warennie ad parcum custodiendum venit idem Thomas cum vi sua et multitudine armatorum cum arcubus et sagittis et assultaverunt eos et traxit ad ipsum Willelmum de una sagitta ita quod percussit eum in crure, unde obiit de plaga illa infra nonum diem, et quod hoc fecit nequiter et in felonia et in pace domini Regis offert probare versus eum sicut curia consideraverit per corpus suum sicut ille qui interfuit et hoc vidit. Dicit eciam quod secta fuit facta secundum legem terre et quod uthesius [4] levatus fuit, et quod xij. juratores eum indictaverunt coram justiciariis itinerantibus ultimo in partibus illis de morte illa, et quod idem Willelmus in vita sua post plagam ei factam cognovit quod idem Thomas eum percussit sicut predictum est et mortem suam super eum posuit.

Et Thomas venit et defendit totum sicut clericus qui est ordinatus. Et super hoc venit Robertus de Den' [5] frater ipsius Thome et profert literas clausas Episcopi Cicestrensis in quibus continetur quod idem Thomas coram

---

[1] Coram Rege Rolls Nos. 3 and 5. These rolls, which are duplicates, are here referred to as A and B respectively; the text is from A.
[2] A, m. 11; B, m. 8 d.
[3] Interpolated in A; not found in B.
[4] *Sic*, in full, A, B.
[5] Supply *clericus*, B.

IV. PLEAS BEFORE THE JUSTICES OF THE BENCH IN HENRY THE THIRD'S REIGN.

PLEAS OF HILARY AND EASTER TERMS IN THE FOURTH YEAR OF HENRY III. [A.D. 1220].

189. Hugh Hoppeoverhumbr' appeals Thomas of Dean, for
Sussex that on St. Giles's day, between the hours of prime and terce [6–9 A.M.], in the second year of the reign, as he with William of Leigh his cousin was in the park of the Earl of Warenne at Cuckfield in charge of the park, the said Thomas came with his force and with a multitude of armed men with bows and arrows, and assaulted them, and aimed an arrow at the said William and hit him in the leg, so that he died of the wound within nine days; and that he did this wickedly and in felony and in the king's peace he offers to prove against him by his body as the court shall consider, as one who was present and saw this. He adds that suit was made according to the law of the land, and that the hue was raised, and that twelve jurors indicted [Thomas] of that death before the justices at their last eyre in those parts, and that the said William after the wound and while yet alive declared that Thomas hit him as aforesaid and charged him with his death.

And Thomas comes and defends all of it as a clerk who is ordained. And upon this comes Robert of Dean his brother, and produces letters close of the Bishop of Chichester, in which is contained that Thomas has suffi-

eo sufficienter probavit per testes etc. quod idem Thomas tempore congruo a Sefrido[1] quondam Episcopo Cicestrensi ad ordinem acolitatus fuit promotus, et ideo petit eum ut clericum ut de eo omni querenti in foro ecclesiastico justiciam exhibeat.

[2] Thomas committitur R. Cicestrensi Episcopo ut eum habeat recto, quia clericus est. Et sciendum quod Dominus Cantuariensis qui ipsum Thomam prius receperat in custodia inde quietus.[2]

190.
x
[3] Willelmus Smalwude appellat Hugonem le Large de Weltumestawe quod ipse receptavit eum cum duobus equis quos habuit de camberlano Baldewin' de Gynnes[4] quem occidit, ita quod idem Hugo habuit in camera sua illos duos equos per octo dies et habuit pro custodia illa sex solidos, et quedam femina in hospitio sex denarios pro ferenda aqua ad equos ne viderentur, et quod ipse scivit quod hoc fuit latrocinium et illum tali modo receptavit offert probare per corpus suum.

Et Hugo defendit totum versus eum prout curia consideraverit, et ponit se super patriam[5] quod tenetur fidelis homo.[5] Committitur villate de Weltumestowe ad habendum eum ad summonicionem.[6]

Idem appellat Nicholaum de Trumpiton' de receptamento, scilicet, quod ipse receptavit in domo sua duos equos quos furatus fuit, scilicet, j. nigrum equum et j. ferrandum, et multociens venit ad domum suam et ibi moram fecit per octo dies aliquando, aliquando plus, aliquando minus, cum sociis suis, et bene scivit quod fuerunt malefactores et quod

---

[1] Seffrid was bishop from 1180 to 1204. The present bishop is Ralph of Warham. The see was vacant in 1217, which may account for the fact that Thomas has been in the custody of the archbishop.

[2-2] Not in B.

[3] A, m. 13; B, m. 10. This membrane of A is headed *Rotulus Latronum*; a batch of criminal cases from Hertford, Kent and Essex seems to have been brought before the Bench at Westminster.

[4] *Gisnes*, B.

[5-5] *quod fidelis homo est*, B.

[6] William, the approver, has many appeals to make. The justices do not decide what is to happen to the various appellees until all the appeals are before them. It chances that the approver fails in his first battle.

ciently proved before him by witnesses etc. that he was promoted in due season by Seffrid, Bishop of Chichester, to the order of acolyte, and therefore he demands him as a clerk, in order that he [the Bishop] may do justice respecting him to everyone who shall complain in the ecclesiastical court.

Thomas is committed to R[alph], Bishop of Chichester, that he may have him to right, for that he is a clerk. And note that the Archbishop of Canterbury, who had taken Thomas into his custody, is quit thereof.

190. William Smallwood appeals Hugh Large of Walthamstow, for that he received him [William] together with two horses which he had from the chamberlain of Baldwin of Guines, whom he [William] killed, so that Hugh kept those two horses for eight days in his chamber and received six shillings for keeping them, and a woman at the inn had sixpence for bringing them water, so that they might not be seen; and that [Hugh] knew that the horses were stolen and received him in manner aforesaid, he offers to prove by his body.

Essex

And Hugh defends all of it against him as the court shall co ider, and puts himself upon the country that he is held to be a lawful man. He is committed to the township of Walthamstow, so that it may produce him when summoned.

[William] also appeals Nicholas of Trumpington of receipt, to wit, that he received in his house two horses which [William] had stolen, to wit, a black horse and a dapple-grey, and [William] often came to [Nicholas's] house and stayed there, sometimes for eight days, sometimes more, sometimes less, with his companions, and [Nicholas] well knew that they were evil doers and that the horses

equi furati fuerunt. Committitur villate de Cestrehunte etc. Nondum fuit [1] inquisicio de eo.

Rogerus de Watham serviens manucepit habendi die Lune filios presbiteri appellatos.[2]

Idem appellat de receptamento Robertum Wudecoc' et Willelmum filium ejus. Set dicit quod ipsi nesciverunt de homicidio quod fecit cum sociis suis in domo sua. 'Juratores ad hoc summoniti dicunt quod nichil sciunt de eis nisi bonum. Idem dicunt de Almero de Mapelderested' et Willelmo de Colevilla de receptamento appellatis. Et ideo vicecomes capiat plegios de eis.'[3]

ertford Idem appellat Willelmum filium Henrici juxta Warre[4] de receptamento, set adeo senex est quod vix potest ire, et preterea loquitur ficte versus eum. Et ideo loquendum. Juratores dicunt quod nichil sciunt de eo, et ideo eat quietus quia senex est.

Idem appellat Johannem et Adam filios Presbiteri[5] de societate et homicidio, ita quod ipsi simul cum eo occiderunt unum hominem Aluredi Gernu' et eum escaudaverunt[6] in domo Roberti Wudecoc'[6] et habuerunt de suo ad valenciam iiij. librarum esterlingorum. Item ipsi occiderunt in eadem domo unum alium hominem, et tercium inter Writel' et Chelmereford'. Item Adam simul cum eo fregit domum Michaelis de Smalwude fratris sui et eam robavit, ita quod idem Adam habuit unum pallium de blu[7] cum penula de bisse[7] ad valenciam dimidie marce, et hoc offert probare per corpus suum, et capit se primo ad Adam.

Et ipsi veniunt et defendunt totum de verbo in verbum et ponunt se super patriam. Et vicecomes dixit quod fecit inquisicionem et inquisicio dixit quod sunt de malo retto. Idem testati sunt legales[8] milites de comitatu.

---

[1] B has no verb.
[2] More of these persons below.
[3] This verdict is postscript.
[4] *Ware*, B.
[5] Supply *de Legh'*, B.
[6-6] Omit, B.
[7-7] *furratam de bassis*, B.
[8] Om. *legales*, B.

were stolen. [Nicholas] is committed to the township of Cheshunt etc. No inquest has yet been made about him.

Roger, the serjeant of Waltham, has undertaken to produce on Monday the sons of the Priest who have been appealed.

[William] also appeals as receivers Robert Woodcock and William his son, but says that they did not know of the homicide committed in their house by [William] and his companions. (The jurors summoned for the purpose say that they know nothing but good of them. And they say the same of Ailmer of Maplestead and William of Colville who have been appealed as receivers. Therefore let the sheriff take pledges for them.)

[William] also appeals William, son of Henry of Ware, as a receiver. But he is so old that he can hardly walk. Also the count against him is fictitious. Therefore the matter must be further discussed. The jurors say that they know nothing of him. Therefore let him go quit, for he is aged.

[William] also appeals John and Adam, the Priest's sons, of being his companions and of homicide, to wit, that along with him they slew one of Alfred Gernun's men and scalded[1] him in Robert Woodcock's house and had of his property to the value of four pounds of sterling monies. Also they slew another man in the same house, and a third between Writtle and Chelmsford. Also Adam along with [William] broke the house of [William's] brother Michael of Smallwood and robbed it, and Adam had [from that robbery] a blue cloak with a linen hood, value a half-mark; and this he offers to prove by his body, and he betakes himself against Adam in the first instance.

And they come and defend all of it word by word and put themselves upon the country. And the sheriff said that he had made an inquest and the inquest said that they are of ill fame. The lawful knights of the county testify the same.

---

[1] *excaudare, excaldare*, means 'to scald'; perhaps it here refers to some means whereby the dead body was disposed of.

duell' Et ideo procedat duellum primo versus Adam quem appellat de morte predictorum et de roberia domus fratris sui et de pallio predicto¹ precii septem solidorum¹ et qui totum defendit per corpus suum.

Vadiant duellum et Adam committitur in custodia Hugoni de Illeg', Ade de Illeg' et Rogero de Watham servienti ad respondendum de corpore suo die Martis et tunc veniat armatus. Johannes committitur eodem modo eisdem.²

susp' 'Willelmus Smalwude victus est et susp', et Adam et Johannes dimittuntur per plegios et predicti Hugo, Adam et Rogerus sunt plegii ejus et inveniat³ plures plegios vicecomiti in comitatu.'

191.
Hertford

⁴ Alicia uxor Willelmi Blac' cognoscit quod⁵ interfuit [cum] viro suo⁵ occisioni trium hominum et j. femine apud Bernet'. Et ideo comburatur. Reginaldus Comber, Thomas de Grantham et Matillis uxor ejus et Reginaldus frater ipsius Matillidis quos ipsa indictavit de homicidio committuntur Willelmo de Husseburn' senescallo [Abbatis S. Albani⁶] ad ponendum eos in gaola pro libertate sua.

192.
Hertford

⁷ Philippus filius Hereuici, Robertus filius Unfridi, Henricus filius Andree et Willelmus filius Ricardi iiij. liberi homines de curia Comitis Britannie⁸ de Cesterhunt' summoniti ad faciendum recordum de duello vadiato in curia sua inter Hamonem de Mora appellantem et Eliam Pyion⁹ appellatum de j. equo furato unde idem Hamon appellat, veniunt et recordantur quod Hamon de la Mare questus

---

¹⁻¹ *ad valenciam dimidie marce*, B.
² B has no more of this case.
³ *eorum et inveniant* would be better.
⁴ A, m. 12; B, m. 10.
⁵⁻⁵ Om. B.
⁶ *Sic* B; in A the words are illegible.
⁷ A, m. 13; B, m. 10 d.
⁸ The manor of Cheshunt belongs to the honour of Britanny and Richmond. The present earl is Peter Mauclerc. For this manor see Clutterbuck, Hist. Hertfordshire, vol. ii. p. 79.
⁹ *Piggun*, B.

So let the battle proceed, in the first place against Adam whom [William] appeals of the death of the persons aforesaid and of breaking his brother's house and of the said cloak, price seven shillings, and who defends all of it by his body.

They wage battle. Adam is committed to the custody of Hugh of Eleigh, Adam of Eleigh, and Roger, serjeant of Waltham, who must answer for his body on Tuesday, and then let him come armed. John is committed in the same manner to the same persons.

William Smallwood is vanquished and hanged, and Adam and John are dismissed upon pledges, and the said Hugh, Adam [of Eleigh] and Roger are pledges for them and they must find other pledges before the sheriff in the county [court].

191. *Hertford.* Alice, wife of William Black, confesses that she was present along with her husband at the slaying of three men and one woman at Barnet. Therefore let her be burned. Reginald Comber, Thomas of Grantham and Maud his wife and Reginald, Maud's brother, whom [Alice] indicted of homicide, are committed to William Hussebourne, steward of the Abbot of St. Albans, to be imprisoned by him in accordance with his franchise.

192. *Hertford.* Philip, Hervey's son, Robert, Humfrey's son, Henry, Andrew's son, William, Richard's son, four free men of the court of the Earl of Britanny of Cheshunt, summoned to make record of a battle waged in their court between Hamo Moor, the appellor, and Elias Piggun, the appellee, touching a stolen horse, whereof Hamo makes appeal, come and record that Hamo Moor complained in the Earl's court

fuit in curia Comitis de Philippo le King' quod furatus fuit unam equam suam in communi pastura sua nequiter et in felonia et latrocinio in pace Dei et in pace Comitis domini sui, et hoc optulit probare per corpus suum sicut curia consideravit [1] in j. hora diei.[2] Et Philippus venit et defendit nequitiam et feloniam et latrocinium, et dixit quod habuit inde warantum et illum haberet ad horam scilicet quendam Edwardum, et habuit diem habendi eum. Post tria essonia que idem Philippus fecit, venit ipse et produxit warantum suum Eduardum qui se fecit warantum de illa equa, et quando Hamon vidit eum seisitum [3] de equa sua locutus fuit versus eundem Edwardum per eadem verba que prius, adjiciens quod nescivit alium latronem quam ipsum Edwardum quem vidit seisitum et qui warantum se fecit de equa, et optulit probare versus eum per corpus suum etc. Et Edwardus defendit totum de verbo in verbum, et vocavit inde ad warantum Eliam Pyion,[4] quem secum produxit. Et cepit equam et warantum se fecit et dixit quod vendidit illam ipsi Edwardo ut proprium catallum suum. Quando Hamon vidit ipsum Eliam seisitum de equa locutus fuit versus eum, et dixit quod nescivit alium latronem quam ipsum Eliam quem vidit seisitum et qui se fecit warantum versus eum, et dixit quod nequiter et in latrocinio in pace Dei et Comitis furatus fuit illam equam sicut prius, et hoc optulit probare per corpus suum etc. sicut curia etc. Et Elias defendit totum de verbo in verbum et optulit facere de illa equa ut de proprio catallo suo versus illum Hamonem sicut curia consideraret.[5] Consideratum fuit quod Elias daret vadium ad defendendum se et Hamo ad disracionandum.

Et Hamon dicit quod in quadam parte recordantur bene et in quadam parte parum,[6] quia quando Elias vocatus fuit

---

[1] *consideraret*, B.
[2] This means that he will prove it before nightfall; Bracton, f. 142. The formula appears in the Norman books; see Brunner, Schwurgerichte, p. 179.
[3] The warrantor takes the chattel into his possession, and when he is so seised of it the plaintiff counts against him.
[4] *Piggun*, B.
[5] *consideraverit*, B.
[6] Other instances of this mode of challenging the correctness of a record will be found in Bracton's Note Book, Cases 40, 212, 243, 592,

against Philip King, for that he stole a mare of his in his common pasture wickedly and in felony and in larceny, in the peace of God and in the peace of his lord the Earl, and this he offered to prove by his body one hour of the day as the court should consider. And Philip came and defended wickedness, felony and larceny, and said that he had a warrantor and would produce him in due season, namely, one Edward; and a day was given him to produce [Edward]. Then Philip, after casting three essoins, came and produced Edward his warrantor, and Edward took up the warranty of the mare. And when Hamo saw [Edward] seised of the mare, he counted against him by the same words that he had used before, adding that he knew no other thief than Edward, whom he saw there in seisin and who had taken on himself to warrant the mare; and he offered to prove against him by his body etc. And Edward defended all of it word by word, and vouched to warranty Elias Piggun, whom he produced. And [Elias] took hold of the mare and took up the warranty and said that he sold the mare as his own proper chattel to Edward. And when Hamo saw Elias seised of the mare, he counted against him, and said he knew no other thief than Elias, whom he saw there in seisin and who had taken up the warranty against him; and he said that wickedly and in larceny, in the peace of God and of the Earl, [Elias] stole the mare, using the same words as before; and this he offered to prove by his body etc. as the court etc. And Elias defended all of it word by word and offered to behave against Hamo as regards the mare as though it were his [Elias's] own proper chattel, as the court should consider. It was thereupon considered that Elias should give gage to defend himself and Hamo gage to deraign.

And Hamo says that [the four recorders] do in part record well, but in part too little, for when Elias was

ad warantum et warantizavit equam Edwardo, ipse calumpniatus fuit quod ipse Elias fuit campio locatus, et quod idem Edwardus conduxerat eum pro pecunia sua ut deveniret warantus, et inde produxit sectam sufficientem, et quod hoc verum sit, probat per quendam audientem et alium videntem, et offert domino Regi si hoc non sufficit j. marcam pro habenda inde inquisitione, unde dicit quod hoc non potuit ei allocari desicut petiit ut hoc ei allocaretur.

Et predicti iiij. pro curia dicunt quod tale est recordum sicut ipsi recordantur et non sicut ipse Hamon dicit, et quod tale sit sicut ipsi dicunt offerunt disracionare per corpus cujusdam liberi hominis de curia, vel prout curia consideraverit, vel ad defendendum quod tale non est sicut idem Hamon dicit sicut curia consideraverit.

Et Elias quesitus ubi habuit equam illam, dicit quod ante guerram[1] data fuit ei apud Cardif' in Wallia cum porcis a quodam homine per sicut doceret ei de skermia, et quod illam habuit per sex ebdomadas, et quod illam duxit de Wallia[2] usque in partes istas, et quod illam vendidit eidem Edwardo pro iij. sol. et j. den. extra Waltham ad Crucem. Set de venditione illa nullam sectam producit, immo cognoscit quod solus fuit cum ipso Edwardo. Et idem dicit Edwardus. Dicit eciam Edwardus quod equam illam habuit ipse per v. annos.

Et Hamon dicit quod equa ei pullenata fuit et quod adhuc habet matrem ejus et quod furata fuit ad Pascha anno Regni Regis Henrici tercio et inde habet sectam sufficientem.

Et Elias quesitus quomodo cognovit equam illam post tantum tempus dicit quod per *mercum* scilicet per fissuram auris.

Et octo de hominibus ville de Cestrehunt et totidem de villa de Watha' et de Wurmel et de Enefeld summoniti ad certificandum justiciarios.

Isti sunt plegii Elie Pyion habendi eum die Lune ante[3]

955, 1019, 1486, 1672; see Glanvill, lib. 8, cap. 9, and the statute 1 Edw. III. statute 1, cap. 4, which altered the procedure.

[1] The civil war of 1215_7.
[2] B has no more of this case, except the names of the pledges.
[3] Supply *mediam*, B.

vouched to warrant and warranted the mare to Edward, [Hamo] challenged him as being a hired champion, whom Edward had hired for money to become his warrantor, and of this [Hamo] produced sufficient suit; and that this [account of the proceedings] is true, he now proves by one who saw and by another who heard, and if this be not enough, he offers the king one mark for an inquest thereof; for he says that he could not get this [challenge] allowed him, though he craved that it might be allowed.

And the said four [recorders] on behalf of the [Earl's] court say that the record is as they record, and not as Hamo says; and that it is as they record they offer to deraign by the body of a free man of the court, or as the [King's] court shall consider, or to defend that the record is not as Hamo says as the court shall consider.

And Elias being asked where he got that mare, says that before the war she was given him at Cardiff in Wales together with some pigs, by a certain man in consideration of lessons in sword-play, and that he possessed her for six weeks, and brought her from Wales into these parts, and sold her to Edward for three shillings and a penny, outside Waltham at the cross. But as to the sale he produces no suit, but confesses that he and Edward were alone together. And Edward says the same. Edward also says that he has had the mare these five years.

And Hamo says that the mare was foaled to him, and that he still has her mother, and that she was stolen at Easter in the third year of the reign, and of this he has sufficient suit.

And Elias, being asked how he knew the mare after so long an interval, says that he knew her by a mark, namely, a slit in her ear.

And eight of the men of the vill of Cheshunt, and as many of the vill of Waltham and of Wormley and of Enfield, are summoned to certify the justices.

The following are pledges to produce Elias Piggon on

Quadr', Thomas de Muleton', Petrus de Nereford' et iiij. predicti milites cum recordo.

Dies datus est eis de audiendo judicio suo die Lune ante mediam Qudragesimam, et tunc veniant dearmati. Et ad diem illum venerunt, et Elias committitur gaole de Flete per consilium domini Regis.

Plegii Hamonis de prosequendo, Willelmus le Tanur de *London*'[1] et Johannes del Hale.

[2] Octo homines de Watham jurati dicunt super sacramentum suum quod ut credunt, quia omnes de patria ita dicunt, equa pullenata fuit Hamoni, et quod capta fuit in communa de Cestrehunt' et quod Hamon eam invenit in caruca Philippi le King, et quod Eduardus illam dederat in maritagium cum filia sua ipsi Philippo ' et quesiti quando '[3] et quod idem Philippus post placitum istud motum in curia de Cestrehunt commisit[4] equam illam Elie *Picon* qui se facit warantum ut sic posset secure jurare, et bene dicunt quod alio modo non fuit equa ipsius Elie nec illam duxerat in partes illas. Dicunt eciam quod equa ivit in caruca Philippi per duos annos ut credunt, et melius credunt quod Edwardus illam cepisset in pastura per mesprisionem et ingnorantiam quam dicto modo.

Homines de Cestrehunt' jurati dicunt quod nesciunt si pullenata esset Hamoni, set melius credunt quod non esset ei pullenata, set bene sciunt quod Edwardus illam dedit in maritagium Philippo sicut predictum est, set non credunt quod Elias unquam illam vendidisset ipso Edwardo, bene autem sciunt quod coram tota parochia de Cestrehunt dixit idem Elias quod hoc fecit pro Deo[5] et rogavit omnes homines ut precarentur pro eo adeo veracissime sicut hoc fecit

---

[1] This word, illegible in A, is supplied from B.

[2] A, m. 14.

[3] These words are interlined. Apparently the jurors do not answer the question thus put to them.

[4] Substituted for *vendidit*. Edward made a sham gift or sale of the mare to Elias, in order that the latter when taking up the warranty might swear with safe conscience that she had been his own proper chattel.

[5] Elias protested before the parish that he entered into the warranty for conscience sake, i.e. because he really was under an obligation to warrant the mare. The mention of the parish (not township), and the prayers, suggests that Elias took occasion of divine service to make this declaration of his innocence.

Monday before [Mid] Lent: Thomas of Multon, Peter of Nereford, and the four knights who brought the record.

A day is given them to hear their judgment, on Monday before Mid Lent, and then let them come without their armour. At that day they came, and Elias is committed to the Fleet gaol by the king's council.

Hamo's pledges to prosecute: William the Tanner of London and John of Hale.

Eight men of Waltham being sworn say upon their oath that, as they believe (for all the countryside says so), the mare was foaled to Hamo, and that it was taken in the common of Cheshunt, and that Hamo found her in the plough of Philip King, and that Edward had given her by way of marriage gift with his daughter to Philip; and that after this action had been begun in the court of Cheshunt, Philip handed over the mare to Elias Piggun, the would-be warrantor, in order to enable him to swear safely; and they say positively that in no other way did the mare ever belong to Elias, nor had he brought her into those parts. They add that, as they believe, the mare went in Philip's plough for two years, and they rather think that Edward had taken her from the common by mistake and in ignorance, and not in manner aforesaid [i.e. not in felony].

The men of Cheshunt being sworn say that they know not whether the mare was foaled to Hamo, but they rather think that she was not; but they know well that Edward gave her to Philip as a marriage gift in manner aforesaid; but they do not believe that Elias had ever sold her to Edward; but they know well that in the presence of the whole parish of Cheshunt, Elias said that he [took up the warranty] for God's sake, and asked all men to pray for him so truly as true it was that he did this for God's sake

pro Deo et non pro denariis, unde melius credunt quod hoc fecit pro Deo quam pro alia causa. De maritagio filie Edwardi nichil audiverunt.

viij.

Homines de Wirmele jurati dicunt quod nesciunt si pullenata fuit Hamoni nec ne, set bene sciunt quod Edwardus illam dedit in maritagium Philippo cum filia sua, et bene credunt quod Edwardus illam emit et nesciunt a quo, set non credunt quod Elias unquam illam vendidisset Edwardo.

viij.

Homines de Enefeld' dicunt super sacramentum suum quod bene credunt quod equa fuit Hamonis et ei pullenata quia omnes homines ita dicunt, et quod Edwardus dedit eam in maritagium sicut prius dictum est, et bene sciunt quod Elias nunquam illam vendidit Edwardo, immo pro denariis hoc fecit Elias, scilicet pro x. marcis unde credunt quod habuit v. marcas et v. marce ei adhuc aretro sunt, et quidam eorum dicunt quod credunt quod hoc fecit pro filia ipsius Edwardi habenda in uxorem simul cum denariis.

Comes Britannie habet iterum curiam suam per consilium domini Regis de Hamone et Edwardo 'qui habent licenciam concordandi,' et Elias habeat judicium suum in curia domini Regis. 'Consideratum est quod amittat pedem et sciendum quod misericorditer agitur cum eo per consilium domini Regis cum majorem penam de jure demeruisset.'[1]

amittat pedem

193.

Essex

[2] Willelmus de Barrevilla captus et inprisonatus pro malo retto ponit se super comit' Essexie vel Norfolkie [vel] Suhantone vel super omnes de fidelitate sua ita quod si eum aquietent quietus sit, sin autem convincatur. Postea ponit se super comitatum Surreie vel super omnes homines

---

[1] Bracton, f. 151 b, speaks of this case. 'Sometimes a man enters into defence and warranty maliciously, fraudulently, and for reward, as a hired champion. If this be discovered before the justices, the duel will not go forward, but inquiry shall be made by the country whether he has taken reward or no. And if it be found that he has, then he shall lose foot *and fist*. Case of Elias Pigon, a hired champion before Martin Pateshull, Hil. A. R. 4, com. Essex.'

[2] A, m. 14.

and not for lucre; and so they believe rather that he did it for God's sake than for any other cause. As to the marriage portion of Edward's daughter they have heard nothing.

The eight men of Wormley being sworn say that they know not whether the mare was foaled to Hamo, but they know well that Edward gave her as a marriage gift with his daughter to Philip; and they believe that Edward bought her, they know not from whom; but they do not believe that Elias had ever sold her to him.

The eight men of Enfield say upon their oath that they well believe that the mare was Hamo's and foaled to him, for all men say so, and that Edward gave her as a marriage gift as aforesaid; and they know well that Elias never sold her to Edward, but [Elias] has [taken up the warranty].for money, to wit, for ten marks, whereof, as they believe, he has had five marks and five are still due to him. And some of them say that they think that [Elias] has done this to get Edward's daughter to wife as well as the money.

Cognizance of the case between Hamo and Edward is restored to the court of the Earl of Britanny by the king's council, and they have leave to compromise, and let Elias have his judgment in the king's court. It is considered that he do lose his foot, and be it known that by the action of the king's council he is dealt with mercifully, for by law he had deserved a worse punishment.

193. *Essex* William of Barreville, arrested and imprisoned for ill fame, puts himself upon the county of Essex, or of Norfolk, or of Southampton, or all of them, as to his good character, so that if they acquit him he shall go quit, and if not he shall be convicted. Afterwards he puts himself upon the county of Surrey, or upon all the men of England that

Anglie qui eum cognoscunt, et dicit quod appellatur Willelmus de Verly et non de Barrevilla.

A die Pasche in xv. dies venerunt xxiiij. milites de comitatu Surreie per summonicionem Regis, et dicunt super sacramentum suum quod credunt ipsum esse latronem et malum hominem et quod multa mala fecit tempore pacis et post pacem¹ et presertim de latrocinio facto in domo Roberti de Barrevilla. Et quia posuit se super eos, suspendatur etc.

194. ² Robertus Devoniensis captus pro malo retto apud London' cognovit in gaola coram tribus servientibus custodibus gaole quod si quidam capellanus de Derteford' qui venit ad gaolam ad inquirendum de pannis et aliis rebus quas amiserat et que ei furate fuerunt, ipsum deliberasset de prisona, monstraret ei pannos suos et illos ei redderet. Et capellanus venit et cognovit quod res sue furate fuerunt et quod fuit ad gaolam sicut dictum est, set non vult plus dicere ' quia sacerdos est.'³ Et preterea testatum est quod pluries alienavit loquelam suam, et dictum fuit quod abjuravit terram coram justiciariis itinerantibus in Devonia. Et quia cognovit coram servientibus domini Regis quod predictum est qui in hoc habent recordum,⁴ suspendatur.

195. ⁵ Testatum est per vicecomites Londonie et alios legales homines quod Rogerus le Waner inventus fuit seisitus de j. capa furrata et j. supertunica et j. toallia que extracta fuerunt de domo Fulconis le Wayder per fenestram cum j. longa virga habente croco⁶ ad capud, et quod cognovit coram eis quod ei invadiata fuerunt a quodam latrone qui suspensus fuit. Postea cognovit furtum et devenit proba-

---

¹ This refers to the peace which ended the civil war of 1215-7.
² A, m. 14.
³ He will not reveal any confession that has been made to him; or perhaps he will not admit that the lay court has any jurisdiction over him.
⁴ This means that no one can be heard to contradict their testimony as to a confession made in their presence.
⁵ A, m. 14.
⁶ *Sic.*

know him, and says that his name is William of Verly and not of Barreville.

On the quindene of Easter came twenty-four knights of the county of Surrey at the king's summons, and they say upon their oath that they believe him to be a thief and a bad man and that he has done many ill deeds in time of peace after the peace was made, and in particular a robbery in the house of Robert of Barreville. And since he put himself upon them, let him be hanged etc.

194. Robert of Devon, arrested at London for ill fame, confessed while in gaol before three serjeants, the keepers of the gaol, that if a certain chaplain of Dartford, who came to the gaol to inquire after some clothes and other things which he had lost, would get him [Robert] out of prison, he would show him where his clothes were and deliver them to him. And the chaplain came and confessed that his things had been stolen and that he went to the gaol as aforesaid, but he will not say more, because he is a priest. And also it is testified that [Robert] has often changed his story, and it was said that he had abjured the realm before the justices in the Devonshire eyre. And because he confessed before the king's serjeants as is aforesaid, and they have record in such a matter, let him be hanged.
Kent

195. It is testified by the sheriffs of London and other lawful men that Roger Wainer was found seised of a furred cape and a surcoat and a towel which were extracted from the house of Fulk Woader through the window by means of a long stick with a crook at the end, and that [Roger] confessed that these things were pledged with him by a certain thief who has been hanged. Afterwards he confessed the
Lond.

tor. Post retraxit se versus unum de recept', et alii non inveniuntur. Et ideo suspendatur.

¹ Robinus le Soper' cognovit coram eisdem quod invadiaverat predicto Rogero unum chalonem qui furatus fuit predicto modo cum virga in domo Hugonis le Rede, pro tribus denariis et obolo. Non potest contradicere ballivos domini Regis, et ideo suspendatur. Inventa fuerunt in camisia sua croca similia illi qui fuerunt ² in virga. 'Postea devenit probator et cognovit totum et eosdem appellat quos Rogerus *et eciam unum alium.*'³

196. ⁴ Gilibertus de Talestorp' captus apud London' eo quod vendiderat j. equum in Smithefeld' et debuit invenisse plegios et non rediit cum plegiis suis nec denarios suos habuit ⁵ et postea ·j. equam eodem modo, ita quod arestatus fuit, et evasit per mediam ecclesiam et iterum captus, non vult ponere se super patriam suam set petit quod possit abjurare regnum. Et abjuravit.

197. ⁶ Robertus de Wauilla appellat Thomam filium Alienore de Baiocis quod ipse die Lune proxima post festum S. Michaelis sicut Willelmus de Tillebroc dominus suus fuit at prandium suum apud Lue in domo Rogeri Fittel et idem Thomas cum eo ut armiger suus, idem Thomas fecit illuc venire unum exploratorem, scilicet, Thomam Mustel per consilium predicte Alienore, et tantum fecit quod idem Thomas una cum exploratore illo fecerunt Willelmum pre-

---

¹ A, m. 14.
² *Sic.*
³ Robin's fate is left in some uncertainty, but apparently he turned approver after he had been sentenced to death.
⁴ A, m. 14.
⁵ Probably the horses were stolen, and apparently Gilbert did not succeed in getting money for them. When asked by the buyers to find sureties for the warranty of title, he went away and did not come back, perhaps because he dared not; he may have been anxious to get the horses out of his hands, even though he could get no money for them. After he was arrested he escaped into a church, but instead of staying in sanctuary, ran out on the other side and was again captured. The marginal venue *Leic.* may be a mistake for *Lond.*
⁶ A, m. 28; B, m. 22 d.

theft and became an approver. Afterwards he withdrew from his appeal against one of those whom he charged as his receivers, and the others cannot be found. Therefore let him be hanged.

Robin Soaper confessed before the same [sheriffs and others] that he had pledged to the said Roger for threepence halfpenny a counterpane stolen in the said fashion by means of a stick from the house of Hugh Rede. He cannot [be heard to] contradict the king's bailiffs, so let him be hanged. Some crooks like that on the stick were found in his shirt. Afterwards he became an approver and confessed all and appealed those whom Roger appealed and one more also.

196. *Leic.* Gilbert of Talesthorpe was arrested at London because having sold a horse in Smithfield he was to find pledges [to warrant the title], and he never came back with his pledges nor did he get his money, and afterwards he did the same thing with a mare, and being arrested he escaped through a church and was then again caught. He will not put himself upon his country but prays that he be suffered to abjure the realm. He has abjured.

197. *Linc.* Robert of Waville appeals Thomas, son of Alienora of Bayeux, for that he on Monday next after Michaelmas when William of Tillbrook his lord was at dinner at Louth in the house of Roger Fittel and the said Thomas was with him as his esquire, the said Thomas, by the counsel of the said Alienora, caused a spy to come thither, namely, Thomas Mustel, and so contrived that he and the spy made William

dictum ire apud Tyrington' post prandium, et cum illuc venisset ad domum suam, idem Thomas et {uxor sua et [1]} socii sui inebriaverunt ipsum Willelmum, et cum inebriatus esset et jacuit in lecto suo, venit idem Thomas cum vi sua et percussit dominum suum dormiendo in fronte cum una hachia ad pik', ita quod incerebravit eum, unde si alium ictum non habuisset inde mortuus esset,[2] et quod hoc fecit nequiter et in felonia et in pace domini Regis etc. offert disracionare per corpus suum sicut curia consideraverit sicut ille qui interfuit et hoc vidit et fuit homo suus de manibus suis et nepos[3] suus et de manupasto suo. Dicit eciam in appello suo quod idem Thomas cepit de domino suo j. anulum cum j. rubi precii xl. marcarum simul cum aliis catallis suis, et quod quando mortuus fuit ipse ejecit eum de lecto et cooperuit eum litera[4] sua et putavit eum comburere.

Rogerus de Chelueston'[5] appellat Eustachium de Bokering' eodem modo et per eadem verba, quod ipse percussit eundem Willelmum dominum suum cum quadam hachia ad pik' in lo*nn*ia[6] ita quod de illa plaga mortuus esset si aliam non haberet.[7] Et hoc offert probare per corpus suum sicut curia consideraverit sicut ille qui interfuit et hoc vidit etc. [8] et dicit quod fuit homo suus et filius sororis sue et de manupasto suo.[8]

Et Thomas venit et defendit feloniam et mortem ipsius Willelmi et plagam et totum de verbo in verbum sicut curia consideraverit, et petit sibi allocari quod quedam inquisicio inde facta fuit in comitatu per preceptum domini Regis[9] per quam credit quod non possit habere appellum versus eum.

Et quesitus si manducavit cum Willelmo predicto apud

---

[1] Struck out in A, but stands in B.
[2] Several persons are to be appealed of having killed the same man; therefore it is well to assert that each gave one blow which by itself was a death-blow; Bracton, f. 138.
[3] *cognatus*, B.
[4] *litera*, B.
[5] *Chalueston'*, B.
[6] *luigna*, B.
[7] *habuisset*, B.
[8] Omit, B.
[9] A writ of January 30, 1220, directing that the appellees may be delivered from gaol on finding pledges, will be found in Rot. Cl. vol. i. p. 410; perhaps an inquest was taken before this writ was issued.

go after dinner to Torrington, and when he had come there to his house the said Thomas {and his wife} and his companions made William drunk, and when he was drunk and lay on his bed, the said Thomas came with his force and struck his lord while asleep on his forehead with a pickaxe and brained him, so that even if he had received no other blow he would have died; and that he did this wickedly and in felony and in the king's peace etc., he offers to deraign by his body as the court shall consider, as one who was present and saw this and was the man of [William's] hands and his nephew and of his mainpast. He adds in his appeal that Thomas took from his lord a ring with a ruby in it, price forty marks, with other chattels of his, and that when [William] was dead he cast him out of the bed and covered him with the bed-clothes and attempted to burn him.

Roger of Chelveston appeals Eustace of Beckering in the same manner and in the same words, that he struck William his lord with a pickaxe in the loin so that he would have died of that wound even if he had had no other; and this he offers to prove by his body as the court shall consider, as one who was present and saw this etc.; and he says that he [Roger] was [William's] man and his sister's son and of his mainpast.

And Thomas comes and defends the felony and William's death and the wound and all of it word by word as the court shall consider, and craves that it be allowed him that a certain inquest was made of this matter in the county [court] by the king's command, in consequence whereof, as [Thomas] believes, [Robert] can have no appeal against him.

And being asked if he dined with William at Louth, he

Lue, dicit quod revera manducavit cum eo et venit cum eo ad hospitium[1] apud Tyrinton' et quod supavit et bibit coram lecto suo et [2] coram domino suo, set dicit quod dominus suus misit eum nocte illa ad custodiendum quendam campum cum fabis pro porcis cujusdam Fabri qui solebant venire ad fabas illas comedendas, et cum redisset de campo illo cum sociis suis, scilicet, cum quodam Dicke Smithe et Radulfo de Nergvilla,[3] venit ipse per domum Thome Mustel et invenit eum extra domum suam, ita quod idem Thomas dixit ei quod habuit sitim et quod libenter biberet, et idem Thomas respondit quod non habuit aliquam sitim, set tamen si vellet libenter cum eo biberet, et intraverunt domum Thome Mustel et biberunt, et cum exirent de domo illa, idem Thomas Mustel dixit quod audivit clamorem, et cito post dictum fuit eis quod dominus suus fuit occisus, quo audito petiit idem Thomas consilium a Thoma Mustel et aliis[4] sociis suis quid inde faceret, et illi consiluerunt[5] ei quod non iret illuc, et ipse voluit illuc ire, set ipsi non permiserunt eum, et cum non ausus esset ire, ad hospitium[6] ipse ivit ad domum Petri de Beckerinck' avi sui et hoc factum monstravit ei et statim mane duxit eum illuc. Et dicit quod idem Robertus fuit eadem nocte apud Stiueton'.[7]

Et Eustachius venit et[8] eodem modo venit et defendit totum de verbo in verbum sicut curia consideraverit, et idem dicit de inquisitione, et petit sibi allocari et dicit sicut Thomas quod idem Rogerus fuit nocte illa apud Stiueton'.

Et Alienora venit et defendit consilium et assensum et totum de verbo in verbum sicut curia consideraverit et petit inquisitionem illam sibi allocari.

Idem Robertus appellat de vi Rogerum prepositum de

---

[1] Supply *suum*, B.
[2] Omit *et*, B.
[3] *Nogvill'*, B.
[4] Omit *aliis*, B.
[5] *consuluerunt*, B.
[6] Perhaps this means an inn or hospice where William's retainers slept; but more probably it means William's house. Beckering is close to Torrington.
[7] This last allegation is directed against the appellor's statement that he saw the crime. Stewton is close to Louth, and some fifteen miles from Torrington.
[8] Omit *venit et*, B.

says that in truth he did and came with him to his house at Torrington, and that he supped and drank in the room with the bed on which his lord was lying: but he says that his lord sent him that night to guard a certain field of beans because the pigs of a certain smith used to come and eat the beans, and when he returned from the field with his fellows, namely, Dicky Smith and Ralph of Nergville, he came by the house of Thomas Mustel, whom he found outside his house, and who said that he was thirsty and would like a drink, to which he replied that he was not thirsty but still would like a drink with him if that was his wish; and they entered Mustel's house and drank, and when they were leaving, Mustel said that he heard a cry, and soon afterwards it was told them that his lord was slain; thereupon Thomas [who is speaking] asked the advice of Mustel and his other companions as to what he should do, and they advised him not to go thither, and he wanted to go thither, but they would not suffer him, and since he dared not go to the house he went to the house of Peter of Beckering, his grandfather, and told him what had happened, and straightway in the morning took [Peter] to [where William was]. He adds that on that night Robert [the appellor] was at Stewton.

And Eustace comes and in the same manner defends all of it word by word as the court shall consider, and says the same as regards the inquest [in the county court], and craves that this be allowed in his favour, and says (as Thomas does also) that on the said night Roger [the appellor] was at Stewton.

And Alienora comes and defends counsel and consent and all of it word by word as the court shall consider, and craves that the said inquest be allowed in her favour.

Robert also appeals as an accessory Roger the reeve of

Stiueton' quod fuit cum ipso Thoma ad forciam illam etc., et hoc offert probare per corpus suum prout curia consideraverit. Remanet[1] in custodia in qua prius fuit in comitatu quousque illi de facto convincantur.

Et predictus Rogerus appellat Walterum filium Anketilli de Stiueton' eodem modo de vi quod fuit in forcia cum ipso Eustachio, et hoc offert etc. Remaneat sub custodia qua fuit quousque Eustachius appellatus de facto convincatur.

Et Robertus de Tillebroc appellavit Johannem fratrem predicti Thome qui est infra etatem quod percussit dominum suum de piko unius hachie in oculo etc. Set Robertus non venit, et Johannes qui fuit in domo ubi Willelmus occisus fuit et hoc cognovit et vidit plagas committitur gaole de Flete. 'Dicit eciam quod fuit in domo quando dominus suus cubavit et quod firmavit hostium camere quodam flagello,[2] et quod homines ville venerunt ad clamorem ad extinguendum ignem, et quod in flamma vidit plagas post ubi jacuit.'[3]

Et quia idem Thomas cognoscit quod fuit in villa ubi dominus suus occisus fuit, et scivit de morte ejus, et nullum inculpavit de morte ejus nec mortem ejus secutus fuit, nec adhuc sequitur, et eadem nocte coram lecto suo comedit et bibit etc., consideratum est quod duellum sit inter eos et quod Thomas det vadium defendendi se et Robertus probandi. Plegii ejus, Alanus de Wauilla et Stephanus de la Strande. Plegius Thome, gaola de Flete.

duellum

Eodem modo consideratum est de Eustachio etc., et ideo det vadium defendendi se et Rogerus probandi. Plegii ejus, Alanus de Wauilla et Stephanus de la Strande. Plegius Eustachii, gaola de Flete.

duellum

Dies datus est eis in Oct. S. Trin. et tunc veniant Robertus et Thomas armati, et Rogerus et Eustachius similiter. Et sciendum quod inventi fuerunt in laico habitu 'et sine tonsura'[4] et ita liberati gaole, et nullus

---

[1] Corr. *Remaneat*, B.
[2] *Flagellum*, which generally means a flail, is known also as meaning a bar for fastening a door; Du Cange.
[3] Postscript in A; not found in B. This seems to record an assertion by John that he saw nothing until after his lord was slain.
[4] Interpolated in A; not found in B.

Stewton, for that he was with Thomas in that force etc. ; and this he offers to prove by his body as the court shall consider. Let him remain in custody in the county as hitherto until the principal appellees be convicted.

Roger [of Chelveston] also appeals Walter, son of Anketil of Stewton, in the same manner as an accessory who was in the force with Eustace ; and this he offers etc. Let him remain in custody as hitherto until Eustace, the principal, be convicted.

And Robert of Tillbrook has appealed John brother of the said Thomas, who is under age, for that he struck his lord with the pick of an axe in the eye etc. But Robert does not come, and John, who was in the house in which William was slain and confesses this and saw the wounds, is committed to the Fleet gaol. (He says, too, that he was in the house when his lord went to bed and that he fastened the chamber door with a bar, and that the men of the vill came to the cry to put out the fire, and that then he saw the wounds as he lay in his bed by the light of the flames.)

And because the said Thomas confesses that he was in the vill where his lord was slain, and knew of his death, and charged none with that death, and made and yet makes no suit, and on that night ate and drank before the couch [on which his lord was] etc., it is considered that there be battle between them and that Thomas do give gage to defend himself and Robert to prove. [Robert's] pledges, Alan of Waville and Stephen of the Strand. Thomas's pledge, the Fleet gaol.

Like judgment is given as to Eustace, so let him give gage to defend himself and Roger to prove. [Roger's] pledges, Alan of Waville and Stephen of the Strand. Eustace's pledge, the Fleet gaol.

A day is given them, on the octave of Trinity, and then let Robert and Thomas come armed, and Roger and Eustace likewise. And note that they were found in lay dress and without tonsure and were delivered to gaol in

essoniavit ante vadia data quod fuerunt clerici, nec aliquis eos petiit ut clericos, set post vadium datum dixerunt quod fuerunt clerici. Et sciendum quod Thomas cognovit quod Thomas Mustel et duo alii prius nominati fuerunt cum eo quando audivit de morte domini sui in eadem villa.

Sciendum quod testatum fuit ibi quod quidam serviens de wappentachio, scilicet, Thomas de Luset habuit et adhuc habet capam ejusdem Willelmi furratam et quod fuit amicus predicte Alienore que de precepto et consensu a predictis appellata est.[1]

198.
Midd.

[2] Gilibertus de Suff' cognoscens se esse latronem appellat Thomam de Hereford' quod ipse simul cum eo occidit quendam hominem juxta Reygate in quodam bosco et invenerunt cum eo xx. denarios unde habuit medietatem ad opus suum, et hoc offert probare versus eum per corpus suum etc.

Et Thomas defendit totum de verbo in verbum per corpus suum sicut curia consideraverit. Et ideo det vadium defendendi se et Gilebertus probandi. Plegius utriusque, *duellum* gaola. Veniant die Jovis armati.

199.
Her.

[3] Thomas de Docking cognoscens se esse latronem appellat Ricardum le Champaneys de S. Albano de societate et latrocinio, scilicet quod simul furati fuerunt j. tunicam de burello unde habuit ad partem suam tres solidos de quibus emit unam capam, et eum receptavit in

---

[1] It would seem that the appellors were successful in their first battles, for on the roll for Trinity term the appeals of Roger of Chelveston against Walter of Stewton, and of Robert of Waville against Roger of Stewton, are proceeding, and it is there recorded that Walter vanquishes Roger, who is condemned to pay the recreant's fine; the fine, however, is forgiven, *quia pugnavit pro Rege*; see Bracton's Note Book, Case 1460. In Rot. Cl. vol. i. p. 424, is a curious writ dated July 25, 1220, relating to this matter; the Constable of the Tower is told that so long as Walter of Stewton is in his custody he is to be treated liberally, is to be *in libera prisona*, is to be allowed to live honourably of his own, and may learn sword-play (*et discere eskirmire*). It seems that Walter learnt *eskirmire* to some purpose.

[2] A, m. 29 d; B, m. 24.

[3] A, m. 29 d; B, m. 24.

that guise, and no one before the gages were given [for battle] essoined them as being clerks, nor did anyone demand them as clerks, but after battle was waged they said that they were clerks. And note that Thomas said that Thomas Mustel and two other persons named above were with him when he heard of his lord's death in the said vill.

Note that it was there testified that a certain serjeant of the wapentake, to wit, Thomas of Lunet had and still has a furred cloak of the said William and that he was a friend of Alienora who is appealed by the said persons as commanding and counselling the crime.

198. Gilbert of Suffolk, confessing himself a thief, appeals
Midd. Thomas of Hereford, for that he along with him slew a man in a wood near Reygate, and they found on [the slain man] twenty pence, whereof [Thomas] had one half to his use; and this he offers to prove against him by his body etc.

And Thomas defends all of it word by word by his body as the court shall consider. Therefore let him give gage to defend himself and Gilbert to prove. Pledge for both of them, the gaol. Let them come armed on Thursday.

199. Thomas of Docking, confessing himself a thief, appeals
Hertf. Richard Champneys of St. Albans of fellowship and larceny, to wit, for that together they stole a tunic of burell, whereof [Richard] had for his share three shillings, with which he bought a cape, and for that [Richard] received him in his

hospitio suo et scivit de latrocinio illo et de aliis rebus, et hoc offert probare per corpus suum etc.

Et Ricardus defendit societatem et latrocinium et receptamentum et totum de verbo in verbum etc. per corpus suum etc. Et quia est de mala fama consideratum est quod duellum sit inter eos, et Ricardus det vadium defendendi se et Thomas probandi. Plegii eorum, gaola. Veniant die Jovis armati.

¹ ' In Octabis S. Trin. venit vicecomes et custos gaole et dicunt quod Thomas simul cum aliis fregit gaolam et quod j. *rasurus* inventus fuit sub lecto ipsius Thome. Et Thomas hoc cognoscit. Et ideo suspendatur.'

susp'

200. ² Thomas de Luminges qui captus fuit cum latronibus apud S. Albanum venit et dicit quod non habet dominum nec est in franco plegio, nec aliquem plegium habet. Et preterea ³ testatum est per senescallum Abbatis de S. Albano et per probos homines quod cognovit latrocinium in curia Abbatis. Et preterea ⁴ cognovit in banco quod nullum hominem scivit qui tantus latro fuit sicut Robertus de Bermundes' senescallus Archiepiscopi,⁵ et postea retraxit se. Et quia omnia bona ei deficiunt nec vult ponere se super patriam, consideratum est quod suspendatur.

Kent

susp'

201. ⁶ Johannes Blakeman captus pro malo retto cognovit quod alias captus fuit apud Faveresham et quod inprisonatus fuit in carcere domini Regis apud Cantuariam, et quod evasit de carcere per auxilium *vicecomitis*. Et super hoc veniunt vicecomes Kancie et Willelmus de Esse qui tunc fuit constabularius Cantuarie et *recordantur* quod idem Johannes fuit in profundo carcere, et quod ibi fregit carcerem et quod fere potuit exire, [et quum] hoc percep-

Kent

---

¹ What follows is not in B.   ² A, m. 29 d; B, m. 24.
³ *postea*, B.   ⁴ *postea*, B.
⁵ Thomas thought of turning approver and therefore charged the Archbishop's steward.
⁶ A. m, 29 d.

house and knew of that larceny and of other things; and this he offers to prove by his body etc.

And Richard defends the fellowship and larceny and receipt and all of it word by word etc. by his body etc. And because he is of ill fame, it is considered that there be battle between them, and let Richard give gage to defend himself and Thomas to prove. Their pledge, the gaol. Let them come armed on Thursday.

On the octave of Trinity come the sheriff and the keeper of the gaol and say that Thomas along with others broke the gaol and that a razor [or other sharp instrument] was found under his bed. And Thomas confesses this. Therefore let him be hanged.

200. Thomas of Lyminge, who was arrested along with robbers at St. Albans, comes and says that he has no lord and is not in frank-pledge and has no pledge. Afterwards it is testified by the steward of the Abbot of St. Albans and by good men [of the Abbot's court] that he confessed himself a robber in that court. Afterwards he declared in the Bench that he knew no one who was so big a thief as Robert of Bermondsey the Archbishop's steward, and afterwards he withdrew this charge. And because there is no one point in his favour and he will not put himself on the country, it is considered that he be hanged.
Kent

201. John Blackman, arrested for ill fame, confesses that he was once before arrested, at Faversham, and put in the king's prison at Canterbury, and says that he escaped thence by the help of the sheriff. And upon this come the sheriff of Kent and William of Esse, who was the then constable of Canterbury, and they bear record that the said John was in the deepest dungeon and he broke prison and had almost got loose; and when this was discovered,
Kent

tum fuit, positus fuit in turri in tribus paribus firgiarum, et ibi fregit firgias *et exivit*, et tali modo evasit. Et Johannes non potuit hoc dedicere, et ideo suspendatur.

susp'

¹ PLACITA DE TERMINO S. TRINITATIS ANNO REGNI REGIS HENRICI QUARTO.

202.
Hertford

² Willelmus de Knappwell' ballivus S. Comitis Wintonie ostendit quod sicut homines domini sui scilicet quidam Stephanus et Philippus duxerunt quandam domicellam nomine Matillidem que fuit in custodia domini sui et unde fuit seisitus die quo iter suum arripuit versus terram Jerosolyme³ ut de illa cujus terram habuit racione terre quam Gaufridus de Bernevilla pater ipsius Matillidis de eo tenuit, venit Johannes de Merstona cum Willelmo fratre suo et cum aliis inter Hiche⁴ et S. Albanum⁵ die Martis ante Ascenscionem Domini⁵ in chimino domini Regis et in pace domini Regis et in felonia assultaverunt eos et vi et armis abstulerunt eis predictam domicellam, et nequiter et in felonia robaverunt predicto Stephano 'de catallo proprio'⁶ j. capam et j. chalonem et duo lintheamina et j. scapularium precii dim. marc. et plus et quod hoc fecit nequiter et in felonia et in pace etc. offert probare per corpus suum prout curia consideraverit.

Et Johannes venit et defendit pacem domini Regis etc. et feloniam et roberiam⁷ set verum vult dicere. Dicit etiam quod Gaufridus de Bernevilla predictus habuit duas filias scilicet illam Matillidem et quandam aliam primogenitam Aliciam nomine. Idem Gaufridus tenuit de predicto Comite

---

¹ The rolls here indicated as A and B respectively are Coram Rege Rolls Nos. 6 and 7; the text is from A.
² A, m. 10; B, m. 6.
³ The Earl has gone on the crusade; in this same year he dies at Damietta.
⁴ A little south of St. Albans Hedge Farm is marked on the map.

⁵⁻⁵ Omit, B.
⁶ Omit, B; interlined in A. It seems that the property was laid in Stephen, and that it was Stephen, not William, who offered battle. William represents himself as pleading on Stephen's behalf.
⁷ Supply *et totum de verbo in verbum*, B.

he was put in the tower and loaded with three pairs of fetters, and he broke his fetters and got away, and this was the manner of his escape. And John could not deny this. Therefore let him be hanged.

PLEAS OF TRINITY TERM IN THE FOURTH YEAR OF HENRY III. (A.D. 1220).

202.
Hertford

William of Knapwell, the bailiff of S[aher] Earl of Winchester, shows that as the men of his lord, to wit, Stephen and Philip were conducting a certain damsel named Maud (who was in ward to his lord and of whom his lord was seised on the day when he started for the Holy Land, as of her whose land he had by reason of the land which her father, Geoffrey of Berneville, held of him), came John of Marston with William his brother and with others between Hedge and St. Albans on the Tuesday before Ascension Day in the king's highway, and in the king's peace and in felony assaulted them and by force and arms took from them the said damsel, and wickedly and in felony robbed the said Stephen of one cape and one counterpane and two sheets and one scapulary, price a half-mark and more, of his [Stephen's] own proper chattels; and that this he did wickedly and in felony and in the peace etc., he offers to prove by his body as the court shall consider.

And John [of Marston] comes and defends the king's peace etc. and the felony and the robbery, but is willing to tell the truth. He says that the said Geoffrey of Berneville had two daughters, to wit, the said Maud and an elder daughter, Alice by name. Geoffrey held of the Earl, and

et predictus Comes concessit custodiam illarum Matillidis et Alicie cuidem Johanni de Litlebir' qui habuit amitam Abbatis de S. Albano[1] in uxorem, ut inde maritaret Johannem[2] filium suum et heredem, scilicet de Alicia, et de Matillide Saherum postnatum filium suum. Idem Johannes filius duxit in uxorem Aliciam predictam et de ea[3] habuit jam iiij. pueros. Contigit vero postea quod quedam ecclesia de eodem feodo vacavit, et placuit eidem Sahero postnato filio melius promoveri in ecclesiam illam quam uxorem ducere, et presentatus fuit episcopo et admissus ad ecclesiam illam. Quo facto quia Johannes primogenitus frater voluit totam hereditatem earum retinere posuit postnatam filiam Matillidem in Abbatia de Shoplee[4] cum monialibus ut eam ibi faceret monialem. Quum autem ipsa Matillis percepisset quod hoc factum esset ad ejus exheredationem, mandavit ipsa predictum Johannem de Merstona ut ad eam veniret, et cum venisset ostendit ei qualiter eam voluerunt facere monialem predictus Johannes de Litlebir' et amici sui, et in tantum locuta fuit cum eo et ita adamavit eum, quod ipse duxit eam in uxorem in eadem 'Abbatia. Quo facto ipse[5] Johannes de Litlebir' venit illuc et cum hoc audisset quod ita esset desponsata, ipse cum hominibus predicti Abbatis venit et adduxit eam versus Abbatiam de S. Albano. Et in ducendo eam, obviavit eis predictus Johannes de Merston', et cum ipsa eum vidisset, clamavit et dixit ei quod inimici ejus cum vi adduxerunt ut eam interficerent vel facerent eam monialem. Et ipse vidit multitudinem gentium et respondit ei quod noluit pro ea pugnare. Et ipsa hoc audiens sponte cecidit de equo suo et secuta fuit eundem Johannem virum suum, et tali modo recuperavit ipse

[1] It appears below that some of the Abbot's men took part in the quarrel; hence this notice of his kinship to John of Littlebury. The Abbot was William of Trumpington; he seems to have owed his position to the fact that he was a kinsman of the Earl of Winchester's steward; he scandalised the monks by his very secular behaviour. See Walsingham, Gesta Abbatum, vol. i. p. 250.

[2] *Willelmum*, B; but *Johannem* seems correct.

[3] *ea*, not in A, but in B.

[4] This seems to be the nunnery of Sopwell, which was situate a little south of St. Albans, and which was a cell of the Abbey of St. Albans.

[5] B has *duxit eam in partes suas ad domum suam*; but these words are struck out.

the Earl granted the wardship of Maud and Alice to one John of Littlebury (whose wife was the aunt of the Abbot of St. Albans), that he might marry John his son and heir to Alice and his younger son Saher to Maud. John the son married Alice and has already had four sons by her. Afterwards it chanced that a certain church belonging to the same fee fell vacant, and Saher, the younger son, chose to be promoted to that church rather than to marry a wife, and was presented to the bishop and admitted to the church. Thereupon John, the elder brother, wished to retain the whole inheritance [of the two damsels] and therefore placed Maud the younger of them with the nuns in the Abbey of Sopwell, intending to make her a nun of that house. But when Maud perceived that this was done to her disherison, she sent for the said John of Marston to come to her, and when he had come she showed him how the said John of Littlebury and his friends wished to make a nun of her, and talked and made love to him to such effect that he married her in the said Abbey. After this, John of Littlebury came thither, and when he had heard that she was thus espoused he with the men of the Abbot [of St. Albans] came and took her off towards the Abbey of St. Albans. And as they were conducting her, he, John of Marston, met them, and when she saw him, she cried aloud and said to him that his enemies were carrying her off by force that they might slay her or make a nun of her. And he saw that numbers were against him and answered that he would not fight for her. When she heard this, of her own free will she slipt off her horse and went after the said John [of Marston], her husband; and this was the way in which he recovered his wife.

uxorem suam. Postea vero venit predictus Johannes de Litlebir' cum Johanne de' Shelford' et aliis hominibus Abbatis ad domum de Shoplee et ceperunt ibi j. chalonem et duo lintheamina et illa asportaverunt versus S. Albanum. Et tunc obviavit eis quidam Gaufridus Hopeshot homo predicte Matillidis et ipsi interrogaverunt cujus homo esset et ipse respondit quod fuit homo ipsius Johannis de Merston' et debuit ire ad domum de Shople propter j. chalonem et duo lintheamina. Et Johannes de Litlebir' statim dixit ei quod panni illi sui fuerunt et quod ipse latro fuit et ceperunt eum et ligaverunt pannos [1] super eum et eum adduxerunt apud S. Albanum et ibi eum tenent in prisona [2] et faciunt eum appellare de hoc eodem facto quo nunc appellant istum Johannem. Et bene dicunt [3] quod hoc appellum faciunt per odium et athiam, et petit sibi allocari quod appellum illud faciunt per quendam campionem conductum [4] scilicet predictum Stephanum qui pridie fecit duellum apud Hunt'.

Et predictus ballivus Comitis defendit pro Comite quod nunquam concessit maritagium predicte Matillidis predicto Johanni de Litlebir' set illam retinuit in custodia sua, et [5] die quo iter suum arripuit [6] fuit de ea seisitus [6] et illam fecit committere per ballivos suos in predicta Abbatia et ibi per ipsum Comitem moram fecit donec predicto modo robata fuit, et petunt [7] sibi allocari quod ipse Johannes eam duxit in uxorem sicut cognoscit et bene defendunt [7] quod nunquam fuit desponsata eidem Johanni de Merston' priusquam eam cum vi sua robasset sicut predictum est. De hoc autem quod Stephanus est campio conductus hoc bene defendunt [7] quia ipse est homo domini sui et nunquam cum alio fuit nisi cum domino suo et cum militibus suis per preceptum Comitis. Revera ipse defendit terram Ade de Portu militis domini sui per dominum suum etc., et quod predictam roberiam ei fecerunt sicut predictum est, Philippus

ad jud'

---

[1] Supply *illos*, B.   [2] Omit *in prisona*, B.   [3] *Sic* A, B.
[4] *conducticium*, B.   [5] Om. *et*, B.   [6] Omit, B.   [7] *Sic* A, B.

Afterwards came the said John of Littlebury with John of Shelford and other of the Abbot's men to the nunnery at Sopwell and took there one counterpane and two sheets and carried them off towards St. Albans. And one Geoffrey Hopeshot, a man of the said Maud, met them, and they asked him whose man he was, and he answered that he was the man of John of Marston [Maud's husband], and that he had got to go to the nunnery at Sopwell for a counterpane and two sheets. Thereupon John of Littlebury said that the bedclothes in question were his, and that [Geoffrey] was a thief, and they captured him and bound the bedclothes upon him and led him off to St. Albans, and there they keep him in prison, and they are causing an appeal to be made against [Geoffrey] for the same fact of which they now appeal him [John of Marston]. And he [John of Marston] says of a truth that they make this appeal for hate and spite, and he craves that it be allowed in his favour that they make this appeal by means of a hired champion, to wit, the said Stephen, who the day before fought a judicial combat at Huntingdon.

And the said bailiff of the Earl, on behalf of the Earl, denies that [the Earl] ever granted the marriage of the said Maud to John of Littlebury, but he retained her in his guardianship, and was seised of her on the day on which he started [for the crusade], and he caused his bailiffs to commit her to the said Abbey of Sopwell, and there she stayed by the Earl's appointment, until she was stolen thence in manner aforesaid; and he craves that it be allowed in his favour that John [of Marston] confesses that he has married her; and he denies that she ever was espoused to the said John of Marston before he carried her off by force in manner aforesaid. And as to Stephen being a hired champion, this he fully denies, for he is the man of his [William's] lord [the Earl] and was never with any other save with [the Earl] and with [the Earl's] knights by the Earl's commands, though true it is that he [Stephen] has by the Earl's command defended [in battle] the land of Adam of Port, one of the Earl's knights. And that they [John of

Boiard cui roberia facta fuit offert disracionare per corpus suum versus ipsum Johannem sicut curia consideraverit, et bene defendit captionem pannorum sicut idem Johannes dicit et quod nunquam captus fuit Gaufridus cum pannis sicut predictum est.

Et Philippus quesitus¹ si ita sit sicut Willelmus senescallus pro eo narravit, dicit ² quod ita est et Stephanus ³ hoc idem cognoscit.

Et Johannes de Merston' quesitus quo waranto duxit eamdem Matillidem in uxorem, dixit quod revera per voluntatem ipsius Matillidis, set dicit quod ipsa in custodia Johannis de Litlebir' patris per Comitem qui eidem Johanni custodiam concesserat de ipsa Matillide et de terra sua cum maritagio, unde dicit quod non cepit eam de custodia ipsius Comitis, set de custodia Johannis exivit ipsa eo quod voluit eam facere monialem.

Et ballivus Comitis dicit, quod ipsa fuit in custodia Comitis domini sui die quo iter suum arripuit etc. et quod Comes ejus custodiam non dimiserat Johanni de Litlebir' ad maritandum⁴ set maritagium Alicie ei dimisit tantum, set revera quia confidebat de ipso Johanne et de uxore ejus commisit eis Matillidem ut eam ponerent in predicta Abbatia pro parentela ipsius Comitis que ibi fuit ut ibi salvo custodiretur, et hoc bene patet quia idem Johannes nichil clamat in illa custodia.

Et quia idem Johannes pater absens est, consideratum est quod summoneatur quod sit in Oct. S. Joh. Bapt. ad cognoscendum quid juris ipse clamat in custodia predicte Matillidis etc. et si fuit in custodia sua quomodo exivit de custodia sua etc. Et quia Johannes de Merston' cognoscit quod sine waranto eam duxit, inveniat hos plegios standi recto, Ricardum de Merston' et Reginaldum Tallebois. ⁵ Ballivus S. Albani petit curiam suam.⁵

---

¹ *Philippus et Stephanus quesiti*, B.
² *dicunt*, B.
³ *uterque eorum*, not *Stephanus*, B.
⁴ B inserts *tantum*; but wrongly.
⁵-⁵ Not in B; margin of A.

Marston and his fellows] committed the said robbery against him, Philip Boiard, to whom the robbery was done, offers to deraign by his body against the said John as the court shall consider. And he [Philip] fully denies the taking of the bedclothes alleged by John, and that Geoffrey was ever arrested with the said bedclothes in manner aforesaid.

And Philip, on being asked whether it be as William the steward has counted on his [Philip's] behalf, says that so it is, and Stephen says the same.

And John of Marston, on being asked by what warrant he married Maud, said, 'By Maud's free will,' but he says that she was in ward to the said John of Littlebury the elder by the Earl's grant, for he had granted the wardship of her person and of her land and her marriage; so he says that he did not take her from the Earl's custody, but she escaped from the custody of John [of Littlebury], who wanted to make her a nun.

And [William], the Earl's bailiff, says that she was in the custody of his lord the Earl on the day when he started [for the crusade], and that the Earl had not demised the wardship to John of Littlebury so far as concerned [Maud's] marriage, but had merely demised Alice's marriage; however, as he [the Earl] had great confidence in John [of Littlebury] and his wife, he entrusted Maud to them in order that they might place her in the said Abbey [of Sopwell] for safe keeping, since the Earl had kinsfolk there; and that this is so is evident, for John [of Littlebury] makes no claim to the wardship.

And because John [of Littlebury] the elder is not present, it is considered that he be summoned to be here on the octave of St. John Baptist, to declare what right he claims in the wardship of the said Maud etc., and if she was in his custody, how she went out of his custody etc. And for that John of Marston confesses that he married her without warrant, let him find pledges that he will stand to right, namely, Richard of Marston and Reginald Taillebois. The bailiff of St. Albans craves cognizance of the case.

¹PLACITA DE TERMINO S. MICHAELIS ANNO REGNI REGIS HENRICI QUARTO INCIPIENTE QUINTO.

203. ²Rogerus de Kyrkele queritur quod Henricus de Ver venit ad domum suam in Mutford'³ de nocte die Lune in prima ebdomada Quadragesime et fecit portare coram eo unam torchiam⁴ de candela illuminatam et fregit hostium et intravit domum suam, et interrogavit ubi esset filia ipsius Rogeri quam ei sepius pepigerat, et cum illam non invenisset in domo illa, intravit in cameram suam et quesivit eam per totam cameram, set mater sua ipsam filiam suam emiserat per quandam fenestram de camera,⁵ et cum illam non invenisset in camera, exivit versus grangiam suam que plena erat blado scilicet de ordeo, et invenit hostium clausum et firmatum sera, et fregit serruram et hostium, et intravit et quesivit per totum filiam suam, et cum ipsam non invenisset, apposuit candelam in blado et combussit totum bladum et grangiam, et hoc fecit nequiter et in felonia et in pace domini Regis, et hoc offert disracionare per Thomam de Braddel'⁶ qui habet filiam ipsius Rogeri in uxorem, per corpus suum prout curia consideraverit sicut ille qui amisit de suo in grangia unam archam cum pannis suis, et si de eo male contigerit, idem Rogerus offert probare versus eum⁷ sicut curia consideraverit.

Et Henricus venit et defendit pacem domini Regis et feloniam et combustionem et totum de verbo in verbum sicut curia consideraverit, set verum vult dicere. Dicit eciam quod idem Rogerus est villanus suus, et revera quedam domus combusta fuit per infortunium, et predictus Thomas duxit filiam ipsius Rogeri in uxorem contra voluntatem suam desicut ipsam maritare non potuit sine assensu suo, et quia noluit concedere maritagium, nec facere

---

¹ A and B are Coram Rege Rolls Nos. 9 and 8 respectively; the text is from A.
² A, m. 19; B, m. 12.   ³ *Mutfeud*, B.   ⁴ *thorchiam*, B.
⁵ Om. *de camera*, B.   ⁶ *Bradel*, B.   ⁷ Om. *versus eum*, B.

PLEAS OF MICHAELMAS TERM IN THE FOURTH AND FIFTH YEARS OF HENRY III. (A.D. 1220).

203. Roger of Kirkley complains that Henry de Vere came to his [Roger's] house at Mutford by night, on Monday in the first week of Lent, and had a lighted torch of wax carried before him, and broke the door and entered his house and asked where was Roger's daughter, whom [Roger] had often promised him; and when he could not find her in the house, he entered her chamber and sought her throughout the chamber; but her mother had got her out of the chamber window; and when he could not find her in the chamber, he went out towards [Roger's] barn, which was full of corn, to wit, of barley, and he found the door closed and bolted, and he broke the bolt and the door, and entered and sought her everywhere; and when he could not find her, he set the torch to the corn, and burnt all the corn and the barn; and this he did wickedly and in felony and in the king's peace; and this [Roger] offers to deraign by the body of Thomas of Bradley, who has Roger's [said] daughter to wife, as [by the body of] one who himself lost property in the burning of the barn, namely, a chest with his clothes in it; and in case any mischance shall befall [Thomas], Roger offers to prove against [Henry] as the court shall consider.

And Henry comes and defends the king's peace and the felony and the burning and all of it word by word as the court shall consider, but desires to tell the truth. He adds that Roger is his villein, and true it is that a building was burned, but this was by misadventure; and the said Thomas married Roger's daughter against [Henry's] will; and whereas [Roger] could not give her in marriage without [Henry's] consent, and he [Henry] would not consent nor would he

ipsum liberum,[1] facit ipse hoc appellum per odium et atiam, et petit sibi allocari quod appellat eum de combustione alterius domus quam sue, et de hoc quod idem Rogerus est villanus suus qui hoc appellum facit.

[2] Et Henricus quesitus quando domus combusta fuit, dicit quod ut audivit combusta fuit predicta die Lune de nocte et quod ipse captus fuit proxima die Sabbati ante festum S. Michaelis.[2]

Et Rogerus quesitus si secutus fuit comitatus, dicit quod fuit ad quemlibet comitatum et quod comitatus fuit de mense in mensem.

Et quia Thomas appellat eum de combustione alterius domus sue et preterea idem Rogerus cognovit quod die quo domus combusta fuit tenuit de eodem Henrico, consideratum est quod appellum non jacet, set xij. liberi et legales et discreti homines sum' per quos etc. et qui nec ipsum Henricum nec predictos Rogerum vel Thomam affinitate[3] attingant et qui nec odio nec amore veritatem celare velint quod sint a die S. Hillarii in xv. dies ad recognoscendum si predictus Henricus venit predicta die Lune de nocte ad domum ipsius Rogeri et domum suam fregit et grangiam suam combussit necne et ita se interim inde certificent ne nos ad eum[4] capere possimus.[5]

---

[1] Possibly *ipsam liberam*, A, B. It seems that *ipsum* refers to Roger; it is Roger who could not *maritare* the girl; at least *maritare* commonly means to give in marriage. On the other hand, it seems to be Thomas whom Henry charges with making an appeal touching a house that is not his; for see the judgment.

[2-2] Om. B.

[3] *affirmitate*, B.

[4] *Sic*, A, B; but seemingly it should be *eos*.

[5] Bracton refers to this case on f. 146. Search has unsuccessfully been made for later proceedings. Henry de Vere is elsewhere accused of abduction and robbery (Bracton's Note Book, Case 1597); as to his dealings with the manor of Mutford, see Rot. Hund. vol. ii. p. 192. His plea suggests that the right of prohibiting the marriage of villeins was liable to gross abuse, and that in such abuse there may be some little ground of fact for the legends which became current in later times.

enfranchise [Roger], therefore the appeal is grounded on hate and spite; and [Henry] craves that it be allowed in his favour that [Thomas] appeals him concerning a house which is not his [Thomas's], and also that Roger, who makes this appeal, is his [Henry's] villein.

And Henry, upon being asked when the house was burned, says that he has heard say that it was burned by night on the Monday aforesaid, and that he was arrested on the Saturday before Michaelmas.

And Roger, upon being asked whether he attended the county courts, says that he attended every court, and that there were monthly sessions.

And for that Thomas appeals [Henry] of burning a house which belongs not to [Thomas], but to another, and moreover Roger confesses that on the day of the fire he [Roger] was Henry's tenant, it is considered that the appeal does not lie, but let twelve free and lawful and discreet men be summoned by whom [the truth may be made known], and who are not related to Henry, nor to Roger or Thomas, and who will not for hate or love conceal the truth, to be [here] in the quindene of Hilary, to recognise whether on the said Monday Henry came by night to the house of Roger, and broke his house and burnt his barn, or no; and in the meantime, let them certify themselves as to the facts, in order that we [the king or the justices] may have no cause for betaking ourselves against them.

GLOSSARY.

The numbers refer to the Cases, not to the pages.

By Du Cange is meant Léopold Favre's edition of the Glossary, Niort, 1884–7.

abastardare (54), to bastardise; Du Cange has this word.

adreciare (147), to set straight, to set to rights, e.g. to pull down a house which is a nuisance; Du Cange, s.v. adresciare; Skeat, s.v. address, dress.

astela (149), a staff, e.g. the staff of a banner; Du Cange, s.v. astella; Roquefort, astelle; Littré, attelle; a diminutive from hasta.

astrium (149), a pavement. The commoner form is astrum, which see in Du Cange. See also astrea, astracum, astragus. In the English law-books the word astrum means a hearth or hearth-stone, and a child still at his father's hearth is astrarius. The derivation of astrum seems very uncertain; it is discussed by Diez s.v. piastra.

atia, attia, atya (25, 78, 84, 86 etc.), hate, spite. This is the English word hate; see Skeat, s.v. hate, Du Cange, s.v. atia.

attornare (87, 121). In the sense to attorn, to appoint an attorney, this word is common enough; for its etymology see Skeat, s.v. attorney, Diez, s.v. torno. But here and elsewhere (e.g. Pleas of the Crown for Gloucestershire, A.D. 1221, pp. 43, 107) it is used in the sense of to ill-treat, to disfigure. It here seems the French word atourner, v. a., 'parer, mais avec un sens de familiarité ou d'ironie' (Littré); Roquefort gives 'atorner, parer, orner, arranger; et dans un autre sens, changer, défigurer.' Perhaps it comes from ad-ornare and so has nothing to do with our attorn, attorney, attornment.

bersare (88), to hunt beasts; see Du Cange, s.v. bersa, Diez, s.v. bercer. According to Du Cange it means to hunt beasts by driving them into wattled enclosures (see Littré, s.v. bercail, berceau); but bercer, or berser, is used of killing game by other means. The derivation of the word is disputed.

bluet (88), blue cloth; see Du Cange, s.v. bluet, Roquefort, s.v. bloet. There are names similarly formed for other cloths: thus russet, brunet, haberget.

burellus (199), a kind of coarse cloth; Fr. bure, bureau; Du Cange, s.v. burellus, birrus; Roquefort and Littré, s.v. bure; Diez, s.v. bujo. Apparently this cloth gets its name from its dark red (birrus) colour.

GLOSSARY.   143

The numbers refer to the Cases, not to the pages.

see in Du Cange; Italian, pavonazzo, from pavo, a peacock.

pottaur (147), a pottery (?); Du Cange has poteria with this meaning.

rasurus (199), a razor; Fr. rasoir; Skeat, s.v. razor. In Case 199 it is used to describe some instrument whereby an escape from gaol was effected; can it mean a file?

regratarius (137), a regrater, one who buys to sell again at a profit; as to the offence of regrating, see Spelman, s.v. regratarius.

runcinus (84), a rouncey, a small horse; Du Cange, s.v. rucinnus: Diez, s.v. rozza.

skermia (192), **eskirmire** (197, note). We have here evidence that the art of sword-play was professionally taught. The Fr. escrime seems connected with the German schirm; Skeat, s.v. skirmish; Diez, s.v. scaramuccia, schermo.

tensare (43). Apparently made from tenere; to hold, to protect (Diez, s.v. tencer); hence by a transition easy in the middle ages, to tax, and finally, to pillage. In Case 43 Sefrid has exacted toll from the ships. See Du Cange, s.v. tensare; Roquefort, tencer, tenser.

viridis (88). It is not certain that pallium de viridi, or pallium virid' means a cloak of green; for viridis, or viride, seems used to mean vair, spotted fur; it was employed as a Latin translation of the French word vair, which really had its origin in Lat. varius. See Du Cange, s.v. viride; Skeat, s.v. meniver.

INDEX OF MATTERS.

The numbers refer to the Cases, not to the pages.

Abatement of nuisance, 147
Abduction, 202
Abjuration, 48, 49, 77, 89, 107, 116, 142, 143, 161, 169, 194, 196
Accessory, *see* Principal and Accessory
Acolyte, 189
Adulterer, 87
Aid, 158, 168
Ale-tasters, 150
Alibi, 84, 88
Amercement of coroners, 47, 62, 74
  county, 17, 38, 62, 129, 136, 158
  judges, 106
  jurors, 15, 21, 47, 62, 71, 127, 130, 159, 172, 181
  parties, 8, 9, 13, 14, 19, 28, 82, 86, 138, 147
  peers, 44
  pledges, 16, 34, 43, 45, 103, 127, 134, 159, 163
  serjeant, 48
  sheriff, 30, 154, 155
  township, 12, 127, 142, 153, 181
  witnesses, 45
Amercement, distress for, 42
Appeal of arson, 25, 163, 165, 203
  of beating wife, 26, 164
  of homicide, 1, 19, 27, 28, 29, 32, 39, 40, 67, 76, 80, 85, 89, 97, 100, 117, 118, 119, 121, 130, 153, 158, 161, 189, 197
  of imprisonment, 42, 115, 165
  of mayhem, 4, 9, 11, 24, 37, 54, 79

Appeal of rape, 7, 96, 141, 166
  of robbery, 8, 13, 14, 16, 21, 23, 33, 82, 84, 88, 105, 126, 138, 159, 200
  of treason, 115
  of wounds, 41, 87, 155
  by infant, 85
  by maimed man, 4, 9, 11, 24, 79
  by man too old to fight, 19, 27, 165
  by woman, 1, 7, 16, 32, 40, 68, 78, 105, 117, 118, 119, 120, 130, 141, 153, 158
  against infant, 87, 99
  against maimed man, 84
  against man too old to fight, 84
Appeal compromised, 7, 141
Appeal quashed, 1, 3, 13, 14, 23, 25, 26, 28, 29, 32, 37, 39, 54, 67, 76, 84, 86, 97, 103, 121, 138, 161, 165
Appeal, special pleas in, 3, 23, 39, 40, 76, 84, 86, 87, 90, 99, 100, 105, 121, 138, 158, 159, 161, 164, 197, 202
Appeal withdrawn, 9, 27, 135, 155
Appeals, priority of, 99, 121
Approver, 109, 140, 190, 195, 198, 199
Archdeacon, 117, 160
Arrest, summary, 42, 43, 74, 77, 103, 106, 133, 145, 153, 165, 194, 200
Arson, 25, 110, 163, 165, 203
Assize, grand, 46
Assize of bread and beer, 149

The numbers refer to the Cases, not to the pages.

Assize of Clarendon, 1, 5, 6, 8, 10, 12, 107
Assize of cloth, 148
Assize of novel disseisin, 159
Assize of wine, 52, 151
Autrefois acquit, 76, 158

Bail, *see* Pledges
Bailment, 105
Bancum, 115 (p. 75), 177
Battle, 41, 80, 83, 85, 89, 91, 92, 93, 125, 140, 164, 172, 190, 192, 197, 198, 199, 202
Bedell, 26, 178
Bench, the, 115 (p. 74), 177
Bench, justices of the, 18
Bishop's certificate, 123, 189
Books, cartloads of, 139
Boroughs, *see* Municipal bodies
Boycotting, 178
Bracton, cases cited by, 186, 203
Bread and beer, assize of, 149
Bread and beer, demand of, 150
Bridge, county, 176
Burglary, 6, 8, 122, 124
Burial without view of the coroner, 108, 156, 179
Burning as a punishment, 191

Carucage, 17
Castellating house, 115
Certainty in pleading, 60
Certificatio, 115 (p. 73)
Champion, 3, 19, 84, 86, 87, 105, 115 (pp. 71, 72), 202
Champion, hired, 126, 192, 202
Charters, royal, 82, 137, 174
Civil and criminal liability, 159
Clergy, benefit of, 48, 49, 54, 117, 118, 123, 135, 140, 159, 160, 185, 189, 197
Clerk of justices, 18
Clerk of sheriff, 18
Common, 138
Commune of Jews, 103
Compromise, 7, 49, 78, 79, 82, 102, 192
Compurgation, 61, 82, 178

Confession, 77, 111, 118, 119, 140, 144, 184, 191, 194
Confession, seal of, 194
Conquest, Norman, prescription from, 46
Conspiracy, 178
Coroner, 4, 23, 24, 26, 31, 38, 41, 42, 47, 62, 74, 75, 115, 132, 136, 151, 156, 164, 181
Coroners, rolls of, 38, 62
Corruption, 181
Council, the king's, 148, 168, 192
Counselling a crime, 54, 180, 165
County bridge, 176
County court, proceedings in, 4, 15, 21, 47, 60, 88, 106, 115, 121, 126, 153, 156, 160, 172, 176
County, testimony of, 1, 14, 23, 24, 37, 38, 40, 41, 42, 47, 62, 64, 69, 75, 78, 121, 125, 126, 129, 131, 136, 139, 164, 168, 179, 190
Court baron, 42, 192
Court christian, 49, 117, 118, 160, 189
Court, the Great, 177
Crusader's privilege, 202
Custom, local, 3, 46, 128, 131, 139, 149, 152, 173
Customary tenant, 138
Customs, exaction of, 43, 46, 139, 150, 168, 176

Damages, 73
Death, the book of, 91
Delegation of jurisdiction, 186
Deodand, 156
Disseisin, 159
Distress, 42, 88, 90, 105, 159, 165
Distress, misuse of goods taken in, 165
Drawing as a punishment, 179
Dying declaration, 27, 104, 121, 189

Ear mark, 192
Earnest money, 150
Englishry, presentment of, 55, 127, 128, 131, 134, 152, 180
Escape, 10, 154, 155
Escheat, 144, 161, 170

INDEX OF MATTERS. 147

The numbers refer to the Cases, not to the pages.

Essoin de malo lecti, 164
Essoin in criminal cases, 16, 21, 34, 72, 95, 115, 186
Essoinee's duty of staying in bed, 164
Evidence, 20, 38, 43, 45, 106, 169, 170, 184, 192
Exchequer, 40
Exclusive trading, *see* Boycotting
Excommunication, 105
Eyre, cases reserved from, 139, 177
Eyre, justices in, 100, 180

Felony, 67, 114
Feme coverte, *see* Husband and Wife
Fencing lessons, 192, 197 (p. 133 *note*)
Fleet Gaol, 192, 197
Flight, 2, 20, 28, 49, 62, 74, 179
Forest, offences in, 88, 133
Forfeiture of chattels, 2, 28, 62, 74, 75, 153, 161, 170
Franchise, 98, 132, 174, 177, 181, 191
Frank-pledge, 24, 28, 36, 49, 55, 62, 117, 124, 129, 131, 148, 152, 184, 200

Gaol, *see* Fleet Gaol, Imprisonment, Prison
Gaol delivery, 127, 180
General issue, 164
Guardianship in chivalry, 202

Habeas corpus, 115
Hamsoken, 60, 86, 165
Hanging, 111, 112, 119, 125, 140, 143, 144, 153, 157, 179, 181, 182, 184, 190, 193, 194, 195, 199, 200
Hanging the dead, 142
Highway, the king's, 87, 147, 175
Homage, 85
Homicide, 1, 2, 5, 26, 27, 28, 30, 40, 67, 68, 70, 89, 102, 114, 121, 127, 128, 133, 135, 143, 145, 179, 188
Honour, court of an, 192
Horning, 115

Hue and cry, 25, 36, 48, 91, 94, 104, 106, 112, 115, 161, 166, 184
Hundred Court, proceedings in, 15, 36, 42, 48, 115, 119, 181
Hundred, serjeant of, *see* Serjeant
Hundred, testimony of, 19, 20, 42, 108, 110, 111, 119, 186
Husband and Wife, 32, 141, 152, 158, 164

Imprisonment of suspected persons, 30, 40, 42, 74, 103, 115
Imprisonment for false appeal, 26, 30, 35, 45
Imprisonment, false, 42, 45, 95, 115, 165
Indictment, 170, 189, 191, 193, 194
Infancy, 39, 85, 87, 99, 100
Infant en ventre slain, 26, 78, 82
Inquest, after appeal has been quashed, 1, 13, 55, 153
Inquest by sheriff, 96, 186, 197
Inquest, ex officio, 8, 108
Inquest, when appeal not prosecuted, 110, 155, 168
Inquests, repeated, 100
Insanity, 70, 113, 187

Jew, accused of crime, 59, 108
Jews, commune of, 108
Jurors amerced, 15, 21, 127, 130, 172
Jurors consult in private, 36
Jury, constitution of, 105
Jury of twenty-four, 153, 157, 193
Jury, noteworthy cases, 5, 16, 23, 39, 55, 64, 71, 79, 81, 87, 89, 91, 92, 93, 100, 105, 120, 130, 133, 153, 157, 161, 165, 166, 170, 179, 186, 192, 203
Jury, refused, 105, 153, 157, 195, 200
Justices learned in the law, 34
Justiciar, the, 40, 46, 47, 79

King consulted, 113
King, pleas which follow the, 82, 83, 84, 104, 115

148   PLACITA CORONE.

The numbers refer to the Cases, not to the pages.

King's death, imagining the, 115
King's household, 115 (p. 70)
King's peace, 21, 31, 84, 88, 104, 115, 172
Kinsfolk of the slain, 47, 102
Kinship of appellor with slain man, 28, 105
Kiss of peace, 82

Laches, 28, 39, 78
Larceny, 16, 60, 82, 88, 90, 126, 138, 192, 195
Larceny of title deeds, 82
Law, wager of, 61, 82, 178
Liber mortis, 91
Liberty, *see* Franchise
Limitation of actions, 175
Lord and man, 76, 80, 85, 89, 126, 197, 208
Lord and tenant, 115, 208
Lord appeals on behalf of man, 64
Lord's peace, the, 192
Lunatic, 70, 187

Mainour, criminal with the, 72, 90, 106, 112, 125
Mainpast, 121, 161, 197
Malicious prosecution, 170
Manure, 150
Market, 22, 44, 50, 137, 177
Marriage, lord's right of, 202
Marriage of villeins, 203
Married woman, *see* Husband and Wife
Mayhem, 4, 9, 11, 24, 79
Measures, false, 61
Merchet, 203
Mill-monopoly, 177
Misadventure, 81, 114, 132, 156, 188
Misdemeanour, 61
Misnomer, 193
Mitigation of sentence, 77
Monastic profession, 135, 202
Municipal bodies and privileges, 69, 82, 137, 139, 140, 147, 149, 150, 173, 174, 177, 178
Murder, *see* Homicide
Murder fine, 55, 127, 128, 131, 134, 152

Mute, standing, 153, 157, 196, 200
Mutilation, 77, 192

New trial, 100
Nuisance, 147
Nun made so against her will, 202

Odium et atia, 25, 78, 81, 84, 86, 87, 88, 91, 92, 93, 94, 95, 104, 202, 203
Officers, misbehaviour of, 74, 167, 168
Official, bishop's, 123, 160
Ordeal, failure at the, 116
Ordeal of iron, 4, 9, 11, 12, 24, 65, 68, 101, 119
Ordeal of water, 1, 5, 6, 8, 10, 12, 19, 20, 57, 66, 101, 107, 116, 122, 125
Outlawry, 2, 47, 78, 121, 129, 133, 136

Pardon, 47, 114, 134, 136, 147, 171
Payment for aid, 158, 163
Payment for a record, 115
Payment for inquest, 23, 59, 64, 69, 72, 74, 78, 79, 81, 84, 86, 88, 91, 94, 99, 105, 109, 130, 134, 161, 16
Payment for removing a case, 46
Payment ne occasionetur, 185
Peace, *see* King's peace, Sheriff's peace, Lord's peace
Peace pledged in county court, 121
Peace, surety of the, 47
Peers, amercement of, 44, 50
Penance for crime, 102
Pleading, fictitious, 190
Pleading, principles of, 164
Pleas, *see* Appeal, special pleas in
Pleas of the Crown, 35
Pledges for battle, 93
Pledges for keeping the peace, 47
Pledges for prosecution, 110, 134, 136
Pledges for safe custody, 80, 108, 115, 135
Pledges for standing to right, 28, 87, 108, 109, 126
Possession, *see* Property, laying the
Pottery, 147
Precise dicere, 161, 170, 184, 185

INDEX OF MATTERS.   149

The numbers refer to the Cases, not to the pages.

Pre-emption, 150
Premeditated assault, 88
Prescription, 46
Presentment, foolish, 15
Presentment, untraversable, 61, 69
Presentment in local courts, 15, 156
Presentments, written, 62, 71
Price of stolen goods must be named, 60
Price set on injury, 165
Principal and accessory, 4, 9, 76, 84, 155, 164, 197
Priority of appeal, 115 (p. 72)
Prison breach, 154, 155, 199, 201
Prison, private, 142, 191, 202
Property, laying the, 18, 33, 88, 90, 94, 105, 126, 188, 203
Punishment, *see* Burning, Hanging, Imprisonment, Mutilation
Purpresture, 147, 175

Questions put to parties and witnesses, 54, 97, 115, 192, 197
Quid juris clamat, 202
Quit-claim, 76, 79, 82

Rape, 7, 32, 96, 141, 166
Receipt of criminals, 76, 161, 182, 190
Receipt of outlaws, 10, 78, 144, 161
Receipt of stolen goods, 8, 84, 161, 190, 195
Record, 194, 195, 201
Recordari facias, 115
Records of local courts, 115, 126, 169, 172, 192
Reeve, 140
Regraters, 187
Release, 40, 150
Relief, 115
Replevin, 105, 188
Reputation, evidence of, 109
Rescue, 42
Robbery, *see* Burglary, Larceny
Rolls, judicial, 18
Ruby, 197

Sale of chattels, 192, 195

Salt-merchants, 187
Sanctuary, 48, 49, 89, 135, 143, 161
Scotale, 104, 167
Secta, *see* Suit
Seisin of franchise, 137, 177
Seisin of stolen goods, 90, 106, 124, 125, 133, 169, 192, 195
Seisin, simple, 115
Self-defence, 70, 138
Serjeant, 3, 26, 27, 36, 37, 47, 48, 96, 104, 106, 115, 119, 121, 134, 156, 167, 168, 170, 181
Serjeants, improper appointments of, 168
Servants, master's responsibility for, 55
Sheriff, duties and liabilities of, 10, 45, 60, 104, 106, 115, 121, 132, 153, 154, 165, 168, 173
Sheriff, testimony of, 35, 165, 201
Sheriff's peace, 21, 31, 73
Sight and hearing, allegation of, 1, 19, 136
Special pleas, *see* Appeal, special pleas in
Stallage, 187
Standing mute, 153, 157
Stocks, 165
Stolen goods, *see* Receipt of stolen goods
Suit, production of, 87, 184, 192
Sunday, court sits on, 115
Suspicion, grounds of, stated, 66, 101

Tallage, 149
Tallaging ships, 43
Testimony, conflict of, 38, 40, 47, 62, 75, 108, 115, 127, 159, 172, 181, 200
Third party summoned, 202
Tithing, 117, 124, 143, 184
Toll, 69, 139, 176
Tonsure, 43
Township, duties of, 12, 48, 127, 131, 135, 153, 156, 173, 181, 190, 192
Township, guilty of homicide, 2, 179
Township, testimony of, 25, 109, 135, 142, 152, 159, 192
Townships, the four, 5, 6, 10, 12,

u 2

The numbers refer to the Cases, not to the pages.

110, 111, 159, 162, 163, 179, 181, 182, 187, 192
Trail of stolen cattle, 173
Treason, high, 115
Treason, petty, 179, 197
Trespass, 85
Trithing, 26

Usury, 108

Variance, 14, 35, 87, 64, 97, 124, 165, 194
Venue, 27, 94, 133, 161, 179, 186, 193
Verdict, reasons for, 5
View, 92, 175
View of nuisance, 147
Vill, *see* Township
Vill, lord of, 138
Villein, chattels of, 3, 23
Villein, marriage of, 203

Villein, stealing a, 3
Villeinage, 23, 126, 138, 153, 203

Waived goods, 183
Watch and ward, 149
Wapentake, *see* Hundred
War of 1214, 115 (p. 73)
Ward, abduction of, 202
Warranty, 90, 105, 121, 146, 192, 196
Warranty of stolen goods, 124, 192
Witnesses, 105, 108, 115 (pp. 70, 74), 127, 169
Witness, appellor must be, 1, 19, 29, 54, 67, 76, 81, 89
Witness, false, 26, 45
'Wolf's head,' 47
Wounds must be shown, 4, 14, 23, 41, 64

Year, day and waste, 144

INDEX OF PERSONS.

The numbers refer to the Cases, not to the pages.

Abeton', Osbertus de, 62
Abetot, Osbertus de, 135
Achard, Robertus, 126
Acle, Stephanus de, 80
Acton', Reinerus de, 80
Aelker, Johannes, 109
Ake, Gillebertus de, 95
Akerman, Rogerus, 179
Aketon', *see* Acton'
Alanus, Magister, 123
Alba Mara, Comes de, 50
Albus, Robertus, 75
Alegenny, Abbas de, 181
Alfolc, Johannes, 143
    Osbertus, 143
Alrigg', Mauricius de, 170
Ambreslega, Ricardus de, 70, 75, 135
Amundevilla, Elias de, 93
Apelton', Henricus de, 112
Ar, Robertus de, 185
    Walterus de, 185
Araby, Radulfus, 164
Arceles, Segerus de, 84
Armiger, Thomas, 45
Arund', Johannes de, 108
Arundel, Nicholaus de, 179
Aubeni, Robertus de, 54
    Willelmus frater Roberti de, 54
Auceps, Ricardus de, 72
Audeley, Walterus de, 89
Aula, Edwardus de, 97
Aunestowe, Simon de, 54
    Simon filius Simonis de, 54
Aurifaber, Adam, 103

Aurifaber, Milo, 103
    Walterus, 103
Awelton', Johannes de, 108

Bacheler, Robertus le, 96
Bagot, Rogerus, 164
Baiocis, Alienora de, 197
    Thomas filius Alienore de, 197
    Willelmus de, 98
Balistarius, Hubertus, 134
Balraue', Nicholaus, 165
    Willelmus, 165
Banastre, Gilebertus, 89
Barba, Thomas cum, 134
Bard', Hugo, 89
Barrevilla, Robertus de, 193
    Willelmus de, 193
Baryl, Rogerus, 181
Baskervilla, Radulfus de, 85
    Thomas de, 85
Bassecherche, Willelmus de, 170
Bathoniensis, Episcopus, 128
Beaupennie, Ricardus, 108
Bedeford, Bonefand Judeus de, 59
    Hugo de, 61
    Matillis uxor Hugonis, 61
    Robertus Decanus de, 49, 54
Bedell', Willelmus le, 96
Bekeringe, Petrus de, 81, 197
Bello Monte, Philippus, 126
Belne, Hugo de, 135
    Willelmus le Brun de, 135
Belraie', *see* Balraue'
Benetleg', Alardus de, 136
    Ricardus de, 136

The numbers refer to the Cases, not to the pages.

Ber', Walterus de la, 108
Berdeston', Alanus de, 158
    Rat' de, 158
Bere, Alwardus, 8
Bermundes', Robertus de, 200
Bernevilla, Alicia de, 202
    Gaufridus de, 202
    Matillis de, 202
Bertherton', Ricardus de, 62
    Simon filius Ricardi de, 62
Berton', Engelr' de, 158
    Simon de, 158
Betecote, Willelmus de, 185
Bigot, Nicholaus le, 160
Bisseleg', Lithulfus de, 131
Blac', Alicia uxor Willelmi, 191
    Willelmus, 191
Blake, Robertus de, 146
Blakeman, Johannes, 201
Blesebi, Ricardus de, 26
Blewin, Reginaldus, 2
Blundus, Henricus, 101
Bodiha', Margaria de, 99
    Willelmus filius Margarie de, 99
Bokering', Eustachius de, 197
    Petrus de, 197
Bomini, Auluredus de, 16
    Herebertus prepositus de, 16
    Nicholaus frater Aluredi de, 16
Bonum, *see* Bunum
Bordesl', Abbas de, 135
Bore, Almaricus de, 90
Bosco, Agnes uxor Roberti de, 153
    Matheus de, 135
    Ricardus de, 179
    Robertus de, 153
Bradeleg', Thomas de, 203
Brai, Robertus de, 178
Braibroc, Robertus de, 91
Brancestria, Robertus de, 102
Brasey, Willelmus, 135
Brekeherte, Willelmus, 179
Bremele, Willelmus de, 80
Bremesgrave, Rogerus de, 135, 136
Brente, Ricardus de, 187
Brienon', Willelmus de, 87
Brimesgrave, Rogerus de, 135
    annie, Comes, 192

Brochamton', Reginaldus de, 119
    Sibilla uxor Reginaldi de, 119
Bruges, Willelmus de, 147
Brun, Osbertus, 169
    Robertus, 124
    Wille, 107
Brunesland, Willelmus de, 83
Bunum, Henricus, 49
    Pirot, 49
    Willelmus, 54
Burchton', *see* Burton
Burel, Margeria uxor Willelmi, 26
    Petrus, 14
    Willelmus, 26
Bureweston', Andreas de, 66
Burgeis, Ricardus, 186
Burgo, Abbas de, 44, 91
    Hubertus de, 124
Burguunin, Willelmus le, 124
Burmesland', *see* Brunesland
Burnelle, Willelmus, 6, 170
Burton', Godricus de, 164
    Robertus de, 164
    Simon de, 164
    Unfridus de, 164
Buscell', Johannes, 49
    Henricus, 49
    Osbertus, 49
    Walkelinus, 49
Buuennie, Willelmus, 95

Calvus, Rogerus, 3, 115
Camerarius, Johannes, 102
Cantilupo, W. de, 154, 155
Cantuariensis, Archiepiscopus, 123, 200
Cape, Hugo filius Hugonis, 179
    Johannes filius Ricardi, 179
    Ricardus, 179
Capellanus, Gervasius filius Walteri, 185
    Walterus, 185
Cardun, Galfridus, 46
Caretarius, Benedictus, 88
Carpentarius, Simon, 55
Catteshull', Walterus de, 188
Caune, Willelmus de, 121
Cave, Hugo, 105
Cerysaus, Ricardus de, 115

INDEX OF PERSONS. 153

The numbers refer to the Cases, not to the pages.

Cestrie, Comes, 105
Champaneys, Ricardus le, 199
Chelueston', Rogerus de, 197
Cherlecot, Gaufridus de, 158
Chiewer, Radulfus de, 120
Chilleu, Agnes de, 5
Chimilli, Leticia uxor Willelmi de, 86
Chimilli, Willelmus de, 86
Cicestrensis, Episcopus, 189
Cimiterio, Reinerus de, 81
Cithyarista, Willelmus, 88
Clara, Comes de, 44
Clendon', Ricardus de, 100
    Sibilla de, 100
    Stephanus de, 100
    Willelmus de, 100
Clericus, Alanus, 21
    Johannes, 115, 146
    Radulfus, 61
    Ricardus, 115
    Robertus, 123
    Thomas, 95
    Willelmus, 72
Clodder', Willelmus, 129
Cnatton', Johannes de, 80
Cochtan', Simon de, 156
    Simon filius Simonis de, 156
Cocus, Willelmus, 42
Cofin, Gaufridus, 115
Colethorp, Gaufridus de, 106
Colevilla, Willelmus de, 190
Comber, Reginaldus, 191
Congham, Gaufridus de, 102
Convintrensis, Archidiaconus, 160
    Episcopus, 160, 165
Cophin, Ricardus, 121
Corbin, Rogerus, 124
Cote, Reginaldus, 43
    Sefridus filius Reginaldi, 43
Covintria, Aunfridus de, 166
    Prior de, 168
    Reginaldus filius Aunfridi de, 166
    Walterus de, 105, 166
Craft, Rogerus de, 168
Cranfeld', Oliverus de, 56
    Rollandus de, 56
Crapin, Hugo, 82

Crawe, Albrea uxor Petri, 56
    Malot, 7
    Petrus, 56
Credewell', Ricardus de, 104
Cretton', Juliana de, 84
Critele, Walterus, 188
Crithecreoh', Alec' de, 77
Croo', Philippus, 89
Croxebi, Walterus de, 82
Cruce, Ricardus de, 146
Cruitur, Willelmus de, 115
Cruk, Johannes de, 184
Cumbrinton', Emma uxor Rogeri, 127
    Rogerus, 127
Cumin, Johannes, 151
Cumine, Rogerus de, 115
Cumpton', Beatricia uxor Henrici de, 160
    Henricus de, 160
Curteis, Willelmus le, 146

Decanus, Laurencius, 95
Dene, Robertus de, 189
    Thomas de, 189
Depeford', Matillis uxor Osberti de, 120
    Osbertus de, 120
Devenesbi, Rannulfus de, 115
Devoniensis, Robertus, 194
Diggelford', Robertus de, 179
Dilun, Gaufridus, 76
Dimok', Osbertus de, 4
Dives, Reinbaldus, 81
Dobin, Hugo, 101
    Mariona uxor Hugonis, 101
Docking', Henricus de, 102
    Thomas de, 199
Draicot', Philippus de, 64
Dreintun', Johannes de, 110
Drueri, Robertus, 88
Dugingehal', David de, 127
    Ricardus de, 127
Dumberton', Elias de, 126
Duneham, Ricardus de, 83, 84
    Thomas de, 84
    Willelmus de, 20.
Dunestapel', Jordanus de, 52
    Petrus Vinitor de, 52

The numbers refer to the Cases, not to the pages.

Dunger', Rogerus, 138
Dunham, *see* Duneham
Dunstanvilla, Alanus de, 115
Duredent, Walterus, 95
Duuedale, Thomas de, 135
Duuekedale, Johannes de, 88

Eboraco, Milo Judeus de, 103
Ecclesia, Osbertus de, 19
Edlinton', Simon de, 24
Eghe, Willelmus, 143
Eia, Elias filius Stanard de, 48
    Stanard de, 48
Eliensis Episcopus, 98
Emme, Gaufridus, 105
Engaine, Henricus, 91, 92, 93
Ercalawe, Willelmus prepositus de, 78
Erdint', Thomas de, 62
Ernlly, Robertus, 146
Espeke, David, 60
Esse, Willelmus de, 201
Essexie, Comes, 79
Estocke, Henricus de, 95
Eston, Willelmus de, 126
Estretenton', Andreas de, 36
Eton', J. de, 170
    Walterus de, 95
Etton', Hugo de, 112
    Reginaldus filius Hugonis de, 112
Evereswic, Robertus de, 110
Exoniensis, Episcopus, 2
Extraneus, Johannes, 76

Faber, Adam, 136
Fale, Robertus, 57
Fauchonberge, Eustachius de, 18
    Willelmus clericus Eustachii de, 18
Faudingestorp', Ingerus de, 116
Feltrarius, Robertus, 88
Ferrariis, Robertus de, 64
    Robertus filius Roberti de, 64
    Rogerus homo Roberti de, 64
Ferrator, Willelmus, 147
Filia,
Filius,
    Admeri, Martinus, 81
    Aggi, Radulfus, 40
        Ricardus, 40
    Aier, Robertus, 76

Filia,
Filius,
    Ailrici, Margeria, 166
    Alani, Hugo, 29
    Alicie, Gilibertus, 105
        Robertus, 105
        Rogerus, 109
    Andree, Henricus, 192
        Hugo, 110
        Willelmus, 89
    Ascelin, Willelmus, 61
    Audani', Alanus, 89
    Baldewini, Adam, 63
    Bere, Robertus, 110
    Botild', Ricardus, 121
    Chaut, Rogerus, 121
    Derwin', Henricus, 188
        Hugo, 188
        Mabilia, 188
        Nicholaus, 188
        Willelmus, 188
    Dinisii, Radulfus, 28
    Engelardi, Sibilla, 73
    Ernwici, Willelmus, 143
    Fot, Seilda, 106
    Gamel', Hernaldus, 110
    Gaufridi, Gilebertus, 25
        Johannes, 84
        Matillis, 96
        Ricardus, 61
        Rogerus, 48
    Gervasii, Nicholaus, 60
        Willelmus, 164
    Gill', Henricus, 109
    Godefridi, Robertus, 7, 13
    Godelr', Willelmus, 88
    Godwini, Thomas, 63
    Goldine, Robertus, 186
    Gudred', Johannes, 81
    Haldengi, Ricardus, 23
    Hawisie, Willelmus, 23
    Henrici, Willelmus, 190
    Hereberti, Thomas, 162
    Herewardi, Ricardus, 41
    Hervici, Philippus, 192
        Ricardus, 3, 115
    Holdewini, Gilebertus, 128
    Horin, Andreas, 109
        Gilebertus, 109

The numbers refer to the Cases, not to the pages.

FILIA,
FILIUS,
Huberti, Henricus, 153
  Thomas, 153
Hugonis, Walterus, 41
Hukeman, Bruning', 109
Johannis, Cristiana uxor Willelmi, 40
  Emma uxor Ricardi, 164
  Petrus, 82, 165
  Ricardus, 164
  Willelmus, 40, 80
Josce, Willelmus, 163
Laising, Johannes, 109
Lamberti, Dionisius, 61
Lefwini, Petrus, 45 .
Nicholai, Rogerus, 86
Normanni, Gaufridus, 109
Odonis, Robertus, 163
Osberti,
  Ricardus, 135
  Thomas, 20
Paie, Norman, 188
Patric, Robertus, 140
Petri, Galfridus, 40, 46, 47, 79
Philippi, Johannes, 133
  Leoninus, 138
Podrich', Henricus, 131
Presbiteri, Adam, 190
  Johannes, 190
Prioris, Willelmus, 121
Radulfi, Rannulfus, 88
  Walterus, 29
  Willelmus, 109
Ricardi, Adam, 94
  Herebertus, 188
  Lucas, 21
  Willelmus, 192
Roberti, Alanus, 81
  Gilebertus, 23
  Paulinus, 88
  Simon, 116
  Warinus, 3
Rogeri, Willelmus, 80
Rumfar', Augustinus, 88
  Willelmus, 38
Saxi, Augnes, 82
Sibille, Nicholaus, 136

FILIA,
FILIUS,
Simonis, Ricardus, 20
  Thomas, 141
Suain, Johannes, 132
Sureman, Andreas, 45
Swein, Rogerus, 70
Sweyn, Thomas, 155
Symonis, *see* Simonis
Thenard, Walterus, 135
Tholy, Robertus, 159
  Willelmus, 159
Thurkilli, Hugo, 45
Thurstani, Galfridus, 47
Turstani, Hawisia, 82
Unfridi, Robertus, 192
Ursell', Benedictus, 103
Walteri, Alienora uxor Ricardi filii, 134
  Claricia uxor Laurencii filii, 61
  Jordanus, 4
  Laurencius, 61
  Ricardus, 134
War', Willelmus, 130
Warini, Fulco, 78
  Jordanus, 79
• Willelmi, Albanus, 109
  Andreas, 172
  Gaufridus, 115
  Henricus, 84
  Herewardus, 41
  Osbertus, 61
  Philippus, 13
  Ricardus, 21
  Robertus, 115
  Rogerus, 85, 109
Win', Willelmus, 109
Fisman, Willelmus, 5
Fittel, Rogerus, 197
Flagellator, Ailwinus, 108
Flandrensis, Bartholomeus clericus
  Ricardi, 18
  Johannes, 82
  Ricardus, 18
Flecherus, Petrus filius Roberti, 49
  Robertus, 49
Fletcher, Willelmus le, 88
Flich', Ricardus de, 90
Flitte, Gilebertus de, 49

The numbers refer to the Cases, not to the pages.

Foke, Ricardus, 146
Foliot, Wido, 115
Forestarius, Alanus, 8
   Godardus, 130
   Nicholaus, 146
   Stephanus, 122
Fortescu, Ricardus, 13
Fougeres, Robertus de, 163
Franccenat', Robertus de, 82
Franceys, Ricardus le, 186
Francus, Ricardus, 119
Frater Joelis, Willelmus, 24
Fremantel, Gamell', 111
Frokemere, Matilldis soror Roberti de, 12
   Robertus de, 12
Fulebroc, Edwardus de, 155
Fullo, Hugo, 74

Gamages, Herbertus serviens Mathei de, 67
   Matheus de, 67
Gamel, Ricardus, 136
Gant, Gilebertus de, 82
Gardinarius, Godwinus, 60
Gering, Willelmus, 42
Gernu,' Aluredus, 190
Giffard, Radulfus, 14
Gille, Radulfus, 88
Girmunvilla, Gilebertus de, 115
Gisnei, Willelmus de, 90
Gisnes, Baldewinus de, 190
Gisorcio, Alanus de, 97
Glastonie, Abbas, 186
Glin, Johannes de, 19, 20
Gloucestrie, Comes, 132
   Martinus ballivus Comitis, 132
Godspere, Walterus, 88
Goiz, Johannes, 115
Goky, Ricardus, 181
Golichtly, Hobbe, 157
Goman, Willelmus, 162
Goseberchurch', Petrus de, 41
Grafton', Hugo filius Walteri de, 47
   Walterus presbyter de, 47
Grantham, Matillis uxor Thome de, 191
   Thomas de, 191

Gratteshuil', Walterus de, 130
Gropin, *see* Crapin, 82
Guberant, Willelmus, 29
Guldene, Ricardus, 108
   Walterus, 108
Guldenema', Johannes, 74
   Willelmus, 74
Gule, Radulfus, 87
Gynnes, Baldewinus de, 190

Hagel', Nicholaus de, 143
Hairu', Hugo, 94
Hairun, *see* Heyrun
Haket, Lucia filia Walteri, 130
   Margeria uxor Walteri, 130
   Radulfus, 130
   Walterus, 130
Hal, Robertus de, 104, 155
Hale, Johannes del, 192
Hallere, Jordanus de, 179
Hanekesford', Willelmus de, 162
Hanleg', Warn' Constabularius de, 146
Harlatriee, Johannes de la, 144
Harstan', Alicia de, 169
Hasceby, Johannes de, 35
Hautein, Theobaldus, 36
Hawenes, Robertus de, 60
Hay, Odo, 11, 12
Heglo', Laurencius de, 108
Helesham, Baldewinus de, 88
Heligan, Henricus de, 115
Henchirche, Beinild de, 65
Hereford', Thomas de, 198
Herigen, Hervicus de, 115
Herthal', Robertus de, 70
Hethe, Thomas de la, 157
Herwinton', Henricus, 135
   Philippus, 135
   Robertus, 135
Heyrun, Johannes, 163
   Radulfus, 163
   Willelmus, 163
Hicha', Hugo de, 88
Hideford, Robertus de, 8
Hinton', Ricardus de, 46
Hnokel, Gocelinus, 182
Ho, Thomas de, 86

INDEX OF PERSONS. 157

The numbers refer to the Cases, not to the pages.

Hobbe, Radulfus, 159
  Robertus, 159
  Willelmus, 159
Holecumbe, Aylbriht de, 179
  Ricardus de, 179
  Willelmus de, 89
Holeworth', Juliana de, 117
  Willelmus filius Juliane de, 117
Hopeshot, Gaufridus, 202
Hoppeouerhumbr', Hugo, 189
Hopton', Petrus de, 77
Hose, Radulfus, 80
  Walterus filius Radulfi, 80
Hospitalis Jerosolyme, Prior, 149
Hoth, Radulfus, 88
Hotham, Gefridus de, 27
Hottot, Thomas de, 93
  Walterus de, 93
Hou, Osbertus de, 87
Hugeford, Walterus de, 75
Hugenhull', Henricus de, 64
Hulecumbe, *see* Holecumbe
Hulle, Ricardus de la, 186
Huntedun', Humfridus de, 60
Husseburn', Willelmus de, 191

Iberniensis, Willelmus, 120
Illeg', Adam de, 190
  Hugo de, 190
Ingaldestorp, Thomas de, 102
Ingwarthi', Willelmus de, 172
Inneskathan, Serlo de, 4
Ippeleg', Alditha de, 154
  Sirias de, 154

Jordanus, prepositus Episcopi Exoniensis, 2
Judas, Petrus, 142
Judea, Kelina, 103
Judeus, Milo, 103
  Vinantus, 103
Juvenis, Robertus, 181

Kade, Rogerus, 148
Kam, Nicholaus, 1
Kantinton', Ricardus de, 180
Karlebi, Alicia uxor Gaufridi de, 30
  Gaufridus de, 30
Kaul, Rogerus de, 115

Kenetton', Thomas de, 146
Kenleia, Odo de, 170
  Willelmus filius Odonis de, 170
Kennel, Reginaldus de, 19
  Rolandus filius Reginaldi de, 19
Kewerion, Johannes de, 20
Killio, Rollandus de, 16
Kima, Prior de, 22
Kinardesleg', Hugo de, 143
King, Philippus le, 192
Kittere, Hobbe, 136
Knapwell', Willelmus de, 202
Kurnic, Ogerus de, 20
Kylgath, Ricardus de, 115
Kynebaut, Johannes, 162
Kyrkele, Rogerus de, 208

Lalleford', Joias de, 163
Lancell', Rannulfus de, 83
  Ricardus de, 84
Lancuc, Rogerus de, 115
Landa, Euriwynus de, 20, 115
  Willelmus de, 24
Lankarf, Petrus de, 16
Large, Hugo le, 190
Le, Reginaldus del, 80
Lega, Juliana uxor Walteri de, 55
  Walterus de, 55
Legh', Willelmus de, 189
Leircestrie, Abbas, 160
Lekeburn', Robertus de, 105
Lelman, Rogerus, 109
Lidiard, Radulfus de, 186
Lihtfot, Henricus, 181
Lilleshull', Abbas de, 176, 178
  Aldit de, 77
  Elyas de, 77
  Eva de, 77
  Gaufridus de, 77
  Robertus de, 77
Litlebir', Johannes, 202
  Saherus, 202
Littlingeton', Willelmus de, 141
Lond', Ricardus de, 134, 144
London', Johannes de, 184
Longo Campo, Willelmus de, 42
Longus, Baldewinus, 45
  Radulfus, 88
Ludelaw', Edelina de, 72

The numbers refer to the Cases, not to the pages.

Lunet, Thomas de, 197
Lurdingestrete, Robertus de, 99
Lutreworthe, Willelmus de, 163

Makeblith', Willelmus, 103
Malecumb', Gaufridus de, 125
Malesoures, Willelmus, 45
Malherbe, Adam, 89
Malus Vicinus, Aluredus, 20
Mannebi, Willelmus de, 26
Mapelderested', Almerus de, 190
Mara, Willelmus de, 126
Marchaunt, Jacobus le, 161
Marchis, Howel le, 145
Mare, de la, *see* Mora, de
Marescallus, Comes, 144
  Ricardus, 136
  Thomas, 136
  Walterus, 136
  Willelmus, 28
Marham, Robertus Decanus de, 32
Marisco, Robertus de, 48
Marmiun, Robertus, 130
Martel, Martinus, 82
Maugis, Willelmus, 49
Maynard, Willelmus, 161
Medicus, Osbertus, 12
  Ursell', 103
Meisac, Drogo de, 115
Mentenge, Robertus, 105
Merc, Eudo de, 80
Mercator, Robertus, 8
Merle, Adam de, 34
Merston', Johannes de, 202
  Ricardus de, 202
  Michael serviens de, 36
Mertherin, Radulfus de, 20
Messarius, Alanus, 37
  Emma uxor Alani, 37
Meverell', Ricardus, 64
Middelton', Johannes de, 133
Miner, Adam le, 105
Molendinarius
  Gaufridus, 121
  Henricus, 121
  Hugo, 121
  Lambertus, 61
  Robertus, 121
  Walterus, 61, 121

Molendinarius, Willelmus, 12, 32, 101
Molendino, Johannes de. 108
Molton, Editha de, 120
Monacus, Walterus, 105
Monoculus, Ricardus, 179
Mora, Hamon de, 192
  Henricus de, 192
Morand', Rogerus, 12
Morcoc, Walterus, 26
Morel, Nicholaus, 82
Morton', Hugo de, 84
  Robertus de, 134
  Rogerus de, 84
  Willelmus de, 29, 55
Mortuo Mari, Rogerus de, 85
Morwestewa, Lucia de, 16
Motton, Robertus de, 144
Mukeleston', Adam de, 80
Muleton, Thomas de, 192
Musard, Radulfus, 169
Muscegros, Walterus de, 72
Mustel, Thomas, 197

Nedler', Petrus le, 169
Nereford', Petrus de, 192
Nergvilla, Radulfus de, 197
Neuna', Agnes uxor Willelmi, 130
  Willelmus, 130
Niger, Ossulfus, 19
  Ysaac, 103
Niweton', Adam de, 31
Noreis, Willelmus le, 165
Norensis, Ricardus, 36
Norf', Gaufridus de, 101
Not, Willelmus, 138
Notte, H. le, 158

Oildene, Willelmus, 45
Oliver, Jordanus, 186
Ounebi, Robertus de, 39

Painell', Johannes, 135
  Radulfus, 135
  Robertus, 135
Paiseie, Ricardus de, 179
  Walterus de, 179
  almarius, Ricardus, 6
Palmerius, Goditha uxor Walteri, 68
  Walterus, 68

INDEX OF PERSONS. 159

The numbers refer to the Cases, not to the pages.

Pantulf, Hugo, 78
Parco, Willelmus de, 126
Parisius, Johannes de, 82
    Petrus de, 82
Parles, Willelmus de, 135, 158
Parmentarius, Nicholaus, 8
    Walterus, 108
Parvus, Henricus, 19
Pateshulla, Martinus clericus Symonis de, 18
    Symon de, 18
Patesle, Herebertus de, 102
Patinton', Herebertus de, 171
    Juliana uxor Johannis de, 171
    Johannes de, 171
Paumer, Thomas le, 81
Paumerius, Willelmus, 163
Pauncefot, Ricardus, 186
Pecche, Ricardus, 178
Pech, Henricus, 117
    Hugo, 117
    Rogerus, 117
    Willelmus, 117, 118
Pedewell', Gervasius de, 122
Peissi, Adam de, 183
Pempol, Serlo de, 115
Penant, Henricus, 19
Penwithen, Edmerus, 9
    Martinus, 9
    Robertus, 9
Penwithen, Thomas, 9
Penwur', Rollandus de, 115
Petra Ponte, Alanus de, 76
Picot, Willelmus, 74
Piggun, Elias, 192
Pilardinton', Gaufridus de, 159
    Hugo de, 159
    Iveta uxor Ricardi de, 159
    Rogerus de, 159
    Willelmus de, 159
Pilate, Radulfus, 37
    Robertus, 36
Pin, Petrus, 178
Pincebec, Prior de, 41
Pipin, Willelmus, 74
Pistor, Ricardus, 179
Place, Hugo, 146
Pleidur, Walterus le, 144
Plested, Osbertus de la, 146

Plunton', Nigellus de, 106
Poher, Hugo le, 180
    Rogerus le, 180
Pollard', Petrus, 81
Pomeria, Henricus de, 115
Ponte, Rogerus de, 121
Ponte Gode, Wulwardus de, 12
Portehors, Nicholaus, 45
Praeriis, Henricus de, 126
Prepositus, Gaufridus, 60
    Johannes, 105
    Ricardus, 162
    Stephanus, 179
    Wimundus, 60
Prestehop', Rogerus de, 171
Pride, Robertus, 147
Pridias, Rogerus de, 3
Pring, Simon, 62
Pudifot, Herbertus, 109
Puintulf, Hugo, 168
Punbelee, Stephanus, 175
Pyion, Elias, 192

Ranam, Lefchildus de, 8
Rasene, Robertus de, 27
Rede, Hugo le, 195
Reigni, Johannes de, 183, 186
Reinfridi, Philippus frater, 9
Reninton', Alanus de, 3
Revel, Ricardus, 10
Reyny, *see* Reigni
Ritero, Osbertus, 11
Rockeby, Henricus de, 163
Rodenicht, Hugo filius Roberti, 155
    Robertus, 155
Rodknicht, Ricardus, 165
Rombaud, Robertus de, 47
    Rogerus de, 47
Roppele, Robertus de, 138
Ros, Robertus de, 3
    Willelmus de, 3
Ruffus, Elias, 96
    Johannes, 147
    Rein', 79
    Stephanus, 143
Rulesdon', Radulfus de, 126
Rumbaud, *see* Rombaud
Ruperes, Hugo de, 85

The numbers refer to the Cases, not to the pages.

Russell', Adam frater Willelmi, 60
    Willelmus, 60
Russiadic, Radulfus, 76
Russodic, Radulfus, 126

Sakebrich', Henricus de, 163
Salopia, Abbas de, 175, 177
Samford', Radulfus de, 73
Samson, Johannes, 136
Sancta Brigida, Adam de, 76
Sancti Albani, Abbas, 191, 200, 202
Sanford', Edwardus de, 179
    Jacobus ad capud ville de, 179
    Stephanus Prepositus de, 179
Sanguinel, Willelmus, 61
Saureb', Walterus de, 106
Saxebi, Simon de, 39
Saxelebi, Rannulfus filius Ricardi de, 39
    Ricardus de, 39
Scaccis, Robertus de, 10
Schirreve, Willelmus, 143
Scotus, Johannes, 104
Segrave, S. de, 159
Senex, Ricardus, 76
Serviens, David, 105
    Eudo, 105
    Gaufridus, 96
Seuerebi, Robertus de, 84
Shine, Willelmus, 134
Shireford', Gaufridus de, 164
    Robertus de, 173
    Thomas de, 164
    Wakelinus de, 164
Shiterok, Simon de, 184
Shortenhal', Robertus de, 153
Siageberi, Wido de, 80
Sigerid mater Denis, 28
Smalwude, Adam de, 190
    Willelmus, 190
Smithe, Dicke, 197
Solario, Willelmus de, 61
Soper', Robinus le, 195
Sowe, Johannes de, 67
    Jollanus de, 164
    Reginaldus de, 164
    Ricardus frater Johannis de, 67
    Simon de, 164
    Willelmus Forestarius de, 164

Spernour', Michael Prepositus de, 153
    Patecoc' de, 153
    Simon de, 153
Spina, Stephanus de, 45
Sproufford', Hynge de, 111
Stanchard, Alicia filia Walteri, 141
    Walterus, 141
Stanes, Ricardus, 188
    Willelmus de, 135
Stanford', Johannes de, 93
    Rogerus de, 93
Stapelton', Robertus de, 133
Staunleg', Ricardus de, 160
Staverton', Gaufridus de, 164
Steinton', Rogerus de, 114
Stiuecle, Simon de, 94
Stiueton', Rogerus Prepositus de, 197
Stoddon', Hugo de, 83, 84
Stokes, Ricardus clericus de, 115
    Robertus de, 146
    Thomas de, 135
Strande, Stephanus de, 197
Stures, Radulfus de, 24
Stutevilla, Willelmus de, 139
Suff', Gilibertus de, 198
Suham, Henricus de, 163
    Radulfus de, 163
Sukebergh', Willelmus de, 134, 135
Suldham, Prior de, 98
Sulee, Radulfus de, 105
Sullee, Ricardus de, 135
Sumercot', Ricardus filius Roberti de, 23
    Robertus de, 23
    Rogerus villanus Roberti de, 23
Sumeri, Willelmus de, 135
Summonitor, Adam, 163
Sundiherst, Ricardus, 99
Sutor, Edwardus, 188
    Willelmus, 125
Sutton', Ricardus Prepositus de, 162
    Robertus de, 59
Swele, Ricardus, 106

Tailur, Warinus le, 179
Talestorp', Gilibertus de, 196
Tallebois, Reginaldus, 202

INDEX OF PERSONS. 161

The numbers refer to the Cases, not to the pages.

Tameton', Willelmus, 106
Tanton', Prior de, 121
Tanur, Willelmus le, 192
Tassell', Willelmus, 99
Tatteswarhte, Ranulfus de, 64
Teinus, Reginaldus le, 10
Thurbern, Adam, 187
Tikenbret, Willelmus de, 115
Tillebroc, Robertus de, 197
    Willelmus de, 197
Tirel, Baldewinus, 20
Tiwardeni, Warinus de, 20, 115
Toki, Walterus, 184
Toli, 82
Toller, Hugo le, 189
Torberti, Alanus, 108
    Gaufridus, 108
Torell, David, Edwardus, Eilardus,
    Johannes, homines Willelmi, 87
    Willelmus, 87
Torp, Rogerus de, 24
Tregadec, Rogerus de, 14
Treleuth, Radulfus de, 19
Trelewith, Radulfus de, 20
Trenchebof, Walterus, 116
Trenchefoille, Willelmus, 86
Trethac, Drogo de, 115
Trevithov, Rogerus de, 19, 20
Trig, Willelmus, 88
Trilleg', Willelmus de, 101
Tropinel, Willelmus, 121
Trumpiton', Nicholaus de, 190
Turroc, Clemens de, 96
    Rogerus frater Clementis de, 96
Turz, Robertus, 124
Tyrell, Baldewinus, 20, 115

Utlaga, Robertus, 10

Vabadun, Jacobus de, 102
Vautort, Juelus de, 115
Vavassur, Maugerus, 106
    Robertus, 106
Ver, Henricus de, 203
Verdun, Robertus de, 153
Verly, Willelmus de, 193
Visorz, Warinus de, 97

Wabode, Thomas, 167
Wadinton', Simon de, 31

Wake, Wido, 29
Waleis, Simon le, 146
Waller', Johannes le, 129
Walo, Robertus, 25
Walteri, Tebb', 88
Waltervilla, Gaufridus de, 93
    Robertus de, 91, 92, 93
Waner, Rogerus le, 195
Ware, Henricus juxta, 190
Warennie, Comes, 189
Wareslete, Stephanus de, 135
Warewici, Comes, 161
Warewico, Kettellus de, 161
Watervilla, *see* Waltervilla
Watham, Rogerus Serviens de, 190
Wayder, Fulco le, 195
Waur, Rogerus de, 163
    Willelmus de, 163
Wavilla, Alanus de, 197
    Robertus de, 197
Wederake, Adam de la, 143
    Reginaldus de la, 143
Welle, Lucas de la, 6
Wellebi, Robertus de, 33
Welleton', Elias de, 26
Wene, Adam filius Roberti, 147
    Robertus, 147
Wenne, Edwardus de, 2
    Odo de, 2
    Philippus de, 2
    Rollandus de, 2
Wery, Hugo, 186
Westmonasterio, Abbas de, 90
Weston', Rogerus de, 102
Westwod', Priorissa de, 150
Whiteford', Rogerus de, 135
Wiard, Henricus, 108
Wifin, Walterus, 8
Wiflingham, Gilebertus de, 25
Wigornie, Ricardus Decanus, 139
Wigun, Ricardus, 78
Wik', Walterus de, 121
Wika, Rogerus de, 20
Wiles, Alanus, 82
Wilebbye, Walterus, 151
Wilekebi, Gaufridus de, 95
Wililega, Warnerus de, 170
Wiliton', Ailbricus de, 60
Wilton', Alanus de, 105

The numbers refer to the Cases, not to the pages.

Wilton', Thomas de, 105
Winewic', Willelmus de, 88
Wingeli, Anketillus de, 14
Winielton', Johannes de, 20
Wintonie, S. Comes, 202
   Philippus homo Comitis, 202
   Stephanus homo Comitis, 202
Wischard, Gilebertus, 148
Wispinton', Astinus de, 24
   Osgotus de, 24
Witham, Godardus de, 27
   Umfridus frater Godardi, 27
   Willelmus de, 89
Wither, Matillis, 119
   Petrus, 119
   Richolda, 119
Wither, Robertus, 119
   Walterus, 119
   Willelmus, 119
Witingham, Hugo, 88
   Willelmus, 88
Winelestorp, Robertus de, 106
Wnchcht, Osbertus, 19
Wradere, Henricus, 88
Wreneford', Gaufridus de, 186
Wrotham, Willelmus de, 2
Wuburn', Abbas de, 55
Wudecoc', Robertus, 190
   Willelmus filius Roberti, 190
Wulward, Rogerus de, 158
Wykewau', Magister Radulfus de, 147

INDEX OF PLACES.

The numbers refer to the Cases, not to the pages.

H = Hundred ; W = Wapentake.

Acford', 124
Aili, 125
Alencestr', 156
Almath, 115
Almthechierche, 143
Asewardechirn', W, 34
Asle, 104
Attingeham, 176
Awelton', 108

Balrichweie, H, 152
Baxterleye, 162
Bech', 90
Bedeford', 61
Benetleg', 136
Bernet', 191
Bisseleg', 131
Bobi, W, 31
Bomine, 11, 12
Bomini, 8
Bradeford', H, 77, 169
Brente, 187
Brimesgrave, 138
Brimstre, H, 74
Bruges, 172, 174, 181
Burneham, 187

Calwat, H, 23
Cantuaria, 201
Cardif', 192
Caunpeden', 157
Caunwic, 82
Cesterhunt, 192

Chaddeleg', 12
Chaddesleg', 13
Chaunedon', 11
Chelmereford', 190
Chippi', 88
Cicestria, 104
Claile, H, 47
Clipton', H, 59
Cnihteton', 144
Cochtan', 156
Coutun', 109
Covintria, 166
Credewell', 104
Cruk, H, 184
Cukefeld', 189
Cumbrinton', 127
Cunedour', H, 170
Cuthuluestan', H, 62

Derteford, 194
Dimidii Comitatus, H, 133
Dovoria, 143
Dunclent, 135
Dunestapell', 52

Eboracum, 103
Ellesmere, 71
Enefeld, 192
Eston', 89
Estwivelesir', H, 5
Etindon, 159
Eton', 95

Faveresham, 201
Fekeham, 141
Fleta, gaola de, 197
Flitte, H, 48
Forieta, H, 80
Freston', 42

Givele, 188
Grafhow, W, 88

Hacton', 59
Hagema', foresta de, 80
Hamme, 182
Hanleg', 146
Harcha', 105
Haunleg', 131, 132
Hecham, H, 46
Herefordia, 146
Hethe, 135
Hiche, 202
Hornicast', 24
Hunteworth', 182

Ivelcestria, 179

Kantinton', H, 180
Kareinton, H, 185
Kerior, H, 1, 19, 20
Kideministr', 140
Kintan', H, 158
Kirketon', W, 40
Knichtelawe, H, 16
Kris, 181

PLACITA CORONE.

The numbers refer to the Cases, not to the pages.

Lalleford', 163
Lancaueton', 84
Lancell', 84
Langeshag', 88
Leicestria, 41
Leng', 181
Lichefeld', 69, 133
Lileshull', 77
Limpelesham, 187
Lincolnia, 81, 82
Lindesle, W, 26
Lisniwet, H, 13
Londonia, 97, 137, 194, 195, 196
Ludelaw', 72
Lue, 197
Luiton', 50, 52

Malvernia, foresta de, 128, 131
Malvernia, Magna, 128
Parva, 128
Manlei, W, 82
Markel', 101
Merston', 159
Milvertone, H, 179
Musselawe, H, 171
Mutford', 203

Nesse, W, 29
Neuha', 97
Neunham, 163
Niwenton', 181, 182
Norhtperiton', H, 181, 182
Northoury, 181
Norton, 188

Offelawe, H, 67, 69
Oswaldeslauwe, H, 143
Our, H, 70

Peenge, 90
Pehenhull', H, 167
Penwith, H, 19, 20
Periton', 94
Persor', H, 127
Pidelsir', H, 8
Piderair', H, 19
Pilardinton', 159
Pirhull', H, 65
Powdesir', H, 8

Redburnestok', H, 54
Reygate, 198
Rowell', 44

Salop', 79, 167, 175, 176, 177, 178
Sanctus Albanus, 200, 202
Sanctus Austellus, 115
Sanctus Botulfus, 81
Scardeburg', 115
Schirbec, W, 42
Scistok', 162
Selton', 57
Seysten', H, 133
Shoplee, 202
Siberton', 91, 92, 93
Sixle, 28
Smithefeld', 196
Sowe, 164
Spernour', 151
Stafford', 133
Stanes, 135
Stanes, H, 188
Stiueton', 197
Stottesdun, 76
Stratton', 163
Suckeleg', 146
Suham, 163
Sumercot', 23

Suthbir', 147
Suthbrente, 187

Tamewurthe, 69, 162
Tanton', H, 179
Thameworth', 69, 162
Thatemanneslowe, H, 64
Theokesbiria, 181, 182
Tregeny, 115
Trehow, W, 83
Trigesir, H, 14
Triueru, 115
Tyrington', 197

Undele, 44

Wainflet, 22
Walecroft, W, 39
Waltham, 192
Warewicus, 154, 155, 161
Well', W, 25
Weltumestawe, 190
Wenne, 2
Whitacr', 162
Whitstan, H, 186
Wichebaud, 187
Wichio, 137, 150
Wigornia, 72, 127, 135, 137, 139, 146, 147, 151
Wileton', H, 183
Wimeresle, H, 45
Winewich', 46
Wirmele, 192
Witheleg', H, 187
Wivelingham, 25
Wlericheston', 163
Wragho, W, 27, 28
Wristanestre, H, 60
Writel', 190
Wurmel, 192

Printed by photo litho in Great Britain
by William Clowes and Sons Ltd., London and Beccles
for
Spottiswoode, Ballantyne & Co. Ltd., London & Colchester

Lightning Source UK Ltd.
Milton Keynes UK
UKHW011225070119
335144UK00006B/978/P